PRAISE FOR MANAGING BIOTECHNOLOGY: FROM SCIENCE TO MARKET IN THE DIGITAL AGE

"We can sometimes forget why technology matters beyond helping us do our work faster and cheaper; it is because technology tools help us connect with patients, our most important end customers. By including a discussion on patients and patient centricity in their book, Simon and Giovannetti remind us that technology is a powerful way to connect us with them. The recent emergence of patient engagement, sophistication and empowerment means that any healthcare leader must be prepared to genuinely understand the needs of patients, and be prepared to engage with them to improve their health outcomes. This book nicely maps out how technology can be used to meet those goals."

Olivier Brandicourt, MD, Board Member, Pharmaceutical Research and Manufacturers of America

"Biotech innovation is rapidly embracing digital technologies in the discovery, validation, clinical and product commercialization phases. The Internet of Things is bringing forward the Internet of Medical Things and the opportunities to build value with combinations of molecules, software and devices have never been so evident. Personalization, precision, data analytics and elements of consumer convenience are making their way into product pipelines. Industry participants can use this book as a modern roadmap to innovation and commercialization."

Donald Jones, Chief Digital Officer, Scripps Translational Science Institute and Chairman, Cardiff Ocean Group

"This is an unprecedented moment in the healthcare industry. Simon and Giovannetti have captured the tremendous potential of the period in this innovative and well-informed book, where they have brought to life the need to leverage digital technology and patient centricity to drive better health outcomes."

Lynn O'Connor Vos, CEO Greyhealth Group

"If you want to know where biopharma is going, read this book! Our industry is facing unprecedented opportunities driven by major scientific breakthroughs, while transforming itself to address accelerated landscape changes driven by digital revolutions and the emergence of value-based healthcare worldwide. In this ever-changing context, we all need to focus everything we do on the patients. They are why we exist as an industry, and this is ultimately what this insightful essay is really about."

Emmanuel Blin, former Chief Strategy Officer and Senior Vice President, Bristol-Myers Squibb

"This expert and thorough analysis of the journey from biomedical investigation to patient care presents an innovative blueprint for streamlining, redesigning, and amplifying the process. Specific examples of success stories support the recommendations for improved networking among the various players in the medical arena. Essentially, the authors predict a shift from emphasis on drug development to a broader collaborative system focused on the individual patient. The book is an interesting and important read for anyone involved in the prevention and treatment of disease."

Marianne J. Legato, MD, PhD (hon. c.), FACP, Emerita Professor of Clinical Medicine, Columbia University Founder and President, Foundation for Gender-Based Medicine

"*Precision Medicine, Patient Centricity, Digital Health, Value-Based Reimbursement, Risk-Sharing*—these terms were virtually unused in biopharma even five years ago. This book provides essential grounding and concepts to consider for anyone interested in healthcare, drug development and patient access in the 21st Century."

Ron Cohen, MD, Former Chairman, Biotechnology Innovation Organization

MANAGING BIOTECHNOLOGY
From Science to Market
in the Digital Age

FRANÇOISE SIMON, PhD
*Professor Emerita, Columbia University
and Senior Faculty,
Icahn School of Medicine at Mount Sinai,
New York, NY*

GLEN GIOVANNETTI
*EY Global Biotechnology Leader
Cambridge, MA*

The rights of **Françoise Simon** and **Glen Giovannetti** to be identified as the authors of this work has been asserted in accordance with law.

Registered Office
John Wiley & Sons, Inc., 111 River Street, Hoboken, NJ 07030, USA

Editorial Office
111 River Street, Hoboken, NJ 07030, USA

For details of our global editorial offices, customer services, and more information about Wiley products visit us at www.wiley.com.

Wiley also publishes its books in a variety of electronic formats and by print-on-demand. Some content that appears in standard print versions of this book may not be available in other formats.

ISBN: 978-1-119-21617-9

Cover image: © LAWRENCE LAWRY/Gettyimages
Cover design by Wiley

Set in 10/12 pt TimesLTStd-Roman by Thomson Digital, Noida, India

SKY10024901_021121

In memory of my parents, Yvonne David and Louis Simon
—Françoise Simon

To my wife Lisa, who has been a companion on the
Life Sciences journey for over 30 years in multiple cities,
with tremendous flexibility, support and patience,
including with this project
—Glen Giovannetti

TABLE OF CONTENTS

FOREWORD

The healthcare sector is undergoing unprecedented change. Aging populations and the rising incidence of chronic diseases have strained budgets, resulting in policy reforms that are changing the way healthcare is provided, consumed and paid for around the globe. The traditional contrast between the European universal payer system and the US freer market model is starting to fade, as more than half of US reimbursement now comes from public entities such as Medicare and Medicaid. In emerging markets, despite the rise of middle-class populations, challenges remain, from intellectual property to manufacturing quality, drug pricing. and patient access to health services.

Major players in the health ecosystem—patients, providers, manufacturers, and payers—are changing their behaviors in response by assuming more financial responsibility for improving health outcomes, adopting new technologies, and leveraging data to drive innovation and care delivery. In parallel, the confluence of radical advances in biotechnology and information technology is leading to a new model of precision medicine. It gives unprecedented power to individuals, and it allows the deep integration of the customer voice into innovation, from product co-creation to continuous monitoring.

As it has happened in many other industries, the entrance of nontraditional players is poised to disrupt the health industry and its incumbents, creating a cadre of new potential leaders. Some of these include consumer, telecom, and tech power-houses; Apple, IBM, Google, Intel, and QualComm have all made major invest-ments in health. A plethora of start-ups, particularly in the data analytics space, is also upending business as usual. Today, health data is fragmented and in silos.

While consumer data collected on smartphones and biosensors are still not connected to medical offices and electronic health records, there is great promise in eventually providing seamless care to patients, from research to the clinic, and moving from treatment of illness to prevention and prediction. Consumers have become accustomed to the convenience of personal technologies and will increas-ingly demand the same from their health providers, including more remote care and data sharing. With health budgets already under strain, the value generated by these insights may come at the expense of healthcare industry incumbents.

The global biopharmaceutical industry finds itself in the middle of this storm. In a world where payment will be based on demonstrating real value, the industry's traditional development and commercial strategies are no longer fit for purpose. Commercial-stage biopharma companies are beginning to adapt their strategies, reducing their dependence on large sales forces that promote undifferentiated products. They now seek to unlock value across their operations—from how they approach R & D (leveraging data and focusing on precision medicine and orphan diseases), to the evidence they collect to support value arguments, to providing "beyond-the-pill" solutions that may require partnerships with nontraditional entrants.

Emerging biotech companies working on exciting new science must also adapt their financing strategies to this new reality. No longer is it enough to sell investors on the promise of new scientific approaches. Biotechs must also articulate why their scientific advances will result in differentiation in a competitive global market. In *Managing Biotechnology: From Science to Market in the Digital Age*, Françoise Simon and Glen Giovannetti provide a comprehensive overview of the new business context and global strategies for biotechnology companies. The book is an important source of insight into critical topics such as networked innovation, alliances, commercialization, and digital communications. It serves as a roadmap to take concepts and products from science to market, and it captures the range of knowledge that students and managers need to leverage emerging technologies. It can also help interested policymakers aiming to grow and support biotech clusters worldwide to understand the risks, opportunities and challenges of the biotech industry.

This in-depth examination, based on the authors' broad experience, will be useful in teaching and inspiring current and future leaders across sectors driven by biotechnology. It will contribute high-value guidance for all stakeholders, from providers and payers to manufacturers. Most importantly, it may play a part in helping to bring new medicines to market and improving patients' lives and outcomes.

For biopharmaceutical firms, the future may hold an enabling scenario of optimized research, but it could also be a disruptive one, of disintermediation by infotechs of patient/provider communications. As the authors point out, success will depend on a melding of new cross-industry business models and of leading edge science, to improve the standard of patient care on a global scale.

By Philip Kotler
S.C. Johnson & Son Distinguished
Professor of International Marketing
Kellogg School of Management
Northwestern University

PREFACE

Since its founding four decades ago, the modern biotechnology industry has been a source of significant innovation across many parts of the economy, especially in the area of human health. Once-fatal diseases—ranging from HIV and hepatitis C to many cancers—are now chronic conditions or have been effectively cured, due to the introduction of innovative biotech medicines. Many of these medicines were discovered and developed by nimble entrepreneurial companies. New techniques and technology platforms under development by companies both large and small (and in academic, government, and private research labs) continue to create optimism that many more poorly treated, or untreated, conditions will soon be addressed, including many diseases prevalent in aging populations.

Over the same four decades, the rise of digital technologies has restructured the order of many industries, giving a majority of the global population access to enormous computing power and information, while simultaneously enabling previously unimaginable connectivity through social media platforms. These technologies have had an impact on the delivery and consumption of healthcare, although the pace of change in this industry has lagged many other parts of the global economy.

While scientific innovation remains at the core of the biopharma industry, the long-term trend of constrained health systems budgets and persistent public pressure on drug prices has put the traditional biopharma business model under tremendous strain. Biopharma companies understand that this new reality requires them to objectively demonstrate the real-world value of their products. They also realize that, to address significant unmet medical needs, they must expand their traditional focus on physicians to include engagement with patients and payers; in short, to think "beyond the pill." Adoption of digital technologies and access to, and effective analysis of, data will be key enablers as proof of outcomes becomes the industry benchmark. At the same time, many information technology (infotech) companies view healthcare as an untapped growth area ripe for digital disruption, as was previously seen in the financial and retail sectors. As a result, they are committing significant resources to developing new health offerings. Biopharma companies will have to understand whether these relatively new entrants in healthcare represent collaborators, competitors, or both.

The convergence of these trends is altering the biopharma value chain and ultimately the industry's business model. Traditionally, that value chain was linear, starting with scientific inquiry, product identification, clinical development, and, for those drugs that successfully progressed through regulatory approval, commercialization. As development milestones were achieved, responsibility for the product was handed off from function to function, with little integration and information sharing (or one-way sharing at best). Strategic decisions, including budgets and capital allocation, often occurred within functional silos. This structure worked in a world in which "me-too" drugs that did not provide much, if any, incremental value could still generate a return on investment through effective sales and marketing.

This fundamentally product-centric view of biopharma drug development is outdated. It is no longer tenable for companies to invest in products that, even if proven safe and effective by regulators, do not provide measureable value to patients and health systems. Patient expectations, driven by growing reliance on digital technologies and the connectivity they provide, are also changing. As a consequence, the biopharma value chain has reoriented around a fundamental understanding of patient needs, with data and insights flowing not just in one direction from the lab to the market but also from the market back to the lab, as depicted in the figure.

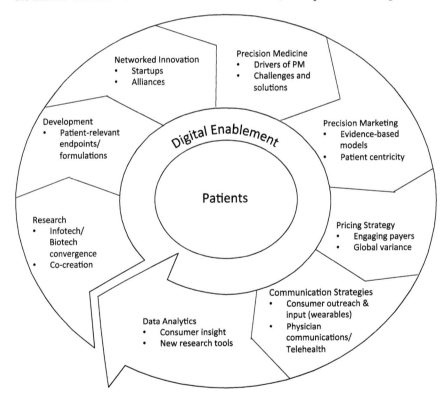

Managing biotechnology—framework

The innovation end of this cycle begins with a deep understanding of disease, including both the biology and the care pathways that patients experience. These insights are informed by a company's own experiences in a disease area (again, from research and commercial perspectives). The need to develop this depth of expertise is a factor causing many larger companies to fundamentally rethink their portfolios in order to specialize in fewer areas, increasing the likelihood of true differentiation. This is also resulting in broader adoption of precision medicine strategies to target more precisely patient populations that can be segmented by genetic or other characteristics to identify those more likely to respond to a particular drug therapy. In addition, technological convergence will also be a source of insight. For instance, artificial intelligence technologies developed by infotech companies can assimilate and analyze a range of patient and health data to generate new drug development hypotheses.

Understanding the patient care pathway in the actual health setting is important for effective clinical trial designs that support not just a regulatory approval but also negotiations with payers. Patient input is also becoming essential at the clinical development stage where patient relevant endpoints can be considered as part of a strategy to demonstrate effectiveness to a regulator and value to a payer. Connectivity to patients and patient advocacy groups also has the potential to facilitate trial recruitment.

In commercialization, making the case for the value of a product to payers and marketing a drug to providers and patients will be based on a combination of clinical data and "real-world" data that takes into account actual patient experiences, co-morbidities, and care delivery models. In some sense, the innovation phase of the cycle never really ends, as payers put more focus on real-world data over that generated in randomized clinical trials with selective enrollment criteria. Companies entering into risk-based reimbursement models in which payment is based on the achievement of defined outcomes will especially need a deep understanding of the patient journey and what other lifestyle factors might impact those outcomes. In some circumstances, this will drive the need for education, monitoring or other "beyond-the-pill" solutions.

Digitally enabled strategies will result in new ways to connect with patients. They will provide both structured and unstructured data from electronic health records, wearables, monitoring of social media, and other channels for analysis. These data will inform interactions with payers, providers, and regulators and will also feedback into R & D, completing the cycle.

BOOK STRUCTURE

The structure of this book largely follows the above framework. We have left a detailed discussion of the scientific breakthroughs underpinning the biopharma sector to others. Our book follows the triple transformation of the biopharma sector: networked innovation, including the convergence of infotech and biotech; new digital strategies; and patient centricity through the value chain.

In Chapter 1, we address the impact of technology convergence and the strategies of big infotech players on the biopharma value chain, as well as the barriers to further convergence. As most of the industry's innovation comes from, or is advanced by, start-up biotechnology companies, in Chapters 2 and 3 we provide information for entrepreneurs around financing and connected innovation through alliances with large companies and other entities. Chapter 4 discusses the impact of an expanding view of precision medicine on drug development and commercialization strategies, including significant market and organizational barriers that must be overcome to promote more widespread adoption.

As a companion to precision medicine, in Chapter 5, we introduce the concept of precision marketing. As payers, physicians, and consumers increasingly expect clinical and economic data to support a medicine's use, biopharma companies can make their product profiles more compelling via evidence-based marketing. This chapter also discusses product launch strategies, multichannel marketing approaches, sales force deployment, and product sustainability. Complementing material in Chapter 5, Chapter 6 explores what patient-centricity means today, discussing in greater detail the concepts described above, as well as the challenges biopharma companies encounter as a result of regulations and a lack of trust by the public.

In Chapters 7 and 8, we discuss approaches to engage with payers on a more strategic (versus transactional) basis, including understanding the needs of various payers and the patient populations they serve. We also develop drug pricing concepts, including novel risk-sharing pricing structures that can be based either on financial or clinical outcomes.

Chapter 9 covers digital health trends among patients and physicians and how digital technologies are impacting the biopharma value chain as well as digital strategies being deployed by biopharma and health systems. Finally, Chapter 10 addresses the data analytic core competencies that companies will need to develop in order to access and extract value from the data that surrounds the product during both development and commercialization.

Leading the biopharmaceutical enterprise is becoming a more complex proposition because of changing market dynamics, including the growing power of the patient and the emergence of increasingly powerful and accessible digital technologies. This book is intended to highlight these changes and help students, prospective entrepreneurs, and management teams identify both the risks and the opportunities that come from operating in the Digital Age.

RESEARCH METHODOLOGY

The research material for this book was derived from a variety of public and private sources including peer-reviewed and industry journals, media reports, and financial databases. This research and analysis were supplemented though qualitative interviews conducted over a two-year period with over 150 industry and academic experts, biopharma and infotech executives across research and commercial functions, venture capitalists, and public and private payers.

ACKNOWLEDGMENTS

This book is based on several years of research, and it is also a field study of biopharma strategy through the value chain, including many executive interviews and company case studies. We benefited as well from management seminars and academic executive programs that allowed us to test our models and concepts.

A global network of academic and industry leaders brought great value to our book. At the risk of overlooking several, we first note the experts and executives who contributed thoughtful comments and case studies: Philip Kotler, whose seminal work in healthcare strategy inspired us, and Charlotte Sibley (former SVP, Shire), who generously provided in-depth reviews and expert insights throughout our book; Olivier Brandicourt (Board Member, PhRMA), Roch Doliveux (former CEO, UCB), Wendy Gabel (former VP, Biogen), and Bernard Poussot (Board Member, Roche) also provided valuable comments.

John Maraganore (CEO Alnylam), Michael Pehl (President, Hematology and Oncology, Celgene), and Jacqualyn Fouse (Executive Chair, Dermavant and retired President and COO, Celgene), as well as Emmanuel Blin (former SVP, Bristol-Myers Squibb) contributed company case studies.

In Europe, we benefited from a case study from Maryvonne Hiance, Dominique Costantini, and Emile Loria at OSE Immunotherapeutics, and thoughtful reviews and insights from Philippe Latapie, François Meurgey, and Catherine Parisot.

Françoise Simon would also like to extend her appreciation to her academic colleagues: At the Icahn School of Medicine at Mount Sinai, Dean Dennis Charney; Annetine Gelijns, Professor and System Chair, Population Health Science and Policy; and Senior Associate Dean, Brian Nickerson, for their support, and Dr. Bruce Darrow, Mount Sinai Chief Medical Information Officer, for his technology expertise.

At Columbia, Françoise Simon would like to acknowledge Deans Linda Fried at the Mailman School of Public Health and Glenn Hubbard at the Business School, and she thanks Professors Kamel Jedidi, Don Lehmann, and Michael Sparer for their support, as well as Emerita Professor Marianne Legato for sharing her expertise in gender-based medicine; in Europe, she thanks Professors Nathalie Angelé-Halgand and Frantz Rowe at the Université de Nantes, Martine Bellanger at EHESP, Claire Champenois at Audencia, Pierre Lévy at Université Paris-Dauphine, and Christine Coisne and Loïc Menvielle at EDHEC for providing an academic testing ground for the book.

At INSEAD, Françoise Simon also thanks Professor Stephen Chick and Research Program Manager Ridhima Aggarwal for the use of the PatientsLikeMe case, which she co-wrote with them and excerpted in the book.

Both authors give a special acknowledgement to Ellen Licking, Senior Life Sciences Analyst at EY, for her insights, her network and for her research and editorial contributions. Ellen worked with great dedication to advance the research for the entire book, with particular emphasis on the following areas: precision medicine, data analytics, new pricing models, and strategic payer engagement.

In addition to Ellen, Glen Giovannetti would like to thank many colleagues at EY including Global Life Sciences Sector Leader Pamela Spence, Susan Garfield, Kristin Pothier, and Ryan Juntado for their contributed articles. EY Life Sciences specialists Jeff Greene, Scott Palmer, Mahala Burn, Alan Kalton, Todd Skrinar, Jamie Hintlian, and Adlai Goldberg also provided invaluable insights. Melanie Senior, a life sciences writer and analyst, provided support for the precision medicine and payer engagement sections of the book. Jason Hillenbach and Rajni Sadana ably led a research team who also provided support for many of the figures in the book, and Angela Kyn provided marketing support.

Finally, we would like to thank our publisher, John Wiley & Sons, and our editor, Bob Esposito, and Editorial Director, Justin Jeffryes, for their expert guidance through our book.

ABOUT THE AUTHORS

FRANÇOISE SIMON

 Françoise Simon is a Professor Emerita at Columbia University and Senior Faculty at the Icahn School of Medicine at Mount Sinai. She also manages her own international consulting group. Her teaching focuses on executive programs and won her the Chandler Award for Commitment to Excellence from the Columbia Business School.

Dr. Simon has more than thirty years of experience in consulting and marketing management in the Americas, Europe, Asia, and Africa. Her clients include many Fortune 500 companies as well as new venture firms, several governments, and the United Nations.

Prior to joining the Columbia faculty, Dr. Simon was a Director of Arthur D. Little, and developed a global strategy practice serving clients in the Americas, Europe, and Asia.

Previously, Dr. Simon was a Principal of Ernst & Young, where she led a strategy practice in the health and consumer industries in the United States and Europe. Her corporate experience includes an appointment as New Product Manager in International Diagnostics for Abbott (now Abbvie) in Chicago. Prior to that, she was a Marketing Development Manager for Novartis in Switzerland.

Dr. Simon holds an MBA from Northwestern University and a PhD from Yale University. She has held faculty positions at the University of Chicago and New York University, as well as Columbia University and the Icahn School of Medicine at Mount Sinai.

She has published more than twenty articles and conducted more than 200 management seminars in the Americas, Europe, Asia, and Africa. She is the co-author of *Building Global Biobrands: Taking Biotechnology to Market*, with Philip Kotler (Free Press, 2003), *Winning Strategies for the New Latin Markets*, with Fernando Robles and Jerry Haar (Prentice-Hall, 2002), and *Europe and Latin America in the World Economy* with Susan Kaufman Purcell (Rienner, 1995). She is a past Vice President and Director of the American Marketing Association, and has served on the International Council of the American Management Association.

Dr. Simon has also served as a member of the Council on Foreign Relations.

GLEN GIOVANNETTI

Glen Giovannetti is a Partner at Ernst & Young LLP and the EY Global Biotechnology Leader. He has more than 25 years of experience serving clients in the biopharmaceutical industry, primarily in Silicon Valley and Boston. He has extensive experience in assisting clients from start-ups to market leaders around issues of growth, global expansion, and strategic transactions including initial public offerings, R&D collaborations, and acquisitions.

Glen has led the development of the EY Biotechnology Annual Report, *Beyond Borders*, for more than a decade. He is a past member of the Board of Directors of the Biotechnology Innovation Organization and a member of the Board of Directors of Life Sciences Cures. Glen has a BA in Accounting from Linfield College, where he is also a member of the Board of Trustees, and is a Certified Public Accountant in California and Massachusetts.

PART *1*

NEW MODELS
FOR NETWORKED
INNOVATION

CHAPTER 1

DIGITAL EVOLUTION OF BIOTECHNOLOGY

For nearly four decades, biotechnology has driven the transformation of many sectors, from healthcare to food and energy, and it has grown into a global industry. It is now being transformed itself by its convergence with information technology (infotech). Biotechnology has been defined as "the use of living systems or molecular engineering to create and manufacture biologic therapies and products for patient care" [1], but it can be more broadly seen as the application of molecular biology across industries.

From the start, biotechnology grew together with other sciences. A first inflection point, Watson and Crick's 1953 discovery of the structure of DNA, depended on the development of X-ray crystallography by Franklin and Wilkins. By 1986, the first automated gene sequencer by Hunkapiller at Applied Biosystems supported Venter's National Institutes of Health (NIH) research, and a later-generation ABI sequencer, introduced in 1998, further enabled his research at Celera. This led to a second inflection point, in 2000, with the draft of the human genome by Celera and the Human Genome Project. The synergy between computing and bioscience continued with the emergence of bioinformatics and the 2003 launch of IBM's Blue Gene supercomputer, with a focus on structural proteomics.

Another technology has evolved over the past three decades, supported by the optimization of gene sequencing: CRISPR (clustered regularly interspaced short palindromic repeats). This nucleotide sequence was first identified in Japan in 1987, but it took decades to define its function as a molecular scalpel and an RNA guide capable of editing genes. By 2007, it was shown that spacer DNA could alter microbial resistance, and by 2012, a team including Doudna and Charpentier showed that a simpler CRISPR system relying on the Cas9 protein could work as an editing tool in human cell culture. In 2014, Platt used a Cas9 mouse to model lung adenocarcinoma. CRISPR may be first developed for monogenic diseases such as beta thalassemia, but challenges include safety (avoiding activity in unintended parts of the genome), delivery (via methods such as lipid-based nanoparticles or virus-based particles) and manufacturing [2].

Unlike computing, bioscience has not progressed in linear fashion, due to the inherent risk of working with animal and human biology. After the 1953 discovery of

Managing Biotechnology: From Science to Market in the Digital Age, First Edition. Françoise Simon and Glen Giovannetti.
© 2017 John Wiley & Sons, Inc. Published 2017 by John Wiley & Sons, Inc.

the DNA structure, it took 29 years for the launch of the first recombinant human insulin, discovered by Genentech and licensed to Eli Lilly. Monoclonal antibodies, developed by Köhler and Milstein in 1975, were not marketed until the introduction of IDEC's Rituxan (rituximab) in 1998, after several failed attempts by firms such as Hybritech.

Similarly, the first genotype-specific oral therapy, Novartis's Gleevec (imatinib) for Philadelphia—positive chronic myeloid leukemia, was approved in the United States, Europe, and Japan in 2001, but it took decades to develop it; the abnormal Bcr-Abl gene coding for tyrosine kinase, stimulating leukemia cell growth, was identified in 1985, and the molecule was first synthesized in 1992 (Figure 1-1).

DISCOVERY		COMMERCIALIZATION
US NIH approves first CRISPR-Cas 9 trials in cancer	2016	
	2014-2017	FDA immuno-oncology approvals; BMS's Opdivo (nivolumab) and Merck's Keytruda (pembrolizumab) in 2014 for melanoma; other indications in lung, bladder cancer, and for Keytruda solid tumors with same genetic type (2017).
Human embryonic stem cells through cloning, Oregon Health Sciences University; US Supreme Court rules that genes cannot be patented – Myriad Case	2013	European Commission approves first biosimilar MAbs; Hospira's Inflectra and Celltrion's Remsima (infliximab)
CRISPR as genome editing tool in human cell culture (Jinek, Doudna et al.); CRISPRs shown in 2005 as templates for RNA (Mojica)	2012	FDA approves Vertex's Kalydeco for cystic fibrosis and Roche's Perjeta for metastatic breast cancer (genotype-specific)
First complete map of a food plant genome (Rice)	2001	Novartis' Gleevec (imatinib), first genotype-specific oral therapy, approved in the US, EU, and Japan
Draft of human genome (Celera, Human Genome Project)	2000	Development of "Golden Rice" with provitamin A
First complete animal genome sequenced (C. elegans)	1998	UniQure's Glybera gene therapy approved in EU
Sheep cloning from adult cells (Wilmut & Campbell)	1997	Genentech's Rituxan (rituximab), Herceptin (trastuzumab) are FDA approved
First gene therapy (Anderson, NIH Clinical Center, for adenosine deaminase deficiency)	1990	
First patent for transgenic mouse (Harvard in 1988)	1988/1989	Amgen's Epogen (erythropoietin) approved in 1989, then Neupogen in 1991
	1986	Automated DNA sequencer, introduced by Applied Biosystems
DNA fingerprinting (courtroom use in 1985)	1984	
	1982	First rDNA drug approved by FDA (human insulin, Genentech)
First patent in genetics (Diamond v. Chakrabarty)	1980	Amgen formed as Applied Molecular Genetics; first biotech IPO (Genentech)
Recombinant human insulin (Genentech)	1978	Biogen, Genzyme, and Hybritech founded
	1976	Boyer and Swanson found Genentech
Monoclonal antibodies (Kohler & Milstein)	1975	
Recombinant DNA (Cohen & Boyer)	1973	
	1971	First biotech founded-Cetus, developed Proleukin (Interleukin-2)
Genetic code defined as a sequence of codons (nucleotide base triplets), specifying 20 amino acids (Khorana, Nirenberg)	1966	
Structure of DNA (Watson & Crick, from Franklin & Wilkins X-ray crystallography)	1953	

Source: Françoise Simon

Figure 1-1   Biotechnology milestones

INDUSTRY APPLICATIONS

Today, biotechnology has matured and is driving innovation across sectors, from medicine and food to agriculture and biomaterials (Figure 1-2):

- In healthcare, *red biotech* has led to novel biologic therapeutics, including recombinant proteins such as insulin and growth hormone, monoclonal antibodies such as Genentech's Herceptin (trastuzumab) for HER2-positive breast cancer, vaccines, molecular diagnostics, gene and stem cell therapy, tissue engineering, and regenerative medicine.
- In food and agriculture, *green biotech* has improved crop efficiency and used bioremediation for environmental reclamation. It has blurred the distinction between food and medicine, with the emergence of medical foods and innovations such as a strain of "golden rice" yielding provitamin A [3].
- Marine biology has led to *blue biotech*, with food products and ingredients derived from algae, invertebrates, and fish; diagnostic agents such as fluorescent reporter protein; and marine extract additives in cosmetics.
- In industrial processes, *white biotechnology* has produced biodegradable plastics, renewable chemicals, pollution-eating bacteria, and advanced biofuels [4].

The following chapters will focus on red biotech, including the transformational impact of digital technologies and the convergence with infotech. A new form of digital convergence has emerged, which presents both an opportunity and a

Red biotech / Healthcare	• Therapeutics: Recombinant proteins (insulin, growth hormone), monoclonal antibodies (Genentech's Rituxan and Herceptin) • RNA interference (Isis' Vitravene), gene therapy, stem cell therapy (Osiris, Prochymal for graft versus host disease) • Diagnostics: molecular diagnostic tests and biomarkers (Abbott, Vysis companion test for Herceptin) • Tissue engineering (skin for burn treatments, scaffolds for organ replacement)
Green biotech / Food & Agriculture	• Medical foods (Golden Rice with pro-Vitamin A) • Herbicide- and pest-resistant crops (transgenic corn, cotton, and soybeans) • Animal breeding and cloning • Molecular farming (vaccine production from transgenic plants)
Blue biotech / Marine Biology	• Bioactive substances (antiviral and anticancer compounds from marine sponge *Cryptotethya crypta*) • Diagnostic agents (Fluorescent reporter protein from bioluminescent jellyfish, *Aequorea victoria*) • Cosmetics (marine extract additive in skin creams)
White biotech / Industrial Applications	• Biocatalysts including enzymes for chemical synthesis, with detergent and food production uses • Biofuels (ethanol from corn starch) and plastics (biodegradable food packaging) • Bioremediation (use of plants and microorganisms for environmental reclamation)

Source: Françoise Simon

Figure 1-2   Biotechnology across industries

threat for the biopharmaceutical sector. From mobile devices, such as the Fitbit wristband biosensor, to R & D analytics tools such as IBM's Watson, infotech companies are playing a key role in meeting consumer and researcher communication needs.

IMPACT OF MEGATRENDS

Multiple trends are disrupting business models and leading the industry to define value differently. For consumers, longer life spans are increasing the incidence of chronic conditions such as diabetes and heart disease, across developed and also emerging markets, driving demand as incomes rise. However, this is also placing manufacturers on a collision course with resource-constrained payers, who are increasingly defining value in terms of outcomes achieved by new therapies. For researchers, postgenomic science is driving precision medicine, which has already yielded a new wave of targeted therapies but is struggling to handle an explosion of data: at the individual level, "small data" from biosensors, monitors, smartphones, and smartwatches; at the population level, "big data" from genomic, clinical trial, and insurer databases. These conflicting trends have led to a disconnect within the biopharma space.

Consumer-generated health data need professional interpretation, which medical offices largely cannot provide online due to liability and reimbursement issues and which cannot be transmitted to most hospital electronic health records (EHRs). Researchers now access an overwhelming amount of health data, well beyond clinical trial databases, which has led to the entry of information technology leaders into healthcare. Apple is partnering with the Mayo Clinic with its HealthKit and ResearchKit software that links patients, physicians, and EHRs. IBM aims to streamline R & D with its Watson Health unit and has made significant acquisitions in data analytics, including Explorys, Phytel, and Merge. Alphabet is partnering through its Verily unit with Sanofi, Dexcom, and Medtronic in diabetes, and in 2013 it launched Calico, a biotech company focused on longevity. Qualcomm and Novartis have set up the dRx Capital joint venture to invest in digital startups and optimize clinical trials. The interaction of these transforming forces is summarized in Figure 1-3.

DIGITAL HEALTH OPPORTUNITIES

From research to postmarketing surveillance, digital health has the potential to greatly improve R & D and manufacturing efficiency, as well as product co-creation and communication with patients:

- In R & D, digital health can optimize diagnostics through integrated biomarkers, increase speed to market, and streamline data analytics.
- In manufacturing, digital technology can adapt processes to reduce costs.

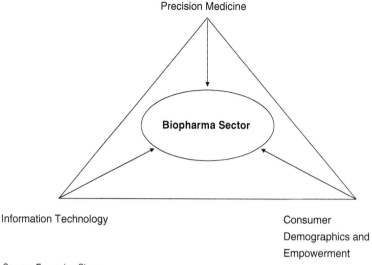

Source: Françoise Simon

Figure 1-3   Transforming forces

- From a regulatory and reimbursement standpoint, it can enable real-time drug monitoring and support health economics dossiers with real-world evidence.
- At the commercial end, digital health can allow deep integration of the customer voice, from drug co-creation to postlaunch communications, and it can help collect real-world evidence to support economics dossiers (Figure 1-4).

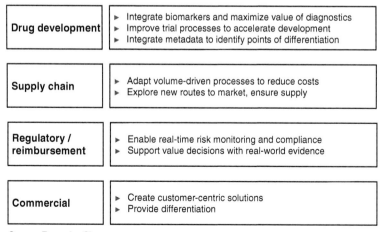

Source: Françoise Simon

Figure 1-4   Impact of digital solutions on the value chain

INFOTECHNOLOGY INITIATIVES IN HEALTHCARE

The health sector has been slower than other industries such as banking and retail to adopt digital technology, due to regulation, physician concerns about liability and reimbursement, and upfront costs and resistance to changing workflows, as well as consumer concerns about data security and privacy.

By contrast, infotechs have entered this space rapidly, for various reasons. Companies such as IBM may grow their businesses by addressing large database interpretation problems that require platform technologies such as Watson. Consumer-focused firms such as Apple are responding to market demand for online healthcare information by adding health apps on their mobile devices.

While infotech leaders are reluctant to become directly involved in healthcare due to the heavy burden of regulation and long development cycles, they still have the potential to disrupt the sector, for instance, if digital interventions prove more effective than some drug therapies. To support their healthcare penetration, infotechs have the added advantage of massive resources. Apple's market capitalization passed $800 billion by May 2017, well above that of Johnson & Johnson, which led biopharmas at nearly $346 billion at the same time. A key advantage for Apple is its brand value among consumers. Alphabet combines advertising revenue from Google with strong gains in mobile search, and infotech growth, in general, is driven by the rise of the cloud, that is, the shift of many computing operations to online services [5].

As mobile health (mHealth) comes to dominate the sector, through the fast growth of mobile devices versus PCs or laptops, infotechs play a key role in all of its aspects. As defined by the World Health Organization (WHO), mHealth is "medical and public health practice supported by mobile devices such as mobile phones, patient monitoring devices, personal digital assistants and other wireless devices" [6]. At the consumer end, infotech provides hardware and software from biosensors and smartphones and also enables real-time interactions via social media. At the research end, infotech aims to optimize predictive analytics to gain deeper insights into the origin of diseases, diagnostics, and treatments.

A hybrid category of mHealth includes Food and Drug Administration (FDA)-approved medical devices such as WellDoc's BlueStar to measure glucose levels and AliveCor's mobile electrocardiogram machine. More broadly, Apple's HealthKit and ResearchKit aim to address the current lack of interoperability by linking consumer biomarkers with medical offices and EHRs (Figure 1-5).

DISRUPTION RISK FROM INFOTECH

In addition to opportunities, the rising dominance of infotechs in healthcare may pose significant risks for biopharmas. What makes their convergence uncertain is

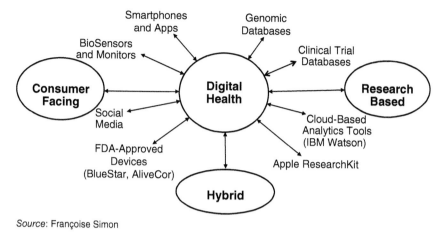

Source: Françoise Simon

Figure 1-5   Digital health landscape

the significant variance between the business models of biopharmas, device companies, and technology firms:

- R & D is profoundly different in the biology and engineering cultures, where biotech timeframes may span 10 years, in contrast to the rapid cycle times and iterations for technology products. Firms such as Apple may release new or upgraded products twice a year.
- Success metrics also vary: in biopharma they are rigidly defined by FDA-validated safety and efficacy, whereas in technology they are driven by network effects and viral diffusion.

As patients manage more of their healthcare, companies such as Apple may be better positioned to own the consumer relationship. In addition, with the rising role of social media such as the PatientsLikeMe website, conducting member-driven observational trials, biopharmas may lose partial control of clinical data and cannot interactively join the online dialogue with product messages, due to regulatory restrictions.

Economic models are just as divergent, as drugs and devices depend on public or private payer reimbursement, with some consumer copays, whereas tech products rely on direct selling through app fees, licenses, or subscriptions, or indirect selling such as advertising revenue from search engines (Figure 1-6).

Another nontrivial barrier to the convergence trend is a different cultural attitude toward risk. Silicon Valley, unlike Big Pharma, has an inherent tolerance for risk. Risk itself is also increased by the digitization of healthcare. In addition to the extreme product attrition seen in biopharma R & D, the cloud-based diffusion of data may pose significant security problems. A study of 1,000 US consumers showed that 43 percent were not comfortable with sharing their

	Biopharmaceutical	Medical Device	Technology
Technology cost	Very high	Moderate	Initial cash flows may be limited
Development time	10 years or more	3–7 years from conception to approval	Rapid cycle times and iterations
IP protection	Composition / utility / other patents Market exclusivity for rare disease	Utility and design patents	Broad portfolios / design patents
Success metrics	Safety and efficacy	Safety, efficacy, convenience	Ramp up in number of users, consumer appeal, viral diffusion
Delivery	Medical or consumer channels	Medical or consumer channels	BtoC or BtoB channels
Validation	Clinical trials / regulator approval (FDA/EMA/Other)	Clinical trials / 510(k) submission	Beta testing, agile development, fast customer feedback
Economic model	Reimbursement by government or insurers, patient copay	Reimbursement by governments or insurers, consumer payments	Software licenses, subscriptions, indirect selling (advertising revenue from search)

Source: Adapted from Steinberg D, Horwitz G, Zohar D. "Building a business model in digital medicine." Nature Biotechnology. 2015; 33 (9): 910–920.

Figure 1-6   Business model variance

personal data online [7], and this trend is reinforced by recurring media exposure of security breaches. In 2015, Anthem, the second-largest US health insurer, revealed that its records had been compromised by hackers, posing a potential risk for Social Security numbers and employment data for up to 80 million past and present members [8]. In addition, Silicon Valley has so far remained wary of health regulators. Devices such as the Apple Watch are not therapeutic and are therefore seen by the FDA as wellness-related and not subject to its regulation.

Because a convergent business model has yet to emerge, the following questions for infotech companies entering the health space are worth considering:

- *Product or service*: Is it a wellness support tool like the Fitbit wristband sensor, a medical device like the BlueStar glucose monitor, or a true therapeutic product?
- *Validation:* What is required, from randomized clinical trials to user acceptance?
- *Technology:* Does the product include hardware (smartphones), software (apps), and/or cloud-based analytics platforms? What information is transmitted, from small data (individual biomarkers) to big data (population-level genomics)?
- *Customer/end user:* Who is the customer? For wellness tools, it is primarily the consumer. For medical devices, there are hybrid targets (patients or physicians). For researchers, analytics platforms reflect the greatest need.

- *Economics:* Will revenue come from payer reimbursement, patient copays, or full out-of-pocket consumer expenditure [9]?

TECHNOLOGY STRATEGIES

Rise and Limitations of Wearables

According to Forrester Research, the average US online adult uses more than four connected devices (from desktops to tablets and eBook readers), 70 percent use a smartphone, and this usage cuts across age groups, from Millennials (born 1981 to 1997) to Boomers (born 1945 to 1964). However, the generation gap is evident for wearables, with usage by 34 percent of Millennials versus only 7 to 11 percent of Boomers [10]. This may be linked to the limited functionality of apps: While their number exceeds 165,000, from Apple iTunes and Google Play (Android), most are only wellness tools, and less than a quarter focus on disease and treatment management. Over half of apps have low functionality, such as simply providing information.

A major barrier to true "scientific wellness," including data analysis by healthcare professionals, remains the lack of interoperability, with only 2 percent of apps linking patients to physicians and healthcare systems. Other adoption barriers are a lack of scientific evidence, limited reimbursement, and privacy and security [11].

The mHealth sector is beginning to evolve from consumer gadgets to prescribed devices, but full integration into EHRs is so far confined to a few pilot programs (Figure 1-7). Despite these limitations, infotech-enabled innovations are being introduced by players of all sizes, from startups to multinationals.

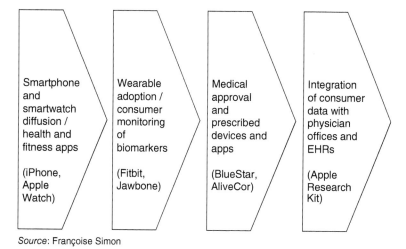

Source: Françoise Simon

Figure 1-7   Evolution of mHealth

New Entrants

WellDoc was first to launch an FDA-approved, physician-prescribed, and payer-reimbursed mobile medical device. Its BlueStar software for continuous glucose monitoring (CGM) was validated with a randomized trial of more than 150 patients, showing a capacity to reduce glycated hemoglobin, that was published in *Diabetes Care* in 2011. FDA clearance via a 510(k) submission supported reimbursement, and WellDoc was able to raise funding from sources such as Merck.

AliveCor, founded in 2010, adopted a hybrid model. While its mobile electrocardiogram (ECG) device was also FDA approved and validated by trials, including those of the Cleveland Clinic, it is marketed online directly to consumers, without a prescription. It can also be sold to physicians, with reimbursement for point-of-care use [12].

Proteus Digital Health innovated in a different way, as it gained in 2012 the first FDA clearance for a medication adherence function for its Ingestible Sensor, a capsule that records and sends to a smartphone the time of ingestion, activity, and heart rate. The adherence indication requires a new drug application filing, but its potential market is significant, as up to half of patients may not be compliant. The company is working with Otsuka to use its sensor with the psychiatric drug Abilify (aripiprazole). Proteus also plans to target common conditions such as cardiometabolic syndrome and high-value drugs such as those for hepatitis C [13].

On a larger scale, Dexcom competes with Medtronic in diabetes, a condition that affects a 29 million population in the United States alone, with estimated direct medical costs of $176 billion and indirect costs of $69 billion, according to the US Department of Health and Human Services. In April 2015, Dexcom announced that its Platinum glucose sensor would be linked to the Apple Watch, to be followed by an integration with Android platforms.

An advantage Medtronic has over Dexcom is that it is the only firm with both a CGM device and an insulin pump. Its MiniMed Connect device was cleared by the FDA in June 2015. Medtronic is also partnering with Samsung to allow CGM and pump data on Samsung devices [14].

BIG INFOTECH STRATEGIES

Technology leaders have entered healthcare with different strategies that reflect their core strengths. Apple remains focused on consumers, whereas Qualcomm and IBM are expanding within a business-to-business (B to B) perspective, and Alphabet may be seen as a holding company with a broad portfolio, from its core Google search engine to biotech Calico.

Apple: Building a Consumer Ecosystem

Apple has become the world's most valued company, with 2016 revenues of nearly $215.6 billion, gained through innovation-driven growth and a role as a category maker. In the same way that it redefined digital music with iTunes, it broke new ground in mobile devices, from the iPod to the iPhone and the iPad, while spending vastly less on R & D than biopharma companies. This is linked to Apple's talent for perfecting through superior design and bringing to the mainstream existing products: MP3 players before the iPod, smartphones before the iPhone, and tablet computers before the iPad.

The power of the brand is such that the "killer app" may be the Apple name itself; in the first 24 hours after the Apple Watch launch, sales reached 1 million devices, and within a few weeks, developers had introduced more than 3,500 apps for it [15].

Apple retains in healthcare its consistent overall strategy: focus on a limited number of products, target the high end of the market, and keep building the Apple brand equity.

As Michael O'Reilly at Apple mentions, "we are committed to making great consumer products with great user experience in the marketplace" [16]. Apple's consumer focus is also apparent in the fact that, after consultation with the FDA, the agency considered the Apple Watch as a wellness tool not subject to regulation. It may now move toward more medical applications, as it is increasingly used in clinical trials. In this context, infotech companies may need to play a future role in screening third-party apps, and data security remains key. Health data collected on Apple devices will not be stored on servers, but instead on IBM's Watson Health cloud, where it will be de-identified and stored for data mining and predictive analytics.

Together, the HealthKit, ResearchKit, and the Apple Watch are meant to constitute a continuous learning environment, linking individual data to health systems.

FROM APPLE TO EPIC: THE ROAD TO DATA INTEGRATION

HealthKit evolved as Apple realized that, with the proliferation of healthcare apps, different apps did not communicate with each other. For this iOS framework introduced as a wellness tool, Apple first formed a partnership with the Mayo Clinic, followed by other health systems, including integration with the Epic EHRs.

The follow-up ResearchKit aims to turn the iPhone into a medical tool helping physicians and scientists gather patient data more frequently and accurately. With it, trial participants can access an interactive consent process, complete active tasks, and submit survey responses. With user permission, researchers can access biomarkers and gain insights on mobility, motor impairment, speech, and memory.

GlucoSuccess, one of the five initial apps, prompts users to log their finger-stick blood glucose levels, and gives visual and text summaries. The app can determine a patient subset whose glucose is more responsive to exercise and can even track the impact of time of day for exercise. This has a potential for biopharma disruption, as exercise could bypass drugs for prediabetes cases, for instance.

Other projects include, in dermatology, a study at Oregon Health and Science University on iPhone images to measure moles over time and allow globally collected data to help create new detection algorithms.

The Apple Watch links to ResearchKit. The EpiWatch app from Johns Hopkins will test whether biosensors can detect the onset and duration of epileptic seizures, capture their digital signature through activity and heart rate data, and send an alert to caregivers. The app also aims to track medication adherence and side effects. In addition, the CareKit now allows developers to build apps to track symptoms and monitor treatment effectiveness, facilitate medical dosing, and permit patients to share data with family members and providers [17].

While ResearchKit is already used by leading health systems, some issues remain. Monetization is not one of them, however, as Apple views it largely in philanthropic terms and does not have proprietary claims to the related apps, because it was released as an open-source platform.

Portability to Android and other platforms will need to occur through third-party developers. Selection bias exists in two ways: the relatively upscale iOS demographics versus those of Android users (who are more numerous, especially outside of the United States) and the "active/take-charge" behavior profile of customers. While the Apple Watch may lead to higher user engagement, it still has a fairly limited worldwide market. Misrepresentation may also pose a problem, as is the case for all social media. ResearchKit participants may disguise their gender, age, or medical condition. This may be addressed through patient identification by physicians in clinical trials.

What remains to be seen is whether these mobile devices can actually impact outcomes, and whether there is enough user incentivization for them to graduate from niche to mainstream products. Will consumers worldwide want to diligently monitor their health, or will many wearables sit on shelves after novelty fatigue, information overload, privacy concerns, and lack of time prevail over health activism?

Qualcomm: From Chips to Health Ventures

Within an overall strategy of "end-to-end two-way connectivity," Qualcomm Ventures has made investments in companies as diverse as Fitbit, AliveCor, AirStrip Technologies, Telcare (disease management), Sotera (wireless telemetry), and ClearCare (mobile platforms for home care providers).

In healthcare, Qualcomm is in three lines of business:

- *Venture investments:* Through the Life Fund and the dRx Capital Fund, a joint venture with Novartis with a capital commitment of up to $100 million, for early stage investments in companies including Omada Health (digital behavioral medicine), Science 37 (clinical research) and Cala Health (bio-electronics to develop therapies in neurology).

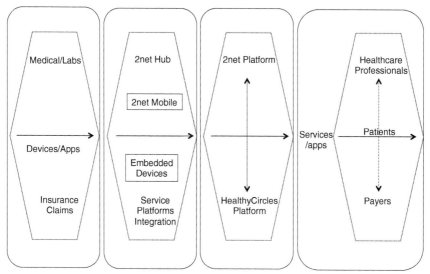

Source: Adapted from Qualcomm Ventures

Figure 1-8   Qualcomm Life ecosystem

- *Platforms:* With its 2net system (acting as middleware between patient and claims data, and healthcare professionals), and the HealthyCircles care coordination platform, monitoring a patient's status at home and optimizing care management.
- *Licensing and acquisitions:* Among others, Qualcomm Life acquired Capsule Technologie, a French provider of medical integration, with more than 1,930 hospital clients in over 38 countries. This supports an extension into acute and ambulatory care, with the goal of leading to the Internet of Medical Things (IoMT) for the company (Figure 1-8).

While, in its core chip business, Qualcomm competes directly with Intel, its technology overlaps that of other players such as Samsung. The company can be seen as a technology enabler rather than a business-to-consumer (B to C) player [18].

IBM: From Hardware to Software and Cloud Services

IBM first formalized its healthcare involvement with the Life Sciences Solutions unit it formed in 2000 and its early partnerships with Spotfire and Agilent in data management and MDS in proteomics. These complemented IBM's long-term development of its Blue Gene computer and academic collaborations with universities including Duke, Georgia Tech, and Johns Hopkins [19].

Since then, IBM has continued to evolve from a horizontal technology company to one delivering comprehensive vertical solutions. This is shown by extensive acquisitions and partnerships, from Apple to Medtronic, and the introduction in April 2015 of its Watson Health unit, with its own budget and R & D.

Through the Watson ecosystem, IBM may provide B to B to C solutions, aggregating clinical and claims data at the population health level and from the medical literature, and combining them with individual genomic data to support precision medicine. Within IBM, distinct groups also cover health systems and biopharmaceuticals [20]. Watson Health leverages broad datasets, including 100 million electronic health records, 200 million claims records, and 30 billion medical images. Watson for Genomics absorbs 10,000 new medical articles and data from 100 trials every month, and it is available through Quest Diagnostics to oncologists in the United States.

Current strategic objectives are the management of data (which IBM views as the world's new "natural resource"), cloud computing, and customer engagement through mobile and social technologies. IBM has made multiple acquisitions to build its capacity in data analytics. This includes the acquisitions of Explorys (spun off in 2009 from the Cleveland Clinic), Phytel (with cloud software for hospital data), and Merge Healthcare in October 2015 for $1 billion (in radiology and imaging services), as well as Truven in 2016 (analytic solutions for healthcare utilization, quality, and cost data).

For cloud services, which IBM sees as a "catalyst for innovation," the company has invested more than $8 billion to acquire 18 companies [21]. To expand its global footprint, the company has been partnering with many others across countries.

Apple and IBM in Japan   In April 2015, the two companies announced a collaboration with Japan Post group, the largest health and life insurer in Japan, to deliver iPads with IBM-developed apps to an intended target group of 4 to 5 million seniors by 2020. Japan has one of the world's fastest-aging populations, with 33 million seniors accounting for a quarter of the population, and a projected growth of 40 percent over the next 40 years. Custom-built IBM apps include exercise and medication reminders, access to community activities, and supporting services, with data stored by the cloud services of the IBM MobileFirst for iOS platform [22].

While this is a global priority, as the elderly will increase from 11.7 percent in 2013 to 21 percent of the population by 2050, several questions remain regarding security, outcomes, and global rollout. Some consumer segments may not wish to release their individual data, even though these are de-identified; multiyear studies will be needed to determine the project's actual impact on health outcomes, and such a large-scale national rollout may be possible in single-payer systems in Europe but not in the fragmented US insurance market.

Medtech and Pharma Alliances   IBM now has a wide range of life sciences partnerships. In diabetes, it announced in April 2015 a collaboration with Medtronic, using Watson to create an "Internet of Things" around its devices.

This aims to support real-time care management plans and to explore closed-loop algorithms intending to mimic a healthy pancreas function [23]. Other initiatives include a Johnson & Johnson partnership, applying Watson to prepare patients for knee surgery and help afterwards with care management.

Watson Partnerships The Watson cloud service is rapidly gaining customers. By May 2015, 14 cancer centers had already signed on to combine genetic databases and the medical literature to optimize treatments. These ranged from the Cleveland Clinic and Duke Cancer Institute to the University of Washington and the Yale Cancer Center. IBM plans to integrate Watson's cognitive abilities with the Epic EHR system and decision-support technology [24].

With the resources of partners such as Memorial Sloan-Kettering, Mount Sinai, and MD Anderson, IBM aims to apply Watson's cognitive computing in several areas:

- At the point of care, it may facilitate evidence-based medicine for providers.
- For researchers, it may optimize drug discovery and standards of care.
- For consumers, it may enhance activity and adherence via real-world sensing.

While these applications impact the entire healthcare area, IBM has a key objective to create a new middle layer in the system, linking EHRs and R & D centers with a new cloud-based architecture.

Alphabet: Expanding a Healthcare Portfolio

While Apple's identity is that of a consumer-focused company, and IBM's main business is within the B to B realm, Alphabet is expanding a broad range of activities, from its core consumer-centered Google Search to its Verily unit and the Calico biotechnology company, founded in 2013 under the leadership of Art Levinson, the former Genentech CEO.

Among infotech leaders, Google has shown a great willingness to innovate and explore far-reaching growth avenues, at the risk of facing failures in the process. It introduced Google Health in 2008 with the goal of helping customers set up online personalized health records, but it may have been ahead of the market. Early users found it burdensome to manually enter their own data, and the initiative did not have a compelling value proposition. As a result, Google abandoned this service three years later. By 2011, an IDC survey showed that only 7 percent of consumers had tried online health records, and fewer than half of them continued to use them. Suppliers of similar services included Microsoft and WebMD, but the more successful services have often operated through alliances with insurers and providers [25].

This history of mixed success in vertical businesses including healthcare may explain, in part, Alphabet's new structure. While the company has more than 80 units covering everything from robotics to fiber optics, virtual reality, and

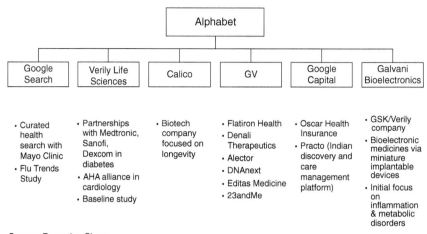

Source: Françoise Simon

Figure 1-9   Alphabet healthcare portfolio

self-driving cars, the reorganization enables them to be more independent and entrepreneurial. Healthcare initiatives span the core search business (a curated search project with the Mayo Clinic and other health systems), the Verily unit (biopharma alliances in diabetes), the Calico biotechnology company, and a portfolio of investments by GV (initially known as Google Ventures) and Google Capital (Figure 1-9).

Alphabet does not appear to envision becoming a healthcare company overall, largely because of concerns shared by many infotechs about pharma regulation, and is pursuing many related initiatives through partnerships.

Google Search and Mayo Clinic   In its core search business, Alphabet announced in February 2015 a partnership with the Mayo Clinic to provide enhanced information, to be curated by Mayo doctors and delivered on PC and tablet browsers as well as Google mobile apps on the Android and iOS platforms. This may cover conditions ranging from diabetes to the measles. The service does not include actual medical advice, but it intends to address the current problem of pseudoscience on the Internet [26].

Google has sought for several years to leverage its successful customer engagement to deliver more granular healthcare information. In 2008, it announced a predictive flu-tracking model, correlating its own searches with flu data in 2003 to 2007 from the CDC (Centers for Disease Control). A 2014 academic review pointed to a possible overestimation of flu prevalence, inasmuch as some correlations may have been unrelated to actual flu history [27]. While Google updated its model, there may be further potential for a collaboration with the FDA for adverse event tracking, because the sheer volume of related postings on social media like Twitter and Facebook does not allow accurate monitoring.

Verily Partnerships   The Verily unit has a wide range of acquisitions and alliances, and it is adopting a disease-centric viewpoint, with a first focus on diabetes. In 2014, the unit partnered with the Novartis subsidiary Alcon to develop a contact lens that could noninvasively track glucose levels in tears, obtaining a patent in 2015. The device includes miniaturized versions of a chip, sensor, and antenna, aiming to transmit data every second. Clinical trials were initiated, with a goal of obtaining FDA approval.

The focus on diabetes was strengthened in August 2015 with two new partnerships with Sanofi and the Joslin Diabetes Center, and with Dexcom for a glucose monitoring device. The Sanofi alliance aims to develop new tools to integrate previously siloed components of diabetes management, including indicators such as blood glucose and hemoglobin A1C, patient-reported information, and medication regimens. Objectives include helping physicians understand daily trends in blood sugar and offering patients real-time information and guidance in diet and medication dosage [28]. The alliance was formalized in September 2016 as Onduo, with a joint investment of about $500 million.

At the same time, Verily teamed with Dexcom to develop a bandage-like disposable sensor, linked to a smartphone app for CGM, with a first version planned in two to three years and another generation in the next five years. Verily is expected to limit its role to R & D, with Dexcom handling sales and distribution. The deal includes an initial upfront payment of $35 million, R & D milestone payments up to $65 million, and revenue-based royalties of 5 to 9 percent from Dexcom [29]. Although these partnerships are separate, as they lead to commercial products, the goal will be to integrate miniaturization technology, sensors, and data analytics, with a potential to disrupt diabetes care management. In another area, Verily formed in December 2015 Verb Surgical, an independent company with Johnson & Johnson, focused on developing surgical instruments for a new robotics-assisted platform.

In addition to these efforts, Verily is engaged in several broader studies. In November 2015, it announced a five-year, $50 million collaboration with the American Heart Association (AHA), with each partner contributing half of the funding, and a single team working on new approaches to research the causes, treatment, and prevention of heart disease.

An earlier initiative announced in July 2014 is a Baseline Study, collecting thousands of individual genetic data to identify patterns of genetic mutations, with a goal to define a healthy human body and to identify new biomarkers to detect conditions such as cancer and heart attacks at earlier stages. Google was to collaborate on the study with the Duke and Stanford medical schools. Verily's long-term opportunity is to build chronic disease models as a path to better outcomes; for diabetes, this includes disease management and medication dosing, and also behavioral changes such as diet and activity [30].

Galvani Bioelectronics   Verily and GlaxoSmithKline (GSK) announced on August 1, 2016, an agreement to form Galvani Bioelectronics, aiming to develop and commercialize bioelectronics medicines. This fairly new field targets a range of chronic diseases, using miniaturized implantable devices that can modify electrical signals along nerves. GSK has researched this since 2012, and Verily brings expertise in data analytics, the miniaturization of low-power electronics, software, and device development. The initial goal is to reach clinical proofs of principle in inflammatory and metabolic disorders, including type 2 diabetes. GSK is to have 55 percent equity in the venture, and Verily will hold the rest [31].

Calico Partnerships   In addition to the wide-ranging initiatives from the Verily unit, Calico has started several biopharma alliances since its start in 2013. Within its focus on longevity, it started in September 2014 a collaboration with AbbVie to create an R & D facility in the San Francisco Bay Area, specialized in age-related diseases, including cancer and neurodegeneration. Each partner was to initially provide up to $250 million, with the potential to contribute an additional $500 million. AbbVie is to provide scientific and technical support, as well as commercial expertise in bringing products to market [32]. Other partnerships include C4 Therapeutics (protein degradation), QB3 (age-related diseases), as well as the Broad Institute of MIT and Harvard, the University of Texas Southwestern Medical Center, and the University of California in San Francisco.

Google Investments   To complete these initiatives, Alphabet has also broadly invested in healthcare through its two investment arms. GV was founded as Google Ventures in 2009 and has since accumulated more than $2 billion under management in 300 companies, including the Uber car service and the office messaging system Slack. The fund's objectives are financial return and also access to operational help for its portfolio companies. It has moved strongly into healthcare since 2014, with more than a third of its current funding in this sector. This includes more than $100 million in Flatiron Health (applying analytics to oncology data), Editas Medicine (genome editing firm with expertise in CRISPR/Cas9 technology), and DNAnexus (next-generation cloud-based sequence data management).

Biotech companies include Alector and Denali Therapeutics in neurodegenerative diseases, Compass Therapeutics in antibody discovery, Rani Therapeutics for the oral delivery of large molecules, and SynapDx (blood test for autism). GV also invested in 2017 in Arsanis (monoclonal antibodies), Magenta Therapeutics (stem cell research for cancer) and Science 37 (mobile technology and clinical trial provider).

In addition, Google Capital was formed in 2013 as a late-stage growth venture capital fund. It has since invested in a dozen companies, in areas such as big data, financial technology, security, and e-learning. Its 2015 healthcare investments include Practo in India (healthcare discovery and practice management platform) and Oscar Health Insurance, with $32.5 million in funding for the latter [33].

Oscar competes against UnitedHealthcare, Anthem, and other insurers by focusing on Internet services for individuals, including free fitness-tracking and unlimited telemedicine, and signs up customers through online exchanges created by the 2010 Affordable Care Act (ACA). A potential goal of the partnership is for Oscar to help distribute new Google products to its members [34].

The scale of these investments does not obscure the fact that Alphabet, like other infotech leaders, is keeping its core business at a safe distance from heavy biopharma regulation.

In the same year as Google closed Google Health, Microsoft folded its Health Solutions group into the Caradigm joint venture with General Electric (GE). Caradigm is a population health company with an enterprise software portfolio including healthcare analytics, data control and security, care management, and patient engagement. Its partnerships include the Geisinger Health Plan and the Eliza Corporation for health engagement management [35].

Microsoft has, for now, stayed away from vertical business forays, leveraging instead its Windows platform dominance with partnerships. These include a collaboration with Johns Hopkins, announced in October 2015. Based on the latter's Project Emerge, the new solution will apply data analytics to show when a patient in intensive care requires treatment to prevent complications; it will scale existing workflows and care concepts into an integrated system for patients, families, and care teams, with a move to Microsoft's Cloud for real-time intelligence. It will also link with Microsoft Azure to connect disparate devices into an Internet of Things. The goal is to deliver this to health systems nationally and to transform the management of intensive care [36].

A new entrant into healthcare is Amazon. It has stated its interest in the pharmacy business, and it joined Johnson & Johnson, Bristol Myers Squibb, Merck, Varian Medical Systems, and China's Tencent for an investment totaling $900 million in Grail. A spin-off in 2016 from gene sequencer Illumina, Grail was set up to develop a comprehensive cancer screening test for asymptomatic patients, sequencing tumor DNA in blood samples and combining it with datasets from its population-scale clinical trials. Its first trial plans eventually to enroll 10,000 participants. Together with IBM's Watson Health, this illustrates the growing importance of integrating knowledge from large databases into diagnostic and drug development [37].

CONCLUSION

The convergence of infotech and healthcare may lead to a profound transformation of biopharma business models, and infotech companies may gain a dual role as enablers and disrupters. They are most likely to do so as external players, due to concerns about regulation, long development cycles, and different cultures.

Areas of opportunity include the optimization of clinical trials, as cognitive computing tools such as Watson aggregate data from multiple sources and apply them to individuals to enable precision medicine. Real-time data streaming from biosensors may also help optimize trials; the use of Apple's ResearchKit has already enabled broad enrollments [38]. It may also disrupt biopharma, as diurnal variations in biomarkers, linked to exercise patterns, may allow patients with conditions such as prediabetes to bypass early drug therapy.

For biopharma companies, there is, so far, a lack of a clear value proposition for significant investments in digital health. They may therefore need to view it not as a classic investment but as a hedging of the risk that infotech leaders and new entrants will own a dominant position in that space.

The next two chapters will further examine financing and alliance strategies for biopharma companies, including possible partnerships with infotech firms.

SUMMARY POINTS

- Biotechnology has now matured and is driving innovation across sectors, from medicine and food to agriculture and biomaterials.
- Information technology companies have rapidly entered the health space in a new convergence that presents both an opportunity and a threat for biopharma firms.
- Infotechs are playing a key role, with digital solutions through the value chain; in R & D, digital tools can optimize clinical trials and streamline data analytics; at the commercial end, these tools may allow deep integration of the customer voice, from product co-creation to post-launch communications.
- Infotechs are entering healthcare with different strategies that reflect their core strengths, from Apple to IBM and Alphabet.
- Apple is building a consumer ecosystem, from its HealthKit partnership with the Mayo Clinic to its Apple Watch that tracks vital signs and aims to optimize outcomes.
- IBM is extending its vertical solutions through acquisitions such as Explorys and Phytel; Watson Health may provide BtoBtoC solutions, aggregating clinical, claim, and journal data for researchers, and combining them with individual genomic data to support precision medicine.
- Alphabet has built a large portfolio, from its core Google Search to Verily and longevity-focused Calico Life Sciences; Verily has several diabetes alliances with Novartis, Sanofi, and Dexcom; GV and Google Capital investments range from Flatiron Health (oncology analytics) to Oscar Health Insurance.
- These investments do not obscure the fact that infotech business models differ greatly from those of biopharmas, from rapid production times to a greater tolerance for risk and a wish to avoid healthcare's heavy regulation.

- Convergence barriers are also significant, from consumer privacy and security concerns to physician reimbursement, liability, and lack of infrastructure to handle massive patient data flows.
- The objective of providing seamless patient care remains elusive, given the siloed nature of digital innovation and the lack of interoperability between consumer biosensors, physician offices, and hospital electronic systems.
- Despite these uncertainties, the new convergence is profoundly transforming biopharma business models; this may evolve into an enabling scenario (optimized research and clinical trials), but it could also be a disruptive one (disintermediation by infotechs of patient/physician/researcher communications).

CHAPTER 2

BIOTECHNOLOGY FINANCING STRATEGIES

The primary way that biotechnology companies create long-term value for society and their investors is through the development of innovative products that address significant unmet medical needs. This is an inherently high-risk, high-reward activity. The simple fact is that most drug development efforts do not result in a product approval [1]. Founders and funders must contend with a number of different types of uncertainty, including scientific risk, regulatory risk, financial risk, and, increasingly, payer risk. As a result, a core competency entrepreneurs must develop is the ability to market the company's story to investors, including addressing how inherent risks will be mitigated. Among these risks is how the product or technology under development will result in improved outcomes (and therefore differentiated value) for patients and increasingly value-conscious payers, even if that result is a decade or more away. As Ed Mathers, a partner at NEA Ventures, notes

> "We still ask 'will it work?', but now we also ask 'will it matter?'. If a new product or platform doesn't matter to payers and pharma companies, then we are unlikely to invest in it. Nowadays, the product must not only work clinically and provide some measurable benefit relative to the standard of care, it must also offer economic advantages in terms of impacting the overall cost of therapy" [2].

Further, the value of a product may only be fully realized through novel business models that go "beyond the pill," which, as described in Chapter 1, may require novel collaborations with infotech firms and other "nontraditional" partners.

THE LONG GAME

Despite significant advances in scientific understanding and advanced clinical development strategies that leverage the latest digital and other enabling technologies, drug development, on average, still requires a decade or more and

Managing Biotechnology: From Science to Market in the Digital Age, First Edition. Françoise Simon and Glen Giovannetti.
© 2017 John Wiley & Sons, Inc. Published 2017 by John Wiley & Sons, Inc.

significant amounts of capital—all before the first dollar of profit is realized [3]. Indeed, including the expenditures associated with failed drugs and the cost of capital, in November 2014, the Tufts Center for the Study of Drug Development estimated that it costs $2.6 billion to successfully develop a drug [4]. Even if one counts only the costs of successfully bringing a specific drug to market, as companies tackle increasingly complex diseases and development times lengthen, it is not uncommon for companies to require more than $500 million (and at times, substantially more) prior to launching a first product. For example, companies such as Vertex Pharmaceuticals, Regeneron Pharmaceuticals, and Incyte Pharmaceuticals all raised in excess of $1 billion from the issuance of equity securities prior to their initial product, and Pharmacyclics, which elected to sell itself to AbbVie for $21 billion soon after the launch of its first product, raised in excess of $800 million [5]. Thus, companies need to recognize a central truth: because multiple kinds of financing amassed over many years will be required to bring a product to market, each financing transaction is just a piece of an overall long-term strategy.

Because of these long time frames and capital intensity, while most infotech companies have significant healthcare businesses as noted in Chapter 1, they have not been frequent investors in biopharma companies pursuing drug development. However, as data and analytics capabilities and technologies such as artificial intelligence become more critical to the creation of value in biopharma, this could change. In addition, we can expect to see more companies formed with business models focused on amassing health data to create new insights for drug development and patient care which, like Grail discussed in the previous chapter, will be of interest to infotech players.

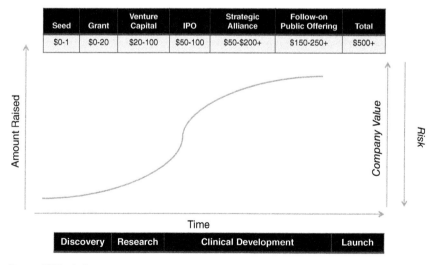

Seed	Grant	Venture Capital	IPO	Strategic Alliance	Follow-on Public Offering	Total
$0-1	$0-20	$20-100	$50-100	$50-$200+	$150-250+	$500+

Source: EY Analysis

Figure 2-1   Biotech company funding sources and representative amounts (US$, millions)

Year	Grants*	Venture Capital	IPO	Strategic Alliances*^	Follow-on Public Offering	Total
2002		$17				$17
2003		28		$7		35
2004			$30	12		42
2005				72		72
2006	$12			5	163	180
2007	12			331	60	403
2008	7			140		147
2009	4			21		25
2010	2			20		22
2011				19		19
2012				53	87	140
2013				39	174	213
2014				763		763
2015				89	496	585

Source: EY Analysis based on Alnylam Pharmaceuticals' financial statements
*Approximate cash flow per year.
^Includes equity purchased by strategic alliance partners of approximately $930 million.

Figure 2-2   Biotech company funding—Alnylam Pharmaceuticals

Figure 2-1 presents typical financing ranges by source of capital and stage of development. Figure 2-2 presents the case study of Alnylam Pharmaceuticals, a pioneer in RNAi technologies, which has raised in excess of $2.6 billion since its founding in 2002 (also see the text box, "Financing Strategies for the Long-Term at Alnylam"). Alnylam, with a lead product in Phase III development, has leveraged its broad technology platform to raise more than $1.5 billion from 10 strategic alliance partners, including over $900 million from the issuance of equity to select partners (through December 2015). The majority of biotechnology companies will not have a technology platform as broad as Alnylam's and thus would expect to raise more from public offerings of equity than from collaborations.

FINANCING STRATEGIES FOR THE LONG TERM AT ALNYLAM

By John Maraganore, Chief Executive Officer, Alnylam Pharmaceuticals

Founded in 2002, Alnylam Pharmaceuticals develops therapies based on RNA interference (RNAi), a distinct mechanism for targeting and turning off genes that play fundamental roles in disease development. Specifically, our technology "silences" messenger RNA (mRNA) that encodes disease-causing proteins. RNAi was discovered by researchers at the Carnegie Institution and the University of Massachusetts, who were awarded a Nobel Prize in 2006. Alnylam unlocked the full therapeutic potential of RNAi, first showing that the pathway can be harnessed in animals and, ultimately, in humans.

As of mid-2017, we have 8 RNAi therapeutics in clinical trials that address serious, life-threatening illnesses with limited treatment options. Many of Alnylam's investigational therapeutics target rare diseases with significant unmet patient needs. Our company, which went public in 2004 at an approximately $100-million market value and traded for some years at less than cash value, now has a market capitalization of approximately $7.5 billion.

We sometimes relate the Alnylam story to a classic children's book, *The Carrot Seed*, by Ruth Krauss, which captures simply and elegantly the challenges of biotechnology development generally and Alnylam's success specifically:

A child plants a single seed in bare ground. As he diligently waters and weeds, each member of his family expresses doubt that it will grow. For quite some time, the seed does not sprout, but the child continues to water and weed against the continued doubt of others. Eventually, it sprouts and delivers an enormous carrot, just as the child always knew it would.

At Alnylam, we appreciate that skepticism can be healthy, particularly in the biotech arena where there are enormous technical hurdles and risks. But when you trust your science, vision, and people to deliver great things, perseverance becomes an indispensable quality for converting promise into reality.

So what are the key principles that steer Alnylam's financing strategy so that we can realize the promise of our science while protecting the integrity of the company and its top-line objectives?

Plan but Remain Opportunistic

Markets are sometimes open and sometimes closed, and investor interest in technologies or therapeutic areas ebbs and wanes over time, so flexibility is crucial. The key is to do the best possible deal at the right time. Ultimately, both raising equity and giving away product rights in a partnership cause economic dilution to shareholders that must be more than made up for in potential future upside.

Establish What Is Nonnegotiable

We appreciate that deals are necessary to fuel the organization and its development programs. We also understand that transactions always involve giving up something of value to secure both current and future financing to advance scientific programs and keep the lights on. But we have some firm boundaries as well—internal assets we consider "untouchable" for ensuring that we continue to control the company, its strategic direction, and the core intellectual property around which all our success revolves. We consider these core assets our children and, no matter how well-intentioned the surrogate, no one is going to love and nurture our children as we do.

Do Not Give Away Too Much

Once we determine which assets are "off the table," we negotiate deals that further our financial goals without compromising our independence. Raising cash is imperative to our progress, but we need to maintain a balance between securing necessary funding and ceding control. We pursue terms—whether selling whole pieces or percentages—that maintain our strategic advantage and never trade off anything that undermines what we are trying to build. Likewise, we are mindful that geographies matter, so we ensure that we retain rights in global markets of prominence in the pharmaceutical business, such as North America and the European Union.

Prioritize Value-Creating Alliances

Of course, certain monetary goals can be reached through equity offerings, which if timed and priced properly, can offset dilution with the promise that ready cash affords for advancing development programs. But we are most interested in deals that forge alliances with partners who bring expertise, resources and market access to either complement our own strengths or open entirely new vistas. What we tend to avoid are deals with limited long-term benefit, such as those involving single products that do not contribute to our universal strategies.

Passing the Baton

Given the magnitude of the capital required for drug development, many players must participate in the successful funding of a start-up biotech company, with no one player having the capacity to fund the entire amount on its own. These different players have a unique role to play in the capitalization of the biotech, depending on its maturity. The sources of capital typically include many of the following:

- Angel or other "seed" stage investors
- Venture capital firms
- Corporate venture capital
- "Crossover" investment funds
- Public investors such as mutual funds, hedge funds, and retail investors
- Grants from governments and disease foundations
- Collaborations with larger pharmaceutical or biotechnology companies

In the future, new sources of capital from crowdfunding platforms and non-traditional backers, including information technology or healthcare services companies, may play a larger role as well. While not strictly drug development, the Grail financing transaction noted in Chapter 1 is a relevant example.

At the start-up stage, this journey is analogous to a relay race in which the job of management is to cultivate relationships and market the company's story so that the next group of investors is ready to "take the baton" when needed. But even experienced management teams with strong business and financing strategies can be subject to the inevitable ebbs and flows of the biotech financing market. Some of this volatility is inherent in all sectors as investors look broadly for value-creating opportunities and periodically shift their investment focus to sectors that appear poised for a rise in value. As noted earlier, however, drug development is a particularly high-risk, high-reward proposition, with risks coming from many parts of the business model.

Worries about general economic trends, or sector-specific concerns, such as the growing influence of healthcare payers on drug prices, may drive investors to look for relatively safer investments. This situation tends to result in pronounced fluctuations in the availability of capital for biotech companies and can lead to protracted periods during which the public financing market is virtually closed, especially for initial public offerings (IPOs) (Figure 2-3). This has happened on multiple occasions over the history of the biotech industry.

At a macro level, the biotech financing ecosystem breaks down if one class of investors is not available or interested when needed. For example, in periods in which a market for IPOs is not available to biotech companies, venture capital investment comes under enormous strain as venture capitalists (VCs) must continue to fund their portfolio companies for longer than anticipated. This, in turn, has an impact on their rate of return, which can result in fewer dollars invested in such venture capital firms and, therefore, fewer start-ups financed down the road.

First-time biotech chief executive officers (CEOs) are frequently surprised at the amount of time they spend raising capital and communicating with existing investors, both as private enterprises and especially following an IPO transaction. But, given the underlying risks, drug development and company building require both scientific and financial optionality. Management teams must build in the financial optionality to ensure that there are sufficient resources to enable the scientific pivots that may be necessary as greater knowledge regarding a technology or product candidate is obtained. Katrine Bosley, CEO of gene editing pioneer Editas Medicine, notes, "Even if the CEO thinks two or three steps ahead, the reality he or she responds to will be different from the plan. By thinking through multiple scenarios over several years, the

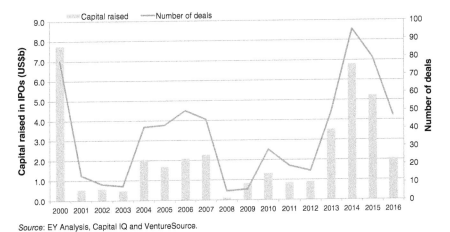

Source: EY Analysis, Capital IQ and VentureSource.

Figure 2-3   US and European biotechnology IPOs (2000–2016)

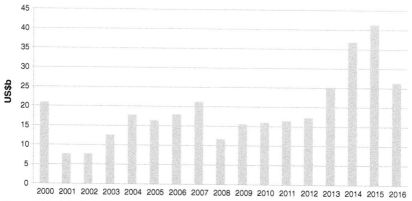

Source: EY Analysis, Capital IQ and VentureSource.
Innovation capital is the amount of capital raised by companies with revenues of less than US$500 million.

Figure 2-4   Capital raised by US and European biotechs with revenue of <$500 M (2000–2016)

CEO has a better grasp of how much capital will be required to reach the next value-creating milestone" [6].

Successful companies must have two core capabilities: first, the discipline of understanding the interests and needs of investors and strategic collaborators; second, the ability to explain the company's story. Both capabilities are critical from a company's earliest days and never lose importance.

While the total amount of equity financing for pre-commercial companies has recovered since the global financial crisis in 2008 (see Figure 2-4), it is also true that the investment is heavily concentrated, with approximately one-third of all companies raising equity capital in the United States in 2015 commanding 80 percent of capital raised. For pre-IPO, venture capital-backed companies, the picture is similar [7]. Thus, devising and executing the right fundraising strategy can be a source of significant competitive advantage, allowing companies to pursue multiple technologies or therapeutic areas.

STRATEGIC DECISIONS

How Much Capital to Raise

There is an adage in biotech to always "take the money" when it is available, although the reality is often more nuanced. When raising capital—whether as a privately held company or following an IPO—it is the responsibility of the management team to have formulated a plan that clearly explains to investors how the available invested capital will be utilized to provide a return commensurate with the risk.

In difficult financing environments, a company may only be able to raise enough capital to take its lead product to the next scientific or clinical milestone (referred to as a value inflection point). In this situation, it is critical that companies raise sufficient capital to reach this point, building in a cushion that accounts for potential unanticipated hurdles. That is because it is extremely difficult, not to mention dilutive to the interests of current shareholders, to be forced to return to investors for additional capital to complete the necessary research effort. At the same time, in periods where capital is relatively more available, it may not be advisable to take capital at levels well beyond the company's needs or managements plans to create value for shareholders. The greater the sum raised, the more difficult it is to achieve the high rate of return that investors (especially VCs) require, which may result in unforeseen pressure on a company's strategy or even pressure to sell the business entirely. Said another way, the financing and capital allocation strategy of the company must be closely linked to the research and development and business strategy, including defining priorities (reallocation of capital if a product candidate is delayed or fails during development), related budgets, and key milestones. Editas Medicine's Katrine Bosley notes, "In flush times, raising more money is tempting because it's easy. Still the CEO must understand why she is raising the money. Will the capital allow the company to pursue productive activities at a faster pace, or is the additional money simply more runway? Both options are legitimate, but the CEO should be able to articulate why she is raising that specific amount of money and how it fits with the company's overall capital strategy particularly alongside business development and grant activities" [8].

Pricing and Dilution

Equity capital is the lifeblood of every biotech company and is necessary to maximize the creation of value. That said, each financing transaction dilutes the holdings of founders and existing investors. As a result, determining the price per share can be a sensitive negotiation. Given the serial nature of biotech fundraising (i.e., companies need to return to the same investor groups repeatedly), it is important for management teams to balance the desire to maximize the price per share at each fundraising (thereby minimizing their own dilution) with the reality of needing to leave some room in the valuation for shareholders to earn a satisfactory return.

So-called nondilutive capital can be an important complement to the sale of equity. Most commonly, this term refers to out-licensing of some of the company's technology in exchange for a license fee and other consideration. While not dilutive from the perspective of voting equity securities, these arrangements do "dilute" the value of the enterprise by transferring ownership of a potential income-earning asset to the licensee. Nevertheless, for a variety of reasons discussed in greater detail below and in Chapter 3, strategic alliances are a critical component of any financing strategy.

True non-dilutive capital, in the form of research grants from government agencies or from disease foundations, can be an important component of an overall financing strategy, especially for companies working in areas of high unmet need or where governments have a strong public health interest (e.g., in infectious diseases). These sources of capital are discussed later in this chapter.

When to Raise Capital

The reality is that biotech management teams typically feel like they are always in the process of raising capital because of the need to be in continuous dialog with existing and potential future investors. The timing of successive rounds of financing is an important consideration, however. While financing after a value-creating event (e.g., an important proof of concept or a clinical trial readout) is most desirable from a valuation and dilution standpoint, it is important not to underestimate how long it may take to close a financing round, even in a healthy investment climate. Management teams that delay too long may find that they are left with fewer options. Further, a company is in a stronger negotiating position with potential investors if it has a comfortable cushion of cash on its balance sheet. In fact, it is not uncommon for companies to close a financing round in advance of a value-creating event, accepting a lower overall valuation in exchange for removing the risk of not being able to close a deal if the event outcome is either unclear or negative.

Adaptations to Preserve Capital

Most companies follow a traditional financing model, consisting of multiple rounds of venture capital, one or more strategic collaborations with larger pharmaceutical or biotech companies, an IPO, and then a series of follow-on public equity offerings. However, biotech companies have, because of necessity, become adept and creative in accessing nontraditional sources of capital and developing new business models to minimize net cash outflows.

Through the experience of managing difficult financing cycles (or closed "windows," as they are referred to in the industry), companies and investors have devised various strategies preserve scarce capital, including:

- Outsourcing certain noncore functions to lower-cost markets
- Developing new sources of cash flow by broadly licensing a core technology on a nonexclusive basis or performing research services for other companies (a strategy that gained traction in Europe in periods of relative scarcity of capital)
- Pursing orphan or ultra-rare diseases, which typically require smaller, less expensive clinical trials
- Utilizing biomarkers or other precision medicine techniques to more precisely identify patients likely to benefit from a particular therapy
- Adopting "fail-fast" (and cheaper) development models in which experiments and trials are designed to find the flaw in a particular technology as early as possible and certainly before expensive late-stage clinical trials

- Participating in precompetitive industry consortia that are working on shared (underlying) scientific issues or combining data to discover new insights and improve efficiency
- Repurposing existing drugs for new markets

Whether developing a broad technology platform or adopting a more targeted approach, companies and their investors must be single-minded in the execution of their chosen strategy

GEOGRAPHIC CONSIDERATIONS

As in real estate, in biotech fundraising, location matters. The United States is by far the most open and dynamic financing environment for biotechnology, with a deep and experienced group of venture capital investors and a public market characterized by pools of institutional capital (e.g., mutual funds and pension funds) and investors that possess a higher risk appetite for research and development stage investments, with all their incumbent risks. Equity market regulation is also focused on disclosure, rather than limiting the kinds of companies that are allowed to raise capital, as is the case in some other countries. Clearly, biotechnology innovation and investment occurs in many regions around the world, but the sums raised and deployed in the United States dwarf all other countries. Thus, in the sections that follow, most of the discussion focuses on the dynamics of the US financing market, although most of the concepts are also applicable in Europe and other regions with significant concentrations of biotechnology companies.

SOURCES OF FINANCING

Seed Capital

Sometimes referred to as the "friends and family" round, small, pre-venture capital financings are actually less common in biotech than in high technology, where it is not uncommon for a company to reach the market and begin generating revenue with a relatively small amount of equity capital. Given the product development timelines and the substantial capital needs that are the norm in biotech, most companies begin with a round of venture financing that, as discussed in greater detail below, typically comes with at least a soft commitment to provide additional capital in the future. That said, if a start-up company requires some capital to achieve an early research milestone or early proof of concept in order to interest venture investors, there are a few sources beyond mortgaging the house or tapping friends and family.

Angel Investors Angels are typically wealthy individuals who chose to invest in start-up companies alone or in a network with other investors. These investors frequently are veterans of the industry and understand the risk profile of the biotech business model. Angel networks operate in many cities in the United States and Europe. Life sciences–specific angel networks are typically found in areas of significant industry concentration, for example, Boston (Mass Medical Angels) and San Francisco (Life Science Angels) [9]. According to annual research performed by the Center for Venture Research at the Peter T. Paul College of Business and Economics at the University of New Hampshire, investments in biotech companies by angel investors comprised between approximately 5 and 15 percent of total angel investments between 2000 and 2014 [10].

Crowdfunding   Not to be confused with crowdsourcing, which has grown in popularity as a means to bring many minds with diverse backgrounds to consider a particular challenge (scientific, design, business, etc.), the objective of crowd-funding is to find individuals willing to commit capital to a particular idea. Crowdfunding can further be divided by whether the funding party receives equity in the venture (i.e., an investor), some other consideration (i.e., a customer), or nothing at all (i.e., a donor). Equity-based crowdfunding is regulated by the securities laws of individual countries and is typically conducted through an Internet website. Many crowdfunding sites have been launched in recent years—including a few specifically focused on life sciences—in countries all over the world. Examples include Polliwog in the United States [11], the UK's Syndicate Room, and WiSeed in France [12], to name just a few. Companies seeking to raise capital in this manner need to consider both the securities laws of the country where the crowdfunding service is based and the laws of their own country so as not to run afoul of disclosure or other requirements. Most equity crowdfunding sites specialize in modest-sized investments of several thousand dollars to low millions of dollars.

A word of caution: while equity crowdfunding is only in its infancy in most markets around the world and will likely gain more visibility and acceptance over time, biotech entrepreneurs need to bear in mind the *The Long Game* discussion above regarding the magnitude of capital needed to bring a biotech drug through development. Early seed funding of this type may allow a company to complete an important proof of concept necessary to access larger pools of capital, most likely from VCs. That said, VCs typically prefer a "clean" deal with no or only a few non-founder shareholders. A capital structure that includes several hundred equity holders may add a layer of operating complexity and management distraction that is enough to scare off an otherwise interested venture capital investor. As a result, entrepreneurs considering crowdfunding should weigh this risk as well as the ability to secure other types of financing, such as research grants (discussed below).

Government Grants   Covered in more detail later in this chapter, many early stage start-up biotech companies have accessed government grant funding from sources such as the US government's Small Business Innovation Research (SBIR) program (www.SBIR.gov), to demonstrate the potential viability of their technology in order to attract venture capitalists or other equity investors.

Venture Capital

The vast majority of biotechnology companies receive their start-up funding from VCs. In the early days of the industry, the leading venture capital firms were typically high-technology focused or diversified firms that saw biotechnology as the next frontier of innovation. As the industry matured, and the business models and risks associated with biotech investing became better understood, life science–focused venture firms became much more common. These funds frequently include partners with substantial investing and operating experience in the industry.

While biotech entrepreneurs seeking to start a company continue to meet with many potential investors before securing an initial financing round, it is also common for a VC firm to do its own research into a promising new technology area, license the necessary intellectual property, identify the management and scientific advisory team, and launch the company. This co-creation model makes fundraising at scale a much more challenging prospect for the first-time entrepreneur. Thus, it is important to understand which venture firms may have interest in a particular technology and to establish relationships as early as possible, even before formally incorporating a company. Biotech entrepreneurs should expect those potential venture investors who express interest to perform extensive due diligence about the technology, the underlying patents, the competitive landscape in a chosen therapeutic area, potential reimbursement challenges, and the experience of the management team.

In the traditional investment model, the company founders hold shares of common stock and the VCs invest in convertible preferred stock. A company typically closes between three and five rounds of venture capital investment (labeled Series A, Series B, Series C, etc.), prior to undertaking an IPO. According to company financial statements, the 224 biotech companies in the United States and Europe that completed an IPO in the period from 2013 to 2015 raised a median of $62 million of venture capital prior to the IPO transaction [13].

Upon the IPO, the preferred stock automatically converts into common stock based on the terms defined in each series. Preferred stock derives its name from the fact that it has certain features that give its holders rights in preference over the holders of common stock. Such rights typically include:

- The right to receive a specified amount upon the sale or liquidation of the company before any return is provided to common shareholders (liquidation preference)
- The right to have the shares repurchased by the company after a specified event or date (redemption right)
- The right to receive dividends, if declared, prior to common shareholders

- The right to be represented on the board of directors
- The right to vote on all matters on which common shareholders vote and to approve certain transactions, including the sale of the company and the issuance of new shares
- The right to receive additional shares of common stock upon conversion if the company sells shares at prices below the original amount paid by the VC (anti-dilution protection)

Frequently, later series of preferred stock may have terms that are more beneficial than an earlier series; for example, upon sale of the company, holders of Series C may be entitled to receive a full liquidation preference prior to the Series B, Series A, or common stockholders receiving any return.

Although certain venture firms may choose to invest in the entire Series A round themselves, more typically, two or three firms will invest as a syndicate. Upon making the Series A investment, these firms will also reserve some of their capital in order to participate in future rounds of financing (the terms of preferred stock agreements often include significant penalties for firms that do not invest their pro-rata share of future rounds, including the automatic conversion of existing rounds to common stock at a less favorable exchange rate). It is common for one or more new investors to be added to the syndicate in subsequent financings to help establish a price for that round of financing. It is also increasingly common for a particular venture capital round to be invested into a company in tranches. For example, in a Series A financing with an announced value of $10 million, investors may agree to contribute $5 million upon closing and the remaining $5 million upon the achievement of a specified objective (e.g., hiring of management or achieving an early clinical result) or upon the passage of time. Investing in this manner allows the VC firm to mitigate its risk a bit and to improve its overall rate of return.

Most of the preferred stock preferences described above serve to provide a degree of protection should the company not end up being as successful (or as valuable) as originally anticipated. Each of these preferred stock preferences must be negotiated by management and the investors. Given the complexity of these terms, it is important to engage outside legal counsel with appropriate experience in negotiating such arrangements. A side benefit from the issuance of preferred stock is that, on a comparative basis, the company's common stock will be worth a lower amount per share. This allows the company to issue options to employees to acquire common stock with a lower exercise price, which can be a critical recruitment and employee-retention tool.

Venture capitalists are, by and large, not passive investors—they expect to be closely involved in overseeing the company's strategy and operations and leveraging their networks to bring value to the company. As such, just as VCs will perform company diligence, it is important for entrepreneurs and early stage management teams to perform their own inquiries into potential investors. While a company's negotiation leverage may vary considerably with the investment climate, there are several important factors to understand about a potential investor including:

- *Investment philosophy*: Does the firm typically invest in technology platforms with broad product opportunities, or more targeted single product candidates?
- *Relevant experience:* What can the firm and the individual VC bring to the company beyond the cash invested in terms of industry experience and network?
- *Future rounds:* How much has been committed to future rounds and the decision-making process at the firm related to those rounds?
- *Age of fund:* Venture capital funds typically have 10-year lives and become fully invested (including committed funds for future rounds) in the first 5 years. To avoid divergence of strategy within the funding syndicate, it is better if all members are investing from funds with similar remaining lives.

Corporate Venture Capital

In recent years, venture capital investment from the venture arms of large pharmaceutical companies has become a more significant source of capital for biotech companies. These groups have different missions depending on the pharmaceutical company; some are managed solely for return whereas others have a dual mission of helping the company stay informed about new and emerging technology areas. Corporate venture capital is most typically invested as part of a syndicate with traditional VCs and rarely leads or controls a financing round. Because many of these early stage companies will be acquired by larger pharma players in the future, start-ups often want to have more than one corporate investor in the syndicate. This helps the company to stay closer to potential acquirers' interests and needs. It is also a hedge; multiple corporate venture groups have an interest in the entity so the company is not viewed as being captive to single big pharma investor. There also can be a perception that having a corporate investor provides an aura of scientific validation to the company's technology, although there is little correlation between a corporate venture investment and a later strategic alliance with, or acquisition by, the same entity [14].

As noted in Chapter 1, information technology companies have become very active in health and also have active venture capital units that invest in health technologies. While this investment has primarily been targeted to Internet and software entities focused on healthcare, certain companies (including Alphabet) have also invested in traditional drug development companies [15].

Venture Debt

In the United States, certain lenders have created loan products targeting pre-revenue biotech companies. While it may seem counterintuitive that a company with no cash flow would borrow additional funds, the thesis for these arrangements is built around the idea of extending the funding runway to increase the chance that the company will hit its next value-enhancing milestone. The loans are typically secured by all of the company's assets, which may include, or specifically exclude, its intellectual property. The banks that provide these loans base their decision, in part, on the company's technology and its management team, but more fundamentally on their perception of the quality of the venture capital syndicate, including the likelihood that they will provide additional rounds of financing (enabling the loans to be repaid). The lenders seek a return both from the interest and fees they earn on the loan and from receiving warrants to purchase shares of preferred stock.

Crossover Investors

In recent years, it has been more common for biotech companies to close a final private round of financing immediately before launching an IPO with certain "crossover" investors—firms that invest in both private and public entities. In addition to strengthening the company's financial position, these transactions serve to strengthen a company's overall chance of successfully completing the IPO by adding a group of investors who will likely also be purchasers in the IPO transaction. The investors benefit by acquiring a portion of the investment at (lower) private valuations.

Public Investors: The IPO Process

An IPO is an important milestone in the life of a company, not just due to the funds raised in the transaction, but because it opens up the opportunity to access even greater sums of capital from public investors in the future. An IPO is often described as an exit event for investors, however, in biotechnology, it is more appropriately referred to as a liquidity event. In fact, it is not uncommon for venture investors in a biotech company (and the crossover investors mentioned above) to purchase shares in the IPO to signal to the market their support and to ensure the company raises sufficient funds to meet its near-term R & D objectives. Eventually, venture investors do sell (or distribute to investors) their shares, and most will then transition off the board of directors in order to focus on new investments.

Broadly speaking, there are two types of investors that acquire the majority of shares offered in an IPO: dedicated specialist investment funds that focus on the sector and generalist investors who invest across sectors. The generalist investors, including large diversified mutual funds, represent much larger pools of capital. When an IPO "window" opens wide for biotech, as it did in the period from 2013 to 2015, it is frequently driven by enthusiasm of generalist investors looking for market-beating returns.

The management teams behind successful transactions frequently start by building relationships with key specialist investors on so-called "non-deal road shows" months before the formal IPO process commences. The purpose of these meetings is to allow investors to become familiar with the company's management, its technology, the market opportunity, and key upcoming milestones. When management teams visit these potential investors during the more time-compressed IPO process, the conversation can focus on progress made as opposed to an initial introduction to the company and its technology. This process also can build the credibility of management in the eyes of investors who will have seen the company deliver on its strategy.

The actual IPO process (Figure 2-5) typically kicks off with the selection of investment bankers and is a multi-month process involving many players and significant expense. Beyond the capital raised in the IPO transaction itself, the IPO event sets the stage for companies to raise substantial future capital through subsequent follow-on offerings. Management teams should recognize, however, that this access comes with the high cost of complying with public market listing requirements and the expectations of public investors. This translates into the need for more administrative employees and higher legal, accounting, insurance, and other external costs. Operating as a public company also requires a significant time commitment by the CEO, chief financial officer (CFO), and other members of management to communicate with shareholders, as well as enhanced transparency regarding the affairs of the company. Lack of compliance with disclosure and communication obligations can result in significant penalties and a loss of market confidence.

IPO Preparation		IPO Execution		IPO Realization
1. Analyze strategic options	5. Evaluate organization's IPO readiness	9. Finalize IPO/deal team (bankers/ lawyers/ auditors)	14. Obtain regulatory approval and securities admission to exchange	17. Maintain active investor relations efforts
2. Prepare investor pitch deck	6. Formalize supporting readiness team (internal/external)	10. Set timetable, start due diligence	15. Complete book building, order book analysis, issue price and allocation	18. Manage analyst and investor expectations
3. Develop transaction calendar	7. Establish public company structure and governance	11. Fine-tune business plan, fact book, presentation, equity story	16. Price on stock exchange, IPO ceremony	19. Maintain reliable forecasting, reporting, and disclosures
4. Conduct "test the waters" meetings with investors	8. Execute readiness roadmap, people, process, systems	12. Operate like a public company (quarterly closes)		20. Deliver on IPO promises
		13. Finalize offering prospectus/filings		
18 to 36 months before IPO	12 to 18 months before IPO	6 to 12 months before IPO		Post-IPO

Source: EY Analysis

Figure 2-5   The IPO journey

In addition, management teams must take into consideration the expectations of public investors and regulators. As such, prior to or coincident with the IPO, companies should identify gaps between current practices and regulator/investor expectations to develop a plan to close any gaps. Common areas to be addressed include:

- The composition and independence of the board of directors
- The bylaws or corporate charter, which address issues such as the frequency of election of directors
- Board committees (audit, compensation, etc.) and related committee charters
- More formalized lines of reporting and employee policies
- Strengthening the overall internal control environment and processes

Companies typically select three to four investment bankers to participate in the IPO transaction. One of the bankers is selected as the overall lead or "book running manager." The role of the investment bankers is to underwrite the IPO (i.e., agree to buy all of the shares and then resell them to investors). To accomplish the task, the bankers perform extensive diligence on the company and, along with management, market the company to prospective investors. In addition to the bankers, the IPO transaction team typically includes legal counsel, external auditors, patent counsel, and an investor relations/communications firm. The investment bankers are also represented by their own legal counsel, which assists in the due diligence process and participates in the drafting of the offering document (the drafting is led by the company and its legal counsel). The investment banks are paid a percentage of the transaction proceeds (typically 6 percent) and certain out-of-pocket expenses for their services. In addition, the company can expect to pay an additional $2–3 million in professional services costs related to the transaction.

As noted previously, following the close of the transaction, the company must stay in full compliance with all securities laws including those around quarterly and annual disclosures and communications with shareholders. A company that remains in good standing can then raise subsequent rounds of capital with far less effort and time required.

JUMPSTART OUR BUSINESS STARTUPS (JOBS) ACT

The United States is the most robust equity market for biotech companies: the total capital raised each year in the United States dwarfs all other markets. This is the result of numerous factors, including a deeper pool of experienced investors who understand the risks associated with biotech investing, experienced management teams, and equity markets (and regulations) that are conducive to financings by pre-revenue emerging companies. This last point is illustrated by the Jumpstart Our Business Startups (JOBS) Act, which was enacted in April 2012.

One reaction to the 2008 financial crisis was a significant decrease in IPO activity, especially among innovative emerging companies. As a result, the US Congress sought to create a climate to encourage IPOs and the innovation and job creation that can result from an IPO financing. Among other things, the act created a new category of company called an emerging growth company (EGC). An EGC is defined as a company with total annual gross revenues of less than $1 billion in its most recent completed fiscal year. Certain regulatory requirements are phased in for EGCs during a five-year period known as an IPO "on-ramp."

In a major change from past practice, the JOBS Act allows an EGC to submit its IPO registration statement and subsequent amendments to the SEC on a confidential basis. Through the confidential registration statement submission process, the SEC staff can comment and companies can respond and submit confidential amendments before filing publicly if the EGC ultimately decides to proceed with an IPO.

Importantly, the JOBS Act also permits companies to hold "test the waters" meetings with potential investors to share their story and gauge interest in a future IPO transaction. These meetings can occur prior to a company incurring the cost of preparing a registration statement.

Finally, the JOBS Act exempts an EGC from certain requirements during the on-ramp period. These scaled disclosures generally allow for temporary, not permanent, relief from a number of reporting requirements, including:

- A reduced number of audited financial statement periods
- Reduced executive compensation disclosures
- Delayed compliance with auditor attestation of internal controls over financial reporting under Section 404(b) of the Sarbanes-Oxley Act

An issuer with EGC status loses its eligibility as an EGC five years after its common equity IPO or earlier if it meets certain size criteria related to its revenue, issuance of debt, or overall market value. In combination, the above factors have lessened the cost and burden of the IPO process for small biotech companies, and, in turn, have contributed to the increase in biotech IPO activity during the period from 2013 to 2015.

SOURCE: EY Technical Line November 7, 2013, Implementing the JOBS Act.

Government Grants and Disease Foundations

Grants from government and private sources such as foundations and, increasingly, patient advocacy groups and disease-focused foundations are an important source of non-dilutive funding. All of the parties have an interest in seeing innovative science and research advance for reasons that go beyond a pure financial return. For governments, it is often a matter of economic development or achieving broader health outcomes for society, including preparedness for infectious disease epidemics or warfare. Grants can frequently be sourced at national, regional, or local levels. Private philanthropic sources may also seek specific health outcomes (e.g., the Bill and Melinda Gates Foundation focuses on eradicating malaria) or to advance promising but high-risk therapies to address significant unmet medical needs. In addition to funding, working with patient advocacy groups and disease foundations may provide access to a qualified pool of potential clinical trial participants, which is especially important if the company is pursuing a rare disease. In addition, involving interested patients in the development process may provide the company with invaluable information on how to develop truly patient-centric therapies by more fully understanding the real-world challenges of patients, for example, around drug administration and adherence (see Chapter 6 for more discussion on this topic).

While funding from these sources may be modest in size—for example, enough to offset a portion of the cost of a clinical trial—in many cases, the sums received have been quite significant, at times exceeding $100 million. Many companies have become adept and creative (see the Vertex Pharmaceuticals case study that follows) in accessing these sources of capital.

VENTURE PHILANTHROPY: CYSTIC FIBROSIS FOUNDATION AND VERTEX PHARMACEUTICALS

Cystic fibrosis (CF) is a hereditary disease that is caused by a defective gene that makes the body produce abnormally thick and sticky fluid, called mucus. This mucus builds up in the breathing passages of the lungs and in the pancreas. The buildup of mucus results in life-threatening lung infections and serious digestion problems. The disease may also affect the sweat glands and the male reproductive system. Millions of people carry a CF gene but do not have symptoms. This is because a person with CF must inherit two defective genes, one from each parent. About 1 in 29 Caucasian Americans have the mutant CF gene [16].

The Cystic Fibrosis Foundation (CFF) has sponsored much of the research into the condition, with significant impact on the life expectancy of those with the disease. The foundation has sponsored academic research and has provided more than $425 million to several leading biopharmaceutical companies [17].

One company whose CF research was funded by CFF beginning in 1999 was Aurora Biosciences [18]. Aurora performed high-throughput screening to try to identify compounds that would be active against CF and was subsequently acquired by Vertex Pharmaceuticals, which was primarily interested in assets other than the CF research. However, CFF and Vertex subsequently struck an innovative deal that resulted in approximately $150 million of research funding to Vertex from CFF, in exchange for royalties of up to 12 percent on any future drugs developed as a result of the funding. Vertex officials have commented that such funding was crucial to their decision to continue developing CF therapies [19].

That research has led to two approved drugs thus far—Kalydeco (ivacaftor) and Orkambi (lumacaftor/ivacaftor)—which have been described as transformational for patients as they address the underlying mechanism of the disease and not just the symptoms. Based on the expected future sales of these drugs, in November 2014, CFF sold its rights to receive future royalties to Royalty Pharma, Inc., for an eye-catching $3.3 billion [20]. In addition to supplying CFF with a sizeable reserve to provide funding to many other academic institutions and biopharmaceutical companies, this success has many other disease foundations seeking to emulate the CFF model.

Strategic Alliances

Strategic alliances, which are covered in greater detail in Chapter 3, have been an integral part of the biotech financing landscape since the birth of the modern biotechnology industry and are a critical component of virtually every biotech company's financing strategy. In fact, each year billions of dollars of license payments, R & D support payments, and milestone payments flow from big pharma to emerging biotech enterprises.

Asset-Based Financing

A variation on the strategic alliance that has emerged from time to time in the industry is asset-based financing. In these structures, a financial investor provides R & D funding to a biotech company, in exchange for taking an economic interest in the product under development. This interest could be in the form of the right to receive future success payments and royalties as the product progresses toward and eventually enters the market. The total return may or may not be capped, but is intended to reward the investor for the risks taken (in other words, a higher overall return is required, the earlier a product candidate is in development). In one form of these arrangements, the biotech company out-licenses its technology to a new company founded by an investment fund. The investment fund then pays for the continued development of the product, including at times engaging the sponsoring biotech company to perform R & D services for a fee. If the development progresses as planned, the biotech company can exercise an option to reacquire the technology at a premium to the amount invested by the investment fund. If the option is not exercised, the investment fund owns the product and can seek a different partner, chose to develop it itself, or shut down all R & D.

The rationale for a biotech company to enter into such arrangement is based on access to capital and value arbitrage. If the company perceives that its stock is undervalued by the market and is concerned about raising capital at a depressed value, then this structure allows the research to continue with funds provided by a third party. If the R & D effort is successful and relevant milestones are achieved, the theory is that the public market will recognize these events and the stock price will rise, allowing the company to finance the milestone payments or buyback of the technology at an overall lower level of dilution. Given the complexity and risks, these structures have not been widely adopted and tend to be more common when the IPO market is closed to biotech companies. However, these structures remain an available option with several investment funds interested in providing the capital.

A WORD ABOUT MERGERS AND ACQUISITIONS

In the history of the industry, only a handful of the thousands of biotech companies that have been founded have matured from start-up to commercial leader. The fact is that most companies that have enjoyed a measure of clinical or early commercial success have been purchased by a larger company seeking growth and/or the opportunity to leverage their commercial infrastructure. These mergers and acquisitions (M & A) events have provided strong returns to shareholders and are thus a critical part of the overall financing ecosystem for the industry.

While a sale of the company may be the ultimate destination, it is not a strategy that is in the control of management inasmuch as it requires another interested party willing to pay a reasonable sum to gain the interest and approval of the investors. Management teams must therefore build their business and financing plans, with an idea of reaching the goal of full commercial operations (with or without an alliance partner) and profitability, while remaining open to the possibility that a sale of the company may represent the best value-creating option for shareholders at any one point in time. This is especially true when one considers that companies today must build additional commercialization and patient engagement capabilities to succeed as value-based drug pricing takes hold, which is described in later chapters of this book.

SUMMARY POINTS

- Drug development, on average, requires a decade or more and significant amounts of capital, all before the first dollar of profit is realized. It is not uncommon for companies to require more than $500 million (and, at times, substantially more) prior to launching a first product.

- Given the magnitude of the capital required for drug development, many players must participate in the successful funding of a start-up biotech company, with no one player having the capacity to fund the entire amount on its own.

- Management teams must build in the financial optionality to ensure that there are sufficient resources to enable the scientific pivots that may be necessary as greater knowledge regarding a technology or product candidate is obtained.

- Successful companies must have two core capabilities: first, the discipline of understanding the interests and needs of investors and strategic collaborators; and, second, the ability to explain the company's story. Entrepreneurs must develop the ability to market the company's story, including addressing how inherent risks will be mitigated.

- The financing and capital allocation strategy of a biotech company must be closely linked to the research and development and business strategy, including defining priorities (reallocation of capital if a product candidate is delayed or fails during development), related budgets, and key milestones.

- Biotech management teams typically feel like they are always in the process of raising capital because of the need to be in continuous dialog with existing and potential future investors. The timing of successive rounds of financing is an important consideration, however. Management teams that delay too long may find that they are left with fewer viable options.

CHAPTER 3

SUCCESS THROUGH COLLABORATION

A significant portion of FDA drug approvals in recent years have been the product of collaborations between biotechnology and pharmaceutical companies [1]. In addition, a majority of the most promising late-stage assets under development originated at firms other than the current owner [2]. Pioneering biotechnology companies such as Amgen and Genentech started this collaboration trend by licensing their first products (Epogen/Procrit in the case of Amgen and Humulin in the case of Genentech) during development to large pharmaceutical companies, setting a pattern that most biotech companies would pursue in the decades that followed. The drivers of these early transactions—including access to, and validation of, new technologies and techniques—remain relevant today. In fact, strategic alliances have proliferated in number and variety precisely because they can be structured to meet the specific needs of the participants.

This flexibility will be relevant as the sector moves toward a future of being compensated primarily based on the value delivered, either through improved health outcomes or improved efficiency. Larger companies are more likely to develop the commercial expertise and critical mass necessary to structure and monitor outcomes-based payment arrangements. Further, as the industry moves beyond selling single drugs to creating solutions that focus on the needs of patients, one can imagine new forms of collaboration that may integrate multiple products (e.g., in a multidrug "cocktail" to treat specific types of cancer) and related services (which might be provided by an infotech company with complementary technologies or data). In some cases, a single company may own all of the components of such an offering, but more likely will assemble the relevant pieces through alliance transactions.

ALLIANCE EVOLUTION: MORE PLAYERS AND NEW STRUCTURES

As the biotech industry has matured, larger commercial-stage biotech companies have become active licensees, often in competition with traditional pharmaceutical

Managing Biotechnology: From Science to Market in the Digital Age, First Edition. Françoise Simon and Glen Giovannetti.
© 2017 John Wiley & Sons, Inc. Published 2017 by John Wiley & Sons, Inc.

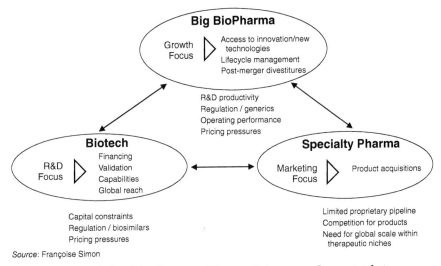

Figure 3-1   Biopharma alliance drivers and constraints

partners and so-called specialty pharma companies that have a strategy of acquiring late-stage or approved drugs to the exclusion of performing most R & D (Figure 3-1). In addition, large pharmaceutical companies have collaborated with each other around a particular therapeutic area either to create new combination therapies or to manage overall development risk across a portfolio of competing products.

As drug development time frames and costs have continued to rise, and the rate of successful drug approvals has remained stubbornly low [3], it is not surprising that alliance structures have evolved in response to these challenges and are now a critical component of the R & D, business, and financing strategies of biopharma companies of all sizes. Scientific complexity, significant unaddressed public health challenges such as Alzheimer's disease and other neurodegenerative diseases, and the move to compensation based on value, as described above, suggest that new forms of collaboration will also be necessary.

From the standpoint of research and development, many have suggested that the movie industry and the Hollywood model of development would be more appropriate to the R & D challenges facing the biopharma industry [4]. The studios (analogous to pharmaceutical companies) were once fully integrated operations that owned or employed all aspects of the movie business, from the creative side (screenwriters, directors, and actors) through to marketing and distribution. Over time, the system has fragmented, with the creative development talent (analogous to academics, biotech companies, and key service providers involved in drug discovery) operating independently and coming together for short periods around specific development opportunities that best fit their individual talents, whereas the studios focus on financing, marketing, and distribution across geographies and platforms. The time to discover and develop a new drug is obviously much longer than the time to produce the average movie, nevertheless, the necessity of seeking innovative ideas and capabilities externally is widely recognized. Some have even gone as far as to say that large pharma companies should abandon early research altogether and adopt a "search and development strategy" in which all product candidates would be sourced externally, with pharma concentrating on the areas where it can provide the most value through scale (large clinical trials, manufacturing, marketing and distribution) [5].

Of course, there are challenges with any model. For instance, bringing individuals with specific talents together for short periods of time would require new compensation models (in Hollywood, the creative talent frequently is entitled to a portion of the revenue from the resulting movie) and employees who are comfortable working on a freelance basis or working for firms that act as the equivalent of a Hollywood agent. Similarly, a pharma company lacking deep research insights in a particular therapeutic area would likely not be able to consistently identify breakthrough advances early enough to be able to sustainably acquire such innovations at a reasonable price.

While R & D stage product licensing and development alliances have been, and will likely remain, the most common type of transaction in the industry, emerging drug pricing challenges and the move to outcomes-based pricing arrangements will require alliances with a broader range of players, including payers, providers, patients, and nontraditional players. In some cases, such alliances will be needed to access new capabilities ranging from advanced data analytics to a deeper understanding of consumer behavior. For example, biopharma companies can be expected to enter into alliances with nontraditional partners to access and analyze real-world data necessary to demonstrate the value of their products. Moreover, if biopharmas are to build holistic "beyond-the-pill" solutions that improve outcomes and lower costs, they must extend their business models and align with health providers, infotech and telecom companies, and others. Particularly as it relates to the relationship between biopharma companies and payers, these new models will require a mind shift change away from the transactional (maximizing price per unit) to the collaborative (shared success based on improved patient outcomes and system-wide cost savings). Figures 3-2 and 3-3 provide examples of alliance transactions classified by the underlying driver, from the traditional product focused alliances to newer forms of collaborations.

Biopharma companies large and small understand how to structure and manage traditional product development alliances given their long history of collaboration. It is a different story for deals involving biopharmas and nontraditional collaborators such as infotech companies and healthcare payers and providers. As described in Chapter 1, infotech companies often have very different expectations regarding product cycle times and the ability to interact with

Structure	Examples	Objective
Product license and development	▶ Multiple examples	Larger biopharma licenses drug candidate and parties share responsibilities to develop and launch drug in specified markets. Most traditional form of alliance
Nonexclusive license	▶ Roche/Alnylam	Licensor gains broad access to the intellectual property to conduct its own R&D within a defined therapeutic area
Platform deal	▶ Celgene/Agios ▶ Celgene/Juno	Broad exclusive alliance based on a technology. May include elements of other alliances (e.g., equity associated with big sibling alliance or option to acquire)
"Big sibling" alliance	▶ Roche/Genentech ▶ Sanofi/Regeneron ▶ Bayer/CRISPR	Broad pipeline alliance (all products in one or more therapeutic categories) in which larger company takes significant or controlling equity position to insulate biotech from capital market volatility
Option to acquire	▶ Actavis/Rhythm ▶ Novartis/Proteon ▶ Sanofi/Warp Drive Bio ▶ Takeda/PVP Biologics ▶ Takeda/Maverick Therapeutics	Pharma company has the right to acquire the biotech company for a predefined price upon the achievement of an agreed-upon milestone
Therapeutic area scale	▶ GlaxoSmithKline/Pfizer	Companies contribute HIV assets to new company (ViiV) that is broader in scope than each company's individual business
Academic partnerships	▶ Sanofi/UCSF (Diabetes) ▶ Pfizer/Harvard ▶ Celgene with UPenn, Columbia, Johns Hopkins, and Mt. Sinai	Pharma partners with a university lab, supports research, and may receive right of first negotiation for developed technology
Precompetitive R&D	▶ TransCelerate (clinical trials standards) ▶ Biomarker consortia	Consortia of biopharma companies combine human and financial resources to address defined common challenges in research and clinical development.

Source: EY Analysis

Figure 3-2   Alliances to access innovation: strategic objective defines deal structure

Business Need	Objective	Examples	Analysis
Demonstrating product value	Accessing real-world evidence	▶ AstraZeneca/HealthCore	Partnership enabled AZ to use RWE to solidify favorable formulary placement for its branded drugs in multiple instances
	Developing around the pill solutions	▶ AstraZeneca/Exco InTouch ▶ Novartis/Verily	Collaboration to use a suite of interactive mobile and Internet-based health tools for COPD patients Novartis in-licensed Verily's "smart lens" technology to help diabetic patients continuously measure glucose levels
	Measuring outcomes	▶ Fresenius Medical Care/Aetna	Partnership creates collaborative care model for end-stage renal disease patients
Expanding access	Innovating distribution	▶ Novartis/Indian Post Office ▶ Merck/Optum	Boosting access through proposed concept to sell OTC medicines from rural post offices Partnership to create a Learning Lab to scale value-based payment models based on measuring outcomes
	Creating awareness	▶ Novo Nordisk/World Diabetes Foundation/Chinese Ministry of Health	Program to improve diabetes awareness among local Chinese communities in Tier 2 and Tier 3 cities. Communication aimed at patients, physicians, and public officials
	Developing biosimilars	▶ Biogen/Samsung ▶ Amgen/Actavis/Synthon	Established biotech companies contribute manufacturing expertise for development of biosimilars
	Enhancing affordability	▶ Roche/Swiss Re	Developing specific insurance coverage for cancer to improve access to expensive drugs in China
Exploring new business models	Patient-centricity	▶ Merck & Co. Inc./ Health Management Resources ▶ Pfizer/IBM Watson	Offers evidence-based weight management interventions Develop innovative remote monitoring solutions aimed at transforming how clinicians deliver care to patients with Parkinson's disease
	Supply chain innovation	▶ Pfizer/CVS Caremark	Provides in the US a direct-to-patient supply chain model for selling the erectile dysfunction drug Viagra

Source: EY Analysis

Figure 3-3   Alliances to meet evolving commercial needs

consumers in a regulated setting. Similarly, payers typically are constrained by an annual budget, whereas the benefit of a drug may be realized through reduced treatment costs over time. It remains to be seen whether the business arrangements involving nontraditional partners will be fee for service (or product) or will involve sharing the risks and the benefits based on cost savings realized or some other measure.

Dividing the spoils in these relationships will also prove challenging. For example, the parties will have to agree on how much value each component— the drug or perhaps a mobile device that helps ensure the patient takes the medicine as prescribed—actually generates. As a result, a significant number of the alliances between biopharma and nontraditional players to date can be described as pilot programs as both parties seek to experiment with new business models and understand what types of arrangements will be able to achieve meaningful scale.

The history of alliances in the precision medicine arena (see Chapter 4) between drug and diagnostic companies may be instructive in this regard. Biopharma companies are increasingly pursuing a strategy of developing drugs for segmented patient populations that, because of their genetic makeup, are more likely to respond. This strategy should enable shorter and less costly clinical trials with a higher likelihood of success, as well as help companies prove the value of their therapeutics to payers. Many of the diagnostic companies that develop the biomarker tests to identify the appropriate patients initially believed that they would capture more of the overall value of the diagnostic-drug combination. However, structuring risk-sharing arrangements has proven difficult, and most diagnostic procedures continue to be done on a fee for service basis.

STRATEGIC ALLIANCES: A STALWART OF THE BIOPHARMA INDUSTRY

Alliances are common in the biopharma industry because they effectively address strategic issues faced by each participant. For biotech companies, alliances provide:

- An important source of capital to fund R & D
- A means of sharing risk
- Validation regarding the relevance of the company's technology to investors
- Access to capabilities not present in the biotech company or too expensive to build (e.g., managing large-scale clinical trials, manufacturing, regulatory affairs, and commercialization on a global scale)

For pharma companies, alliances provide:

- Access to innovative products—a significant portion of pharma pipelines are represented by product candidates that were discovered by alliance partners—and insights about new technology areas
- Access to cutting-edge technologies (e.g., RNA interference or gene editing) that cannot be replicated in-house either because of intellectual property considerations or a lack of expertise
- A reduction in risk, enabling companies to take ownership rights to a particular product rather than requiring them to acquire the entire enterprise

For specialty pharma companies, alliances provide:

- Access to products—either innovative products that fit a therapeutic focus or established products currently marketed

As noted previously, the proliferation of new technologies and drug development strategies from academia and biotech has made external sourcing of products and technologies critical to long-term sustainability. In addition, following the consolidation within big pharma that has occurred over the last 20 years, companies also learned that R & D did not benefit from economies of scale in the same way as manufacturing or commercial functions. The resulting R & D productivity crisis (more spending with no increase in the number of approved drugs) further convinced companies that looking outside their walls for innovative ideas was essential. In addition to actively pursuing biotech collaborators, big pharma companies have adopted various open innovation strategies, including the following:

- *Innovation hubs*: Johnson & Johnson has established regional innovation hubs in key biotech research clusters around the world to identify promising science and technology at an early stage and develop collaborations with local academics, entrepreneurs, and emerging companies [6].
- *Alliances with external venture groups:* GlaxoSmithKline and Johnson & Johnson jointly invested in a venture fund managed by Index Ventures (now called Medicxi) that will involve each pharma bringing both capital and expertise to entrepreneurs [7].
- *Alliances with academia:* Pfizer launched Centers for Therapeutic Innovation (CTI), a unit dedicated to developing drug candidates through collaborations with academic scientists. CTI launched in 2010 with a broad collaboration with the University of California, San Francisco, and has since established sites in New York City, San Diego, and Boston, each linked to up to eight academic institutions [8].
- *Crowdsourcing:* UCB Pharma sponsors a Hack Epilepsy effort aimed at getting to more innovation in epilepsy (as well as developing patient-centric R & D) [9].

JANSSEN AND OSE IMMUNOTHERAPEUTICS: DEAL STRATEGIES IN A EUROPEAN CONTEXT

By Claire Champenois, Associate Professor Audencia Business School, and Françoise Simon

A collaboration between the London Innovation Center of Johnson & Johnson, Janssen Biotech, and Effimune (now OSE Immunotherapeutics) focuses on the development of a novel therapy for autoimmune diseases and transplantation. Johnson & Johnson is growing its immunology portfolio beyond its rheumatoid arthritis (RA) products, Remicade (infliximab), Simponi (golimumab), and Stelara (ustekinumab), partly through alliances such as those with GSK for sirukumab in RA and in-licensing from MorphoSys for guselkumab in psoriasis. Effimune, a biotechnology company based in Nantes, France, offered a possible complement to this portfolio with its preclinical product FR 104, a monoclonal antibody fragment and antagonist of the CD 28 protein, with applications in several autoimmune diseases and transplantation. A competitive product, lulizumab pegol, was in Phase 2 development at BMS, but with a different application (lupus).

Janssen/Effimune Agreement

After a first contact facilitated by the London Innovation Center, Janssen and Effimune signed in September 2013 a global license agreement for FR 104, based on strong preclinical publications, scientific competency, and close links with the Nantes Urology-Nephrology Transplantation Institute (ITUN), a leading European transplantation center, and the National Institute of Health and Medical Research (INSERM). Under the deal terms, Effimune granted Janssen an exclusive option to develop FR 104 and related global rights, with Janssen responsible for all clinical development, registration, and commercialization. The total potential deal value was 155 M euros ($172 million), with milestone payments and a royalty on net sales. In July 2016, the publication of positive Phase 1 results for FR 104 triggered the exercise of the license option by Janssen and a payment of 10 M euros, with development expected to continue to the Phase 2 stage.

Efffimune Evolution: From Licensing to Merger

The company was created in 2007 as a spin-off of ITUN. From 2007 to 2013, it secured funding from private and public sources. It did not rely on venture capital, to avoid possible constraints and because of its low availability in the French context.

Effimune raised about 6 M euros from sources, including 1.5 M euros from the European Commission and 3 M from private funds such as business angels and Family Offices.

Signed on May 31, 2016, the merger with OSE aims to combine portfolios in autoimmune diseases and oncology, with a balanced risk profile and products ranging from preclinical to Phase 3. The OSE lead immuno-oncology product, Tedopi, is in a Phase 3 study in lung cancer, and its preclinical compounds include Effi-7 for autoimmune diseases and Effi-DEM, a new checkpoint inhibitor. OSE had a 2015 IPO on Euronext, raising nearly 21.1 M euros, and signed other deals in France and Israel.

Effimune was helped in early financing by European networks. It belongs to the TRIAD consortium with INSERM, Oxford and Glasgow Universities, and the Primate Research Center in the Netherlands. OSE also benefits from its location in the Nantes biocluster, with strong competencies in gene and cell-based therapies.

This case shows the innovative evolution of a European start-up, without recourse to venture capital, with a significant preclinical licensing deal and a merger diversifying its portfolio.

ALLIANCE VERSUS ACQUISITION

As Figure 3-4 depicts, in the context of drug development, there is a range of considerations in deciding whether a strategic alliance is preferable to an acquisition. For pharmaceutical companies, an alliance structure may be preferable because it allows access to a desired product candidate without having to incur the cost and risk of acquiring the entire entity. The pharma company in a license arrangement typically also has the ability to terminate the relationship with a short notice period if its views on the prospects of successful development change (or if its own therapeutic areas of focus change).

A larger company may also desire to preserve the entrepreneurial culture and operating nimbleness of its alliance partner and may fear that the organization would lose its focus (and, perhaps, key people) if acquired and integrated into a larger corporate structure. On the other hand, an acquisition may be desirable if the

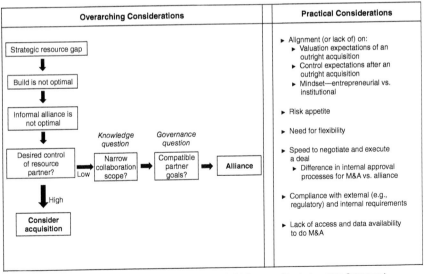

Source: EY Analysis. Overarching considerations adapted from *Build, Borrow or Buy*, by Laurence Capron and Will Mitchell, HBR Press, 2012.

Figure 3-4 Strategic alliance versus merger and acquisition

biotechnology company has created an innovative technology platform and the pharma company wants (or needs) to prevent others from accessing the technology, although meeting the acquisition valuation expectations of the target biotech in this situation may prove challenging, especially for very early stage technologies. As described below, option-based structures, which give the pharma (or large biotech) company the ability to acquire multiple product candidates or the entire company at a later time, have become a common way to address this situation.

From the perspective of a biotech company, the decision to be acquired hinges on an evaluation of the value of the company today versus its potential value in light of known or expected risks (technical, financial, business). Additionally, a biotechnology company developing a single product candidate may prefer to be acquired as there could be limited economic upside remaining for its shareholders once the lead (or only) asset is licensed.

CELGENE: CREATING PIPELINE OPTIONALITY AND SCIENTIFIC LEARNING THROUGH ALLIANCES

Many commercial-stage biotechnology companies have enhanced their pipelines through deal making. Industry leaders such as Amgen and Gilead Sciences have sourced some of their most significant revenue-generating products through acquisitions, and most of the major biotech players have been active in the mergers and acquisitions (M & A) market. However, one firm, Celgene, has stood out from the rest—in terms of number, monetary value, and deal creativity—in its alliance strategy with emerging biotech companies. Celgene has been alone in the prevalence of its investments in early stage science. The company has also been active in collaborations with research institutes such as Sanford Burnham and through academic partnership such as the recently announced consortium with the medical centers at University of Pennsylvania, Columbia University, Johns Hopkins, and Mount Sinai.

On the biotech front, from its 2008 alliance with Acceleron Pharma through to its 2017 deal with BeiGene, Celgene has more than 30 alliance transactions with smaller, mostly private, biotech companies securing access to a broad pipeline of hematology, oncology, and inflammation and immunology product candidates. While the specifics of each deal differ, Celgene has shown a preference for option-based deals in which it receives, typically in exchange for a sizeable upfront payment, options to acquire rights to a specific number of product candidates generated from the partner's R & D efforts, either on a worldwide basis or in specific territories. In many instances, Celgene also acquired equity in the partner, including a 2015 deal to acquire 10 percent of immuno-oncology pioneer Juno Therapeutics for an astounding $850 million. The equity component of these deals provides Celgene with an additional avenue to generate returns beyond the product. Although Celgene's deals have required a substantial allocation of capital, they have resulted in a vast pipeline of innovative science to the point where a shareholder in Celgene effectively owns a share of many of the most exciting technologies under development today.

The Celgene approach to alliances includes the following elements:

- A commitment to the externalization of R & D
- The ability to leverage deep internal expertise to identify promising technologies and platforms being developed by others, typically at an early stage of development
- A nimbleness in decision making and a willingness to be creative in structuring the transaction to meet the needs of the prospective alliance partner
- A willingness to make "big bets" in order to provide the smaller alliance partner with sufficient capital to develop the technology of interest
- The use of options to lock up rights to products emerging from the research of its partners

STRUCTURE CONSIDERATIONS TO MAXIMIZE VALUE

As most biotech companies eventually exit via an M&A transaction with a larger player, biotech management teams must make strategic choices in order to maximize value. Platform-centric companies in particular should consider how best to realize value on the underlying technology and the earlier stage pipeline, even when potential acquirers may only focus on a single lead asset. Management teams need to have a view of the sum-of-the-parts valuation of the company and think through deal structures that will fully reflect the company's total value.

While some have tried to accomplish this goal by spinning off early-stage assets in the face of an acquisition proposal, some start-ups are being proactive about such issues from inception by organizing themselves as limited liability "pass-through entities" which allow for the sale of specific assets in a tax-efficient manner.

While such structures do not work for public companies, the increasing availability of private capital from a variety of strategic and non-traditional sources may make these kinds of structures more common, as an IPO might not be necessary for promising platform companies that can generate and divest multiple product candidates.

DIVESTING FOR FOCUS

In addition to sourcing technology externally, the pressures on drug pricing have resulted in a broader recognition that companies cannot all be winners in every therapeutic category (or adjacent business). This has resulted in a trend of divesting or spinning off to shareholders certain assets or businesses in a targeted fashion in order to focus on the areas where a company can have scale and competitive advantage. The best example of this trend is Bristol-Myers Squibb's sale of its non-pharma businesses (medical devices, nutritionals, etc.) in order to redeploy the capital to acquire innovative technologies and medicines in defined therapeutic areas, in what was referred to as the "string of pearls strategy." More recently, Merck divested its consumer health business to Bayer and redeployed a portion of the proceeds to acquire biotech Cubist Pharmaceuticals and its anti-infective product portfolio, which complemented Merck's existing hospital-based product portfolio. In addition to combining their consumer health businesses, in 2014 GlaxoSmithKline (GSK) and Novartis also swapped businesses, with GSK acquiring Novartis' vaccine business and Novartis taking over GSK's oncology business, with each gaining scale in their respective areas. In the biotech sphere, in May 2016, Biogen announced the spin-off of its hemophilia business in order to focus on its core neurodegenerative disease business.

As multiple drugs with the same mechanisms of action compete for share in a tightly defined patient population, market participants both new and old may sacrifice pricing power to gain or preserve market share. The more crowded therapeutic markets become, the more important it is for companies to soberly analyze their prospects and respond accordingly to build upon strength through future investment or divest or combine in a joint venture in areas where one is likely to be less competitive [10].

DOING THE DEAL

A successful alliance depends on a combination of right product, right partner, and right structure. Figure 3-5 describes the strategic alliance process from gap analysis through execution and monitoring.

Partner Selection

Just as biotech management teams need to sell their story to prospective investors, as discussed in Chapter 2, it is also necessary to begin building awareness and

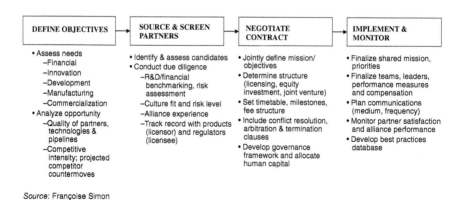

Source: Françoise Simon

Figure 3-5   Strategic alliance process

trust by cultivating relationships with larger biopharma companies that might be future alliance partners well in advance of a particular transaction. These larger companies also have an interest in being seen as the preferred partner in a highly competitive deal environment. Fortunately, from the perspective of an emerging biotech company, all large pharmaceutical and commercial-stage biotech companies have large business development teams whose primary mission is to scout for new technologies and promising product candidates for acquisition and alliance. It is relatively easy to meet these teams at industry events (including a multitude of events that are focused on alliances) and many pharmaceutical companies provide online data regarding their teams and areas of interest [11].

Cultivating relationships beyond the business development team directly with relevant members of the R & D organization through scientific societies and meetings can also be important. This is all the more important the earlier a product is in its development (e.g., prior to proof of concept testing). While the business development team is responsible for deal sourcing and execution, a biotech company's relationship with, and support from, R & D leadership is essential to close a deal and to maximize its value following close.

Once a company has defined the strategic rationale behind a specific alliance transaction, it must further refine the list of potential partners. While much will have been learned from earlier relationship building, the key attributes to be evaluated in partner selection include the following:

- Complementary (or potentially competitive) assets or expertise
- Uniqueness of the partner's assets/attributes
- Degree of strategic alignment
- Exclusivity (inability to acquire or replicate the partner's assets)
- Cultural compatibility
- Prior alliance experience and outcomes

Once this evaluation is complete, the company can assess interest in pursuing a formal relationship based on a prioritized list of potential partners.

Mission and Objectives

For all the participants, alliances pose complex challenges. To be successful, there must be a meeting of the minds that crystallizes the need for the deal and also drives the structure of the transaction. Typically, the signing of a strategic alliance is preceded by many months of discussions and due diligence (by both parties) that encompasses the scientific, financial, and cultural elements of the transaction. A term sheet outlining the general conditions of the arrangement may be circulated fairly early in the process as a basis for continuing discussions. However, prior to defining detailed contractual terms and obligations, it is critical that the partners define the objectives of the alliance inasmuch as such discussions set the framework for the negotiations and the eventual management of the partnership. Indeed, the partners must jointly agree on how they will define success throughout the course of the relationship and where in the relationship they expect to create value. Jumping directly into negotiating a transaction without full agreement on the overall objectives can lead to a lack of flexibility and disagreements down the line as development plans inevitably require alteration.

Structure

The strategic rationale behind the transaction will drive its structure. Figure 3-6 depicts the range of common collaboration structures, from highly informal through to an acquisition, and the key attributes of each. While biopharma companies may have formal or informal alliances with academic institutions and participate in industry consortia to create common standards or address common underlying technological issues, the vast majority of traditional alliance transactions fall under the contractual license category. Such transactions may also include a minority investment; however, it is rare (outside of the context of corporate venture capital described in Chapter 2) for a pharma company to make a minority investment in a biotech company in the absence of a larger strategic relationship. Similarly, formal legal entity joint ventures (JVs) are also relatively uncommon between pharma and biotech partners, although pharma–pharma JVs have been used in certain circumstances. For example, in 2009, Pfizer and GSK launched a JV (ViiV) to combine their

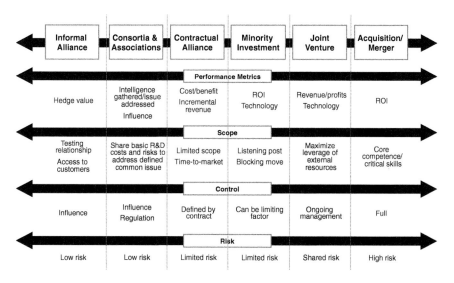

Source: EY Analysis

Figure 3-6   The alliance to acquisition continuum

respective HIV franchises and product pipelines to enhance scale and competitiveness, and various pharmas have entered into JVs with local companies to extend their reach in emerging markets. In general, however, JVs that include a formal legal entity are frequently too cumbersome and difficult to exit, and they typically require the commitment of additional capital and human resources as compared to a contractual alliance.

The most common pharma-biotech alliance—a license and development arrangement—is typically structured as a license to a product candidate or candidates, in exchange for an upfront license payment, the right to receive additional payments upon the achievement of predefined milestones (development, clinical, and commercial), and downstream royalty payments on any eventual sales by the pharmaceutical company of the licensed product(s). In addition, the pharmaceutical company may agree to reimburse the biotech company for its continuing research effort based on an agreed-upon budget.

Alliance transactions are frequently announced as multi-billion dollar transactions, while, in reality, the upfront license payments frequently represent the only guaranteed payments in the arrangement (Figure 3-7).

The licensor (typically the biotech company) can license worldwide rights to its product, or only selected territories. In the early years of the biotech industry, out-licensing worldwide rights to a product was common. As biotechs have gained experience and the balance of negotiating power has shifted, it has become common in recent years for biotech companies to retain the US market (the world's largest and most profitable market for drugs), while licensing the rest of the world rights. Even if the decision is made to out-license a product candidate on a worldwide basis, biotech companies can retain co-promotion rights in certain territories, which provides the option to participate in the commercialization of the product (thereby building internal sales and marketing capabilities) in exchange for

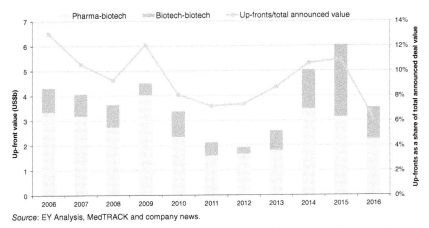

Source: EY Analysis, MedTRACK and company news.

Figure 3-7   US and European strategic alliance trends: up-front payments as a percentage of total value, 2006–2016

enhanced returns. Biotech companies can also pursue a strategy of licensing to several partners on a market-by-market basis, for example, North America, Europe, Japan, and other Asia-Pacific countries. This approach has several disadvantages, including the need to coordinate with multiple partners. Further, such an approach is likely to only attract regional partners and not large multinational pharma companies with globally consistent capabilities and scale.

The structure of the alliance will also be influenced by the nature of the product being developed, for example, a primary care product that requires a significant sales force as compared to a therapeutic treating a targeted or orphan indication where specialist physicians and patients could be covered by a smaller, targeted sales force. An early stage biotech is more likely to fully out-license a primary care product because it would be difficult and possibly prohibitively costly to build its own sales force and medical affairs function. On the other hand, an orphan or highly specialized drug may be best commercialized by a biotech company with an intimate knowledge of the key opinion leaders, patient advocacy organizations, and even individual patients (through clinical trial registries). This was the path pioneered by Genzyme to great success with its enzyme replacement therapies for Gaucher disease and Fabry disease.

A common variation of alliance is the platform technology alliance, which is applicable when the biotech company has a broad drug development technology (or platform) that is expected to generate multiple drug candidates in one or more therapeutic areas. In these arrangements, the partner in the transaction may negotiate for a license to specified number of future drug candidates to be discovered and/or developed by the biotech company. The upfront payment in these arrangements is structured either as a license or an option to license a future product and is used to fund the discovery of the product candidates.

A less common option-based structure—and one that is practically only available to pre-IPO companies—provides the pharma company with the right to acquire the entire biotech company at a predefined price upon the occurrence of certain triggering events (typically a clinical trial result). Examples include Novartis' transaction with Proteon Therapeutics [12] and Genentech's option to acquire Constellation Pharmaceuticals, which expired unexercised in 2015 [13]. Deals of this type are practically only available to pre-IPO companies because the option to sell is technically granted by the shareholders of the company and it would be very challenging to get the dispersed shareholders of a public company to agree to such an arrangement (although there have been notable exceptions, including the Roche-Genentech transaction described below). Further, the option price would put an effective cap on the valuation of the company, which may be reasonable for a venture capitalist looking for a predictable exit but less so for a public investor with multiple entities into which it can invest (with no capped upside). Venture capitalists seeking to increase the predictability of their own investment exits have also adopted "build to sell" structures in which the pharma company acquirer and the acquisition price are known at the founding of the company. Sanofi's deal with Warp Drive Bio and venture capitalists Third Rock Ventures is an example of such a structure [14].

Arguably the most successful relationship ever formed in the biopharma industry, in terms of drugs produced and value created, was Roche's long-standing arrangement with Genentech that originated in 1990 and concluded with Roche's 2009 acquisition of Genentech. Roche initially acquired a controlling interest in Genentech and an option for Roche to acquire the remaining shares of Genentech [15]. The agreement was modified over time to extend the option and provide Genentech shareholders the right to "put" their shares to Roche should Roche not exercise its option [16]. For the period when this arrangement was outstanding, the company's stock traded within a narrow range. Roche eventually exercised the option and immediately sold a significant portion of the shares in a public offering, realizing a significant gain. More critically, this "big sibling" relationship effectively insulated Genentech from the short-term pressures and volatility of the capital markets during a critical period of its development, while allowing it to retain its decision-making autonomy, culture, and employee incentives.

SANOFI-REGENERON: A VALUED RELATIONSHIP

Sanofi first became involved with Regeneron, then an aspiring R & D stage biotech, in 2003 when one of its predecessor companies, the French-German pharma company Aventis, signed an alliance with the biotech to develop its vascular endothelial growth factor (VEGF) Trap technology. Over the succeeding decade-plus, first Aventis and then its successor Sanofi have expanded this relationship numerous times to cover the development of a number of monoclonal antibody technologies and products. The relationship has resulted in two approved products thus far—Zaltrap (ziv-aflibercept), for the treatment of colorectal cancer, and Praluent (alirocumab), for the treatment of uncontrolled high cholesterol—and many clinical stage product candidates.

As Regeneron's product pipeline matured and its products began to reach the market, it would not have been uncommon for Regeneron to either face shareholder pressure to balance R & D investment with the desire for short-term profits or to become an acquisition target. (Note that Regeneron was somewhat protected from the latter because significant voting power remains with management due to a two-class common stock structure.) In part because of these pressures, the history of the biotech industry is one of successful companies being acquired. In fact, with 30-plus years and thousands of start-up companies formed since the industry was founded, fewer than 30 companies with annual revenues of more than $500 million remain independent (including Regeneron). Sanofi played a large role in allowing Regeneron to focus its investment in promising R & D without the pressure of having to repeatedly raise additional capital or confront a takeover by acquiring and holding approximately 20 percent of the company beginning in 2007 (actual ownership percentage has varied with subsequent additional open market share purchases by Sanofi) and by providing significant R & D funding. Not unlike the seminal Roche-Genentech relationship of the 1990s, this significant relationship has allowed Regeneron to pursue its R & D programs aggressively. From the end of 2007 to the middle of 2016, Regeneron's market capitalization increased from $2 billion to nearly $40 billion. A variety of considerations would have influenced Sanofi's decision not to acquire Regeneron in 2007, but a principal reason was to preserve the nimble and highly successful research culture at Regeneron, which may have withered if combined into Sanofi's much larger operations. And the outcome? Praluent was approved, the pipeline remains robust, and the return on Sanofi's shareholding has not been too bad either.

It is somewhat surprising that this structure has not been emulated more frequently, however, it does require a long-term view and willingness to assume more risk than a typical alliance. More recent examples of this genre of transaction include Sanofi's relationship with Regeneron (see text box, "Sanofi-Regeneron: A Valued Relationship"), which began as a more typical alliance transaction in 2003 but expanded over time. Purdue Pharmaceutical's oncology-focused alliance with Infinity Pharmaceuticals [17] (which has since terminated) and the 2014 alliance between Sanofi Genzyme and Alnylam Pharmaceuticals [18] are additional variations on this approach. Each of these transactions included the purchase of a significant (but not a controlling) equity stake (with no option to acquire the balance of the company). Similar to Roche-Genentech, these alliances have provided each biotech company with financial resources and a long-term development and commercialization partner for multiple identified and future product candidates. Roche also recently applied this structure to acquire a controlling interest in Foundation Medicine, which does not develop drugs itself but rather provides data-driven insights regarding possible cancer treatment combinations and regimens based on the genetic profile of a tumor. In addition to an ownership stake, Roche also provides R & D funding for additional genomic profile tests and will utilize Foundation's database to standardize clinical trial testing. This aspect of the relationship is designed to enable comparability of clinical trial results for R & D purposes and ultimately in the clinic [19].

Key Deal Terms

Regardless of the structure being deployed, certain key areas of understanding must be negotiated and included in the alliance contract. These terms include:

- *Scope*: The technology, products, therapeutic areas, and territories covered by the alliance.
- *Responsibilities:* Defining which parties are responsible for research, development (including the design and performance of clinical trials), manufacturing, and commercialization. It is not uncommon for alliance partners to share responsibility (and costs) in areas such as clinical development and commercialization. Given the differences in scale and resources, a biotech company is typically more dependent on an alliance for its success than a

large pharma company partner. Therefore, it is important that the agreement include a diligence provision requiring that the pharma company use all commercially reasonable efforts to purse its responsibilities.

- *Financial terms:* The consideration, both fixed and contingent, that will be paid by the licensing partner. Fixed payments typically include an upfront license or option fee and reimbursement of R & D costs at specified rates per employee or based on a negotiated budget. Contingent payments typically include amounts due upon successful completion of R & D milestones (e.g., identification of a product candidate or successful completion of a clinical trial), regulatory milestones (approval to market in a particular market), and commercial milestones (reaching specified levels of sales in a market), as well as sales-based royalties. The arrangement may also include a simultaneous purchase of equity at a negotiated price.

- *Intellectual property:* Defining the rights to preexisting intellectual property as well as that created as a result of the alliance. It is common for the licensee to receive all rights to develop and market the licensed product, while the licensor receives rights to any underlying improvement in the core platform technology that led to the product under development.

- *Exclusivity:* Defining the extent that the parties may work on competing products (alone or with other organizations) in same therapeutic area or with same mechanism of action during the collaboration term.

- *Governance and dispute resolution:* Defining the mechanisms by which the alliance will be governed and the means to settle any disputes that arise. Most alliances are governed by a joint steering committee (JSC) comprised of two to three representatives from each party. The JSC may also be supported by joint development and commercialization committees. The responsibility of the JSC is to develop and oversee business plans for the alliance, including key milestones and budgets, and to make operational decisions after appropriate review of the facts (e.g., the size and design of a clinical trial). In the event the JSC reaches a stalemate, decisions are escalated to members of senior management for discussion. Ultimately, it is common for one party (usually the licensee) to have ultimate decision making authority.

- *Term and termination:* Defining the term of the arrangement and the rights of each party to early termination, including on change of control of either partner or through breach of a material provision of the agreement. The duration of an alliance is commonly defined as the term of the last-to-expire patent covered by the license. However, an alliance may have a shorter, defined term. Typically, an alliance may be terminated with three to six months of notice by the licensor, whereas the licensee may only terminate because of an uncured breach of contract by the licensor. The dispensation of the underlying products or technology upon termination is also specified. If the licensee (pharma) terminates the arrangement, the technology and all improvements usually revert to the licensor (biotech) company.

Relationships Matter

The language in the contractual arrangement between the parties should clearly spell out responsibilities of the parties and define what happens when there is a dispute. The JSC should build a detailed alliance plan that defines budgets, milestones, timelines, and the project-level division of responsibilities. However, JSCs typically only meet two to four times per year. The success of any alliance, beyond the technical results of the R & D, is based on the quality of the relationship between the partners at multiple levels. Thus, it is important that leadership on both sides be committed to the alliance and that regular communication occurs between formal meetings and issues or questions are addressed timely. Larger companies frequently have alliance management offices that are charged with monitoring the progress of the relationship. On the biotech side, in addition to functionally oriented project managers, management should consider having an alliance manager in charge. The alliance manager should have a different skill set that is tuned to the long-term objectives of the alliance and the strategy needed to obtain them [20].

Monitoring Results and Learning

Because of the strategic importance of alliances in the biopharma industry, companies will likely enter into multiple transactions with various partners. While each transaction will likely have unique attributes, it is important for all companies to establish processes to monitor both individual alliances against expectations (done through the alliance manager and the JSC structure described above) as well as the success of the overall alliance process (Figure 3-8). Measures should be as

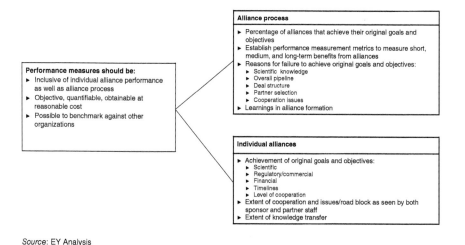

Source: EY Analysis

Figure 3-8   Monitoring alliance results

objective and quantifiable as possible and be both internal and external (if obtainable at a reasonable cost). Knowledge gained from this analysis should be applied to new transactions.

SUMMARY POINTS

- Alliance structures have evolved in response to specific business challenges and are now a critical component of the R & D, business, and financing strategies of biopharma companies of all sizes.

- While R & D-stage product licensing and development alliances have been, and will likely remain, the most common type of transaction in the industry, emerging drug pricing challenges and the move to outcomes-based pricing arrangements will require alliances with a broader range of players including payers, providers, patients, and nontraditional players such as data and other infotech companies and healthcare providers.

- Alliance versus acquisition:
  - For pharmaceutical companies, an alliance structure may be preferable to an acquisition because it allows access to a desired product candidate without having to incur the cost and risk of acquiring the entire entity. A larger company may also desire to preserve the entrepreneurial culture and operating nimbleness of its alliance partner.
  - For a biotech company, the decision to be acquired hinges on an evaluation of the value of the company today versus its potential value in light of known or expected risks (technical, financial, or business).
  - To maximize value, platform technology companies should consider structures that allow for the sale of individual assets in a tax-efficient manner.

- Biotech companies must begin building awareness and trust by cultivating relationships with potential future alliance partners well in advance of a particular transaction, including directly with relevant members of a pharmaceutical company's R & D organization.

- Prior to defining detailed contractual terms, it is critical that the parties define the alliance objectives, including how they will define success throughout the course of the relationship and where in the relationship they expect to create value.

- The strategic rationale behind the transaction will drive its structure, including allocation of responsibilities and territories.

- The success of any alliance, beyond the technical results of the R & D, is based on the quality of the relationship between the partners at multiple levels. Thus, it is important that leadership on both sides be committed to the alliance and that regular communication occurs and issues are addressed in a timely manner.

PART 2

NEW BUSINESS AND MARKETING MODELS

CHAPTER 4

PRECISION MEDICINE

WHAT IS PRECISION MEDICINE?

Precision medicine describes the process of getting the right drug to the right patient at the right time, thereby improving health outcomes. Sometimes called "individualized" or "personalized" medicine, precision medicine most often refers to the use of genetic technologies to determine whether an individual patient is likely to respond to a particular therapy. Today, most approved drugs are effective in only a subset of the patients who take them. Proponents of precision medicine envision a future in which drug therapy is tailored to each patient, leading to better results and lower costs, as wasteful, inappropriate therapy is reduced.

Precision medicine, in the form of molecularly targeted treatments, is already a reality in several types of cancer. But the concept is evolving to include any tools or data that help better tailor medicines and enhance outcomes. In this broader sense, precision medicine is being driven by, and indeed is part of, the many interrelated forces changing the healthcare landscape, including digital technologies, payers' quest for value, and consumer empowerment. Numerous hurdles may delay the widespread adoption of precision medicine. Yet it is already transforming biopharma R & D, commercialization strategies, and business models. Biopharma firms must help address the challenges facing precision medicine by adopting new mind-sets, embracing new digital technologies, and engaging in new kinds of collaborations, both with traditional healthcare stakeholders and new players (Figure 4-1). In doing so, they will ensure that they drive, and are not being driven by, the shift toward more personalized care.

TARGETED MEDICINES MULTIPLY BUT DRUG-DIAGNOSTIC PAIRS ARE RARE

The rapid increase in the number of targeted cancer drugs, designed for patients with particular genetic mutations, illustrates the growth in precision medicine. Therapies such as Genentech's breast cancer drug Herceptin (trastuzumab),

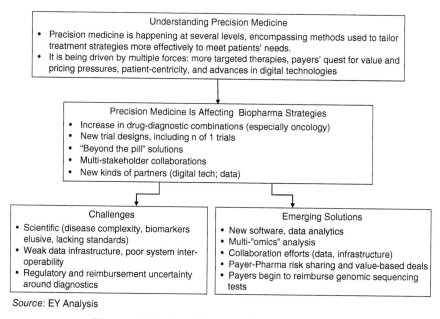

Source: EY Analysis

Figure 4-1   Precision medicine in context

approved for women with high levels of a protein called human epidermal growth factor receptor 2 (HER2), or Novartis's Gleevec (imatinib), approved for chronic myeloid leukemia and gastrointestinal stromal tumors, are used with diagnostic tests that uncover patients' genomic characteristics and thus determine suitability for treatment. These tests are known as companion diagnostics.

In 2006, only five such drug-diagnostic pairs existed, all in oncology, according to data from the Personalized Medicine Coalition. By 2014, as advances in genomics and gene sequencing technologies accelerated, there were well over 100 across several therapy areas, including immunology, cardiovascular disease, gastroenterology, and infectious disease [1]. Among the recent additions: AstraZeneca's non-small cell lung cancer drug Tagrisso (osimertinib) for patients with a very specific mutation that confers resistance to an older kind of targeted therapy, and Vertex's cystic fibrosis treatments Kalydeco (ivacaftor) and Orkambi (ivacaftor/lumacaftor).

More targeted medicines and wider use of biomarkers—measurable substances that can indicate disease incidence and/or whether a drug is having the intended effect—help reduce development time and risk for biopharmaceutical firms by identifying in advance which patients are most likely to respond. A recent study found that drugs developed with a predictive biomarker were three times more likely to be approved than those without [2]. That offers biopharma firms a huge opportunity to increase their R & D efficiency.

However, approved drug-diagnostic combinations remain the exception rather than the rule. Notwithstanding their increased likelihood of regulatory approval, a series of scientific, regulatory, and commercial challenges have hampered the development and widespread adoption of drug-diagnostic pairs. Many of those challenges are being addressed, though this will take time. New genomic sequencing tools and techniques, and the discovery and validation of new and more powerful biomarkers, should support the growth of drug-diagnostic pairs. Important policy initiatives will also accelerate progress, including the United States Precision Medicine Initiative, which promotes research linking genetic information to treatments [3]. This has already spawned a host of data collection initiatives; similar programs are ongoing in other countries.

PRECISION MEDICINE IS HAPPENING AT SEVERAL LEVELS

Precision medicine is not limited to drug-diagnostic combinations. The concept encompasses a wider range of mechanisms and tools used to narrow treatments more precisely to the individual needs of patients and thereby achieve better outcomes. Within the molecular sphere, precision medicine includes various "degrees of targeting": the most targeted are autologous gene and cell therapies that extract and modify a patient's own cells. These treatments represent the ultimate in individualized medicine: unique therapies that must be customized on a patient-by-patient basis. Drug-diagnostic combinations based on particular sets of genetic mutations or aberrant proteins are less targeted than individualized therapies but more so than drugs targeting processes common to many patients, such as angio-genesis inhibitors, which block the growth of tumor blood vessels (Figure 4-2). These molecularly targeted therapies are in turn far more precise than chemotherapy, which acts on both normal and cancerous cells.

Precision medicine is also set to expand beyond the genome, as scientists attempt to unravel the many other biological steps underlying different pathologies.

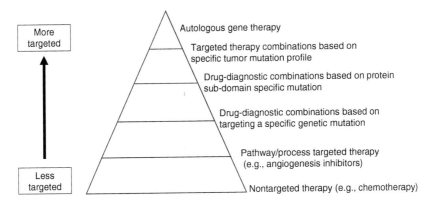

Source: EY Analysis

Figure 4-2   Levels of molecular precision medicine

These include how genes are transcribed (the transcriptome), which proteins they express (the epigenome and the proteome), and which metabolites are produced (the metabolome).

MULTIPLE FORCES, BEYOND SCIENCE, ARE DRIVING PRECISION MEDICINE

This shift toward more tailored therapies is not being driven only by science. It is being driven by payers, providers, and by patients themselves. It is also being enabled by new digital technologies and data sources, including wearable sensors that enable the real-time capture of physiological and other data, sometimes referred to as "digital biomarkers." These additional data can help optimize treatment regimens and medication adherence around the lifestyles and priorities of individuals.

Indeed, some groups are starting to use a new term, *P-medicine*, to describe these broader, yet tightly interlinked, forces driving change across the healthcare landscape, including patient empowerment and digital health. P-medicine envelops personalized, precision, preventative, predictive, pharmacotherapeutic, and patient participatory medicine [4]. Even if many more gene mutations and biomarkers are uncovered, they cannot on their own enable more effective medicine and better outcomes across the board. Only a tiny minority of diseases are understood to be directly linked to particular gene mutations; most result from a far more complex mix of physiological, pathobiological, behavioral, psychological, and environmental factors.

P-medicine encompasses not just the potential of new technologies and science but also a new mindset: toward a greater emphasis on prevention, greater stakeholder collaboration in preempting and solving health challenges, and a greater appreciation for when "no treatment" could represent the best care for a patient. "Precision medicine is technology-inclusive and technology-agnostic in the pursuit of the right therapy for each individual patient," concludes Mara Aspinall, who was CEO of the diagnostics company Ventana Medical Systems (now part of Roche) and is now executive chairman of GenePeeks and CA Therapeutics and cofounder of the School of Biomedical Diagnostics at Arizona State University. "It is not limited to the patient's genomic profile, or any other single data profile. It's about getting the data necessary and sufficient to match the patient to therapies that will work for them," she says [5].

This scientific and cultural shift toward more widespread precision medicine—and, ultimately, P-medicine—has profound implications for biopharma R & D and commercial strategies. It is changing the kinds of medicines they develop, how they develop them, and how those medicines are reimbursed and marketed. Drugs are increasingly specific, often biomarker-linked; trials of such treatments require new designs and may benefit from new tools that facilitate patient recruitment and enable patient-reported outcome measures.

Reimbursement, already shifting slowly from fee-for-service to value-based payment models linked to outcomes, will continue to do so, forcing new kinds of biopharma-payer relationships [6]. Indeed, precision medicine is both driving and demanding a shake-up among all stakeholder relationships within healthcare. The biopharma industry's recent embrace of "patient-centricity"—active patient engagement and input at all stages of drug development—is part of the evolution toward precision medicine [7]. As companies seek to develop solutions that expand "beyond the pill" to include, for instance, adherence support technologies or digital tools that engage patients more closely, they are also building treatments that are more targeted to the needs of patients—more precise medicines.

Payers Apply More Precise Targeting to Control Costs

To control costs, government and commercial payers already apply their own criteria to target treatments more carefully to specific segments of their covered populations. Such nonmolecular segmentation has been happening for years in the United States to limit uptake of certain high-priced drugs. Step-therapy regimens start with the most cost-effective drugs, including generics, before offering patients pricier treatments. Prior authorization, demanded by most payers for high-priced drugs, requires doctors to check with insurers, prior to prescribing, whether a particular patient is eligible for reimbursement. In Europe, reimbursement restrictions are imposed by health technology assessment agencies such as the National Institute of Health and Care Excellence in England and Wales, based on cost-effectiveness criteria [8]. (See Chapters 7 and 8.) Patient registries are also used to help identify eligible patients in certain disease areas and reduce off-label therapy use.

More accurate definitions of disease subtypes and the drive toward specialty medicines with correspondingly high price tags reinforce this payer-driven segmentation. So does tighter drug labeling by regulators. The US Food and Drug Administration (FDA) approved Amgen and Sanofi/Regeneron's PCSK9 inhibitors Repatha (evolocumab) and Praluent (alirocumab), not as a primary prevention for all patients with high cholesterol (akin to statins), but for patients whose cholesterol remains high despite taking statins (as well as for patients with certain genetic disorders characterized by high cholesterol) [9]. Critically, the FDA did not specifically approve the drugs for patients who cannot tolerate statins, saving payers millions by providing the justification for restricting the drugs to second-line therapy. Indeed, utilization management requirements enacted by payers successfully narrowed their use despite the collection of outcomes data showing a reduction in the risk of major adverse cardiovascular events. The uptake of both drugs following launch was below expectations [10].

Providers Experiment with Precision Medicine Programs

Providers, too, are under growing pressure to improve outcomes while lowering costs as part of a broader quest to deliver value-based healthcare. In the United States, established integrated delivery networks such as InterMountain Healthcare or the Swedish Medical Center, plus top-ranking academic medical centers like the Mayo Clinic, Columbia University Medical Center, and Stanford University are among the frontrunners in installing the systems and infrastructure necessary to implement genomics-driven precision medicine–at least in oncology. These organizations want to offer their patients the treatments most likely to be effective, but they also want to use the information to reduce inappropriate medication use and unnecessary costs.

INTERMOUNTAIN: PRECISION GENOMICS FOR CANCER

InterMountain Healthcare's Precision Genomics program for advanced cancer patients has been available since 2013. It uses next-generation sequencing on tumor samples, testing for all possible cancer mutation types. Once these mutations are detected, a panel of experts is assembled to interpret the data and determine the most appropriate treatment. Data interpretation is the hardest part, according to Lincoln Nadauld, Medical Director of Cancer Genomics at InterMountain Healthcare, since most of the genetic alterations picked up by the relatively sophisticated test will be unfamiliar to most oncologists [11].

A matched cohort study of InterMountain's program demonstrated a significantly improved survival rate among patients receiving precision medicine compared with standard chemotherapy, and a nonsignificant (5–10 percent) reduction in weekly therapy costs [12]. For now, "the very best application of precision medicine is in the tough cases," says Nadauld. Among patients with few alternative options, "it's reasonable to try new approaches," based on the growing, but still incomplete, understanding of cancer's genomic footprint and with a limited armamentarium of targeted therapies. During the early stages of many cancers, "we know what gives the best chance of curing, and it's difficult to come in and mess with that gold standard." That will change, though: Nadauld says that expanding the program to earlier stage cancer patients is within InterMountain's three-to-five-year plan.

For now, the majority of precision medicine programs are limited to the most sophisticated, best-funded health systems and medical research centers and to patients with end-stage cancers. But all providers have at their disposal a burgeoning suite of new technologies and data sources to deliver care that is better tailored to the individual needs and priorities of patients, even if these are not all defined at the genomic level. For instance, hospitals or provider groups that adopt electronic health records (EHRs), establish care pathways, and use clinical decision support software and outcomes tracking can provide physicians with the data and support necessary to deliver more patient-appropriate, personalized, higher-quality care across a wide range of conditions. For example, Kaiser Permanente, the largest nonprofit integrated managed care group in the United States, has an EHR system known as KP HealthConnect, which assembles a detailed history for each patient that physicians can access [13].

DIGITAL PRECISION MEDICINE

The scope and depth of non "-omic" patient information will only grow as wearable sensors, remote monitoring tools, online information sources, and social networks provide new kinds of data (both "small" and "big") and new levels of insight into the conditions and needs of individuals. These data, much of it captured in real-time over long periods, include, for instance, activity and movement tracking.

As the kinds of data being collected expand, care of chronic diseases such as rhematoid arthritis and multiple sclerosis will improve, evolving beyond treatment regimens determined by trial-and-error. Sleep and mood patterns can also be captured. Such data may outline behavioral, social, and environmental influences on health and wellness, as well as uncover treatment modality preferences based on lifestyle and/or personal priorities.

All these data may lead to other, potentially lower-cost and more practicable options for segmenting patients to receive the optimal therapeutic regimen: a "digital" form of precision medicine that may be applicable to a wider spectrum of conditions, including chronic diseases such as diabetes and cardiovascular disease. Indeed, in diabetes, the emergence of personalized diabetes management platforms illustrate one possible future direction, where real-time data are used to calibrate therapy advice. To accelerate the use of digital markers in diabetes and other diseases, the US Food and Drug Administration created a digital health unit to clarify and streamline guidelines for connected devices and medical apps.

Digital precision medicine is not here yet: infrastructure, storage, standards, and analytics need to evolve, and strength and relevance of observed influences on disease outcomes must be tested and measured. In the future, however, it might provide an ideal degree of disease differentiation and definition—more detailed than is currently the case across most therapy areas, yet with less granularity (and complexity) than the genomic profile of an individual patient.

This wealth of patient-centric data comes hand-in-hand with greater involvement by patients in their health and well-being – taking precision medicine beyond treatment toward prevention, and toward what scientists at Stanford Medicine refer to as "precision health" [14] (Figure 4-3).

PRECISION MEDICINE IN PRACTICE: LESSONS FROM CANCER

Precision medicine has emerged most prominently in cancer, where the links between genetic changes and disease are relatively strong. Cancer is a complex, multigenic disease, but it is often localized within specific tumors whose genetic signatures can be read and analyzed. Advances in tumor characterization and biomarker identification have helped scientists better understand cancer and to develop better treatments for it, although huge challenges remain. Twenty years ago, the mainstays of cancer treatment were chemotherapy and radiation therapy, which indiscriminately kill both cancerous and healthy cells. Since then, dozens of targeted drugs have emerged, designed to identify and attack specific kinds of

Trends	Stakeholders
Value-based care	⇨ **Payers**: More targeted medicines offer a means of controlling costs.
	⇨ **Providers**:. More targeted medicines support delivery of better patient outcomes. New digital tools (including wearable monitors) enable more accurate patient segmentation. Consolidation means providers have the scale to pursue more ambitious precision medicine programs.
Consumer empowerment	⇨ **Patients**: Precision medicines offer patients improved outcomes and greater likelihood of benefit for the cost. Patient awareness has grown due to democratization of trial and treatment information via websites and advocacy groups (e.g., Cancer Commons, PatientsLikeMe, MyTomorrows).
Rise of specialty medicines	⇨ **Pharma**: More targeted medicines offer greater R&D and commercial efficiency, via smaller, shorter trials. They also offer increased pricing flexibility and product differentiation.
Scientific advances	⇨ Faster, more sophisticated genomic sequencing tools (and lower sequencing costs); advances in biomarker science; improved understanding of disease evolution including via investigation across "-omics" technologies.
Digital technologies	⇨ Digital technologies, wearables, and sensors allow more accurate, real-time measurement and offer feedback options, allowing treatment regimens to be adapted to patients' needs.

Source: EY Analysis

Figure 4-3   Forces driving precision medicine

cancer cells and/or the systems that allow those cells to grow and thrive. Several newer therapeutics help steer the immune system to recognize and fight cancer. Targeted cancer therapies have become the cornerstone of precision medicine, and they continue to become more tightly focused.

In 1997, the FDA approved the first molecularly targeted cancer drug, Rituxan (rituximab), directed at a protein on the surface of immune cells that is involved in the development of cancer. Other targeted drugs quickly followed, including Herceptin (trastuzumab) in 1998, for breast cancer patients overexpressing the HER2 protein, and Novartis's Gleevec (imatinib) in 2001, transforming the prospects for patients suffering from a rare kind of leukemia by counteracting a defect caused by a particular chromosomal mutation. In 2003, AstraZeneca's Iressa (gefitinib) became the first approved drug to inhibit epidermal growth factor receptor (EGFR), a cell-surface protein that, when mutated or overexpressed, can trigger cancer cell growth.

As many cancers were seen to resist existing treatments, a new generation of targeted therapies has emerged. Sprycel (dasatinib) became an option for lung cancer patients resistant to Gleevec, targeting the same mutated protein but via a different mechanism. AstraZeneca's Tagrisso (osimertinib) was approved in November 2015 for lung cancer patients with a mutation that confers resistance to existing EGFR inhibitors such as Iressa and Roche's Tarceva (erlotinib) [15]. Researchers are testing numerous therapeutics combinations: these include regimens that combine targeted drugs or pair targeted drugs with chemotherapy. The goal is to halt the growth of even the most aggressive cancers by simultaneously attacking them via different mechanisms, so there are fewer opportunities to develop drug resistance.

Though targeted, most of these drugs were not initially approved with a companion diagnostic. With a few exceptions (including Herceptin, for which a

HER2 test was approved simultaneously, made by a different company), the companion diagnostics came later.

The Companion Diagnostics Challenge

There are several reasons why few drug-diagnostic pairs have been approved simultaneously. In the early years of targeted medicines, researchers often did not know that mutation profiles of individual patients would significantly affect their chance of responding to a drug. Iressa, for instance, showed highly variable responses among (nonselected) trial patients after its US approval; this led to the drug being withdrawn two years later for lack of efficacy [16].

Even when the variation is understood, integrating diagnostics into drug development is challenging. Developers must understand early on which patients are most likely to benefit from a drug and identify a biomarker that reliably selects those patients. The diagnostic itself must then progress via a separate regulatory path, adding cost and complexity to an already difficult process. Finally, therapies whose use is contingent on a positive test result will have a more limited market than those without such restrictions. In other words, the commercial incentive for biopharmaceutical companies to codevelop diagnostics for their targeted therapies has, to date, been lacking.

This is changing, however. With payers pushing back on high-priced medicines and demanding proof of outcomes, and R & D costs continuing to rise, biopharma firms are starting to use precision medicine to their advantage.

Identifying prospectively the patients most likely to respond to a particular drug can cut development costs by lowering the number of patients required in the clinical trials [17]. It may also shorten the time to approval. (See boxed text, "Tagrisso versus Iressa: From Defensive to Offensive Targeting") Both factors increase R & D efficiency. Having a test will not guarantee the drug works, even in the selected group, but at least it may reduce the cost of failure.

Targeting May Boost Efficacy but Not Necessarily Sales

In principle, drugs that are used with companion diagnostics may also command a higher price, given a narrowly defined target population and high probability of successful outcomes in that group. In practice, pricing will depend on the competition and other market conditions.

Certainly, targeting does not preclude blockbuster status: Herceptin, which includes a companion diagnostic, had sales of $6.7 billion in 2016 [18]. Companion diagnostics can also revive aging drugs: FDA approval of a companion diagnostic for Tarceva in 2013, for instance, helped make Roche's nine-year-old therapy a first-line therapy for EGFR-positive metastatic non-small cell lung cancer [19].

Wider evidence that more narrowly targeted drugs garner higher sales is only now starting to emerge–and for many is elusive. The battle between Bristol-Myers Squibb's Opdivo (nivolumab) and Merck's Keytruda (pembrolizumab) illustrates the current market dynamics. Approved in 2015 to treat non-small cell lung cancer, both drugs target the programmed-death protein, PD-1. But use of Keytruda, unlike Opdivo, is limited to patients that overexpress the PD-L1 biomarker. As described in greater detail in Chapter 5, Opdivo initially won greater market share; however, subsequent clinical trials in the first-line setting failed to demonstrate Opdivo's superiority to chemotherapy, while Keytruda had a positive result. Keytruda's better first-line data gave Merck's drug an advantage, even with the added complexities associated with administering a companion test. Indeed, the May 2017 FDA approval of Keytruda use based on a specific biomarker, not the location where the tumor originated, is an important step in solidifying Keytruda's advantages over rival therapies. More broadly, it is a critical advance for the field of precision medicine itself [20,21].

The unfolding clinical results for Keytruda and Opdivo illustrate the broader challenges associated with effective development and use of drug-diagnostic combinations. Diagnostics are not routinely administered, including the PD-L1 diagnostic approved concurrently with Keytruda. Many physicians are not aware of the diagnostics that are available, nor are they educated in how to use them. Those who have this knowledge do not always have time to wait for the test to be ordered and for the results to return, which can take several days. Furthermore, diagnostics do not always provide clear, binary (yes or no) information: PD-L1 overexpression, for example, is a sliding scale. It provides a suggestion, not a definitive signal, as to whether the drug will work in a particular patient. Some feel, for example, that PD-L1 expression is not a sufficiently robust selection tool. Given those uncertainties, faced with two comparable drugs, one of which requires extra testing, many physicians may, understandably enough, prefer taking the easier route [22].

TAGRISSO VERSUS IRESSA: FROM DEFENSIVE TO OFFENSIVE TARGETING

In the past, some targeted medicines resulted from efforts to resurrect otherwise failed drugs. Today, such medicines have become the end in themselves, promising optimal outcomes and a lower likelihood that payers apply their own patient segmentation strategies. The development of AstraZeneca's lung cancer drugs Iressa (gefitinib) and Tagrisso (osimertinib), approved 12 years apart, illustrates this evolution.

Iressa was first approved in 2003 in the United States as a nontargeted treatment and was withdrawn two years later because of lack of efficacy. Iressa remained on the Japanese market, and a post-hoc analysis of a pan-Asian trial (IPASS) in 2008 revealed that EGFR mutation-positive patients were most likely to benefit from the drug [23]. European regulators approved Iressa in 2009 on that basis, and US reapproval, this time in conjunction with a companion test, took until July 2015. Almost 3,000 patients participated in trials of Iressa, and it took seven years to get from Phase I to regulatory filing [24].

Tagrisso, first approved in November 2015, tells a different story. This drug was codeveloped with a diagnostic, based on a predictive biomarker uncovered before trials began. It was approved in conjunction with that diagnostic for patients with a specific subdomain mutation of EGFR (T790M) whose cancers progressed after treatment with a less specific EGFR-inhibitor. Tagrisso was tested in 411 patients and took just two years to progress from first in human trials to approval.

Tagrisso sold just short of $20 million in its first weeks on the market, but peak sales forecasts start from $1 billion. Iressa reached of its sales peak, $647 million, in 2013; sales are now declining.

The understanding of the target biology was not sufficiently advanced during development of Iressa in the 1990s to allow a precision medicine development approach, even if AstraZeneca had sought it. Nevertheless, Tagrisso's journey to market illustrates the efficacy and efficiency of a proactive precision medicine strategy.

CHALLENGES: SCIENTIFIC, INFRASTRUCTURAL, REGULATORY, AND COMMERCIAL

The conceptual advantages of diagnostic-driven precision medicine are clear: for patients, in avoiding unnecessary treatments; for payers, in avoiding unnecessary costs; for providers, in driving cost-effective outcomes; and for biopharma, in improving R & D economics. But scientific, regulatory, educational, and commercial challenges have hampered the development and widespread adoption of drug-diagnostic pairings [25].

Drug-diagnostic pairs account for a small minority of all cancer drugs. Of the major international biopharma firms, only Roche has embraced diagnostics consistently and wholeheartedly. This was further evidenced by its January 2015 deal to acquire a majority stake in Foundation Medicine, a cancer genomics company.

Genomic sequencing is advancing rapidly, but there are still only a handful, out of many thousands, of genes or gene mutations that can be addressed with current therapies [26]. Additional targeted therapies are making their way through the development process, and the number of biomarker-based tests being ordered is increasing [27].

But the wider use of companion diagnostics requires an educational effort that has so far been lacking. At the most basic level, physicians and patients need to be aware of what tests are available, how they are used, how accurate and reliable they are, and how they can help direct treatment. They also require clarity on what tests are covered by insurance.

Beyond that, physicians must appropriately communicate the benefits and risks of these tests to their patients—whether, for instance, the result can be relied upon to determine treatment choice or indeed the withdrawal of treatment. This can present legal and ethical challenges.

Meanwhile, discovering new, clinically relevant biomarkers is difficult. Recruiting and designing studies of biomarker-targeted medicines, alone or in combination, requires new clinical trial methods and new evidence standards. Adaptive trial designs, whereby trial parameters (dosage, patient selection criteria, drug mix, or other) are altered in response to intermediary results, are gaining traction and have regulatory support. But more expertise and infrastructure is needed for their widespread application [28]. Some argue that studies of a single person—"N of one" trials—will be a critical component of precision medicine, though it is unclear how data from these studies will be used [29]. In short, there is one reason why precision medicine has not advanced as quickly as many believed it would: the regulatory and reimbursement environment for diagnostics needs clarification.

Scientific and Clinical Challenges

Cancer (like many other diseases) is highly complex, heterogeneous, and adaptive. Tumors evolve to resist treatment and often interact with other systems but not necessarily in the same ways in each individual.

This disease complexity makes it difficult to reliably pinpoint predictive biomarkers, even for tightly defined disease subtypes. Increasingly complex drug targets and target combinations will add to the challenge of finding and validating biomarkers that are useful in clinical practice. Furthermore, biomarkers are not always binary (expression/nonexpression); they may offer a sliding scale of expression, similar to what is seen with PD-L1.

To better predict responsiveness across a wider range of therapies or therapeutic areas, additional information beyond the genome may be needed, for instance, protein or metabolite data. Tests themselves can cost several thousands of dollars.

However, this does not concern simply the development of additional tests. Updated evidence standards also are needed to determine when particular tumor biomarkers or genetic read-outs may guide patient management. These are difficult to pin down in a fast-moving field where interpreting complex genetic mutation profiles requires significant expertise. There are calls for a broader dialog to determine evidence standards [30].

New clinical trial designs that can take advantage of biomarker-driven healthcare will be required as well [31]. Basic questions remain to be answered, including how many patients and treatment arms and whether biomarker-negative patients should be included. A key unanswered conceptual question is whether patients will be found for trials, or trials designed for patients.

New tools and scientific insights that will help address these challenges emerge rapidly, but biomarker development, standardization, and trial design challenges will take longer to address.

Infrastructure Challenges

Both electronic health records and clinical decision support tools are required for a pharmacogenomics-based clinical strategy; neither are widespread across most provider networks. In addition, such systems will need to be robust enough to accommodate large volumes of unstructured patient-specific data, presenting data storage, usage, and privacy challenges, topics addressed in greater detail in Chapter 10. An added complexity is the lack of interoperability across health systems and between different stakeholders such as laboratories or imaging centers. As a result, many payers are unable to access data related to precision tests to have a timely impact on treatment decisions.

Overcoming the challenges around data sharing requires cultural and mindset shifts as well as legislative change in some cases. Technology barriers will be addressed by the adoption of emerging technologies such as machine learning and cloud computing, as well as new data analytics approaches (see Chapter 10).

Regulatory Challenges

The separate regulatory and reimbursement pathways for diagnostics versus therapeutics add to the complexity and resources required to bring a drug-diagnostic combination to market. The FDA issued guidance on the development and review of companion diagnostics in 2014, but this fell short of defining precise steps necessary to ensure concurrent drug and diagnostic approval [32]. In addition, FDA standards on clinical relevance for diagnostics lack robustness, even though there is increasing clarity on biomarker-based approaches [33]. Equally problematic, there are no data standards for reviewing the cost-effectiveness of diagnostics, and the processes that do exist lack consistency and transparency. Given the high cost of many of the newer tests, this is a gap that has limited the broader adoption of precision medicine practices.

The expected time frame to overcome regulatory challenges is mid-term (five years). The FDA supports personalized medicine approaches, and the growth in drug-diagnostic submissions will compel change. The emergence of clear health technology assessment (HTA) approaches for diagnostics could take longer, judging by the progress rate of collaborative HTA efforts such as EUnetHTA.

Commercial Challenges

Currently, reimbursement of diagnostics and companion diagnostics is inconsistent across different health systems. Many payers do not reimburse for genetic testing, and some that do restrict it to late-stage cancer patients. Furthermore, drugs and diagnostics may be reviewed by separate teams within payer organizations. There is often a lack of evidence to convince payers (including in Europe) of the savings that may result from the upfront cost of a diagnostic test (up to $5,000). Preventative and screening tests are also poorly reimbursed.

Time constraints have also limited the adoption of companion diagnostics, as clinicians may select an alternative drug with no accompanying diagnostic if therapy is urgent and results from a test do not arrive within an acceptable window.

The difficulty of interpreting complicated test results that don't offer a binary treatment action is a further disincentive. Many specialists and patients are not aware of the tests that are available and how these diagnostics can direct treatment. Uncertainties over test reliability may lead to ethical, and even legal, questions around whether to restrict treatment. Because most diagnostics, to date, have emphasized sensitivity (finding true positives) rather than specificity (correctly identifying true negatives), the tests are biased toward finding a problem rather than giving the "all-clear." This contributes to concerns over inappropriate over-treatment and wasted money and raises evidence hurdles for diagnostic tests. Those evidence hurdles are further exacerbated because sophisticated "multiplex" tests require experts to translate the results into specific clinical actions. As a result, there is uncertainty about who will pay for such analysis and how it will then be used to guide treatment decisions.

For biopharma companies, weak intellectual property protection for diag-nostics means there are real disincentives to paying for diagnostic value. Thus, diagnostic makers have struggled to sign partnerships that can adequately reward them for their development work. These lower valuations have resulted in a cycle, where trials using companion diagnostics are inadequately funded and fail to generate the evidence required for widespread use in the market [34]. Adding to the complexity is the fact that different markets have very different regulations and testing standards for diagnostics. That adds to the cost and complexity of a global drug-diagnostic launch, without providing any obvious positive incentives such as more rapid market uptake.

As evidence of cost savings to health systems mount and biopharmas see greater market share for drugs developed in combination with diagnostics, a positive feedback loop will promote their usage and investment in future therapeutic-diagnostic pairings.

The cultural and educational changes required for greater companion diagnostic usage may take longer. It is important to remember that precision medicine is a new discipline that requires new tools and analytics capabilities. In markets where the approach to new treatments is more conservative, access to targeted therapies and the underlying tests associated with their use may be limited.

FRAGMENTED HEALTH TECHNOLOGY ASSESSMENT APPROACHES

Navigating the health technology assessment (HTA) landscape for diagnostics is challeng-ing. Few HTAs are clear about what kinds of diagnostics require formal review, and few have established processes for assessing molecular diagnostics. Among those that do—including the UK's National Institute of Care and Health Excellence's Diagnostic Assessment Program (DAP) and the Canadian Agency for Drugs and Technologies in Health (CADTH)—the review methodologies, evidence standards, and decision making are rarely fully transparent. Thus, diagnostic manufacturers and their biopharma partners face an uphill battle in determining the most appropriate evidence base to demonstrate value.

As experience grows and evidence emerges around tests for the more common and better-understood mutations, such as EGFR-TK in lung cancer, best practices should emerge. A standalone diagnostics guidance from NICE in mid-2013, for instance, recommended that 5 out of 10 available EGFR-TK test types were cost effective for use among patients with metastatic non-small cell lung cancer [35]. Harmonization efforts may facilitate knowledge sharing across different HTA bodies.

Digitally driven precision medicine will face a similar set of hurdles. Regulation of mobile phone apps, monitoring devices, and tools is still nascent. So is our understanding of how to best analyze and interpret the massive amounts of new data emerging from digital health technologies, not all of which will be relevant to patient care. New technologies must be further tested for reliability and usability and consumers need and must be able to use wearables, sensors, or apps so that they inform and improve treatment. Reimbursement for these digital medicine tools is an unknown.

SURMOUNTING THE HURDLES TO REVOLUTIONIZE MEDICINE

The challenges facing precision medicine are surmountable. Many are already being addressed, and initial successes will provide the evidence required to overcome the rest. Elucidating the science, establishing standards, and facilitating regulation and reimbursement will all help promote uptake and culture change.

Diagnostic tests are becoming less invasive, more accurate, and cheaper, in part due to technology improvements and growing demand. Efforts are being made to make testing more widely practicable and affordable, for instance, by developing multiplex testing kits that can detect, with one test sample, several of the most common gene mutations across certain cancers [36]. This is particularly attractive to payers who would prefer to pay for a single test to tell which of a multitude of drugs approved for similar indications is most likely to work best, rather than paying for several single-drug-linked tests. These consolidated tumor profile tests are underpinned by high-volume, fast next-generation sequencing (NGS) techniques.

Hurdles remain over interpreting the data from such tests, whether such tests are sufficiently reliable at the specific gene mutation level, and, thus, under what circumstances they may be reimbursed. But assuming the tests eventually offer sufficient accuracy and reliability across the targeted mutations, they may emerge as the most practicable real-world solution in selected therapy areas. In November 2015, Thermo Fisher Scientific signed a deal with Novartis and Pfizer to develop a universal, multi-marker NGS test for use across multiple non-small cell lung cancer drug programs, with the goal of allowing tailored treatment approaches. [37] Foundation Medicine is doing something similar.

Meanwhile, more sophisticated testing options are emerging, covering several other layers of information from within the proteome, transcriptome or microbiome (see text box, "Multi-'omics' Analysis").

MULTI-"OMICS" ANALYSIS

As scientists further explore rich data highways within the proteome, transcriptome, and metabolome, companies are starting to offer tools to extract and analyze such "multi-omics" data. Start-up Global Genomics Group (G3) says it is looking at every angle, from the DNA itself to how DNA is expressed at several levels within biological networks. G3 has a deal with Sanofi to find new signaling pathways in atherosclerotic disease [38]. Human Longevity Inc., cofounded and led by genomics pioneer J. Craig Venter and supported by investors including diagnostics group Illumina and the biotech Celgene, is building what it claims is the largest human genotype and phenotype database in the world to tackle diseases associated with aging. In April 2016, it announced a 10-year deal with AstraZeneca to sequence DNA samples from clinical trials. Healthcare IT company NantHealth is taking a similarly holistic approach to examining tumor cells and enabling precision medicine, while Alphabet's Verily Life Sciences has partnered with Duke University and Stanford University to launch the Project Baseline Study, which is designed to collect a broad array of health data to develop a reference of human health [39].

New trial designs are being tested. The Lung Cancer Master Protocol (Lung-MAP) trial, for example, is testing four drugs at once, seeking to match biomarkers in lung cancer tumors with a particular mix of these medicines. The idea is to improve and accelerate drug development; certainly, the wider use of biomarkers should make trials more efficient [40].

Regulators, including the FDA, are encouraging biomarker-driven approaches to enable precision medicine. The FDA's Biomarker Qualification Program guides drug developers in their development of biomarkers, helping them integrate these into regulatory reviews, ensuring reliability and validity, and explicitly seeking to "foster biomarker development" [41].

PrecisionFDA is an R & D portal that allows the scientific community to test and validate ways of processing the large amounts of genomic data collected using next-generation sequencing technology. A beta version was launched in November 2015 [42]. The Biomarkers Consortium, a public-private partnership managed by the Foundation for the National Institutes of Health (NIH), is trying to accelerate the development and regulatory approval of biomarker-based technologies and medicines. The European Medicines Agency (EMA) provides advice and opinions on biomarkers and other new approaches but has not issued specific guidance. It is, however, increasing its collaborations with academia to build expertise in the qualification of biomarkers and other new methodologies.

The FDA is also consulting on how digital health technologies and wearables should be regulated, as the potential of these tools in allowing more appropriate, personalized care becomes clearer. Many of these digital tools are being tested in clinical trials, where the FDA has been "incredibly encouraging," according to Mike Capone, chief operating office at Medidata, which offers cloud-based clinical trial solutions and data analytics [43]. The EMA has not outlined explicitly how it is approaching the digitization of trials and medicines. The organization's 2016 work plan nods to the explosion of new data and tools in healthcare and acknowledges the need for a "robust, agile IT infrastructure" and "new capabilities to manage data" [44].

Building the Precision Medicine Infrastructure

Precision medicine is underpinned by accessible, interpretable data. Millions of data points must be collected systematically and consistently across large cohorts of patients in order to help scientists and clinicians piece together the links between genetics and disease, identify new biomarkers, design targeted therapy trials, and uncover the broader determinants of health outcomes. Collecting and interpreting such data demands multi-stakeholder partnerships. "Rich and highly credible information will be the primary catalyst for the broad adoption of precision medicine, particularly in cancer," pointed out Michael Pellini, CEO of the genomics company Foundation Medicine, in announcing a 2015 collaboration with global information and technology services group IMS Health [45].

Multiple further data collection efforts are underway, including government-sponsored initiatives, to help drive and inform the science behind precision medicine (Figure 4-4). These efforts require robust, integrated information technology (IT) systems, including data analytics software and expertise. They also demand secure storage of the ever-larger volumes of genomic and related personalized data.

The digital and data revolution (discussed in Chapter 10) is providing the infrastructure necessary to accommodate precision medicine. New systems, software, and tools have emerged, both from established technology giants such as IBM, Oracle, Apple, Intel, and Alphabet, as well as from start-ups. Several health

---

Government-Led Programs

- **The UK's 100,000 Genomes Project :** Set up in 2012 to sequence genomes from 70,000 patients with rare disease or cancers and enable genomic medicine in the National Health Service (http://www.genomicsengland.co.uk)
- **The US Precision Medicine Initiative :** Launched in January 2015 to collect genomic, pharmaco-genomic, clinical, and other kinds of data from a cohort of one million or more individuals (https://www.nih.gov/precision-medicine-initiative-cohort-program)
- **US Million Veterans Program :** Observational study and biobank designed to uncover genetic, behavioral, environmental, and health-related linkages. Data have been collected from 400,000 recruits so far

---

Private Programs

- **Project Baseline Study :** Initiative between Verily, Stanford, and Duke to gather data from around 10,000 participants to develop a "baseline" map of human health and the transition from health to disease
- **BGI 1 Million Genomes :** Chinese genomic research company plans to sequence one million human genomes plus one million from plants and animals, and one million from micro-ecosystems. Requires new sequencing technologies under development
- **Human Longevity Instute :** This Craig Venter backed company, focused on aging, hopes to sequence one million genomes by 2020
- **Precision Medicine Exchange Consortium :** Launched by Foundation Medicine in September 2015 with US academic medical centers, regional hospital systems, and community oncology providers. Designed to facilitate exchange of molecular information and to integrate genomic profiling into cancer treatment
- **Multiple Myeloma Research Foundation's CoMMpass** (Relating Clinical Outcomes in Multiple Myeloma to Personal Assessment of Genetic Profile) **:** Longitudinal study aiming to enroll 1,000 newly diagnosed patients. Comprehensive molecular (genomic) profiling will be correlated to clinical outcomes data to better understand responses to treatment

Source: EY Analysis

Figure 4-4   Selected precision medicine data collection projects

systems are already using venture-backed Syapse's precision medicine platform, with its clinical and molecular data integration, decision support, outcomes tracking, and a shared-learning loop that allows best practice to evolve based on real-world results. Oracle launched its own Healthcare Precision Medicine software suite in January 2016 [46].

While data collection partnerships accelerate, some of the regulations and guidelines required to manage and control the use of such data are emerging. US data privacy standards are embedded within the HIPAA (Health Insurance Portability and Accountability Act) privacy rule, which protects patient medical records and other health information and limits how this data can be used. The Genetic Information Nondiscrimination Act also helps protect individuals against misuse of their data. But the issue of data privacy and protection remains challenging, especially in some European markets such as Germany.

Meanwhile, the Clinical Pharmacogenetics Implementation Consortium (CPIC) has created guidelines on how to responsibly use genomic data to inform prescribing. The Institute of Medicine's Roundtable on Translating Genomic-Based Research for Health, established in 2007, holds workshops, discussions, and symposia among experts from all stakeholder groups on how to turn genomics into healthcare applications [47].

Payers Begin to Fund Precision Medicine

Payers such as UnitedHealthcare are beginning to cover molecular profiling for certain patient groups, such as stage IV non-small cell lung cancer patients. Independence Blue Cross announced it would cover whole genome sequencing for patients with limited treatment options: those with rare cancers, triple negative breast cancer, and those with metastatic disease who are not responding to other treatments, as well as children with tumors [48]. Several European payers, including the French government, have begun to fund molecular testing in cancer patients [49]. The advantage of Europe's single-payer health systems is that many have the infrastructure necessary to implement diagnostic-driven strategies.

Meanwhile, more targeted products continue to reach the market. Today, only 15 percent of oncology drugs are considered targeted; earlier in the pipeline, this figure is 50 percent [50]. As these therapies become available and as disease characteristics and subtypes continue to be better understood, the hurdles facing precision medicine will continue to fall.

STAKEHOLDER EXPANSION IN PRECISION MEDICINE

By Kristin Pothier and Ryan Juntado, Parthenon-EY

Unlocking "personalized" or "precision" medicine—the ability to deliver the right treatment to the right patient at the right time—has required an expansion of collaboration between an increasingly complex and varied set of stakeholders who need to partner across healthcare. Additionally, resource constraints within the industry have pushed drug developers to adopt leaner organizations. As a result, in-house capabilities are often diminished or even cut completely, creating a need to outsource various functions such as manufacturing, IT, logistics, and even basic research. Navigating this universe of potential partners is a growing challenge, but it is a challenge that innovators will need to surmount in order to discover, develop, and commercialize the treatments of the future.

First, the universe of potential partners is multiplying. It is impossible to deliver healthcare in the way that it was delivered in the past, with a one-on-one relationship between doctor and patient. Indeed, the number of stakeholders necessary to invent, translate, and deliver care to patients worldwide is ever increasing, bringing with it a series of structural, cultural, and business-related challenges that must be overcome.

The set of potential partners is also growing increasingly varied. Stakeholders in healthcare today, and especially in precision medicine, are seemingly as varied as the therapies being developed for patients. Drug and diagnostics developers go hand-in-hand today to develop targeted drugs where patient access is determined by diagnostics. Payers and policymakers try to make sense of the financial and regulatory implications of all of these discoveries. Finally, patient advocacy groups and patients themselves, fueled by the consumer health explosion, are taking control of their paths with a more united, digital voice that cannot be ignored.

Last, stakeholders are becoming more global. The launch of precision medicine is no longer limited to the United States and developed markets. Today, markets all over the world are clamoring for precision therapies to better treat their infectious disease, cardiovascular, and oncology populations on home soil. However, the implementation and access challenges differ greatly in each region of the world, and stakeholders take on different roles in each region. The delivery of precision medicine in Spain, for example, is drastically different from the delivery of precision medicine in Kuwait—and the appropriate partnership strategies in one region will also vary drastically from those in another.

Increasingly, outsourcing and partnership strategies have offered healthcare innovators an opportunity to survive and thrive in a world with growing economic pressures, instability, and intricacy. These partnerships will enable companies to keep driving toward a more personalized approach to medicine, and we anticipate these partnerships accelerating in the near future—from discovery through development and commercialization. Just as the patient-doctor relationship has changed, so must the rest of medicine to embrace the diversity of enablers, promote successful partnerships, and bring better care to our patients worldwide.

Additional resources: Palmer S, Kuhlmann G, Pothier P, "IO Nation: The Rise of Immuno-oncology," *Current Perspectives in Pharmacogenomics and Personalized Medicine* 2015; 12:176–181. Pothier K, Gustavsen G, "Combatting Complexity: Partnerships in Personalized Medicine," *Personalized Medicine* 2013;10(4):387–396.

BIOPHARMA MUST DRIVE, NOT BE DRIVEN BY, PRECISION MEDICINE

As hurdles are overcome, the forces driving precision medicine will be unstoppable. Payer-driven patient segmentation will continue as costs rise. The digitization of medicine will inevitably increase, along with the shift to outcomes. This leaves biopharma companies with no choice but to embrace precision medicine, in all its forms. The biopharma industry must develop medicines that are sufficiently targeted to drive consistent, reimbursable outcomes, rather than risk having payers restrict them according to their own criteria.

More widespread use of diagnostics may limit the number of patients treated with any particular drug. Yet a smaller, better-defined market may be a worthwhile trade-off for gaining differentiation in competitive markets and to optimize outcomes. Drugs that are effective in broad populations are relatively rare. It may be premature to definitively correlate molecularly targeted treatments with better sales, but prescribing treatments to nonresponders is no longer tenable in a value-based care system, either financially (for payers) or from a reputational standpoint (for biopharma).

Precision medicine ultimately should lead to greater commercial success by offering increased R & D efficiency (because trials will be smaller and less expensive and development times will be shorter), more focused regulatory submissions, and more secure reimbursement and uptake. Precision medicine also demands and encourages greater stakeholder collaboration—including with patients—in a healthcare landscape that calls increasingly for combined expertise and data sharing.

Precision Medicine Demands New Kinds of Collaboration

Implementing precision medicine requires new kinds of partnerships and collaboration, both among stakeholders in healthcare but also with experts across technology, data analytics, and beyond (Figure 4-5). Drug developers are already pairing up with each other to test drug combinations, such as targeted cancer therapies with immuno-oncology approaches. They also need to partner with diagnostics firms that have market-relevant regulatory and commercial expertise. Such partnerships have increased, though not consistently (Figure 4-6).

Incentives between biopharmaceutical and diagnostics firms are not always aligned. Drug developers want an accurate, low-cost test to be available fast in order to open up the relevant patient population for a drug, which could bring in significant revenues, especially if used chronically. Diagnostics developers are only paid when the patient is tested. If the population is too small, the reimbursement math might not work. For larger populations, marketing and education on how to access and use the test may arise, and competing diagnostics are likely to arrive fast, pushing down prices.

Solutions to these divergent incentives include buying diagnostics capabilities, as Roche has done, or signing longer-term deals with large, multi-platform diagnostics firms. Eli Lilly and Janssen both did this in 2014, signing broad-based deals with Qiagen and Adaptive Biotechnologies, respectively [51,52].

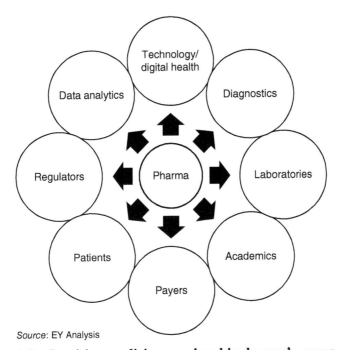

Source: EY Analysis

**Figure 4-5   Precision medicine requires biopharma's engagement
in multiple stakeholder alliances**

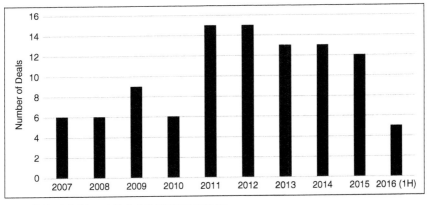

Source: EY Analysis, Informa's Strategic Transactions Database

**Figure 4-6   Evolution of deal making between drug and
diagnostic developers**

Consolidation among diagnostics groups makes this option viable, in terms of accessing the necessary range of capabilities, but also potentially more expensive, as the number of potential partners is reduced.

A Framework for Biopharma-Payer Risk Sharing

Precision medicine also requires biopharma companies to build more collaborative relationships with payers, and it provides a framework for doing so by encouraging outcomes-linked payment deals.

Payers want to see evidence that diagnostic-linked therapies, or digital medicine, are practical and provide value for money before they start paying for tests (which can cost from hundreds to several thousands of dollars) as well as the treatments. One answer is payer-biopharma risk sharing: deals that link drug pricing (and/or reimbursement level) to the real-world outcomes that a treatment delivers. These deals, described in more detail in Chapter 7, were shunned by both sides until recently, but are beginning to gain traction as the broader shift to value-based care takes hold. Tightly defined patient groups and high response rates, as seen with precision medicines, should give both biopharma companies and payers more confidence in tying price to outcomes.

The digitization of healthcare and the concurrent rise of the connected, empowered consumer are already forcing patient-centric approaches among several biopharma firms [53]. They are also driving some of the interdisciplinary collaboration and experimentation required for precision medicine. New technologies, apps, wearables, and burgeoning sources of genomic and non-genomic big data are converging to transform how drug trials are designed and recruited and how therapies are administered, and they are expanding the definition of therapies "beyond the pill." Experiments abound across beyond-the-pill solutions, mobile health, adaptive regulatory pathways and trial designs, and include greater patient engagement, wider use of patient-reported outcomes (PROs) and electronic PROs, and more. These experiments help define and set the rules for a future of more targeted medicines.

Biopharma and diagnostics firms must maintain frequent dialog with regulators, as the latter adjust their processes to accommodate biomarker-based drug development, new kinds of data, and increasingly digital medicines. The priorities of drug regulators are safety and efficacy, but they also, like biopharma, want more efficient drug development and faster access to effective medicines.

PRECISION MEDICINE'S FUTURE

Molecular-driven precision medicine is still in its infancy. It emerged out of cancer drug discovery and it is there, more specifically in late-stage cancers, that it has taken root. As evidence of its success begins to emerge, in terms of both outcomes and costs, it will spread across other therapy areas. The FDA approved 13 novel personalized medicines in 2015, according to the Personalized Medicine Coalition. Eight were in conditions other than cancer, including asthma, schizophrenia, cystic fibrosis, and high cholesterol.

But the spread of diagnostic-driven personalized medicine will not happen overnight. "Changing medicine . . . from over-use and over-treatment to a more accurate precision medicine is a 20-year process," opines Tom Miller, cofounder of GreyBird Ventures, which invests in precision-medicine-focused start-ups [54]. Nor is molecular-based precision medicine likely to be possible, practicable, and affordable across all conditions. For many chronic diseases, "digital" precision medicine, that is, more targeted treatment (and prevention) approaches enabled by new wearable tools and data sources, may prove more fruitful and cost effective. "It's about finding a level of data that defines and differentiates disease in a much more specific way than we do today," sums up Mara Aspinall [55].

Precision medicine will personalize rather than replace traditional, population-based care. The drive toward more specialist, targeted medicines cannot continue ad infinitum. Health systems will not be able to afford the rising prices that would accompany products addressed at ever-narrower conditions. Precision medicine must be applied pragmatically across therapy areas, health systems, and geographies to enable more intelligent *population-based* approaches to treating some chronic diseases, as well as diagnostic-driven, targeted therapies at the *individual* level in other conditions.

Precision medicine may also drive more targeted prevention strategies, in theory helping to control costs. Molecular markers can signal disease risk before symptoms appear, allowing screening efforts to be focused on those at risk. Women with certain gene variations (BRCA1 or BRCA2), for instance, are more than six times more likely to develop breast cancer during their lifetime than those without. Grail, a new spin-off from gene sequencing giant Illumina, is developing a blood test (known as a "liquid biopsy") that can detect tiny fragments of cancer DNA well before any tumor is detected [56]. Others have similar programs underway. Any resulting test would have to be highly accurate, however, and any therapy given to apparently healthy individuals would need to be highly targeted indeed, with no or minimal side effects.

Biopharmaceutical firms must ensure their portfolio includes candidates across disease segments that are sufficiently well defined to allow targeted therapeutic approaches, yet big enough to sustain a business. Companion diagnostic strategies must be planned in advance, with sufficient flexibility to respond to market moves toward multiplex testing and evolving attitudes of payers. Those companies addressing large chronic diseases must access the relevant technologies and expertise to enable digital precision medicine and adapt product pricing, positioning, and marketing tactics rapidly as real-world, often real-time, data emerge on how and by whom medicines are used, and with what outcomes.

Precision medicine is not emerging in isolation but rather alongside other, equally disruptive, changes across healthcare. By adopting flexible, partnership-driven approaches, remaining focused on how to achieve the best outcomes for patients, and opening up to new kinds of expertise, biopharmaceutical firms can emerge stronger, more efficient, and more engaged with their customers.

SUMMARY POINTS

- Precision medicine—getting the right treatment to the right patient at the right time—is growing fast, driven by technological advances (e.g., genomics and sequencing technology) and market forces (e.g., patient empowerment and the need to reduce the costs of inappropriate therapy).

- It is particularly prominent in cancer treatment, where targeted therapies and drug-device combinations are multiplying, offering new options for patients.

- Precision medicine is not only about drug-device pairs; it encompasses a wider range of tools and mechanisms to narrow treatments more precisely to the needs of individual patients and thereby achieve better outcomes. These new tools include a host of digital technologies, such as wearable sensors and smartphone apps that provide patient insights and offer more tailored treatment modalities.

- In the future, these newer digital technologies will enable P-medicine (personalized, precision, preventative, predictive, pharmacotherapeutic, and patient participatory medicine).

- The rise of precision medicine has profound implications for biopharmaceutical firms. It is changing the kinds of medicines they develop, how they develop them, and how they are reimbursed and marketed.

- The commercial model for molecular-based precision medicine is not yet clear. Narrower targeting means smaller patient populations. For now, there is not much evidence correlating more targeted treatments with higher sales. Payers cannot support ever-higher prices, yet prescribing treatments to nonresponders is no longer tenable in an increasingly value-based system.

- Ultimately, precision medicines should enable greater R & D efficiency, via smaller, more targeted trials, and allow more focused regulatory submission and more secure reimbursement and uptake.

- There are scientific, structural, regulatory, commercial, and educational challenges facing the spread of precision medicine. Collecting and interpreting huge volumes of data, and applying it to clinical decision-making, requires new expertise, systems, and processes. Meanwhile, regulations around companion diagnostics are in flux, reimbursement is inconsistent, and uptake is limited.

- These challenges are being addressed. Major data collection projects are underway; regulators are encouraging biomarker-based strategies; and payers are beginning to fund some kinds of molecular profiling.

- The rise of precision medicine requires biopharmaceutical firms to build new kinds of partnerships with diagnostics players, technology companies, and payers. Many such deals are already in place.

- Precision medicine also provides a framework for more robust, data-backed, outcomes-based deals with payers. Furthermore, it embodies and enables the patient-centric approach to medicine that biopharma says it strives to deliver.

CHAPTER 5

PRECISION MARKETING

INTRODUCTION

From consumer trends to regulatory scrutiny, payer power, and portfolios, many factors are leading to a new landscape for biopharma marketing strategy. Drug spending has gained top visibility, triggered in part by Gilead's launches of Sovaldi (sofosbuvir) and Harvoni (ledipasvir/sofosbuvir) and what was perceived as their high price in the large hepatitis C market, and by increased government scrutiny of pricing practices. Aging demographics across countries contribute to pressures on health budgets. Total spending on prescription drugs in the United States rose nearly 6 percent to almost $450 billion in 2016, despite generic utilization rates of nearly 90 percent. Average copays for patients covered by commercial insurers have also grown by more than 25 percent since 2010 [1].

Despite the negotiating power of government payers outside of the United States, the trend is global. According to Quintiles IMS, worldwide medicine spending is forecast to reach nearly $1.5 trillion by 2021, with a compound annual rate of growth declining from recent years but still reaching a 4 percent to 7 percent rate over the next 5 years. In that period, a key spending driver will be oncology with a compound annual growth rate of 9 percent to 12 percent, largely similar to the last 5 years [2]. Consumer pricing concerns have become top issues. According to an online Harris Poll of 2,255 US adults, 69 percent said they would choose a generic more often, if given the choice, and 30 percent said they would always choose a generic. This trend is sharper for older age groups; while 62 percent of Millennials (born 1981 to 1997) preferred generics, 73 percent of Boomers (born 1946 to 1964) and as many as 78 percent of those 70 and older showed that preference [3].

As company portfolios are increasingly dominated by high-priced specialty drugs and biologics, the need is clear for precision marketing (as a counterpart to precision medicine) and specifically for an evidence-based strategy, whereby product positionings are supported by hard clinical and economic data.

This chapter first covers a redefinition of branding models, balancing evidence and experience, targeting new segments such as genotypes, evolving from pills to integrated solutions, and developing dual-targeted and broad branding models. It

Managing Biotechnology: From Science to Market in the Digital Age, First Edition. Françoise Simon and Glen Giovannetti.

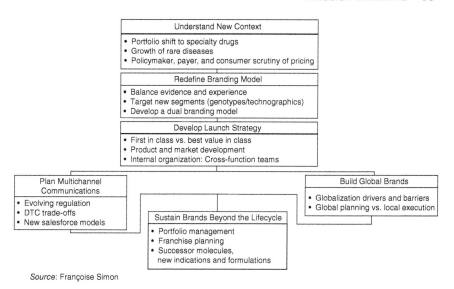

Source: Françoise Simon

Figure 5-1   Precision marketing strategy

next analyzes prelaunch and launch strategies, as well as multichannel outreach. Finally, it assesses sustainability strategies beyond the traditional lifecycle, through portfolio management, multiple indications, and successor molecules (Figure 5-1).

PORTFOLIO SHIFT TO SPECIALTY PRODUCTS

According to a 2016 IMS Health report, spending on specialty drugs doubled in the preceding five years and now accounts for 36 percent of nondiscounted drug spending in the United States, driven by treatments for oncology, hepatitis, and autoimmune diseases. US specialty spending accounted for 42.6 percent of net spending in 2016 [4].

In addition to rising investments in specialty therapies, a key factor has been price inflation. In 2013, more than 100 experts published an article in *Blood* stressing rapid cost increases, particularly in areas such as oncology and blood disorders such as chronic myeloid leukemia [5]. In response, new metrics for comparative clinical value are being developed, such as the American Society for Clinical Oncology's Value Framework and Memorial Sloan-Kettering's Drug Abacus tool [6].

Orphan diseases show especially sharp growth; their small populations drive the need to recoup R & D costs with high prices, and many have become blockbusters, such as Celgene's Revlimid (lenalidomide) in multiple myeloma, with 2016 global sales of nearly $7.0 billion.

As many as 30 million US patients suffer from a rare disease, and this may be understated, as the average patient visits more than seven physicians during almost five years before receiving an accurate diagnosis. The attention to these drug price tags and regulations has increased, in keeping with that growth. The incentives of the Orphan Drug Act, including marketing exclusivity and tax credits, are now under scrutiny.

Orphan drugs now appear on the payer radar, after being lightly treated because their small populations did not impact strongly the total budget costs [7].

These trends support the need for an evidence-based strategy and also close communication with patient groups. The fact that they are globally linked and acutely aware of new therapies may prove to be a double-edged sword: They can provide access to registries and speed up trial recruitment, but they can also harbor overly high expectations, overlook possible side effects, and exert pressure to include patients who do not fit the trial protocol. In response, some companies have opted for open-label studies, while managing expectations and stating eligibility criteria through multiple channels (advocacy groups, conferences, congresses, and social media). Among others, Vertex communicated well that Kalydeco (ivacaftor) should be used only in the very small segment of cystic fibrosis patients with a specific gene mutation [8].

BALANCING EVIDENCE AND EXPERIENCE

While consumer research has shown the importance of understanding the patient journey, a challenge for biopharmas is to balance evidence and experience. Several trends are driving a shift to evidence:

- Regulators worldwide have less tolerance for "me-too" products; France has set up a ranking system based on the innovativeness of new products.
- Payers in most of Europe mandate pharmacoeconomic dossiers, and US groups are developing methods of comparative effectiveness. In July 2015, the nonprofit Institute for Clinical and Economic Review (ICER) launched a program to evaluate new drugs, and it also aims to develop a value-based price benchmark anchored to real benefits for patients [9].
- Physicians have been sensitized to drug recalls, ever since Merck's highly visible recall of its arthritis drug Vioxx (rofecoxib) in 2004, and demand hard clinical data.
- Consumers have online access to scientific data, from search engines to journals.

Given the wide scope of current products, experience-based marketing will continue to coexist with evidence-based approaches. In critical areas such as oncology, evidence will be dominant. In noncritical areas such as allergy, experience will apply, but well-informed consumers will expect it to be supported by evidence as a differentiator, given brand proliferation.

	Regulators	Payers	Physicians	Consumers
Evidence	• Efficacy, safety, tolerability • Randomized trials	• Efficacy/safety vs. standard of care • Competitive products • Comparative effectiveness • Reference pricing	• Hard clinical endpoints on efficacy/safety • KOL influence • Impact on compliance • Market access	• Efficacy/safety • Disease education • Physician and pharmacist influence • Reimbursement/ copay
Experience	• Patient-reported outcomes • Observational trials	• Patient-reported outcomes • Delivery, ease of use and dosing • Cost of companion diagnostic/ease of use • Compliance	• Delivery/dosing convenience • Patient clinical support • CME programs • MSLs/virtual salesforce	• Online community support • Delivery/dosing ease of use • QOL improvement • Social media • Corporate reputation

Source: Françoise Simon

Figure 5-2   Evidence and experience drivers

Experience also partly applies in regulator and payer decisions, as randomized trials are complemented by patient-reported outcomes and observational studies. For physicians and patients, delivery mode, dosing convenience and quality of life also play a role in treatment adherence (Figure 5-2).

A well-known example of the failure to consider stakeholder needs is Pfizer's inhaled insulin, Exubera. For payers, the launch price was perceived as non-competitive with other insulins. For physicians, there was a significant concern about the long-term impact of insulin on the lungs. For patients, barriers included the requirement of a lung function test before the start of therapy as well as a large and inconvenient device. While Pfizer had bought worldwide rights from Sanofi-Aventis for $1.3 billion, it announced its withdrawal in October 2007, after global sales of only $12 million for that year [10]. MannKind recently introduced its Afrezza inhaler, with a smaller size and breath-activated system increasing reliability, but concerns remain about the systemic impact and acceptance of this delivery method [11].

R & D AND COMMERCIAL COORDINATION

A key success factor in this context is the close pairing, early in development, of research and commercial teams. Researchers may not have a clear view of patient needs. For instance, a monthly instead of a daily regimen was used in osteoporosis, to minimize gastric side effects from bisphosphonates such as Roche's Boniva (ibandronate), but a monthly regimen may be a hindrance for older people, who may have difficulty remembering the dosing cycle.

New digital ethnography tools such as video diaries may help uncover drug value in real-life use, but gathering this evidence may face a roadblock with company silos. In particular, target product profiles (TPPs) may be technical documents that do not describe the actual value delivered. In collaboration between scientific and commercial teams, a TPP should include a range of questions:

- *Patients*: Who are the targets and what are their journeys, including pretreatment information and medical, financial, and lifestyle challenges? Which outcomes are most meaningful to them (such as mobility versus brain lesions in multiple sclerosis)?
- *Physicians:* What are key decision criteria across specialties? What outcomes are most relevant, and what are treatment challenges, including lack of adherence?
- *Regulators:* How will the new therapy compare against the standard of care? If it is first in class, what will be the comparator? What is the relative level of innovation and medical benefit?
- *Payers:* How will the new product impact budget costs? Is there less price sensitivity for smaller populations? Will there be cost-effectiveness studies?

For companies to address all stakeholders, a key factor is to adopt an "outside-in" approach, starting with unmet needs and customer experiences.

An example of a close R & D/commercial coordination is Celgene's focus on science as a key driver of growth and successful product development.

SCIENCE IS THE NEW MARKETING

By Jacqualyn Fouse, Retired President and Chief Operating Officer, and Michael Pehl, President of Hematology and Oncology, Celgene Corporation

Biotech companies large and small have been pursuing cutting-edge science for years and bringing that science to patients via therapeutic innovations. The industry is currently riding a new wave of scientific breakthroughs made possible by advances in genomic, proteomic, and immunologic profiling, responding to patient populations through biomarkers and their companion diagnostics and therefore enabling the delivery of more targeted, more effective, and better tolerated therapies to patients across a variety of diseases. These may be most notable in the care of cancer patients—witness treatments based on genetic markers, checkpoint inhibitors, and a plethora of programs underway in the immuno-oncology arena—but significant advances have also been made in the treatment of other serious diseases, including multiple sclerosis and psoriatic diseases.

When we think about the role marketing plays in delivering these therapies to the patients who need them, we have long believed at Celgene that this role must always be grounded in science, and it must put the patient's interest first. What has changed over time is the nature and timing of commercial and market access input into cross-functional, integrated development plans. While, traditionally, these functions played—and still play—a major role in providing an opportunity-based strategic framework for late-stage assets allowing for opportunity optimization, lifecycle prioritization, and product and disease education, commercial colleagues with a strong science and disease background are now sitting at the table with their scientific and clinical colleagues from target identification onwards. For this reason, our early commercialization and market access teams work in cross-functional project teams to understand the science driving our product innovations; to provide input on how science, clinical, and outcomes research can best serve unmet medical needs; and to educate the marketplace through scientific and published evidence with the goal of delivering demonstrable benefits to patients and improved outcomes for the healthcare system.

A representative example is our ongoing development program, together with our partner Agios, of AG-221 (enasidenib), an IDH-2 inhibitor for patients with acute myeloid leukemia (AML) and myelodysplastic syndromes (MDS). Through the thorough understanding of the underlying epigenetic science, we identified a pharmacodynamic marker and a distinct patient segment with IDH-2 mutations. Our in-depth understanding of AML biology, as well as the close collaboration of our translational, clinical, market access, and early commercial colleagues, resulted in a tailored development program that not only maximized the benefit-risk profile for patients and value proposition for payers but also shortened the time period from first-to-man until regulatory submission to only three years.

We believe a number of factors give us a unique approach to this at Celgene. First, we recently established dedicated early commercialization and early project leadership teams to substantively support our cross-functional approach. Second, we leverage our network of collaborator relationships forged through our portfolio of R&D partnerships to further bolster this work. This portfolio of collaborations is distinct from the business development and research model viewpoints.

Our patients and healthcare providers have long demanded this of us and we are fully aligned with them. This approach to drug development and delivering new and effective therapies to patients originated with the transformation of a drug with a checkered past— thalidomide—into a safe, life-extending treatment for multiple myeloma patients that remains in use today. Now with increasingly better access to outcomes data and with a number of parties weighing in on how to assess the value of innovation, payers and regulatory authorities are asking more of us as well.

For us, it has never been acceptable to use anything other than scientific and clinical evidence to support the appropriate use of our products in the markets we serve. Our approach has become even more critical as a number of our products are used in combination therapies across both hematological and solid tumor cancer indications and we must understand the science and clinical data behind these drug combinations to help physicians select the best treatment choices and to work with patients on their treatment options. We must do this even when some of the drugs in these combinations are not our products, and we must do this in a completely objective, data-driven fashion. Today's innovative environment makes this focus on science and data more important than ever, which is why we believe today that our approach to science-based marketing is the right one for our patients, for the healthcare system and for the medical community.

In addition to this focus on science, an understanding of patients' experience is needed to ensure that products and services meet their needs.

VALUE OF EXPERIENCE: THE CONSUMER DECISION JOURNEY

Consumer connections to brands have been researched across industries. While no biopharma brand can match the emotional power of Disney or Apple, a connection pathway may apply in healthcare, as consumers transition from being unconnected to highly satisfied, perceiving brand differentiation and being fully connected. Steps to assess and leverage this emotional connection score include:

- Gathering market research and customer insight data from owned media (websites) to earned media (general platforms and online patient communities)
- Analyzing the best customers—those with the most brand loyalty and advocacy power, such as bloggers and patient community leaders
- Ensuring buy-in from senior leadership, not just brand teams [12].

In addition, a new approach is emerging to address the consumer journey. Instead of the traditional funnel metaphor (awareness, consideration, purchase), starting with many brands and narrowing them down to a final choice, a new journey may progress in four stages—consider, evaluate, buy, and enjoy/advocate/bond:

- The *consider* stage includes a top-of-mind brand set, from exposure to ads, word-of-mouth or professional recommendations.
- In the *evaluate* stage, consumers seek input from peers, online reviewers, and competitor brand communications.
- In the *buy* stage, point-of-purchase factors such as pharmacist input (e.g., switching to a generic) also play a role.
- In the *enjoy/advocate/bond* stage, consumers continue online research; in case of a strong bond, this phase may skip earlier stages and lead to long-term loyalty.

In this context, marketers have three major roles:

- Orchestrator of communications across functions (product development, marketing, customer service, sales, and IT) and channels.
- Publisher and content manager across business units. For instance, Apple has aligned product descriptions and created a library of demonstration videos.
- Market intelligence leader, as market and competitive data are often collected by different functions and business units [13].

In healthcare, the decision flow is especially complex, including "opt-out" steps:

- Pre-diagnosis information—as some symptoms may emerge
- Search for professional help—this may be standard or alternative medicine
- Medical diagnosis—seek to understand treatment or opt for alternative course

- Prescription filling—from benefits versus side effects, continue or abandon treatment
- Condition changes—new decision cycle if no stabilization or cure is achieved.

Companies often do not engage patients at the earliest stage. A Google or YouTube search may include in its top results external sources rather than company information. Similarly, the time a prescription is filled is only one of many touch points, and others may be more influential, such as the pain of a first biologic injection or the difficulty in using an asthma inhaler, which may block adherence.

Consumer insights, in early stages, may come from search engine trends and patient communities and later from pharmacy claims and electronic medical records [14].

MARKETING BEYOND THE PILL

This type of precision marketing through the decision journey changes the biopharma model from detection and treatment to prediction and prevention.

At the prediction stage, genomic databases and tools such as Watson Health allow the early identification of gene mutations and support the joint development of drugs and companion diagnostics (CDx). When Genentech pioneered this model in 1998 with Herceptin (trastuzumab), designed to block HER2 overexpression in metastatic breast cancer, it partnered with Dako to produce the CDx HercepTest.

This requires the coordination of two different processes. Discovery time-lines, approval criteria, channels, customers, and margins are different for diagnostics and therapeutics. Dual salesforces for labs and physicians must be coordinated, and consumer and physician education is needed to communicate the importance of CDx. Postlaunch, monitoring is necessary through biosensor tracking and biomarkers, to support long-term outcomes and Phase IV studies and publications [15]. This dual process is illustrated in Figure 5-3.

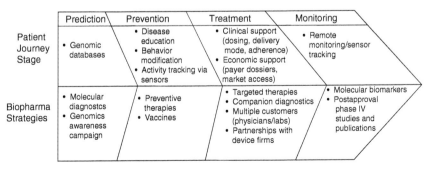

Source: Françoise Simon

Figure 5-3   Marketing beyond the pill

TARGETING NEW CONSUMER SEGMENTS

In precision marketing, the first segmentation base is the genotype, followed by disease state (early to late stage). For biologics, beyond standard demographics such as age and income, location matters. Rural patients far from infusion centers may need to opt for subcutaneous injections, if they have a choice. Ethnicity and gender also matter, as trials increasingly include gender comparisons and ethnic subtypes.

Consumer attitudes are also key, differentiating between a vocal subgroup of activists versus more passive individuals, and mainstream versus alternative medicine–oriented patients. In the HIV area, activists were instrumental in accelerating approvals of antivirals and accessing them prelaunch through compassionate use programs [16]. Technographics are now also an influential segmentation base.

Especially in rare diseases and critical areas, Internet leaders exert a powerful diffusion or criticism role, and can even trigger an observational trial, as was the case for a lithium study in ALS (amyotrophic lateral sclerosis) by members of PatientsLikeMe. The study disproved lithium's effectiveness, and this was later confirmed by a randomized trial.

NEW PHYSICIAN SEGMENTS

These segmentation bases have counterparts among physicians. In rare diseases or those requiring a double specialty, such as hematology/oncology in leukemia, there may be as few as 5,000 relevant specialists worldwide. A prelaunch success factor is the capture of key opinion leaders (KOLs) as trial investigators.

Practice type is also key; many group practices ban sales visits but may remain open to on-demand virtual details or medical science liaisons (MSLs).

Attitudinal segments also matter, as companies must identify early adopters and circumvent the concerns of conservative or cost-conscious physicians.

Technographics follow the same pattern for physicians as for consumers, ranging from web opinion leaders (bloggers or frequent webinar speakers) to passive information seekers and users of medical communities such as Sermo or Doximity. These segmentation bases are shown in Figure 5-4.

Leveraging these bases entails specific planning steps:

- For targeted therapies, investing in predictive tools and early diagnosis of genotypes
- Working with both physician and patient KOLs for medical and observational studies
- Developing prelaunch awareness of genomic screening and CDx
- During and post-treatment, monitoring behavior, adherence, and outcomes via biosensors and biomarkers to support Phase IV studies with real-world evidence

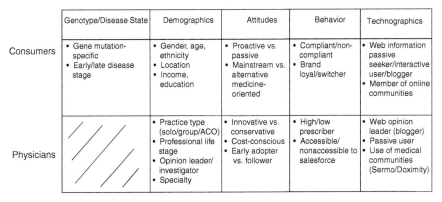

	Genotype/Disease State	Demographics	Attitudes	Behavior	Technographics
Consumers	• Gene mutation-specific • Early/late disease stage	• Gender, age, ethnicity • Location • Income, education	• Proactive vs. passive • Mainstream vs. alternative medicine-oriented	• Compliant/non-compliant • Brand loyal/switcher	• Web information passive seeker/interactive user/blogger • Member of online communities
Physicians		• Practice type (solo/group/ACO) • Professional life stage • Opinion leader/investigator • Specialty	• Innovative vs. conservative • Cost-conscious • Early adopter vs. follower	• High/low prescriber • Accessible/nonaccessible to salesforce	• Web opinion leader (blogger) • Passive user • Use of medical communities (Sermo/Doximity)

Source: Françoise Simon

Figure 5-4   Segmentation bases

DUAL BRANDING MODELS

These evolving segmentation bases are leading to the coexistence of two different branding models for targeted versus mass-marketed products. While many biotechs focus on targeted drugs, this poses a challenge for large pharmas with broad portfolios, such as Sanofi, with insulins addressing more than 350 million diabetics worldwide, versus its Genzyme drugs such as Myozyme (alglucosidase alfa) for Pompe disease, with as few as 5,000 to 10,000 patients worldwide. While their populations are limited, targeted therapies may garner top revenues due to high prices. Roche's Rituxan (rituximab) and Herceptin (trastuzumab) reached, respectively, $8.6 billion and $6.7 billion in 2016 global sales [17].

The superior return on investment for these drugs is supported by several components of their business model: specialists requiring very small salesforces and more reliance on MSLs and patient counselors, no or little use of mass media, and strong links with patient communities supporting product diffusion. Rapid global expansion is also achieved thanks to tightly linked specialist communities and standardized treatment protocols. By contrast, a mass market product such as Crestor (rosuvastatin) faces challenges such as salesforce costs, multiple specialties, and regional treatment variance.

For osteoporosis drugs such as Actonel (risedronate), medical targets may include generalists, endocrinologists, or orthopedists (post-fracture stage), and treatments may vary by country, from biologics such as Amgen's Prolia (denosumab) to bisphosphonates, calcitonin, hormones, or calcium (Figure 5-5).

Despite these differences, a success factor for large pharmas is knowledge transfer across these models, in particular, the application of evidence-based marketing to mass-market products.

	Targeted	Broad
Product example	Kalydeco/ivacaftor	Crestor
Disease type	Specific to gene mutation, small population	Non-gene-specific, large population
Physicians	Specialists	Generalists, family practitioners
Patients	Genotype-specific	Broad market
Treatment variations	Globally coordinated	Regional variations
Economics	High cost, limited competition, patient access programs	Crowded categories/strong competition/payer scrutiny
Communication channels	• MSLs/highly trained small salesforce • Online outreach/patient communities	Segmented large salesforce

Source: Françoise Simon

Figure 5-5   Scope of branding models

LIPITOR'S SUCCESS: EVIDENCE-BASED MARKETING

As Warner-Lambert (later acquired by Pfizer) was preparing to launch its lipid reducer Lipitor (atorvastatin), it faced a handicap as a late follower, reaching the market fifth in the statin class. However, it could have an evidence-based differentiation through its superior reduction of LDL (low-density lipoprotein), and it later became the class leader and top product worldwide, with peak sales of nearly $13 billion. Launched a decade earlier, Merck's Mevacor (lovastatin) and its successor Zocor (simvastatin), introduced in 1992, were the class leaders due to efficacy and tolerability.

Warner-Lambert then designed its trials as head-to-head comparisons and was also granted FDA fast-track status, thanks to a small study showing efficacy in a type of hyperlipidemia. Clinical trials showed Lipitor's better reduction of LDL and triglycerides.

Lipitor was initially marketed only to physicians, and its price (lower than Zocor's) allowed fast formulary inclusion. Warner-Lambert also gained credibility through a partnership with the American Heart Association (AHA) to promote guidelines and educate the public about the risks of hyperlipidemia, in particular in diabetes.

Key success factors included:

- Comparative trial data/evidence-based positioning
- Penetration pricing strategy/Globally coordinated launch
- Initial marketing to physicians/extensive publications and follow-up trials
- Collaboration with medical associations such as the AHA

AstraZeneca also used an evidence-based strategy for Crestor (rosuvastatin), with a value proposition as a highly potent statin. It launched the SATURN head-to-head trial comparing the two statins, led by Cleveland Clinic researchers. Published on November 30, 2011, in the *New England Journal of Medicine* (on the same day as the Lipitor patent expiration), the study unfortunately found similar results for both drugs. It was a calculated risk, in view of possible erosion of Crestor by the generic atorvastatin. Because of this unconvincing cost-benefit ratio, as well as a crowded statin category, Crestor did not equal Lipitor's success. It still generated over $5 billion in 2015 sales, before facing its own patent expiry the following year [18].

NEW LAUNCH STRATEGIES

From early development, launch success relies on a cocreation process, with physician and patient KOL input in R & D and product formulation. For instance, Novo Nordisk has maintained its position against larger competitors such as Sanofi and Lilly with its focus on diabetes and patient needs. Early on, it understood that the differentiator was not insulin, perceived as a quasi-commodity, but the delivery mode; it developed the first easy-to-use autoinjector and branded it as NovoPen.

The launch model itself is evolving. The traditional formula was to be first-in-class with a novel mechanism of action that triggered rapid prescribing from early adopters. This was the case for Gilead's Sovaldi (sofosbuvir), launched as a breakthrough in hepatitis C. While it took months for payers to set up coverage policies in the United States, physicians prescribed it rapidly, and it reached peak worldwide sales of nearly $5.2 billion by 2015. Its successor, Harvoni (ledipasvir/sofosbuvir), then reached peak global sales of almost $13.9 billion by 2015. Both products' sales decreased in 2016, to $4 billion for Sovaldi and $9 billion for Harvoni, as a competitor entered the market, providing more leverage to payers [19].

Once payers started to access restrictions, physicians and patients filed coverage reviews, appeals, and exceptions, and there was a court case for a patient denied Harvoni due to not being symptomatic enough. In future cases, payers may draft some restrictive policies before launch, such as label-only coverage, step therapy, and prior authorizations.

A new standard for market success may then be "best value in class," as defined by comparisons of efficacy, safety, economics, and ease of use. This may allow a dominant position as a category definer such as Xerox or FedEx once were, and is a strong protection against competitive entrants. Physicians are unwilling to switch stabilized patients, and switching to cheaper products may also go against the incumbent's rebates to payers [20].

COMPANION DIAGNOSTICS

In addition to these trade-offs between "first-in-class" and "best-value-in-class," another controversy has emerged about the relative potential of genotype-targeted drugs with or without companion diagnostics.

An example of an oncology drug with a CDx is Pfizer's Xalkori (crizotinib) in 2011. Its challenge, ensuring that drug marketing was directly linked to the diagnostic, remains an issue today. Xalkori addressed a subset of patients with non-small cell lung cancer (NSCLC) with a defect in the ALK gene (anaplastic lymphoma kinase). Pfizer had to coordinate its messaging to multiple stakeholders—from pulmonologists to interventional radiologists, pathologists, and nurses—all of whom had to be convinced to adopt a new hospital treatment system. For instance, this entailed taking more biopsy tissue than normal to ensure patient prequalification.

Abbott Molecular, maker of the Vysis ALK probe test, also aimed to present the drug and test as a single package. This included joint sales calls with Pfizer to "double-team" doctors, as well as rigorous training to ensure science-based detailing.

For patient education, Pfizer also supported the LungCancerProfiles.com website, including patient profiles and interactive tools for questions during physician visits.

While these efforts helped communicate the need for molecular testing, the test may have remained a partial barrier, as Xalkori sales reached only $546 million by 2015 [21].

The controversy has now extended to the new category of checkpoint inhibitor therapies in immuno-oncology.

TO TARGET OR NOT TO TARGET? OPDIVO VS KEYTRUDA

In immuno-oncology, BMS and Merck have adopted different strategies for their respective drugs Opdivo (nivolumab) and Keytruda (pembrolizumab).

As noted in Chapter 4, both target the PD-1 programmed cell death protein, but Keytruda's label restricts it to patients overexpressing the PD-L1 ligand, while Opdivo does not have this limitation. Since their launch, Opdivo has garnered better sales, with 2016 worldwide revenue of nearly $3.8 billion, versus $1.4 billion for Keytruda. While Keytruda' s prequalifying test may have appeal for payers with its more defined patient population, physicians may favor a drug without a companion diagnostic.

Keytruda was first to market, with FDA approvals in refractory melanoma in September 2014, and for second-line NSCLC (non-small cell lung cancer) in October 2015. Opdivo was a fast follower, with FDA approval for refractory melanoma in December 2014, squamous NSCLC in March 2015, non-squamous NSCLC in October, and renal carcinoma in November 2015.

An opportunity was the first-line NSCLC treatment. With more than 1.6 million new cases of lung cancer diagnosed worldwide every year, this would dramatically improve the patient base, especially with BMS's broad approach. However, it was reported on August 5, 2016 that Opdivo was not significantly better than chemotherapy in progression-free survival (PFS) for patients with previously untreated lung cancer.

Merck had a less ambitious strategy with a smaller subset of patients, and in June 2016 it released positive data on progression-free survival versus chemotherapy for Keytruda, which led to an FDA approval in first-line NSCLC.

Both companies are conducting additional trials, but Keytruda led in 2017 with FDA approvals including bladder cancer, and most notably as the first therapy for solid tumors that share a genetic profile, regardless of body location.

Combination trials are showing mixed results: Keytruda had positive results from its combination with Incyte's IDO inhibitor epacadostat in breast cancer, and combined with chemotherapy in lung cancer. However, Merck had to pause enrollment in two Keytruda trials with Celgene's Revlimid (lenalidomide) and Pomalyst (pomalidomide), to investigate patient deaths.

Opdivo showed superior recurrence-free survival versus Yervoy (ipilimumab) in post-surgery melanoma patients, as well as positive Phase 2 results, combined with Yervoy in mesothelioma [22].

Competitive dynamics may change with followers such as Roche's Tecentriq (atezolizumab), with FDA approvals since 2016 for bladder cancer and NSCLC.

A controversial issue remains direct-to-consumer (DTC) advertising for cancer drugs. Physicians argued in JAMA Oncology against this trend and Opdivo promotion in particular, stating that it may foster misinterpretation of efficacy and toxicity, and proposed a "drug facts box" stating risk and benefit data for each indication [23].

This case illustrates new strategic options for targeted therapies in general.

In order for a development model that includes rapid multiple indications to succeed, launch plans must include early-stage milestones and accountabilities. While clinical and commercial teams have traditionally been evaluated with separate criteria, a new scorecard needs to assess their integration, and their incentives need to be aligned in order to gather real-world evidence. There should be coordination to shape the market, company, and product. The product benefits most from early-stage multiple indications and formulations. The market includes physicians, patients, and payers. For physicians, KOL capture as investigators is essential. For consumers, KOLS are equally important as co-creators and can be drawn from advocacy groups. For payers, reimbursement depends on pharmacoeconomics dossiers [24]. These launch success factors are summarized in Figure 5-6.

Product Development	• Cocreation process (patient and physician input in R&D) • Speed of clinical trials (e-recruitment and reporting) • Combination of randomized and observational trials • Multiple indications and patents • Science-driven differentiation
Market Preparation	• PHYSICIANS: Opinion leader capture, education on mode of action, publications and conferences • PAYERS: Real-world evidence, pharmacoeconomics dossiers • CONSUMERS: Disease awareness, partnerships with online patient communities and foundations
Company Organization	• Cross-functional teams • Global planning vs. local execution • Rapid multi-country global rollout

Source: Françoise Simon

Figure 5-6   Launch success drivers

GLOBAL ORGANIZATION

Finally, a key success factor is a well-coordinated global launch, given the need to recover rapidly development costs. The following should be kept in mind:

- As early as in the preclinical stage, a global advisory panel can provide input about unmet needs, including in emerging markets. For instance, China has the world's largest hepatitis C market, but only a small part of its population has reimbursement. The same pattern applies to India across many diseases.
- At later stages, regional KOLs may co-lead and communicate trials.
- Throughout development, close links with global patient communities can speed recruitment, set up multi-country registries and gather evidence worldwide.

A primary challenge remains the trade-off between central efficiency and local responsiveness, and between economies of scale and market focus. Although biologics benefit from pan-European Union registration, biosimilar policies differ by country. Pricing is vastly different, with reference pricing in Europe and elsewhere.

Companies must therefore balance global branding consistency and local adaptation. For instance, Pfizer and AstraZeneca both positioned Lipitor and Crestor worldwide on their potency. However, flexibility is needed to respect pricing and channel variance (the same products sold as prescription or over-the-counter), brand name, and delivery mode variations (e.g., effervescent vitamins versus pills) [25]. These drivers and barriers are shown in Figure 5-7.

Drivers	Barriers
• Global clinical trials and investigators • Globally coordinated specialists, publications, and conferences • Global patient communities • Standardized treatment protocols • Multi-country patient registries	• Global ramp-up production capacity • Country or region-specific regulation (FDA, EMA, Ministries of Health) • Reference pricing/variation in price elasticity • Buying power of middle class • Risk of parallel imports • Variance in prescribing patterns and consumption trends

Source: Françoise Simon

Figure 5-7   Global drivers and barriers

MULTICHANNEL COMMUNICATIONS

Communication strategies are moving from mass media to a multichannel ecosystem, but this expansion is questioned, given the anti-pharma trend among consumers. This is exacerbated by the massive scale and visibility of direct-to-consumer (DTC) promotion in the United States (outside of the United States, branded DTC is only allowed in New Zealand; it was rejected in Europe, where only unbranded DTC is allowed). Total DTC spend in the United States reached $5.8 billion in 2016, with Pfizer, Bristol-Myers Squibb, AbbVie, and Lilly as the top spenders; traditional media led spending, with more than $4 billion going to television versus only $515 million for digital promotion.

Despite the controversy surrounding its pricing policy in hepatitis C, Gilead still spent nearly $102 million on Harvoni, which may risk adding fuel to public protests. While in past years, targeted products such as Novartis' Gleevec were not advertised in the mass media, Bristol-Myers Squibb spent more than $170 million on its campaign for Opdivo [26].

This trend runs counter to a sharp outcry from many stakeholders. Consumers are avoiding print ads, cutting cable television subscriptions, and skipping video ads, and some 10 percent of US desktop Internet users already have ad blockers installed, with a growing trend in mobile. Across sectors, almost half of the 24,000 consumers surveyed in 2015 by GfK/MRI agreed that "much of advertising is too annoying." In a 2016 Accenture survey of 28 countries, 84 percent of respondents said that digital ads are too frequent. Millennials are leading the exodus; they are spending nearly 30 percent less time per week watching television than they were in 2012, according to Nielsen, and the drop is 18 percent for the 24 to 35 age group [27].

For the first time, physicians are officially protesting DTC promotion. On November 17, 2015, the American Medical Association (AMA) called for a ban on DTC advertising of prescription drugs and medical devices out of concern that "a growing proliferation of ads is driving demand for expensive treatments despite the clinical effectiveness of less costly alternatives" [28]. A salient point was the first explicit link between ad spend and drug price inflation.

The government followed suit, with the introduction of a bill aiming to limit DTC for three years after approval. Another bill was introduced with the objective of ending a tax deduction allowing biopharma companies to write off their DTC expenditures [29]. While these bills may not be finalized, the sheer scope of these protests across stakeholder groups may be a sufficient reason for biopharma companies to rethink their communication mix and resource allocation across all channels, with more focus on a product-neutral outreach that is globally acceptable and welcomed from a public health standpoint, such as awareness campaigns for vaccinations or underdiagnosed diseases.

In addition to this stakeholder resistance, multichannel strategies are meeting internal challenges. Because some companies still tend to be product-centric, a multichannel mindset faces barriers such as brand silos (each brand team is not incentivized to contribute to other brands) and a lack of information through a patient's journey, including the pre-diagnosis and post-treatment stages. What is needed is a balance between unbranded disease-oriented programs and brand-specific promotion [30].

Brand messages themselves should be tailored, not only to consumer segments, but also to the different perceived value of a brand by stakeholders. The rise of accountable care organizations (ACOs) has increased the importance of population-level benefits. While a community health center may value a good tolerability profile that supports patient adherence, a teaching institution may focus on an innovative mode of action because of its scientific value. To coordinate a multichannel outreach, marketing may be seen as a matrixed system of functions (innovation, strategic planning, positioning, and marketing mix) and talent factors (marketing as well as salesforce training) [31].

This also applies to new ways of leveraging mobile media, such as location-specific functionality, already used in consumer health. For its 2015 Neutrogena sunscreen campaign, Johnson & Johnson sent mobile banner ads when sun exposure and UV levels were high. The ads, targeting consumers close to beaches or pools, appeared amid beauty or fashion content on a range of websites. Nearly 60 percent of those surveyed said they would be more likely to try the sunscreen [32].

The application of these geofilters to biopharma products raises privacy issues, however, especially in the current context of a consumer backlash against digital intrusion. For this type of outreach, it would be prudent for brand teams to coordinate with medical and corporate affairs departments to ensure a stepwise approach with a possible pilot before a large rollout.

CONTENT MARKETING

For the best examples of content marketing to engage consumers with something relevant and directly useful, biopharmas would benefit from following the initiatives of healthcare systems such as the Mayo Clinic. In diabetes, Novo Nordisk has a disease focus and offers an online portfolio of personalized tools through its Cornerstones4Care support program. Although it includes diet, activity, and blood sugar tracking information, its "Diabetes 101" page remains fairly basic and lacks links to the literature. In addition, its "Medicines" section is limited to its own products, from NovoLog (insulin aspart) for types 1 and 2, to Victoza (liraglutide) for type 2 diabetes.

By contrast, the Mayo Clinic "Diseases and Conditions" website includes not only lifestyle and diet advice but also an extensive array of product-neutral information, from its *Essential Diabetes Book* to a DVD and a full list of type 1 and 2 treatments, from metformin and DPP-4 inhibitors like Merck's Januvia (sitagliptin) to GLP-1 receptor agonists like Novo Nordisk's Victoza (liraglutide), together with efficacy and side effects. The site also has a link to conference presentation summaries and other resources [33].

Alone among biopharmas, Merck has built a worldwide reputation among physicians as well as consumers for comprehensive medical information.

First published in 1899, the *Merck Manual of Diagnosis and Therapy* is the world's best-selling medical textbook, now published online in both professional and consumer versions. The manuals received five eHealthcare Leadership Awards, including a Gold Award for Best Healthcare Content for Professionals, and a Distinction Award for Best Overall Consumer Healthcare Site, at the 2015 Annual Healthcare Internet Conference. Merck has a full portfolio of publications, including a condensed reference guide, the *Merck Manual of Patient Symptoms* [34].

Given the current DTC controversy, it may be beneficial for biopharmas to shift more resources toward unbranded disease information that reflects patient needs through their journey and establishes them as a more trusted education source.

SALESFORCE STRATEGIES

The traditional in-person sales model is no longer sufficient for many reasons.

While salesforces have shrunk and been outsourced, biopharmas remain dependent on representatives, often repurposed as key account managers (KAMs) for health system customers. However, a more comprehensive transformation is needed, given provider consolidation, the rising number of younger physicians joining group practices or networks that ban sales reps, and their demand for digital information. According to the 2015 ZS AccessMonitor survey, only 47 percent of US prescribers permit in-person sales details. In oncology, only 25 percent now see representatives [35].

New Roles for Medical Science Liaisons

In pre-launch stages, medical science liaisons (MSLs) can play a key role as a bridge between scientific and commercial teams, and in driving customer centricity. Far from being a secondary salesforce, MSLs can support existing KOLs and build new ones through investigator-initiated studies. They can communicate in-depth KOL profiles and develop engagement plans based on their information needs, which a representative has no time to assess. According to the Medical Science Liaison Society, the average time for a field representative with a physician is roughly two minutes, while it may be up to an hour for an MSL. This is especially relevant for rare diseases and breakthrough therapies with a new mode of action, where greater medical training is required and where the science must be branded well before launch.

Metrics for MSL effectiveness include quantitative variables (amount of face time) and qualitative ones (medical insights, competitive intelligence, and real-world evidence on patient outcomes). An effective MSL strategy must ensure that they are not siloed, and that they are aligned with medical affairs and marketing teams across all customer-facing channels [36].

As for salesforces, they must reach beyond the traditional "3R" model (right message, right frequency, right target) and engage customers, not only across channels, but also with new content. New channels range from KAM structures to patient/physician portals that may include disease information, social media and digital tools for education. New content may include:

- Budget/outcomes models helping ACOs assess the impact of a new therapy on relevant patient populations
- Value-added services such as education on companion diagnostics and facilitation of remote monitoring though biosensors
- Disease management services enabling coordination between patients, caregivers, nurses, and physicians, especially for chronic conditions
- E-detailing (virtual sales consultations), coordinated with other online brand and disease information
- Innovative pricing and contract agreements, in collaboration with payers and providers; ideally, joint analytic studies with them and possibly with patient communities for real-world evidence on outcomes and comparative value [37]

In sum, successful prelaunch and launch strategies entail a close coordination across all functions, as early as possible in product development. At the preclinical stage (at least seven years before launch), a key factor is the understanding of global unmet needs and the identification of patient and physician KOLs to ensure co-creation of a new product. An assessment of payer views, including a definition of comparators of standard of care, is also needed to undertake possible head-to-head studies.

As a product enters the clinic in Phase I, real-world evidence is possible through patient communities. Global KOL input helps provide an early definition of target product profiles (TPPs). By Phase II, trials should be leveraged as the most effective way to brand the science and, if applicable, the new mode of action. For critical areas, approval may be granted in Phase IIb, and Phase III may serve as part of post-launch studies.

At that stage, efficacy and safety should be well validated, and ease of use, delivery mode, and formulation should have been determined with patient input. Forecasts and pharmacoeconomic dossiers should have been finalized, together with a donation/discount program, in consultation with patient advocacy groups.

Finally, multipronged monitoring should be conducted post-launch, watching patient outcomes, physician and consumer reactions, and competitor and payer responses on a worldwide basis. Multiple follow-on trials and related publications should include new indications and product combinations, both on a randomized and observational basis. This process is shown in Figure 5-8.

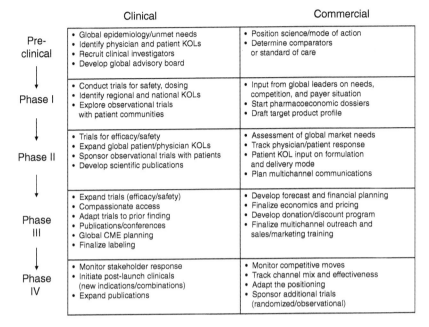

	Clinical	Commercial
Pre-clinical	• Global epidemiology/unmet needs • Identify physician and patient KOLs • Recruit clinical investigators • Develop global advisory board	• Position science/mode of action • Determine comparators or standard of care
Phase I	• Conduct trials for safety, dosing • Identify regional and national KOLs • Explore observational trials with patient communities	• Input from global leaders on needs, competition, and payer situation • Start pharmacoeconomic dossiers • Draft target product profile
Phase II	• Trials for efficacy/safety • Expand global patient/physician KOLs • Sponsor observational trials with patients • Develop scientific publications	• Assessment of global market needs • Track physician/patient response • Patient KOL input on formulation and delivery mode • Plan multichannel communications
Phase III	• Expand trials (efficacy/safety) • Compassionate access • Adapt trials to prior finding • Publications/conferences • Global CME planning • Finalize labeling	• Develop forecast and financial planning • Finalize economics and pricing • Develop donation/discount program • Finalize multichannel outreach and sales/marketing training
Phase IV	• Monitor stakeholder response • Initiate post-launch clinicals (new indications/combinations) • Expand publications	• Monitor competitive moves • Track channel mix and effectiveness • Adapt the positioning • Sponsor additional trials (randomized/observational)

Source: Françoise Simon

Figure 5-8   Pre-launch and launch strategies

In addition to these launch success factors, product sustainability over time depends on the early planning of strategies ranging from portfolio diversification to franchise management, through successor molecules and combination therapies.

SUSTAINABILITY STRATEGIES: BEYOND THE LIFE CYCLE

The traditional life cycle approach limiting a product to its introduction, growth, maturity, and decline can be optimized from early R & D to the post-patent stage.

In the same way as launches are actually won in early clinical stages, life cycles can be extended through portfolio and franchise management approaches. This is especially relevant given the patent expiries of many biologics. The European Medicines Agency has approved 20 biosimilars, and the first US approval occurred in March 2015 with the launch of Sandoz's Zarxio as the biosimilar version of Amgen's Neupogen (filgrastim) [38].

Portfolio Diversification and Franchise Building

Many companies are struggling with dependence on one flagship product, such as AbbVie's Humira (adalimumab). To counter patent loss, the company is counting on its portfolio of more than 70 patents to protect it until 2022. However, generic companies such as Teva have increased in recent years their launches "at risk," that is, before the originator's patent expiry.

The first line of defense is clearly portfolio diversification, as Roche has done with its monoclonal antibodies and its oncology franchise. At the portfolio level, a strategy increasingly used is an asset swap, such as that between Novartis and GlaxoSmithKline (GSK), with Novartis selling its vaccine business to GSK in exchange for GSK's oncology business.

At the franchise level, launching new molecules does not preclude the continued promotion of late-stage brands, as MSLs and salesforces can communicate new prescribing developments. Lower-cost digital programs can target brand-loyal physicians and patient communities and can leverage a brand's name recognition among patients who may be averse to switching to other therapies [39]. A franchise approach may also be useful as a company launches new dosing regimens and enters new markets. Examples include Pfizer's launch of Viagra (sildenafil) as Revatio, with different dosages for erectile dysfunction and pulmonary arterial hypertension, and Merck's extension of Proscar (finasteride), for enlarged prostate, into Propecia for hair loss.

The need for distinct value propositions also applies in emerging markets with high cost constraints and price sensitivity. While Sanofi launched its antimalaria drug as ASAQ in collaboration with the nonprofit Drugs for Neglected Diseases Initiative, which qualified it for the WHO requirements, it sold it as Coarsucam in private markets at a higher price. Similarly, as Plavix (clopidogrel) faced patent loss in 2012, Sanofi launched in Indonesia a lower-priced branded generic version.

In emerging markets, in addition to affordable pricing, biopharmas must also ensure broad utilization, often through distribution partnerships. AstraZeneca entered an agreement in India aiming to market its platelet aggregation inhibitor Brilinta (ticagrelor) through Sun Pharma with the new brand name Axcer [40].

An example of effective franchise management is Roche's approach for its HER2 breast cancer line. Its succession plan includes new molecules like Kadcyla (ado-trastuzumab emtansine), the antibody drug conjugate version of Herceptin, and Perjeta (pertuzumab), which has helped Roche maintain share in the neoadjuvant breast cancer market in the United States. The new drug positioning has been both evidence based, with a trial of a Herceptin/Perjeta combination for second-line therapy, and experience-based, as some patients have switched to the subcutaneous version [41].

LILLY IN DIABETES: A 90-YEAR FRANCHISE

An earlier example of franchise management over time is Lilly's diabetes business, started in 1923 with Iletin, the world's first insulin, invented by Frederick Banting and Charles Best at the University of Toronto. It was followed in 1982 by Humulin, the first recombinant insulin, sourced from Genentech. Before its US patent loss in 2001, Lilly introduced Humalog (insulin lispro), with better dosing convenience and glucose control. A Humalog Mix 75/25 Pen was launched in 2000.

For type 2 diabetes, Lilly licensed the oral therapy Actos (pioglitazone) from Takeda in 1999 [42]. More recently, Jardiance (empagliflozin) was approved in the European Union in May 2014 and the United States in August 2014, as a SGLT-2 agent for type 2 diabetes, with intellectual property through the late 2020s. Although it was third in the market, behind Johnson & Johnson's Invokana (canagliflozin) and AstraZeneca's Farxiga (dapagliflozin), it is the first diabetes drug to show a cardioprotective effect in high-risk patients. However, the FDA issued warnings of ketoacidosis and blood and kidney infections for the entire SGLT-2 class.

Lilly launched Glyxambi in February 2015, a combination of Jardiance (empagliflozin) and Tradjenta (linagliptin), as an adjunct to diet and exercise in patients with type 2 diabetes, as a first US-approved combined therapy. In addition, Trulicity (dulaglutide/GLP-1), dosed once-weekly for type 2 diabetes, was approved in the United States in September 2014, in the European Union two months later, and in Japan by July 2015. While the initial launch focused on specialists, it is now being rolled out to primary care physicians [43].

This illustrates a broad portfolio of extensive in-licensing, new formulations and molecules, and combination products.

Building the Market: New Indications and Formulations

Key success factors are early development of multiple indications and launch of a new molecule well before the initial brand's patent loss to allow for patient base conversion. This is a high-cost/high-reward approach, with the significant expenditure of new trials, but the benefits include long-term added exclusivity, penetration of new segments, and the potential strengthening of physician loyalty through a "one-stop shop" approach.

New formulations should also be planned early, with the potential benefit of dual patents (such as compound and device patents for a smart insulin pen or an asthma inhaler) and the building of an "umbrella equity." Combined products are widely used in areas such as HIV and oncology, but they yield a lower return if one product is externally sourced, as profits are shared.

Mature Strategy: Optimized Customer Penetration

As products reach maturity, an effective approach is to assess value leakages along the patient journey and address them with added services to increase adherence. In diabetes, these leakages include lack of coordinated care, suboptimal treatment of comorbidities, reduced quality of life, and the burden of glucose monitoring. Intervention opportunities include personalized counseling on disease management, co-creation of new formulations and delivery modes, diet and exercise coaching and related apps, and virtual consultations with health professionals [44].

Renewal Strategies: From Patent Protection to Branded Generics

Finally, late-life cycle strategies include maximizing patents and changing product status to branded generics or, if applicable, switches to over-the-counter (OTC) status (Figure 5-9). The most defensible patents are product patents applying to new entities. Formulation and process patents are less protective, and method of use patents covering different indications are least effective, because competing products may be prescribed off-label for the same use.

As noted earlier, orphan drug status yields a seven-year extension in the United States, but it applies only to rare diseases. A trend across countries is for patent litigation to favor generic companies, as most infringement suits fail, and generic challenges increasingly occur before the originator's patent expiry.

Branded generics have been used for decades by companies such as the Novartis Sandoz division and now extend to biologics. Sandoz was first to gain approval for growth hormone Omnitrope, and many other biosimilars have been approved in Europe.

A post-patent strategy with inherent limitations is a switch to OTC status. This only applies to limited cases that meet multiple criteria:

- Can the condition be self-diagnosed and treated?
- Can the patient apply the label properly and monitor the condition?
- Is the product safe and effective, and is the dosage easily delivered?

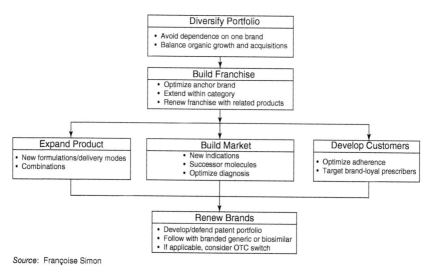

Source: Françoise Simon

Figure 5-9   Sustainability strategies

While this increases patient access and decreases office visit costs, it has risks such as inaccurate diagnosis and drug interactions. A dual status, with different strengths or formulations for prescription and OTC forms, may mitigate risks and reinforce equity [45].

A special case of late-life cycle management concerns the emergence of biosimilars in major markets.

Addressing the Challenge of Biosimilars

The US approval of Sandoz's Zarxio in March 2015 as the biosimilar version of Amgen's Neupogen (filgrastim) was the first step in a potential wave of such products under the new 351(k) pathway set up as part of the 2010 Affordable Care Act. Since 2006, a few products, such as Sandoz's Omnitrope, a biosimilar of Pfizer's growth hormone Genotropin, had been approved in the United States under different pathways—505(b)(2) in the case of Omnitrope. However, Europe leads in terms of regulation and market uptake, as a formal pathway was set up in 2006, and many biosimilars have since been approved by the European Medicines Agency, from filgrastim and epoetin to monoclonal antibodies such as infliximab.

Biosimilars have more limitations than small-molecule generics, requiring at least one head-to-head trial to confirm biosimilarity, and a lack of therapeutic interchangeability allowing automatic substitution by pharmacists. Market uptake varies across Europe. While a generic may reach a 90 percent market share within a year of entry in the United States, biosimilar erythropoietins only gained a 37 percent share across Europe within two years of launch. Germany has seen the highest penetration, partly due to minimum-level quotas set by its 200 sickness funds. By contrast, the United Kingdom has generally seen lower adoption levels, partly due to lower originator prices. Across Europe, discounts range from 15 to 30 percent, and they are expected to be from 25 to 35 percent in the United States.

There are a number of drivers, but also barriers, to biosimilar adoption. While payer pressure will drive them, physicians and patients will face trade-offs. Physicians may be reluctant to switch good responders and, thus, prescribe biosimilars only to new patients. Consumers may welcome lower copays but have safety concerns. An added issue is the extrapolation of original indications. While the FDA approved all five Neupogen indications in the case of Zarxio, for other products this may depend on the existence of real-world evidence. Biosimilars may thus be required to undergo wide post-marketing surveillance to monitor safety, efficacy, and quality of manufacturing, which has been shown to vary for biologics [46].

Further limitations apply to orphan biosimilars. An entire wave of these will lose exclusivity in the next decade. Enzyme replacement therapies such as Sanofi's Cerezyme (imiglucerase) and Fabrazyme (agalsidase alfa) have largely lost patents, as well as protein-based therapies such as Pfizer's Genotropin. Some critical questions apply to orphan biologics, from patient identification and trial recruitment to real-world evidence, reimbursement incentives, and market size threshold. Physician and patient loyalty may also protect originators, as their manufacturers often supply extensive clinical and reimbursement support services. For payers, trade-offs include cost savings versus low total budget impact and safety and efficacy concerns in critical therapeutic areas.

In Europe, regulation varies by country. In Germany, orphan drugs face fairly low scrutiny and there is little intent to cap prices. In the United Kingdom, the centralized National Health Service, rather than regional Clinical Commissioning Groups, regulates orphan drug costs. In France, however, the Paris public hospital system extracted a 45 percent discount on Celltrion's Inflectra, a biosimilar of Janssen's Remicade (infliximab), in exchange for an exclusive contract [47].

While payers may be the most influential drivers of biosimilars, their actions will be mitigated by physician and patient appreciation of the support services of originator companies and by a risk-averse attitude to switching in the critical therapeutic areas that apply to most orphan diseases.

SUMMARY POINTS

- Consumer, regulator, and payer trends are driving the need for precision marketing as a counterpart to precision medicine.

- Payers, physicians, and consumers increasingly demand an evidence-based strategy, whereby product positions are supported by clinical and economic data.

- Biopharmas need to balance evidence and experience across therapeutic areas, with evidence more dominant in oncology and experience more salient in noncritical areas such as allergy, but with the support of evidence as a differentiator.

- Consumer-centered strategies depend on a broad understanding of the patient journey, from pre-diagnosis to post-treatment; new segmentation bases may include genotypes as well as technographics.

- Dual branding models now coexist, from targeted therapies with small salesforces and little or no use of mass media to primary care products with large populations.

- Launch success drivers range from co-creation with patients to the capture of physician KOLs, payer partnerships, cross-functional teams, and global planning.

- Multichannel communications must take into account consumers' resistance to digital intrusion and favor a more product-neutral outreach that meets their needs.

- Salesforce strategies may shift from traditional detailing to new structures such as key account management and value-added services such as patient education and remote monitoring.
- Sustainability strategies go well beyond the traditional life cycle and include portfolio diversification and franchise management, with the early planning of successor molecules, new indications, formulations, and combination therapies, as well as comprehensive patent portfolios.

CHAPTER 6

PATIENT CENTRICITY STRATEGIES

INTRODUCTION

Today, patients are emerging as the central node in the healthcare ecosystem, thanks to multiple technology and market forces, from genomics and data analytics to consumerization and regulator and insurer mandates to improve outcomes. For biopharmas, patient centricity requires a focus on patients through the value chain, from co-creation in R & D to collaboration in clinical trials, input into delivery systems, discussions of market access, and ways to enrich patient/provider communications.

This patient focus is not a single function, it is a mindset that integrates the consumer voice from the start, connects points of care, anticipates future needs, and aims to help create a frictionless care system. It encompasses, but is not limited to, patient advocacy in support of worldwide communities, and patient engagement as a long-term commitment. Engagement solutions include trial recruitment and consent, care management, clinical and reimbursement support, remote monitoring, and adherence programs.

Early research should be informed by a deep understanding of unmet needs, through the identification of patient key opinion leaders (KOLs), patient advisory boards, and codevelopment of trial protocols and endpoints. For biologics, there should a dual development of therapies and patient-friendly delivery systems. In diabetes, Novo Nordisk has led with innovative devices, launching the first insulin autoinjector and branding it as NovoPen, based on the understanding that an easier injection experience was a strong differentiator. In addition to reimbursement counseling, as Sanofi/Genzyme does for rare diseases, companies should aim to involve patients in a consensus on price setting, including donations and discounts for uninsured populations in developed and emerging markets.

At the commercial stage, biopharmas should help develop tools to enrich patient/provider conversations and involve patients in all functions, including non-market–facing ones. For instance, a legal department can play a key role in streamlining consent forms in clinical trials and putting them in clear language, and

Managing Biotechnology: From Science to Market in the Digital Age, First Edition. Françoise Simon and Glen Giovannetti.

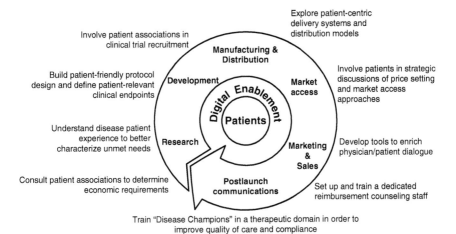

Source: Françoise Simon

Figure 6-1   Patient centricity framework

regulatory affairs and information technology are also needed to ensure clarity and compliance for an electronic consent process.

Several studies of these engagement strategies found that they improved patients' health and reduced healthcare use and costs [1]. A comprehensive patient centricity structure is shown in Figure 6-1.

This chapter will follow patient centricity strategies through the value chain, first focusing on product co-creation at the research stage, as well as on clinical trial collaborations. It will then address information sources and ways to connect patients and providers at the points of care, as well as analyze the entire patient journey, from the pre-diagnosis to the post-treatment stages. Finally, the chapter will address company organization to minimize functional silos, implement cross-functional performance indicators, and develop related metrics, from patient recruitment and retention in trials to salesforce and marketing training.

PATIENT CENTRICITY DRIVERS AND BARRIERS

While multiple factors are driving the move to patient centricity, many barriers remain, from the lack of worldwide regulatory standards to unclear metrics and return on investment.

Regulators in Europe and the United States show growing interest in patient-reported outcomes. The Food and Drug Administration (FDA) has initiated an alliance with the PatientsLikeMe online community, aiming, in particular, to enhance drug safety reporting through patient-generated data. In Europe, patient representatives are involved with the European Medicines Agency (EMA) through advisory groups and as members of committees, including the Pharmacovigilance Risk Assessment Committee and the Orphan Medicinal Products Committee [2].

New digital technologies, including wearable biosensors, are enabling consumers to track their health, but their use remains constrained by their limited functionality and the lack of interoperability from consumers to medical offices and electronic health records (EHRs).

In research, as companies increasingly focus on rare diseases, they must rely on patient communities to accelerate trial enrollment and codevelop protocols. However, these collaborations entail some risks, as uncontrolled patient-to-patient communications during clinical trials may endanger the blinding process of randomized trials.

Consumer trends include the Quantified Self movement, with its focus on health and fitness and continuous tracking of vital signs, but the growth of hacking episodes and website breaches is raising privacy and security concerns. Patient communities have gained considerable power, especially in rare diseases, where some groups have actually cofinanced drug development, as is the case for the Cystic Fibrosis Foundation and Vertex.

Biopharmas themselves need to gain differentiation with "beyond the pill" solutions integrating products and patient services, but their organizations are still functionally siloed, and they lack clear metrics for patient centric initiatives.

Governments and private payers increasingly demand real-world evidence to demonstrate value, as the trend toward outcomes-based reimbursement is gaining ground in Europe, but there is a lack of medical infrastructure to track patient outcomes.

These drivers and barriers of patient centricity are shown in Figure 6-2.

	Factors	Barriers
Regulation	• Regulator interest in patient-reported outcomes • FDA need for enhanced safety reporting	• Legal restrictions on patient communications/compliance • PROs are not always patient friendly
Technology	• New digital technologies	• Limited functionality of wearables • Lack of interoperability (EHRs/medical offices/consumer devices)
Research	• Genomics and precision medicine • Focus on rare diseases/clinical recruitment	• Early development stage of data analytics
Consumer Trends	• Quantified self • Rising power of patient advocacy groups	• Privacy and security concerns • Low public trust in biopharma
Biopharma Disruption	• Shift from volume to value • "Beyond the pill" solutions	• Weak evidence for return on investment/lack of metrics • Siloed organizations
Payer Evolution	• Growing trend toward outcomes-based reimbursement • Need to gather real-world evidence to prove value	• Lack of infrastructure to track outcomes

Source: Françoise Simon

Figure 6-2   Forces impacting patient centricity

DISCOVERY: UNDERSTANDING UNMET NEEDS

Several studies in Europe and the US have shown substantial information gaps between consumers and healthcare professionals. A September 2016 report from the National Academy of Medicine (NAM) noted that, of the four federal health information technology goals stated by the White House in 2004 and updated in in 2009, 2011, and 2015, only one—EHR adoption—has been reached. The three other goals of interoperability, supporting consumers with information, and advancing clinical trials have not been reached, according to NAM. Priority objectives for the next five years include end-to-end interoperability from consumer devices to EHRs, improving patient identification across providers and systems, enfranchising vulnerable populations, and creating a "trust fabric" for privacy and security of health communications [3].

Consumer information gaps have also been reported across Europe. According to an online survey of nearly 7,000 consumers in Great Britain, France, Italy, Spain, Poland, and Germany, more than 75 percent of respondents reported having no or less than good knowledge of medicine R & D. However, 61 percent were interested in learning more, especially regarding drug safety and personalized and predictive medicine. Across countries, respondents were least interested in pharmacoeconomics.

To improve public knowledge, the European Commission and the Innovative Medicines Initiative have funded the European Patients Academy on Therapeutic Innovation (EUPATI). This consortium has 30 project partners, including patient groups, academic institutions, and biopharmas. It aims to improve patient/provider communications, increase understanding of the cost and availability of new drugs, and facilitate the public's involvement in R & D.

It is developing a training course to increase patient experts' capacity to get involved in R & D, a toolkit for patient advocates, and an online library of R & D information [4]. EUPATI and the European Patients Forum are also part, with other patient groups and firms including Amgen, AstraZeneca, UCB, Glaxo-SmithKline, Pfizer, and Merck, of the Patient Focused Medicines Development Initiative (PFMD). This public-private initiative, launched in 2015, aims to develop a framework for patient engagement through the drug life cycle and address cultural, education, and communication barriers.

Biopharmas are recognizing the need for very early insights into a disease natural history. To inform R & D directions, Janssen Research and Development announced in February 2015 new platforms focused on disease prevention and interception, linked to five therapeutic areas as well as external partners. The Janssen Prevention Center focuses on the prevention of chronic diseases including Alzheimer's, heart disease, cancer, and autoimmune disorders. The Disease Prevention Accelerator is an incubator-like group addressing the root causes of disease, to intercept it earlier than the clinically accepted point of diagnosis. It aims to understand genetic predisposition, environmental exposure, and phenotypic alterations, starting with type 1 diabetes, and adding venture teams in areas such as presbyopia/cataracts, perinatal depression, and oropharyngeal cancer [5]. Janssen is partnering with groups such as the Juvenile Diabetes Research Foundation (JDRF), which published with the Endocrine Society and the American Diabetes Association a staging system, noting that type 1 diabetes begins years before clinically observable symptoms, and that early stages can be detected by the presence of islet antibodies [6].

Crowdsourcing Initiatives

In addition to these prediction initiatives, biopharmas are adopting new crowd-sourcing models. For the epilepsy community of approximately 65 million people worldwide and more than 2 million in the United States, UCB staged in April 2015 in Brussels and Atlanta a "Hack Epilepsy" event, where digital experts, specialists, and patients collaborated on building digital tools to inform patients, empower them to talk about their illness, and guide them with questions to providers, following a diagnosis. These events delivered 17 prototype digital solutions, half of which continue in development with startups and UCB support [7].

Patient Insight Research

Uncovering patient needs at early research stages entails technical and legal issues across countries. Data privacy regulations, cultural traits, and digital channel preferences, from smartphone apps to text messaging, vary across regions. There is a need for a comprehensive patient engagement platform, whereby messaging, electronic collection of patient-reported outcomes, health apps/wearable connections, and call center escalation should be coordinated, secured, and proven through global experience [8].

As research moves in to the clinical stage, patient-reported outcomes (PROs) are broadly used, but some gaps remain. The FDA has issued guidelines on the development and validation of PROs, and they are included in some drug labels and observational studies. However, they are not necessarily patient-relevant. Experience in areas such as mobility, cognition, pain, and sleep may not be captured adequately; for example, sleep may be more important to Parkinson's patients than tremor or limb rigidity, and in psoriasis, itchiness may matter more than lesion characteristics.

The understanding of patient experience is most extensive in the small populations of rare diseases. For instance, Shire has established PRO groups to optimize consultation with patient organizations. Even in the large diabetes populations, Novo Nordisk has a long experience of patient engagement, works with regulators to develop PRO tools to optimize quality of life, and conducts cross-disciplinary studies of behavioral and perception challenges in diabetes management [9].

A landmark initiative was announced in July 2016 by the National Institutes of Health (NIH) as the Cohort Program, within the national Precision Medicine Initiative. This longitudinal effort aims to engage one million or more US participants to improve treatment and prevention, based on individual differences in lifestyle, environment, and genetics. Data will be collected through health histories, genomic information, EHRs, and mobile devices, and participants will have ongoing input into study design, as well as access to individual and aggregated results. The program will fund a network of health systems operated by the Veterans Affairs Department to organize enrollment, with initial participation including Northwestern University, Columbia University, and the University of Arizona. It will also support a Data Center (awarded to Vanderbilt University, the Broad Institute, and Verily), as well as a Participant Technologies Center, whereby the Scripps Research Institute and Vibrant Health will create digital enrollment tools. The initial focus will be on genomic testing and next-generation sequencing [10].

DESIGNING PATIENT-FRIENDLY CLINICAL TRIALS

As research moves into the clinic, opportunities and challenges range from trial recruitment, the impact of PROs, the respective roles of randomized and observational trials and the risks of patient communications during clinical trials.

Rare Disease Trials

Rare diseases are now a major focus, numbering over 7,000, with only 10 percent having treatments, and they represent a major opportunity, with estimated worldwide sales of $176 billion by 2020 [11]. However, trial difficulty and cost are highest in this area, since it can be hard to find participants and lead investigators, as well as to organize transportation—sometimes across borders—for patients and their families. For rare disease–focused companies like Sanofi Genzyme and Shire, the first step may be a natural disease history study, through advisory boards and individual conversations; this may help establish which biomarkers, protocols, and endpoints best reflect patient needs. Advocacy groups may also have registries that enable patient identification. To optimize collaboration, companies should create an engagement framework with all relevant functions, from medical affairs, legal and regulatory to commercial; they should build close relationships with key opinion leaders trusted by patient groups, and encourage collaboration between these groups, as several may be active within a specific disease area.

The trade-offs in rare diseases may be the prospect of smaller and faster trials, the incentives of the Orphan Drug Act, and the market potential of many diseases with no treatment, versus poorly understood etiologies, complex diagnoses, difficult recruitment, and increasing payer pressures and public outcry regarding ultra-premium prices.

Trial Recruitment and Retention

Even in diseases with larger populations, enrollment is challenging, as protocols may discourage patients due to the frequency and length of trips to a research center, and as inclusion/exclusion criteria have multiplied. While advocacy groups can help, up to half of rare diseases do not have a specific foundation. In response, companies such as Sanofi Genzyme may help establish and support patient groups and develop networks of investigators and specialized medical centers.

An added challenge is the representativeness of patient KOLs. The most engaged and visible e-patients may be younger and more educated than a general disease population. This concern about tokenism may be partly overcome by stratified recruitment and by a combination of patient inputs with real-world data sources, including medical claims and EHR records [12].

As patient retention is also an issue, predictive analytics (see Chapter 10) may help track demographic and behavior profiles for participants who stay in trials, and time-related burdens may be minimized with simplified consent forms and streamlined visits to research centers.

An underused incentive is feedback to patients about study results, as these are often not communicated or interpreted. This two-way dialogue can take place through in-trial surveys, ongoing advisory panels, and protocol and endpoint codevelopment. Trial optimization may be conducted through sequential steps:

- At the protocol design stage, use large data sets to verify eligibility and inclusion/exclusion criteria, and identify recruitment drivers and barriers (study logistics and frequency of invasive examinations versus burden of symptoms and acceptance of risks to achieve better outcomes).
- At the start of the study, use social listening to identify areas of special patient interest as well as chief complaints.
- During the study, to improve coordination, communicate key patient attitudes and concerns to researchers.
- After the study, ensure that patients have access to study results as well as to their interpretation [13].

Patient-Reported Outcomes

Since the 2009 FDA Guidance on PROs to Support Labeling Claims, these have increasingly been included in trials, especially in oncology, where symptoms such as fatigue, weight loss, and pain have a substantial impact on quality of life. Another PRO driver is the reliance of payers on real-world evidence to support reimbursement, and the role PROs can play in comparative drug effectiveness. This extends to Europe, where the EMA now requires input from patient advocates, as it has direct value for drug tolerability, delivery formulation, and titration. However, a 2016 study showed that only 7.5 percent of reported trials from 2010 to 2014 included a PRO, whereas 24 percent of earlier trials had one.

This may be related to more rigorous standards of review from regulators, as well as a slowing of drug approvals by using PROs to continually adjust dose regimens according to reported side effects [14]. There have been exceptional cases of inclusion of PROs in labels, such as Incyte's Jakafi (ruxolitinib), approved in 2014 for myelofibrosis, where symptom information was included on the label for FDA approval.

Payers also have mixed views on the application of PROs in practice. Medical directors may see engagement as appropriate only in Phase III, whereas pharmacy directors may be divided on all phases. While medical directors are outcomes-driven, pharmacy directors are accountable for budgetary impact and may be more open to patient views of comparative effectiveness.

Another channel for PROs is patient registries; these could be especially useful at the Phase IV post-approval stage, to document the impact of different dosage and titration cycles, and to decide on other treatment regimens than the one already approved. However, patient registries are not generally accepted as evidence to support an FDA label ruling [15].

Clinical trial enhancement and the broader use of patient-generated data are part of the objectives of online patient communities such as PatientsLikeMe.

PATIENTSLIKEME: FROM PATIENT FORUM TO PERSONALIZED HEALTH PLATFORM

Founded in 2004 by Jamie and Ben Heywood, with friend Jeff Cole, after their brother Stephen was diagnosed in 1988 with amyotrophic lateral sclerosis (ALS), Patients-LikeMe has evolved into a major health data platform, with more than 500,000 members and covering 2,700 conditions.

As a for-profit company with an "openness" philosophy, PatientsLikeMe has a dual value proposition of helping patients achieve better outcomes and of improving healthcare with real-world data, allowing more effective treatments and more informed and patient-centric care decisions. For patients, shared symptom and treatment data allow them to learn about their condition, connect with others, and track their disease history and progress over time. For biopharmas, providers, and nonprofit partners, ranging from Biogen and Merck to the FDA, PatientsLikeMe views itself as a measurement company and allows partners to query the network on research questions, consult disease-specific registries, and access patient-reported outcome measures.

Enhancing Clinical Trials
The PatientsLikeMe database can play multiple roles in trials, such as assisting in recruitment and design, assessing drugs in real-world settings, and tracking adverse events over larger populations than those in trials. Several "trial optimization" studies have allowed patients to crowdsource suggestions and take part in "virtual trials" from home. The value of this approach was first shown in 2011, when a PatientsLikeMe patient-initiated observational study of the use of lithium carbonate in ALS refuted an Italian trial (published in 2008 in the *Proceedings of the National Academy of Sciences*) that claimed that it could slow disease progression (Armon 2010). More recently, PatientsLikeMe designed and launched the first virtual trial in ALS, with the Duke ALS Clinic, to study whether a supplement called Lunasin is helpful or harmful to patients living with ALS.

With the growth of wearables, PatientsLikeMe also aims to track data through biosensors. In 2015, it conducted a pilot study with Biogen to monitor activity in multiple sclerosis.

Within the medical community, reactions to PatientsLikeMe vary widely. While some physicians find that PatientsLikeMe membership may improve adherence and information, others feel that they themselves should be the primary source of knowledge and care. PatientsLikeMe has started partnerships with provider networks. In 2015, its alliance with Partners Healthcare in Boston let patients access the database through the patient portal, and in the future will enable physicians to incorporate PatientsLikeMe data into their care decisions.

Business Model Evolution

In keeping with its philosophy, PatientsLikeMe carries no advertising on its website. After receiving seed funding from CommerceNet in May 2005, enabling the website to be launched in April 2006, PatientsLikeMe has developed revenue sources from partnerships. In January 2017, PatientsLikeMe formed a partnership with digital life company iCarbonX, which included an investment in excess of $100 million. iCarbonX was founded in 2015 by renowned genomicist Jun Wang, the cofounder and past CEO of the Beijing Genomics Institute.

Alliance Strategy

Among biopharma companies, Genentech signed a deal in 2014 focusing on oncology. Alliances with Janssen, AstraZeneca, and Novartis allow for testing of patient-reported outcomes measures. With Merck, PatientsLikeMe has conducted a large-scale study of insomnia, examining five years of data and revealing a prevalence among the chronically ill and that these patients are underdiagnosed. PatientsLikeMe has also collaborated with UCB on epilepsy, to better track seizures and understand their early warning signs.

Among providers, PatientsLikeMe signed an agreement in 2016 with M2Gen, a subsidiary of the Moffitt Cancer Center, combining its data with those of Moffitt and Ohio State University to learn about patient experiences in oncology.

Several research collaborations are ongoing with foundations and government agencies. The Robert Wood Johnson Foundation (RWJF) provided two grants, the first in 2013 to optimize measures of patient-reported outcomes and the second in 2015 to develop these with the National Quality Forum (NQF). In 2015, the FDA entered into a multiyear collaboration with PatientsLikeMe to learn how patient-reported data might enhance post-market safety surveillance (Coulter 2016).

Competitive Dynamics

In a social media ecosystem with few entry barriers, PatientsLikeMe has both direct and indirect competitors. In the United Kingdom, HealthUnlocked has a similar model, with 350,000 members and the support of more than 500 advocacy groups. Although the site is free for members, fees are charged for select healthcare organizations.

Disease-specific communities have growing power in rare diseases, where they can actually develop innovative therapies, as was the case for the Cystic Fibrosis Foundation and Vertex for Kalydeco (ivacaftor).

Remaining Challenges

With security breaches on the rise and the risk they pose for patient privacy, Patients-LikeMe hired a director of privacy, security, and compliance in 2016, in addition to the chief privacy officer function led by Ben Heywood for the last decade.

Another issue is "focus versus scale." If the company scaled to a million or more members, trust may be eroded and resources spread too thinly. If it covered more rare diseases, it would compete against related advocacy groups.

An expansion of partners to include insurers may also erode trust among Patients-LikeMe members and lead to concerns about sharing health information. As Patients-LikeMe envisions a future global registry fully integrated into electronic medical records and genomic databases, its business model is still evolving, and the value proposition of patient-generated data would benefit from large-scale validation.

This summary is based on the following case: Aggarwal, R, Chick, S and Simon, F, PatientsLikeMe: Using Social Network Health Data to Improve Patient Care, INSEAD, 2017.

SOURCES

Armon C. "Is the Lithium-for-ALS Genie Back in the Bottle?" *Neurology*. 2010; 75(7): 586-587.

Coulter M, personal communication, 2016; PatientsLikeMe press releases.

The role of observational studies remains controversial. Several publications have focused on "eParticipants" who engage in social media during randomized trials, addressing the potential to undermine their integrity on topics such as eligibility (mutual coaching on how to meet criteria), blinding (advice on how to determine the treatment arm), and safety (sharing adverse effects may stimulate other patients and lead to a false spike in these reports). For instance, during trials for Incivek (telaprevir) from Vertex for hepatitis C, participants had online discussions on sites such as medhelp.org. These included sensitive issues such as suggestions to identify in which study arm patients had been assigned [16]. Forum participants can also pose as self-appointed medical experts and provide advice on dosing, safety, and efficacy, list symptoms that may not be drug-related, and suggest nonadherence.

Preventive measures may include:

- Assessing the size and degree of activity of online communities
- Complementing PROs with objective data from sources such as EHRs
- Educating participants on discussion risks as early as on the informed consent form and through organizations such as the Center for Information and Study on Clinical Research Participation.

In sum, patient centricity strategies in R & D include external and internal processes.

- Externally, gather patient insights on unmet needs early in discovery, through in-person discussions and advisory boards. Also, work with patient groups for recruitment and collect data from multiple sources. In phase IV

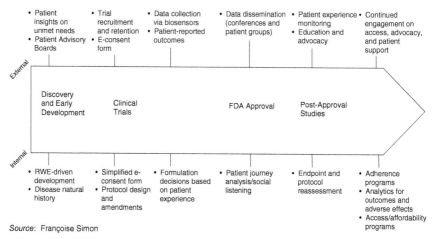

Figure 6-3   Patient engagement through R & D

studies, continue to track the patient experience and provide education and clinical and economic support.

- Internally, analyze at an early stage the natural disease history and drive development with real-world evidence. Facilitate recruitment with simplified consent forms and codevelop protocols and endpoints, which should be reassessed according to PROs. Finally, continue in Phase IV with adherence and access programs. This dual process is shown in Figure 6-3.

CONNECTING THE POINTS OF CARE

While patient engagement initiatives are expanding, there are still inadequate connections between patients, their physicians, payers, and biopharmas. Consumers across countries search online for evidence, but information fluidity remains low in healthcare when compared with sectors such as consumer goods. A 2016 GfK study of 4,900 Internet users in 16 countries, including Australia, China, France, Germany, the United Kingdom, Brazil, and the United States found China in the lead, with 45 percent of the population monitoring health and fitness via wearables and apps; Brazil and the United States came in with 29 percent each, followed by Germany (28 percent) and France (26 percent). Key reasons cited were to maintain or improve fitness and self-motivation for exercise [17].

Questions arise regarding the first point of contact and subsequent information sources. While the first contact has the power of virtual triage and routing, it is rarely a biopharma site and almost never a payer site. A goal would be to gain a higher value position in the consumer mindset by moving up the trust curve and personalizing information according to different recipients (e.g., patients or caregivers) and disease states (e.g., prevention, short-term acute condition, or long-term care). Sites such as WebMD and Everyday Health, as well as health system sites like the Mayo Clinic, attract top traffic, but studies show the importance of additional direct provider links for adequate education and adherence. A project sponsored by the Agency for Healthcare Research and Quality (AHRQ) that convened deliberative groups totaling over 900 participants across the United States found a broad demand for medical evidence in areas such as the inappropriate use of antibiotics, treatment for coronary artery disease, and weight management. Participants wanted personalized information and viewed physicians as arbiters of evidence-based practice. They also stressed the need for more cost transparency [18].

Patient Satisfaction Ratings

Ever since the first *US News & World Report* "best hospital" rankings in 1990, based mostly on physician surveys, rating methods have multiplied, from the launch of Healthgrades in 2004, Medicare's Hospital Compare in 2005, hospital ratings by the Leapfrog Group and *Consumer Reports*, and the ranking of 16,000 surgeons by ProPublica in 2015. Crowdsourced ratings such as Yelp's were found to generally correlate with those of the federal government HCAHPS (Hospital Consumer Assessment of Healthcare Providers and Systems) survey, launched in 2006. The HCAHPS scores drive 25 percent of the financial incentives in the Medicare value-based purchasing program. These surveys are systematically fielded and interpreted, but they suffer from low response rates, entail delays between hospitalizations and public reporting of results, and rarely identify actual problem sources. By contrast, ratings on social media sites are unstructured and have largely uncurated narrative reviews.

In the United Kingdom, the National Health Service operates the NHS Choices site, allowing structured patient reviews. Consumer-generated reviews on sites such as Yelp contain several domains important to users that are not included in HCAHPS, such as cost of hospital visit, insurance/billing, and quality of nursing and staff. While HCAHPS asks, "How often did doctors/nurses treat you with courtesy and respect?," Yelp allows more complete narratives. In response, several health systems have begun allowing direct patient reviews on their sites. Consumer platforms suffer from selection bias and possible false reviews, but they retain the advantage of ease of use and real-time reporting [19].

Even government ratings of hospitals remain controversial. When the Centers for Medicare and Medicaid Services (CMS) released its star ratings in July 2016, the American Hospital Association criticized its confusing format. CMS admitted limitations such as the fact that specialized services including cancer care were not rated, and that measures of deaths and readmissions were based on data from Medicare beneficiaries only [20]. The methodology could also put academic medical centers at a disadvantage, as they treat more complex cases and poorer populations.

Other issues include the lack of a common definition of "patient satisfaction" among the various ratings instruments and the fact that consumer reviews focus on service components of care, such as staff courtesy, that are not correlated with accepted outcome measures such as mortality and readmission rates. Optimally, these two types of measures could be combined, as well as the following steps:

- Public education about the objective components of quality
- Measurement of clinical results that consumers can understand, such as complications and outcomes from surgical procedures
- Inclusion of consumer participation in HCAHPS ratings
- Building into EHRs the capacity to include PROs
- Combining patient experience results, quality metrics, and cost information, and using this more broadly in composite measures [21]

Physician/Patient Dynamics

While there has been significant progress in provider/patient communications, there remain substantial disconnects. The AHRQ defines patient engagement as a set of behaviors by health professionals, a set of organizational policies, and a set of individual and collective mindsets that foster the inclusion of patients and their families as active members of the care team, encouraging partnerships with them, their providers, and communities [22].

To bridge the disconnect between what the patient knows and what the provider thinks he or she knows, shared decision making (SDM) aims to support patient-centered care with these core attributes: education and shared knowledge, involvement of family and friends, collaborative team management, sensitivity for nonmedical/social dimensions of care, respect for patient needs, and free flow and accessibility of information.

In February 2015, CMS approved reimbursement for lung cancer screening with a mandated shared-decision counseling session before the first scan, to determine risks and benefits. Among others, the Mayo Clinic has set up online forums hosting discussion groups, blogs, and events, and providing a non-acute physician/patient platform [23].

In a 2016 NEJM Catalyst online survey sent to clinicians and healthcare executives, respondents saw engaged patients as adhering to a care plan co-created with providers and taking an active role in improving their health. The biggest challenge cited was insufficient time with patients. A majority found patient portals helpful, but there was not strong support for remote monitoring, due to concerns about the burden of handling data streams, and beliefs that, without engagement, technology alone was unlikely to change behavior [24].

Other studies have confirmed communication deficiencies. The 2016 Patient Access and Engagement Report by the nonprofit CancerCare included six surveys with input from more than 3,000 cancer patients, from newly diagnosed to post-treatment. Overall, fewer than half of respondents discussed the cost of follow-up testing with their physicians, only about two-thirds had adequate information about treatment benefits and risks, and only 13 percent felt sufficiently informed about clinical trial opportunities. Fewer than half obtained a second opinion about their treatment plan. Strikingly, communication gaps extended to payers. Only about one half of respondents reported understanding their health plan coverage, despite 58 percent feeling distressed about the financial burdens during treatment [25].

While a broad portfolio of digital engagement tools is available, these generally need further development. Patient portals are most widely used but lack real-time interactivity with providers; patients can access test results but do not have their interpretation in real time. Mobile appointment scheduling is useful, but reminders may be perceived as intrusive. E-consultations provide faster access to care, but have limited applicability, and "doctor on demand" virtual services may vary greatly in quality. Wearables allow continuous data monitoring but without interpretation or connection to medical records. Social networks provide peer-to-peer information and support, but entail potential privacy and security issues. These benefits and limitations are shown in Figure 6-4.

Some health system initiatives now aim to optimize their patient experience with a new organization. Faced with a gap between its good ratings on medical outcomes and uneven patient experience reports, in 2007, the Cleveland Clinic adopted a new care model, creating institutes with multidisciplinary teams treating a single organ system, such as heart/vascular. A new Chief Patient Experience officer position was also established, and outcomes data were published on every surgeon and program, in addition to the HCAHPS ratings available online to consumers. "Managing the 360" defined the patient experience as everyone and everything people encountered, from their decision to choose the clinic until they were discharged. A "Best Practices" department within the Office of Patient Experience identified successful approaches and tested new practices in pilot

Digital Tools	Benefits	Risks/Weaknesses
Patient portals	Real-time information, better education	No/limited provider feedback, no interpretation of diagnostic tests
Online/mobile reminders and scheduling	Time savings for patient and provider staff	Risk of perceived intrusion with reminders
Link of patient-generated data to EHRs	Potential for greater personalization	No interoperability between EHR systems, and between consumer data and medical records
E-consultations	Faster access to care, fewer inappropriate emergency visits	Limited applicability across conditions
On-demand virtual visits	24/7 information	Lack of continuity between providers, uneven quality
Wearables	Better monitoring, potential behavior change	Limited functionality and interoperability, quality and privacy issues.
Social networks	Practical information and support	Contamination risk of clinical trials from peer-to-peer communications, privacy issues
Satisfaction surveys (HCAHPS/CAHPS)	Validated reports on key components of experience	Time lag between hospitalization or consultations and reporting
Consumer ratings (Healthgrades, Yelp)	More extensive narratives than HCAHPS	Not curated, risk of false reports

Source: Françoise Simon

Figure 6-4   Impact of patient engagement tools

projects. A same-day appointment option was mandated for the first time among major US health systems. The full program was launched in 2010, and by 2013, a CMS survey showed that the Clinic was in the 92nd percentile for patient satisfaction, among the 4,600 hospitals surveyed [26].

Biopharma Initiatives for Engagement

Biopharmas have greatly expanded patient communications, but they still face broad distrust among consumers. Traditional direct-to-consumer (DTC) promotion runs against ad-blocking behavior and disruption concerns, especially on mobile channels. While sites such as Fit2Me, launched by AstraZeneca in 2014 to reach the nearly 30 million Americans with type 2 diabetes, offer a wide range of customizable diet and exercise tools, the Fit2Me drug information remains limited to the company's own products, unlike health system sites such as that of the Mayo Clinic.

A 2016 study by researchers at the FDA Office of Prescription Drug Promotion and RTI International focused on 65 oncology websites and found that, while drug benefits and risks were almost equally represented, both consumer and professional sites had uneven quantitative information for benefits and risks [27].

While biopharmas have sought to simplify patient outreach with structures like Shire's OnePath program, assigning a personalized care manager as a single contact point for care coordination and drug access, there is very low consumer awareness worldwide of the range of available patient services.

A 2015 Accenture survey of 10,000 patients in Brazil, France, Germany, and the United States, across seven therapeutic areas including the brain, bones, heart, immune system, metabolism, and oncology, found that only 19 percent of responders were aware of services from biopharmas. They especially wanted more guidance at the pre-diagnosis stage, to know their potential risks before experiencing symptoms. They also wanted a single point of contact for information, and 85 percent preferred it to be their first-in-line team of healthcare professionals; only one percent saw biopharmas in that role [28].

This points to a related need to expand the biopharma/physician range of communications. A ZS Associates survey of physician access by salesforces found that only 44 percent accepted more than 70 percent of sales calls, versus nearly 80 percent in 2008. While a large part of budgets was still focused on the salesforce, more than 53 percent of activity took place through nonpersonal channels such as emails, mobile alerts, and websites. One factor leading to better access was the launch of a truly novel therapy, such as new hepatitis C drugs for gastroenterologists, or oral anticoagulants for cardiologists. These studies suggest that salesforces need to break out of their silos and work with marketing and patient advocacy teams to expand the range and depth of education materials and to communicate these to broader audiences, including nurses and physician assistants, as they are also often more accessible [29].

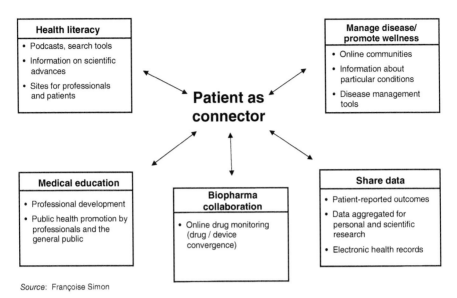

Health literacy
- Podcasts, search tools
- Information on scientific advances
- Sites for professionals and patients

Manage disease/ promote wellness
- Online communities
- Information about particular conditions
- Disease management tools

Patient as connector

Medical education
- Professional development
- Public health promotion by professionals and the general public

Biopharma collaboration
- Online drug monitoring (drug / device convergence)

Share data
- Patient-reported outcomes
- Data aggregated for personal and scientific research
- Electronic health records

Source: Françoise Simon

Figure 6-5   Patient-centric ecosystem

In sum, patients are at the center of multiple points of care with varying degrees of connectivity. Education channels require health literacy, which remains uneven across geographic and demographic populations. Public health communications include ratings such as HCAHPS scores, still inadequately understood by consumers. Online communities are successful with information, support, and even financing of some trials, but they face privacy and security issues. Health data are more easily quantified through wearables but lack connections to medical records. Biosensors are optimizing remote drug monitoring by biopharmas, but these firms need to communicate more broadly the range of their "beyond the pill" services. This communication ecosystem is shown in Figure 6-5.

UNDERSTANDING THE PATIENT JOURNEY

The patient journey encompasses the end-to-end experience of a condition, from a first awareness to diagnosis, primary care and specialist consultations, treatment, prescription fulfillment, drug monitoring, adherence or abandonment of treatment, and follow-up surveillance. Information on these steps must come from multiple sources, as physicians are often not aware of pre-diagnosis experience, prescription fulfillment, and the cost burden of therapies.

Following preliminary research on natural disease history, incidence and prevalence, demographics, and comorbidities, sources may include:

- At the awareness/information search stage, consumer databases and social media analytics

- At the diagnosis and prescription stage, EHR and pharmacy data as well as physician scripts
- During treatment, EHR and insurer claims data
- To track adherence versus abandonment or substitution, co-pays and formulary inclusions, total patient cost burden, and health plan rejection data

This listening and data mining process can provide answers to the following questions:

- What are salient topics and shared experiences in patient-to-patient communications throughout the journey? What are their major information sources? Who are the most-consulted advocacy groups and social opinion leaders?
- How do co-morbidities affect the burden of disease and where are the gaps in patient care across specialists?
- What are unmet needs and frustrations? What may be missing from physician communications?
- What is the perception of brand versus generic options, and alternative medicine? What are drivers and barriers of drug switching or abandonment?
- What is the total disease burden on patients, including treatment cost and impact on family, caregivers and day-to-day living? How can this be alleviated by "beyond the pill" services [30]?

Drivers and Barriers of Behavior

A full understanding of the patient journey requires gathering insights from multiple sources about the drivers of behavior at each step and setting up goals linking value added to the patient and value to the company. This includes increased awareness and screening, better trial recruitment and retention, increased prescribing and fulfillment, reduced switching, and improved adherence. Defining metrics requires coordination between R & D, medical and corporate affairs, health economics, sales, and marketing functions.

There should also be a recognition of barriers at each point of the journey: Initial misconceptions about the condition, decision to seek alternative advice and treatment after diagnosis, abandonment due to side effects or burdensome self-management for multiple conditions, logistical issues, language and cultural barriers, and total cost burden. The intensive continuous coaching that is needed may be outsourced in part. Employers and payers may partner with companies like Omada Health, with services such as professional lifestyle coaches.

The understanding of behavior drivers and barriers may vary across diseases. In the case of depression, a survey of more than 1,200 patients showed that 71 percent took over a month to receive a diagnosis after their first awareness of symptoms, and 38 percent took more than six months. Although antidepressants may take 6 to 12 weeks to be fully effective, the survey showed that 18 percent of prescribed drugs were discontinued in less than one month, with perceived lack of efficacy as the reason for 52 percent of respondents [31].

Given the consumer preference for a healthcare professional as a primary contact point and regulations in some jurisdictions that restrict direct contact with patients, biopharma companies should strive to build high-credibility partnerships with providers and to develop with them online and offline care management tools.

The value proposition for a biopharma then depends on its therapies, services, and provider alliances; it is specific to subpopulations with the most needs based on socioeconomics and disease state; and it is customized to significant moments in the journey, in order to achieve outcomes measures of quality, cost, and patient satisfaction [32].

Adherence Strategies

Adherence can be defined as the extent to which a patient behavior, including taking medication, following a diet, exercise, or other lifestyle actions, reflects agreed-upon recommendations from a healthcare provider. Nonadherence has long been known as having serious health and cost consequences. Studies have shown that 20 to 30 percent of prescriptions are never filled, and that about half of medications for chronic diseases are not taken as prescribed. In the United States, nonadherence is estimated to cause at least 10 percent of hospitalizations, with an increase in mortality and morbidity, and to cost the healthcare system between $100 billion and $289 billion annually [33]. Adherence is a multifactorial behavior that is driven by socioeconomics and demographics, patient knowledge and attitudes, condition and treatment status (disease severity, treatment complexity, and side effects), provider traits (communication skills and resources), and cost issues (drug coverage, co-pay, and access to medication and reimbursement support).

A study funded by the AHRQ found that the effectiveness of interventions varied across diseases. Generally, for chronic diseases, interventions with behavioral support, through continued patient contact over several weeks or months, were most effective for hypertension, heart failure, and hyperlipidemia; other approaches included reminders and pharmacist-led interventions. For depression, collaborative care with in-person visits and counseling appeared effective [34].

Optimizing adherence thus entails both strategic and tactical approaches. Strategies include partnerships with health systems, employers, payers, and pharmacies, as well as alliances with advocacy groups to share experiences and track treatment effect and outcomes. Tactics range from the development of point-of-care tools to nurse-staffed call centers and clinical educator programs for disease management and treatment monitoring. For example, Philips' Health-Suite digital platform has integration capabilities with EHRs and, through a collaboration with Validic, consumer data from wearables. Validic has also partnered with the Sutter Health system of 30 hospitals in California to develop a preventive model of care, including a hypertension management program connecting with blood pressures monitors and activity trackers [35].

However, issues remain at the consumer end, including quality and privacy. A 2016 study published in *JAMA Cardiology* compared the accuracy of four wrist-worn heart rate monitoring devices with that of traditional chest-band electrode systems. While the Apple Watch reached a 91 percent accuracy, other devices, including the Fitbit Charge HR and Basis Peak were, respectively, only 84 and 83 percent accurate, versus 99 percent for the Polar H7 chest band device. Accuracy diminished with exercise intensity, with Fitbit underestimating heart rate during vigorous exercise; the recommendation was for further validation [36].

In sum, adherence strategies follow a step-by-step process, starting with early patient insights, clinical and economic support during treatment (especially with reimbursement dossiers and copay assistance), and continuous tracking of outcomes and quality of life to support the provider/patient dialogue and self-management.

ORGANIZING FOR PATIENT CENTRICITY

While patient centricity is a general mindset that pervades all functions, it may be organized and measured according to different models. It may be centrally located and led by a Chief Patient Officer (CPO). Companies including Sanofi, Merck, and UCB have appointed CPOs in recent years. The patient advocacy function itself may also be centrally located within corporate or medical affairs, allowing for engagement across functions (government affairs, R & D, regulatory, market access, and commercial). It may report to communications or marketing or be decentralized within business units, with a focus on product or disease, but with limited scope due to legal and regulatory constraints. In a newer model, patient advocacy may be embedded within R & D, allowing a strong patient engagement at all development stages, but with the need to coordinate with commercial activities [37].

Whether patient centricity is centrally coordinated or not, it is essential to involve all functions in order to ensure employee commitment. For instance, BMS has a company-wide initiative to promote and track engagement across functions and countries. Measuring engagement and the related return on investment can benefit from a link to existing metrics and department-specific key performance indicators (KPIs).

WHO ARE YOU WORKING FOR? BRISTOL-MYERS SQUIBB EMPLOYEE ENGAGEMENT INITIATIVE

By Emmanuel Blin, Former Senior Vice President and Chief Strategy Officer, Bristol-Myers Squibb

In 2014, Bristol-Myers Squibb was facing a period of significant change; we had just divested our diabetes business as a part of our evolution to a specialty care company, we were transitioning to a new CEO and beginning our evolution of the company to a more efficient structure. We needed to engage our global workforce through this transition. We needed a program that would connect our employees to the work we do for patients.

Our Strategy
We created an initiative to celebrate the commitment of Bristol-Myers Squibb people to our patients, tapping into the key differentiator: the fact that patients are the ultimate motivation for us. Our objective was to ignite a deeper sense of pride and purpose to engage, inspire and motivate colleagues including those from non-market facing functions like R & D. We focused on the power of storytelling to share patients' journeys of overcoming disease with Bristol-Myers Squibb treatments and employee stories of what inspires them to come to work every day.

The internal engagement program was named "Who Are You Working For?" and asked employees a fundamental question of their motivation for working at Bristol-Myers Squibb.

Program Goals
The Who Are You Working For? initiative was designed to meet three key outcomes:

- Colleagues would feel motivated, engaged, and inspired, with a sense of purpose about their jobs
- Colleagues across the globe would feel better connected to each other, to key executives, and to the company
- We would bring an external focus into the company with a stronger connection to patients.

The Power of Storytelling
The initiative came alive through the power of storytelling. We shared stories of patients, their treatment experiences, and outcomes. These patients were facing grim diagnoses and few effective treatments. Most had exhausted all their options when they enrolled in a trial or were prescribed one of our medicines—and these medicines profoundly changed their outcomes.

The most powerful means of storytelling was the live patient presentation. We invited patients to attend team meetings to share their experiences. We also employed the power of storytelling to profile colleagues from around the world.

Program Development
Who Are You Working For? was globally launched in September 2014. Key features that guided the initiative:

- *Internally focused:* Working in a highly regulated environment like the pharmaceutical industry, we recognized that we could tell patient stories to an internal audience in a way that we could not externally.
- *Globally relevant:* It was imperative that the program resonate with global colleagues. We centrally created an initiative that had flexibility to adapt to local implementation and be culturally appropriate in all locations.

Program Launch

The launch events ranged in size from a brief town hall overview to a week of events showcasing the local office's work for patients. Coinciding with the launch of the initiative, we held the first Global Story Contest, asking colleagues to answer the question, "Who Are You Working For?" Over a period of six weeks, we received over 800 contest submissions from 33 countries. Importantly, these stories emanated from all functions, in fact nearly 60 percent were submitted by employees outside of the commercial function, including 28 percent from research and development. Thirty stories were selected to be further developed and published on the Who Are You Working For? internal website. In the first half of 2015, we hosted 28 patient appearances at 20 meetings.

To measure the impact of the program, we surveyed employees and saw substantial increases in areas including a sense of purpose (up 44 percent), understanding the impact our medicines can make on individuals (up 32 percent) and increased knowledge about our pipeline, brands, and therapeutic areas (up 143 percent).

Accelerating the Initiative

We continue to build on the foundation of Who Are You Working For? to reinforce that everything we do is for the patients we serve. We hosted our first Global Patient Week, with 246 events across 65 sites globally. During Global Patient Week, the new external portion of the program, "Working Together for Patients," was launched. On the website we share stories about how and why our employees work for patients. The external website hosts the patient-focused mosaic made up of employee photos, demonstrating that we all do our small part to make a big impact for patients.

2016 and the Future

We are maintaining momentum in the third year of the initiative. We believe that our patient focus drives employee engagement, as well as corporate reputation and talent recruiting. In short, the patient focus is becoming a key reason we both retain and attract talented people.

PATIENT ENGAGEMENT METRICS

At the clinical stage, companies may collaborate with advocacy groups to track the number of patients reached, as well as possible behavior changes, through the patient group database and online forum. For instance, Celgene announced in October 2016 an alliance with Sage Bionetworks for an observational study using the Apple ResearchKit and an iPhone application. For patients with chronic anemia from myelodysplastic syndrome (MDS) or beta thalassemia, who have a disease burden that is difficult to quantify, and where endpoints are typically outside traditional measures, the collaboration will collect neurological data using the BrainBaseline cognitive software. Celgene and Sage are collaborating with the MDS Foundation and Cooley's Anemia Foundation in defining the right elements to be captured in the app, to ensure patient relevance [38]. Specific measures of engagement in trials include patient recruitment and retention. For rare diseases, in particular, advocacy group can greatly improve the speed and scope of recruitment. Advisory boards and individual channels for co-creating protocols can also optimize retention. For instance, reducing the frequency of visits to the research site or providing transportation can help to minimize the burden of trial participation.

While external KPIs include outcomes (trial participation and results, patient and physician feedback), internal KPIs include senior leadership commitment, coordination across functions, and capabilities (employee training and skills). In addition to traditional marketing- and sales-oriented cultures, a barrier to patient centricity remains its unclear impact on business growth and productivity.

A possible approach is a mapping of the value pathway, tracking the increase or decrease in value at each step of the patient journey. For instance, in diabetes, companies would identify first the different disease stages (e.g., potentially or confirmed at risk, prediabetic, onset of complications, diabetic patient, and uncontrolled diabetes). The next step would be to identify the interventions at each stage (e.g., prediction and screening, prevention through diet and exercise, therapy options, monitoring and adherence programs). It would then be possible to identify "value leakages," or points when outcomes suffer due to system failures such as lack of patient education, access, and affordability. Collaborative interventions with providers and patient communities could optimize prevention, early detection, and treatment effectiveness and adherence. These value leakages and interventions in the diabetes case are summarized in Figure 6-6.

Value Leakages	Intervention Options
Pre-diagnosis and Diagnosis • Lack of awareness • Social stigma • Infrequent medical checkups • Total cost burden	• Education through multiple channels (websites, social media, smartphone apps) • Collaboration with patient groups • Access programs (co-pay assistance, discounts)
Treatment Start • Therapy issues (injection pain, side effects) • Burden of frequent monitoring (glucose, etc.) • Lifestyle management (diet, exercise) • Time burden of physician visits	• Clinical support on injections, side-effect management • Innovation therapies (oral, smart insulins) • Personalized coaching on diet and exercise • Glucose monitoring/wireless pumps and sensors
Treatment Continuation • Lack of coordinated care • Lack of motivation • Burden of complex treatment • Management of comorbidities • Decreased quality of life • Pressures on family and caregivers • Lack of insurance/out-of-pocket costs	• Medical team approach to care • Integrated disease management/online support • Education on comorbidities • Alliance with patient groups for emotional support • Access programs (co-pay assistance, discounts, donations) • Integration of patient data with medical records

Source: Françoise Simon and EY Analysis

Figure 6-6   Patient value pathway: diabetes case

At the commercial stage, additional metrics may be applied both to digital communications and salesforce activities. Success factors for digital outreach include relevant content, multiple channels, integration of patient and medical data, and, most importantly, balancing frequency and consumer concerns about information overload and privacy. Metrics for digital communications include:

- For reach and relevance, number of impressions or interactions with the content (reading/downloading)
- Pre- and post-unaided awareness surveys on disease or product
- Percentage of new visitors to a site/time on site
- For engagement, click-through rate or calls to action; on social media, comments/shares/likes, with the caveat that a post may gather many responses, but some may be negative, including adverse events and off-label comments
- For impact, loyalty as measured by repeat visits to a branded or unbranded site, conversion rate (percentage of visitors taking action, such as downloading a doctor discussion guide, and adherence to medication) [39]

Metrics are also evolving for sales activities. A patient-centric sales model would replace prescription targets with a business plan; this would include measuring the quality and scope of services delivered to healthcare professionals, and the collection of patient experience data from them. Sales managers themselves would uncover the needs of medical offices and evaluate representatives, based on a significant amount of time in field work.

ORGANIZATION MODELS

Embedding patient centricity within an organization depends on multiple factors: early listening and incorporating patient insights into the discovery and clinical process, multichannel education and self-management, and access and affordability programs, but also, and most importantly, senior leadership commitment and company culture. This includes visible mission and vision statements, reflected in specific objectives for all functions and KPIs, within employee targets and incentives, including in non-customer-facing departments. Senior commitment is also needed to ensure patient centricity across geographies. For country managers who have been largely evaluated on revenue contribution, it may be perceived as burdensome to add patient-centric KPIs to the traditional metrics. Shaping a new culture includes these activities:

- Transformational leadership defining the mission and vision
- Reinforcing systems and new service designs, such as patient-friendly trials
- Cross-functional coordination to prevent silos, and inclusion of patient-centric KPIs within existing metrics

- Measurement of patient focus at each stage of the value chain
- Capability building through employee selection, continuous training on patient collaborations, and incentivization related to patient outcomes
- Reallocation of budgetary resources toward patient-focused programs

Structure Options

While an appropriate culture is a primary success factor, different structure options each have trade-offs. A decentralized model embedding patient advocacy within business units ensures the diffusion of this capability into franchises, but it does not break down existing silos. A possible evolution may be the reestablishment of cross-functional teams with deep patient-focused experience and skills.

A growing trend is a centralized structure around a Chief Patient Officer. This high-level global appointment helps communicate the corporate mission and vision throughout the company and across regions. It benefits from a clear role as a center of expertise.

At Sanofi, the objective to ensure that patient centricity becomes part of the culture is supported by a three-pillar framework:

- The first pillar is input and understanding, listening to patients through individual and collective channels and designing solutions based on their needs.
- The second pillar is outcomes and solutions, taking those insights and incorporating them into products and "beyond the pill" solutions. This entails a needs-based patient segmentation. Patients' needs vary greatly from first diagnosis to treatment maintenance ten years later. For communications, some patients prefer direct engagement with a nurse, while others are comfortable with apps and digital coaching.
- The third pillar is culture and community, engaging with online groups and ensuring that every employee has a true understanding of how his or her work can impact patients and improve their outcomes [40].

In conclusion, patient centricity is driven by a transformative culture and involves new models and processes at each stage of the value chain, as well as a comprehensive cross-functional and cross-regional coordination.

SUMMARY POINTS

- Patient centricity is a comprehensive mindset that integrates the consumer voice from discovery to post-approval; it connects the points of care and aims to create a seamless system, from patient-generated data to medical offices and health delivery organizations.
- Patient centricity is driven by multiple scientific and market forces, from regulator interest in patient-reported outcomes to digital technologies enabling

consumers to track their health, payer demand for real-word evidence to show value, and the growing power of patient communities, especially in rare diseases.

- Barriers remain, from legal restrictions on biopharma/patient communications to the limited functionality of wearables, privacy and security issues, and the weak evidence of the return on investment of patient engagement.

- At the discovery stage, companies are codeveloping with patients prediction-focused platforms and engaging in crowdsourcing initiatives.

- Clinical trials now largely include patient-reported outcomes, but these have not so far been broadly accepted for product approvals by regulators; collaborations with advocacy groups can optimize patient recruitment and retention.

- Connecting the points of care is challenged by information gaps on prevention and disease awareness across global markets; patient satisfaction ratings are widespread but remain controversial, with weak correlation between surveys and quantitative ratings such as mortality and morbidity; consumer-generated online reviews are not structured or curated.

- Physician/patient dynamics suffer from insufficient time for encounters but may be optimized by shared decision making, e-consultations, and digital education tools.

- Biopharmas have greatly expanded patient collaborations but still suffer from public distrust and a lack of awareness of their support services.

- Understanding the patient journey is key for product co-creation and entails extensive information, from the pre-diagnosis to post-treatment stages.

- Patient engagement metrics remain a challenge but can benefit from patient experience tracking by advocacy groups as well as links with existing performance indicators.

- Senior leadership commitment is key to creating a worldwide patient-centric culture; organization models include decentralization within business units, but they are trending toward centralization around chief patient officers with global responsibilities.

CHAPTER 7

DRUG PRICING IN CONTEXT

INTRODUCTION

Balancing patient access to therapeutics in the face of rising healthcare costs is the central challenge facing healthcare stakeholders. This issue is no longer exclusive to emerging markets, where affordability remains challenging despite government reforms and a rapidly improving economic picture. In developed markets, new waves of scientific innovation have produced breakthrough therapies for grievous diseases such as cancer and hepatitis C. These life-saving products frequently come with list prices near or above $100,000 per patient, and some must be taken chroniclly, straining the budgets of health systems after years of economic austerity. Kenneth Frazier, chief executive officer (CEO) of Merck & Co., notes, "The good news is that [biopharmas] are on the verge of incredible breakthroughs if we don't kill the innovation engine. The bad news is unless we make changes in the system, people won't be able to afford the wonderful things that are coming out of our pipelines" [1]. This comment demonstrates that biopharmaceutical companies understand that getting the patient access/drug pricing balance right is essential.

In recent years, the issue of the affordability of prescription drugs has become more urgent, playing out in the pages of high-profile scientific and medical journals, mainstream news outlets, and, increasingly, on social media sites such as Facebook and Twitter. Oncologists and infectious disease specialists, for instance, have questioned the high costs of new cancer and cystic fibrosis drugs, portraying the potential financial harm as an adverse side effect [2,3].

News outlets have focused their attention on price increases associated with older, established biopharmaceutical products, intensifying public skepticism of one argument manufacturers have traditionally used to justify their pricing practices—the high cost of R & D required to bring new products to market. Indeed, after a series of articles in the US mainstream media about major price increases associated with Mylan's EpiPen (epinephrine injection), the issue has become so contentious that a number of biopharmaceutical companies have promised to be more transparent about their drug pricing decisions [4,5].

Managing Biotechnology: From Science to Market in the Digital Age, First Edition. Françoise Simon and Glen Giovannetti.

The transatlantic disparity in drug pricing, which has resulted in much higher drug costs in the United States than elsewhere in the world, has also been a critical issue. So, too, is the growing influence of social media, which has given consumers new channels to discuss pricing disparities in near real time, even as other digital tools make product pricing more transparent [6,7].

Beyond pricing transparency, advances in digital health will directly affect traditional biopharma pricing strategies. As discussed later in the chapter, biopharma companies will need to use emerging digital tools to capture real-world evidence to demonstrate product value in the data-rich, highly networked environment in which they operate. These data, coupled with powerful analytics capabilities, will help accelerate new pricing models between biopharma companies and payers that are less transactional and more collaborative.

THE ECONOMICS OF DRUG PRICING

The economic drivers that guide the pricing of televisions, mobile phones, and clothing do not apply to the pricing of drugs. There are multiple reasons for this, including market exclusivities. Market exclusivities protect a new branded drug from competition for some limited period of time. These exclusivities are a trade-off that governments—and, by extension, society—make to encourage drug companies and the investors who back them to do the hard and risky work of drug development, which can take up to 10 years and cost billions of dollars [8]. At the end of this period of exclusivity, competitors are free to create alternate versions that, at least for traditional oral small molecules, are much cheaper than the original branded versions.

As a result, biopharma companies have only a limited window to recoup and maximize their research and development investment. If development costs are too pricey or the path to market is too uncertain, it can be difficult for drug companies to justify investment and they will exit a therapeutic area. For instance, beginning in the late 1990s, many drug companies stopped investing in antibiotic research because the space appeared to be well served by existing, low-cost generics; the need for new, higher-powered anti-infectives was less acute and so was the willingness to pay for them. However, a little over a decade later, a public health crisis directly tied to this lack of investment has emerged: the rapid increase in drug-resistant microbial infections. Recognizing this problem, more than 80 biopharma and diagnostic companies called on governments to consider new economic models to reinvigorate antibiotic development [9,10].

Market exclusivities are just one reason drugs are priced differently from other products. Another key reason is that the end user of the medicine—the patient—has traditionally been divorced from bearing much of the cost of treatment as a result of public health systems or private insurance. This scenario has resulted in a situation where patients themselves are not required to prioritize price when making decisions about their prescription drugs, further skewing the market forces associated with healthcare.

But the primary reason for high drug prices stems from the structure of the current fee-for-service-based healthcare system, which relies on unit-based pricing methodology. Indeed, the system is too one-dimensional for the current needs as it does not prioritize payment based on either improved patient outcomes or the ability to reduce total healthcare costs. This has resulted in the creation of incentives that encourage drug companies to adopt pricing practices that are driven by what is possible rather than what others stakeholders might deem reasonable.

Biopharma companies have responded to the existing market incentives in rational and predictable ways. They have established public, unit-based list prices in individual markets and then negotiated specific, undisclosed discounts or rebates based on in-country regulations and health technology assessment criteria. This approach has had two benefits: (1) it is relatively simple to implement and (2) it preserves pricing flexibility, especially in markets where reference pricing is the norm.

Biopharma's pricing model is now under threat (Figure 7-1). As the costs of R & D and sales and marketing continue to accelerate, cost-constrained payers cannot afford to pay for every new innovative product. As a result, they have adopted blunt mechanisms that limit access to therapy for many patients. Moreover, as drug costs have become a bigger line item in national budgets, stakeholders are calling for increased transparency around true R & D and commercialization costs, since those metrics in the past have been used to justify high drug prices [11].

Global Pricing Regulation

Total drug expenditures as a percentage of health costs have remained consistent in most major markets since the 1960s according to the Organisation for Economic Co-operation and Development [12]. Since 2013, however, drug expenditure inflation has started to stand out relative to other healthcare costs, such as imaging, laboratory testing, and in-patient procedures. Much of this can be attributed to a wave of innovative branded products that command high prices [13].

Since 2000, the US Food and Drug Administration (FDA) and the European Medicines Agency (EMA) have each approved more than 500 new medicines. Analysts predict that, by 2020, another 200, primarily high-cost specialty products, defined as complex, often injected, therapies to treat serious diseases, could be approved. If all of these products reach the market, it could result in an additional $600 billion in spending worldwide just on pharmaceuticals. "The budgetary impact of these new innovations is huge," said Douglas Long, vice president of Industry Relations for IMS Health at a November 2015 Pharmaceutical Forum convened by the US Department of Health and Human Services [14].

Already stretched to provide access to existing products, payers worry about the trade-offs required to make room in their budgets for new therapies. Governments in most major markets, meanwhile, have either sharpened existing

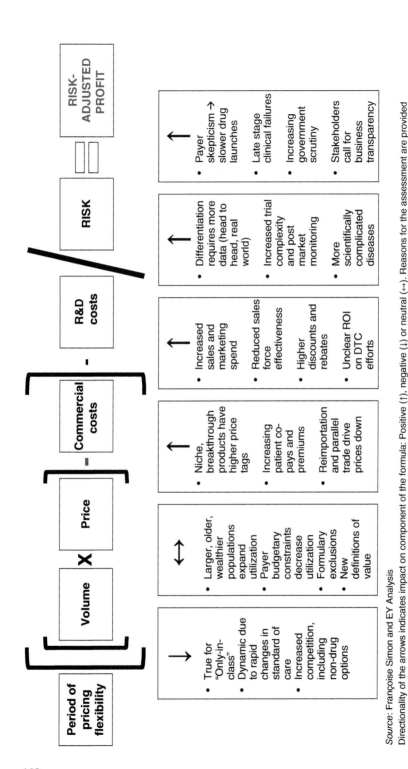

Figure 7-1 Traditional pharma pricing practices under pressure

Source: Françoise Simon and EY Analysis
Directionality of the arrows indicates impact on component of the formula: Positive (↑), negative (↓) or neutral (↔). Reasons for the assessment are provided underneath the arrows.

cost-containment measures or responded with sweeping legislation to keep their systems sustainable:

- In Europe, where a full portfolio of cost-containment measures already exists, countries have tightened and supplemented their policies.
- In Japan, the government has instituted biannual drug price revisions, while promoting the use of generics.
- In the United States, the 2010 Affordable Care Act expanded health insurance to the uninsured and legislated reforms that reward providers for delivering better health outcomes at lower costs, but required biopharma companies to pay additional rebates.

As Figure 7-2 shows, these reforms vary depending on the specific market in question, resulting in markedly different pricing regulations around the globe. As a

	United States	United Kingdom	France	Germany	Japan
Direct price controls	Not currently	No	Yes	No	Biannual price cuts; price caps on generics
Indirect price controls	Discounts to federal agencies; commercial payers negotiate undisclosed rebates	Profit control; price cuts for older drugs	Yes, higher prices granted for strict volume agreements	After one year on market	Price cuts higher for older drugs
External reference pricing	No	No	Yes	For supportive information	Yes
Type of restrictive reimbursement list employed	Use of exclusionary formularies growing, especially at PBMs	Negative list	Positive list	Negative list	Positive list
Cost-effectiveness pricing	No	Yes	Yes	Yes	Yes
Parallel imports	Not currently	Allowed; potential impact depending on how the UK exits from the EU	Allowed (within EU)	Allowed (within EU)	Yes
Prioritization of generics	Yes	Yes	Yes	Yes	Yes
Cost sharing with consumers	Yes	Yes	Yes	Yes	Yes
Use of innovative pricing models	Low but growing	Mostly financial based agreements	Financial based agreements	Driven by AMNOG, German law enacted in 2010 to help control drug prices	Financial based agreements

Source: EY Analysis

Figure 7-2   Pricing regulations in major markets

result of these differing regulations, it is essential for biopharmaceutical companies to develop pricing strategies that are global in scale but can be deployed at the local level. Only by adopting such a global-local mentality will manufacturers be able to address the price sensitivities of the various regions in which they operate, where different degrees of market competition combine with policy and social expectations to allow—or limit—product pricing flexibility.

European Union: A Portfolio of Pricing Controls   Austerity in the wake of the 2008 global financial crisis and a distinctive social contract with citizens have enabled single-payer governments in Europe to take a firm line on drug pricing. Although specific regulations vary country by country, most European Uniton (EU) nations use variations of the following mechanisms to manage drug prices and the costs of medicines:

- Strict health technology assessments (HTAs) to define value based on efficacy, relative therapeutic benefit, and, increasingly, cost effectiveness
- Positive and negative drug lists to control the availability of therapeutics
- Internal and external reference pricing

Before drugs can be marketed, they must receive regulatory approval from the EMA. However, marketing approval is only a first step to coverage. Pricing and access decisions occur at a country level, and most are strongly influenced by HTAs. HTAs are defined as systemic evaluations of the properties, effects, and impacts of health technologies and interventions and are an important step in determining reimbursement. According to a 2015 World Health Organization survey, 80 percent of European countries use HTAs to determine reimbursement and benefits related to medicines, medical devices, procedures, and health services. Each country uses its own guidelines when developing and issuing these value assessments; most prioritize medical need, clinical effectiveness, effectiveness relative to existing therapies, and budget impact. Increasingly, cost effectiveness is also important. To promote sharing and reuse of HTA information, in 2014 the EU created a voluntary network including EU member states, Norway, and Iceland [15]. This initiative builds on EUnetHTA, a network of national HTA agencies, research institutes, and health ministries designed to help inform common approaches to drug assessments and health policy [16].

In addition to using HTAs, many EU member states have positive and negative lists that determine which drugs will be fully or partially reimbursed by the health system (positive lists) and which will not (negative lists). As noted in the above discussion of HTAs, the criteria used to determine reimbursement status vary from country to country and are influenced by health and social policies as well as economic constraints. The United Kingdom and Germany use negative lists; France, Italy, and Portugal are among the countries that use positive lists. Spain uses both positive and negative lists [17].

The final mechanism European countries use to reduce drug expenditures is reference pricing, which comes in two forms, internal and external. Countries that use internal reference pricing set the reimbursement total for a medicine by comparing the prices of equivalent products. Equivalency can be defined narrowly: products that share the same active ingredient. It can also be defined more broadly (and controversially) as products with "therapeutic equivalence," in which the medicines are judged to have the same—or similar—effects. This broader definition is used in Germany and the Netherlands [18].

Active ingredient-based groups are most commonly used to regulate the prices of off-patent medicines. The reference price then applies to all the medicines within these groups of comparable products. In some cases, a generic drug in a particular category may decrease the prices of all comparable therapies, including those still on-patent. This is the case in Germany, where the practice can limit use of on-patent medications that are therapeutically equivalent to lower-cost reference products. That is because patients may have to pay the price difference between the on-patent medicine and the cheaper alternative unless a manufacturer lowers its price to the reference price level [19].

External reference pricing involves using the prices of a medicine in other countries to derive a benchmark price that serves as the basis for further negotiations or pricing decisions. As of 2015, 25 European countries use the mechanism for at least some of the medicines they cover. However, the basket of countries used as a reference varies widely. Countries commonly used in reference pricing decisions include France, Italy, Spain, Germany, and the United Kingdom. Croatia and Greece are also sometimes referenced, but their inclusion is controversial given drug prices in these markets are reduced because of the lower incomes of their citizenries.

A 2013 RAND study suggests that, as a cost-containment strategy, external reference pricing may ultimately have limited impact. That is partly because pharmaceutical companies have responded to the policy by launching their products first in countries with more flexible pricing policies and delaying—or avoiding altogether—countries that would require much lower prices. While that approach avoids any negative effects that might stem from international pricing benchmarks, it has the potential to contribute to drug shortages in certain markets and further complicates the biopharmaceutical industry's reputation as trusted stakeholder [20].

Japan: Direct and Indirect Price Controls   Because of its elderly population and rising chronic disease burden, Japan has also taken a strict line on drug prices as one means of minimizing its health expenditures and the potential pressure on its national debt. One of the government's most prominent initiatives is to increase generic prescribing volume from 52 percent in 2014 to 80 percent by 2020 and to simplify generics pricing, which until 2014 was highly variable. In Japan, generic reimbursement prices are set by the government at a threshold of 70 percent of the branded drug's price or 60 percent if there are more than 10 generic alternatives [21].

Biannual price cuts on products that do not meet an innovation threshold are another mechanism Japan is using to hold the line on drug prices. The government has linked the National Health Insurance (NHI) prices of off-patent medicines to those of generics and will impose statutory price cuts every two years until the rate of generic utilization reaches 60 percent. The country is also contemplating using health technology assessments to re-price already marketed products. If implemented, these assessments will make it harder for biopharma companies to obtain premium pricing for their products unless the medicines are deemed both innovative and cost effective.

At the same time, Japan is taking strides to bolster access to breakthrough medicines. It extended a pilot program started in 2010 that allows premium prices for innovative new medicines and protects them from the biannual price cuts until loss of exclusivity [22].

United States: Prioritizing Value to Control Drug Costs   For now, the highly fragmented US healthcare system remains the most "free" market in terms of access and drug pricing. However, more than 50 percent of US reimbursement is from public payers such as Medicare, Medicaid, the VA, and states. Even here, signs of stress as a result of rising drug costs are evident. A 2017 analysis by the pharmacy benefits manager Express Scripts, which manages prescription utilization for nearly one-third of Americans, estimates price inflation for branded drugs increased 208 percent from 2008 to 2016, compared with a roughly 14 percent increase in the consumer price index during the same period.

As noted, much of this increase was due to greater use of specialty medicines. According to Express Scripts, projected spending on specialty medicines will account for nearly 50 percent of total drug spending in the United States by 2018. To keep a lid on costs and encourage price sensitivity in consumers, payers are piloting new value-based insurance designs; they have also passed along some of their costs to consumers and employers through increased drug co-pays and premiums [23].

Unlike in Europe and Japan, where governments exert some level of pricing control, the US government does not directly negotiate drug pricing via its Medicare and Medicaid programs. US payers and health systems have sought to gain negotiating leverage in this environment by consolidating into larger organizations that have a greater ability to demand price concessions in high cost therapeutic areas. Thus, a wave of acquisitions in the commercial payer space has reshaped their influence in the marketplace, concentrating decision-making power within fewer organizations that represent more Americans [24–26].

Without direct price controls, what has emerged in the United States is a fragmented system in which individual payers or their representatives broker specific deals with biopharma manufacturers to gain a rebate on some portion of the cost of the medicine. In exchange for these rebates, payers give the medicines better positions on their formularies, essentially lists of branded and generic drugs that will be reimbursed by insurance. The better the formulary position, the fewer the market access hurdles for the product, including lower co-pays for patients. As a result of these lower market access barriers, drugs can achieve greater utilization and market share.

Companies typically pay higher rebates—and, thus, have less pricing flexibility—for me-too products in competitive therapeutic areas than they do for first-in-class or best-in-class products, where, traditionally, the reimbursement hurdles have been lower. But even in the United States there are signs that the window of pricing flexibility for best-in-class or first-in-class products is shrinking. Gilead Sciences, for instance, only enjoyed pricing freedom for Sovaldi (sofosbuvir) during its first year on the market when the drug was the sole all-oral hepatitis C regimen. Indeed, on the day a competing product, Viekira Pak (ombitasvir/paritaprevir/ritonavir with dasabuvir), was approved, Express Scripts announced it would no longer cover Gilead's treatment in favor of AbbVie's cheaper product [27]. As a result of its decision, Express Scripts estimated it would save its clients, employers, and some government plans more than $1 billion, while the US healthcare system as a whole would bank more than $4 billion due to an "industry-wide ripple effect" [28].

Increasingly cost constrained, US payers now respond cautiously when determining patient access to new high-priced agents. A case in point is when Praluent (alirocumab) won US regulatory approval in 2015, most payers delayed their coverage decisions until a similar product, Repatha (evolocumab), was approved one month later. In this instance, payers wanted to wait in order to leverage marketplace competition when negotiating access to this class of drugs, which can cost more than $14,000 annually. Since launching, many payers have continued to restrict coverage, even though outcomes studies showed a reduction in the risk of cardiovascular events [29].

COMPETING DEFINITIONS OF PRODUCT VALUE COMPLICATE DRUG PRICING

In most industries, the price of a product reflects its value to the consumer. By and large, the higher the value to consumers, the greater the price. This simple relationship does not hold for drugs. For starters, patients do not necessarily act like consumers (especially when dealing with a debilitating illness). Moreover, patients' notions of value will depend on both their level of medical need and their financial burden.

Thus, a critical challenge when developing balanced pricing strategies is accounting for the different value definitions of stakeholders (Figure 7-3.) It is still true that stakeholders value product efficacy and safety, but, as with improvements in quality of life, these attributes should be considered necessary but not sufficient.

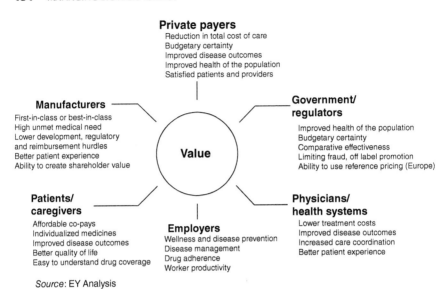

Source: EY Analysis

Figure 7-3   Value is in the eye of the beholder: product attributes stakeholders prioritize

In a world increasingly focused on improved outcomes, the most common and widely agreed-upon components of value include:

- Unmet medical need
- Significant differentiation compared with the standard-of-care
- The ability to subsegment the population most likely to benefit (a topic addressed in Chapter 4)
- Real-world outcomes
- Up-front affordability of the medicine
- Total cost to the healthcare system
- Time required to achieve cost savings

Even in Europe, where health technology assessment organizations delineate value via clinical effectiveness and cost effectiveness, there is no standardized value definition. Not only do the value formulas vary from country to country, but how those formulas are implemented within a given market may be inconsistent. In the United States, where there is even greater payer fragmentation and it has been politically intolerable to use cost-effectiveness measures to determine drug prices, it is even more difficult to reach a universal viewpoint on the subject. That does not mean payers in the United States are disinterested in objective frameworks to define the concept, however. Thus, in 2015, one of the key new developments in the value discussion was the proliferation of third-party tools that compare the efficacy, side effects, and costs of different products (Figure 7-4) [30].

Value Tool (Developer)	Therapeutic Focus	Analysis
ASCO Value Framework (American Society Clinical Oncology)	Selected cancer drugs	▸ Health benefit score facilitates care discussion between provider and patient ▸ Drug cost data presented separately from safety and efficacy data ▸ Not intended for use in coverage decisions ▸ Only allows assessment if treatments have been compared in head-to-head trials
DrugAbacus (Memorial Sloan Kettering Cancer Center)	Selected cancer drugs	▸ Allows stakeholder to define value via six different attributes, including drug cost ▸ Only assesses limited number of drugs in their FDA-approved indications ▸ May facilitate indication-specific pricing
ETAP (Institute for Clinical and Economic Review)	Marketed biopharmaceutical and medtech products	▸ Most similar to European Health Technology Assessment programs ▸ Determines value based on cost-effectiveness threshold and potential budgetary impact ▸ Methods of assessing value not completely transparent
Evidence Blocks (National Comprehensive Care Network)	Drugs to treat specific cancers	▸ Value rated on 1 to 5 scale based on efficacy, safety, affordability, and quality and consistency of evidence ▸ Easy for patients to understand ▸ Designed to facilitate provider-patient conversations about care
RxScoreCard (Real Endpoints)	Marketed and pipeline drugs	▸ Customized value, based on user inputs to create score ▸ Higher scores translate to greater value ▸ Up to 36 different elements used to define value

Source: EY Analysis, public reports.

Figure 7-4   Selected US-based drug valuation tools

While payers and patient advocacy groups in the United States laud these solutions, the different frameworks under development have created analytic challenges for them. As researchers from the Institute for Clinical Research and Health Policy Studies at Tufts Medical Center noted in a November 2015 *New England Journal of Medicine* perspective, "more work is needed to determine how best to consider factors such as adverse events and ancillary benefits that matter to patients" [31].

Ultimately, whether value frameworks originate from health technology assessment organizations or alternative groups, their existence directly affects the pricing of biopharmaceutical products. That is because these different assessments provide credible pricing alternatives that manufacturers must address head on when trying to justify the value of a product. Moreover, in the absence of credible alternative data about product value, payers will use the information gleaned from such tools to demand deeper and deeper discounts in the marketplace. Such payer behavior ultimately limits biopharma value creation, turning drugs into commodities and manufacturers into vendors.

PROVING EFFICACY IN THE REAL WORLD

Although biopharmaceutical companies amass a considerable amount of efficacy data during clinical trials to support regulatory decisions, these data do not necessarily demonstrate real-world value. That requires evidence outside of a clinical trial showcasing improved outcomes against the current standard of care.

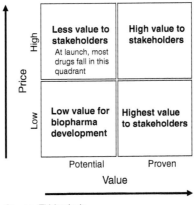

Source: EY Analysis

Figure 7-5   Products have unproven real-world value at launch

With multiple therapeutic options available in almost every drug class, a majority of products now coming to market will be classified as having "potential value" until there is proven evidence. As a result, at launch, many products must bridge a "value gap." As Figure 7-5 illustrates, stakeholders typically categorize newly launched drugs into one of four categories, based on existing data:

- High-price/high-value product
- High-price/low-value product
- Low-price/high-value product
- Low-price/low-value product

Examples of high-price/high-value products include curative therapies such as the all-oral hepatitis C regimens and medicines that provide a step change in the standard of care. These medicines are of high value to stakeholders but, because of the up-front costs, raise concerns about affordability.

High-price/low-value medicines include specialty products that are undifferentiated relative to standard of care or me-too products that offer incremental improvements in efficacy or real-world outcomes. This category may also include chronic disease products that treat broad populations but are not well targeted. Thus, while a given medicine may be very effective in a subsegment of the population, the observed efficacy in the broad population may be underwhelming because a majority of patients are nonresponders. Products in this category are most at risk for pushback from payers and skepticism from providers and patients inasmuch as benefits achieved relative to their costs are harder to determine.

Low-price/high-value products include vaccines and generics and are viewed by stakeholders as having the greatest utility because the benefit/cost ratio is highest. Even products in this category, however, may be susceptible to upfront affordability concerns, depending on the macroeconomic conditions of the market and the number of patients affected.

Low-price/low-value therapeutics, which include over-the-counter medicines and topical ointments, traditionally hold the least value because their therapeutic benefits cannot be broadly attributed across the population. For pharmaceutical manufacturers, these products traditionally have been viewed as the lowest development priority because the likely returns are lower relative to their development and commercial risks.

SETTING THE PRICING STRATEGY

Categorizing a product based on the perception of stakeholders is just one piece in establishing the right global pricing strategy for new biopharma products. To be most effective, companies must also:

- Understand how product and market attributes support—or limit—pricing flexibility
- Refine the pricing analysis, incorporating global-local launch plans
- Link the pricing strategy to the company's overall business strategy

Eight different factors help determine how much pricing flexibility a company has when launching a product. (See Figure 7-6, Figure 7-7, and the text box "Product Factors Determine Pricing Flexibility.")

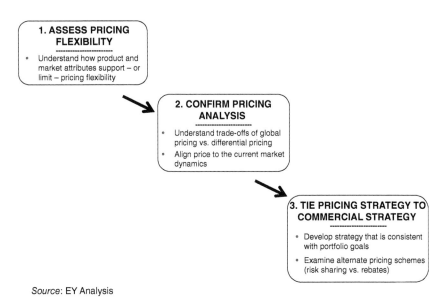

Source: EY Analysis

Figure 7-6   Setting the pricing strategy

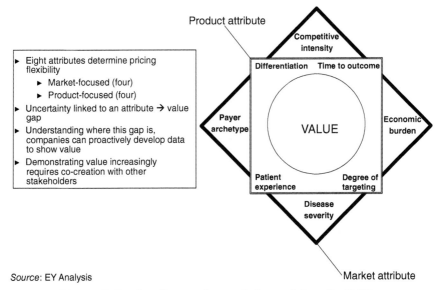

Source: EY Analysis

Figure 7-7   Attributes determining pricing flexibility

Notice that a high degree of uncertainty around any one attribute increases stakeholder skepticism or real-world utility and, thus, the likelihood that there will be a value gap at product launch. By understanding which factor results in the greatest uncertainty, a company can proactively develop data to maximize pricing flexibility. In effect, this attribute becomes the fulcrum for stakeholder engagement around new pricing models, described later in this chapter.

PRODUCT FACTORS DETERMINE PRICING FLEXIBILITY

Given the current complexity of drug pricing and the diversity of payer types, it is difficult to rank order the factors in Figure 7-7 in a decision tree that holds true across all therapeutic areas. Depending on severity of the disease, the total projected costs of treating the indication, and the market competition, certain attributes will be more central than others.

Intuitively, a product that provides a broadly recognized step change in care should also have greater pricing flexibility than a medicine that offers an incremental benefit. However, this flexibility will be affected by other factors, such as the time to outcome and the economic burden of the disease. Therapies that require a longer time to demonstrate a real-world outcome, including demonstrable cost-offsets, will be subjected to more stakeholder skepticism than products that demonstrate outcomes quickly. Similarly, the greater the upfront costs to other healthcare stakeholders, regardless of the demonstrated outcomes, the higher the likelihood that pricing decisions will generate scrutiny. This has been the case for the all-oral hepatitis C regimens that provide up to 99 percent cure rates.

In addition, the greater the number of competing products that can be viewed as comparable therapies, referred to as competitive intensity, the more pricing flexibility is limited. This is especially true for later entrants. Traditionally, biopharma companies have chosen to benchmark their products against comparators that work by the same mechanism of action. In a value-oriented environment, companies must be mechanism-of-action agnostic, instead choosing the comparator that currently provides the best health outcome. This may mean choosing a comparator that is a device or, in the future, a digital app.

Unsurprisingly, products that use precision medicine tools (described in Chapter 4) to narrow the population from all-comers to the highest responders have greater pricing flexibility. Such targeting not only improves outcomes but addresses the budgetary concerns of payer stakeholders. So do medicines treating more severe diseases given the high level of unmet patient need.

Patient-centric attributes, for example, a dosing schedule that facilitates adherence to the treatment regimen, are important factors to consider. However, companies should expect that traditional payers will not prioritize these factors unless there are accompanying real-world data demonstrating improved outcomes.

Finally, the nature of the payer is another critical issue to consider. As explained in more detail in Chapter 8, different types of payers are motivated to make different coverage decisions based on their individual preferences and constraints, including the market dynamics in which they operate. In the United States, for example, Medicaid payers are focused on up-front medication costs because of fixed budgets. Integrated delivery networks, however, might be less sensitive to up-front costs if the medicine results in credible cost offsets in an acceptable period of time. Because integrated delivery networks traditionally keep their members for long periods of time, this particular type of payer may have more flexibility on the time-to-outcome parameter than a traditional commercial payer who will have the patient as a member for only one or two years.

Companies must also refine the analysis relative to the list prices of currently available products and set the product's maximum and minimum prices around the globe. Setting this so-called global price band is as much an art as it is a science. Increasingly, stakeholders are willing to embrace "good enough" innovation if products satisfy basic safety and efficacy requirements but come with lower price tags. This is the value proposition associated with biosimilars and the second and third entrants in the all-oral hepatitis C category.

Moreover, if companies set a price band that is too wide (i.e., there is a big differential between the product's maximum and minimum prices), the company puts its ability to maximize its profits at risk due to reference pricing and parallel trade practices. If the band is too narrow, however, the company may also reduce its global profits because the price range may be unaffordable in certain geographies, ultimately limiting market penetration.

What companies therefore strive to achieve is a price spread that is neither too wide nor too narrow. Within this global price band, regional price bands for major markets (such as the European Union, the United States, and Asia) will exist. Because of external reference pricing, the European price band continues to tighten. The US price band has been more elastic historically; as this market becomes more price sensitive, there may be closer alignment between the maximum price in the United States and in Europe. Asia, meanwhile, continues to have the widest price band as a result of differences in national pricing policies and purchasing power [32].

Finally, successful biopharma companies also strive to link their individual product pricing decisions with the overall business strategy, including assessing downstream consequences on the uptake of other medicines in the portfolio. For instance, the greater a product's importance to a company's overall portfolio, the greater the pressure to accelerate market share and close any existing value gap quickly.

In addition, as more products are used in combination, it will be important for companies to harmonize individual pricing decisions across the portfolio to create a coordinated commercial strategy. Analyzing pricing decisions across a product portfolio enables companies to align product-centric assessments with overarching strategic choices. These include the decision to invest in one business unit rather than another or the potential value creation that might come from divestiture.

ANALYZING NEW PRICING MODELS

Increasingly, product pricing will shift from being a contractual, transactional event to one step in a long-term relationship that redistributes reimbursement risk and is influenced by stakeholder definitions of value that prioritize total costs to the healthcare system in question. Going forward, that means proof of outcomes will be required if biopharma products are to achieve maximum pricing flexibility. Thus, pricing approaches of the future will require companies to work with other stakeholders, especially payers, to co-create data to bridge the value gap. As Len Schleifer, the CEO of Regeneron Pharmaceuticals told the audience at the 2015 Forbes Healthcare Summit, as an industry "we have to think about a different pricing approach that is a little bit more responsible" [33].

These innovative pricing models, which may also be known as managed entry agreements, risk-sharing agreements, outcomes-based contracts, or value-based contracts, generally exhibit the following characteristics:

- The product's price or reimbursement level is linked to an outcome.
- To demonstrate this outcome, drug manufacturers and payers must collect real-world data for some prespecified period of time.
- These data address uncertainties associated with the product's utility outside clinical trials. These uncertainties could be related to efficacy, safety, or the size and value of future cost savings achieved as a result of the drug's usage in a given patient population.

According to researchers at the University of Washington, as of the date of publication, the number of innovative agreements that share product risk is modest, numbering in the hundreds over a two-decade span. Since many of these deals are confidential, it is hard to get accurate numbers. Still, most of these arrangements have been brokered in Europe, where payer austerity and monopsony governments have forced biopharmas to embrace more creative pricing strategies. In Italy, for example, access to most high-priced oncology products requires some kind of pay-for-performance arrangement that requires monitoring via patient registries. In the United Kingdom, financially based risk-sharing agreements are the preferred approach. In the United States, there has been more limited experimentation with innovative pricing due to concerns that novel pricing arrangements would jeopardize government contracts and regulations related to Medicaid prices [34].

The need to broker individual contracts with each payer means these innovative pricing arrangements are both complicated to set up and hard to scale. Both parties must agree, for instance, on the length of time of the arrangement, the data that should be collected and analyzed, and the financial stakes. The need to invest in infrastructure to collect and analyze these data, as well as uncertainty tied to when product revenues can be recognized, are also material barriers to the adoption of novel pricing strategies. Examples of new pricing solutions are summarized in Figure 7-8.

A key factor influencing how fast new pricing models are adopted is new kinds of payers, a topic that is addressed in Chapter 8. In the future, payers will not only be governments or private insurers. Increasingly, physician groups and other providers that are at-risk financially for their prescribing decisions will also by buyers; so will patients themselves. This may add complexity to the payer landscape, but it also presents opportunities for pharma to try out new models with payers whose priorities may be more directly aligned with clinical outcomes.

Solution (Use in marketplace)	Definition	Example
Indication-specific pricing (Emerging)	Differential pricing for a product depending on its performance in specific indications (e.g., lung cancer vs. head and neck cancer)	Express Scripts is piloting a program to test indication specific pricing in United States
Bundled payment (High for procedures and physician services; emerging for therapeutics)	A global payment for all treatment costs including prescription drugs	UnitedHealthcare Group has partnered with multiple physician groups to test the model in oncology
Financial-based risk sharing (Higher in Europe; Emerging in United States)	Designed to provide budgetary certainty to payer via agreements that link price to utilization (oither via script volume or drug dosage)	Gilead Sciences and the government of France agreed to a volume-based cap on Sovaldi in 2014
Performance-based risk sharing (PBA) (Medium usage in Europe; Emerging in United States)	Designed to manage utilization and/or provide evidence of drug efficacy; emphasize clinical outcomes	Bristol-Myers Squibb and the Italian government set up a PBA around Yervoy, in which BMS rebates the full price of the product if a patient fails to respond in a specified time period
Annuity models (Emerging)	Debt financing instrument that covers the acquisition cost of a breakthrough biopharmaceutical product. Can be structured as a bond, mortgage, or credit line. Will include some kind of pay-for-outcome requirement.	Health impact bonds have been structured to improve care delivery of chronic diseases such as asthma. Life sciences companies have not participated extensively to date.

Source: EY Analysis

Figure 7-8   New pricing solutions emphasize real world outcomes

DRUG PRICING IN THE UNITED STATES: THE PRESSURE CONTINUES TO BUILD

By Susan Garfield, Market Access Principal, EY

Concerns about drug pricing in the United States have reached new highs in the media, in the political arena, and among consumers. The United States is unique in its system of relatively free pricing with few controls, collective bargaining, and a mostly market driven approach. Many of the evolving innovative pricing schemes presented in this chapter represent the first step in the reenvisioning of how to align price and value. Moving forward, stakeholder alignment around value-based healthcare will change pricing methods and outcomes. Health systems will leverage real-world evidence sources to better understand the best systems of care, and what value specific drugs deliver within those systems.

Additionally, as treatments become more personalized, so too will the ability of payment systems to evaluate the benefits of treatment paradigms at the individual level. While today coverage and access are provided at the population level for most products and services, in the near future access may be defined by particular genetic makeup, predicted response rate to therapy, family history, or the expertise of the care setting within which one wants to be treated. Put together, these factors represent significant opportunities to evolve our thinking on pricing paradigms. While personalized medicine has not yet translated to personalized pricing, stakeholders are already looking at the implications of this possible future state. For now, it is clear that biopharmas are increasingly aware of the need to change the way they have historically thought about pricing. They are starting to embrace innovative partnerships to deliver value and will be increasingly rethinking their role in the value chain, moving from solo actors to integrated parts of the value continuum.

Today, however, the public protests are real and future change paradigms are not likely to pacify those who believe drugs are too expensive and drug pricing is an unmanaged problem. In the near term, we may see a renewed interest in the government directly negotiating for drugs used in Medicare and other programs. We are also likely to see increased pricing activity at the state level, as legislatures and local constituencies take up the issue on their own and work to address perceived rising costs.

Alongside policy changes and regulatory controls, it is likely that other actors in the drug value chain will be examined more closely. Groups like pharmacy benefit managers (PBMs), group purchasing organizations (GPOs), and specialty pharmacies all play into the end cost of drugs, but very few stakeholders understand their role or the potential value they deliver. As such, pressure is mounting to demonstrate value and rationalize why intermediaries are necessary, especially as large data resources become more ubiquitous and accessible by payers and other direct stakeholders. Further, a value- or outcomes-based payment model for healthcare will drive the need to look at care costs more holistically, including both drug and non-drug interventions.

Ultimately, a rationalization of expenditures is coming. Whether via increased pressures placed on manufacturers directly by payers, or via changes in the structural value chain that reallocate costs among fewer actors, drug pricing is undergoing significant change. As a result, companies must focus attention and resources on partnership models that enhance the value of the drugs they are developing and provide opportunities to be part of the evolving pricing policy debate. Partnerships are likely to include various companies from the technology, financial, data, and scientific communities coming together to help define and deliver value-based care. Biopharmaceutical companies have a role in creating this future state that adequately rewards innovation with a reasonable pricing model, while also allocating scarce resources more rationally.

DEPLOYMENT OF NEW PRICING STRATEGIES

Figure 7-9 arrays innovative pricing solutions based on their complexity and maturity in the marketplace. So-called financial-based agreements (FBAs) represent the majority of the innovative pricing models currently being used in the marketplace. That is because these contracts are among the least complex to implement since they are not associated with complicated monetary clawbacks related to a drug's performance. In addition, such deals also provide budgetary certainty, an important benchmark in a resource-constrained environment.

AstraZeneca's single payment access strategy for Iressa (gefitinib) is a classic example of how biopharma companies can use these financial agreements to enable market access (see the text box, "AstraZeneca's Single Payment Access Strategy for Iressa"). A more recent example is the deal Gilead Sciences brokered in 2014 with the government of France to establish access to its hepatitis C medicine, Sovaldi. At the time, the French government threatened to tax Gilead if it insisted on maintaining the original price tag of Sovaldi; however, Gilead agreed to reduce the cost of the

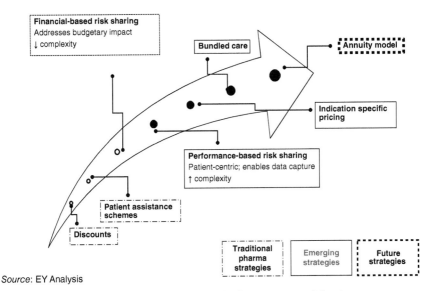

Source: EY Analysis

**Figure 7-9   Redistributing reimbursement risk via new
pricing solutions**

therapy by roughly €15,000, in exchange for no patient co-pays. Gilead also agreed to a volume-based cap on the use of the medicine; thus, if the number of patients exceeded a pre-agreed-upon level, the price of Sovaldi would drop even lower. Both of these conditions helped the French Ministry of Health project the costs it would incur for providing its estimated 200,000 hepatitis C–infected citizens access to a life-saving medicine [35].

ASTRAZENECA'S SINGLE PAYMENT ACCESS STRATEGY FOR IRESSA

The single payment access (SPA) scheme AstraZeneca constructed for its lung cancer drug Iressa (gefitinib) in the United Kingdom in 2010 represents one strategy biopharma companies can employ. As part of the agreement with the National Health Service (NHS), AstraZeneca provided UK-based patients with the first two months of Iressa for free and then as much of the drug as they needed for a fixed payment.

Structuring the SPA for Iressa in this way, AstraZeneca made it easy for the NHS to calculate how much the product would cost annually, without the need for tightly monitoring patient response rates via claims or patient data. Moreover, if patients remained on the drug for at least five months, the NHS stood to save money, at least related to the published list price for the medicine. Real-world data presented in 2012 at the International Society for Pharmacoeconomics and Outcomes Research (ISPOR) conference seemed to confirm the positive economics of the payment scheme: on average, more than 250 patients remained on the therapy for at least 12 months [36,37].

While financial-based agreements shift the reimbursement risk slightly, in many respects they are simply a slightly different spin on straightforward rebates already used in the marketplace. More interesting are performance-based agreements (PBAs), which are designed to manage patient utilization and provide additional product efficacy data. Since Johnson & Johnson negotiated its PBA for Velcade (bortezomib) in 2007, PBAs have been much discussed as a mechanism payers and biopharma companies can use to enable outcomes-based pricing [38].

These kinds of deals have remained rare in the United States and Europe, however, due to the practical hurdles discussed above. As Steve Miller, the chief medical officer of Express Scripts put it, over the course of the last several years, the industry has seen multiple attempts at outcomes-based reimbursement "but most have collapsed under their own weight" [39].

But with drug spending on an unsustainable upward trajectory, payers and drug companies now have increased motivation to make value-based contracts work. In late 2015, both CVS Health Corp. and Harvard Pilgrim, a regional payer based in Massachusetts, announced value-based contracts that give Amgen's Repatha (evolocumab) preferred formulary status in exchange for outcomes- and utilization-based discounts. Entresto (sacubitril/valsartan), a first-in-class therapy to treat congestive heart failure manufactured by Novartis, is another product that has used outcomes-based deals to enable market access. Aetna, Cigna, and Harvard Pilgrim have all signed novel contracts around the drug, which has mounted slower-than-anticipated sales due to reimbursement delays. These examples, though still relatively few in number and limited to opportunities where there is significant product competition, represent an important shift in product pricing strategy [40,41].

By themselves, however, they will not drive a meaningful shift to value-based reimbursement. That is because few of the existing performance-based contracts risk much—either for the payer or the pharma. Moreover, because performance-based contracts are typically structured between a specific payer and manufacturer, it is difficult to expand their use to additional payers and at-risk providers quickly. Ultimately, that makes it challenging to share best practices and lessons learned that would more broadly accelerate the shift to value-based reimbursement in the current regulatory environment.

So-called "Value Labs" are structured collaborations among manufacturers, payers, healthcare systems, data providers, and adjudicators and represent one way to explore value-based contracts in a safe forum. Inherently multistakeholder, Value Labs promote experimentation while mitigating known pain points, such as defining and measuring outcomes and building systems to share data. It is important to note there will not be one Value Lab, but many. Depending on the therapeutic area, different stakeholders will need to be involved. Emerging experiments, such as the Learning Lab created by Merck & Co. Inc. and United-Health Group's Optum division to explore various value constructs, are examples of the trend [42].

EXPERIMENTAL PRICING STRATEGIES

Payers and providers are also experimenting with other solutions that prioritize paying for outcomes while providing patients accessibility to innovative, but potentially pricey, prescription drugs. Two approaches that are worth watching: indication-specific pricing and bundled payment models.

Indication-Specific Pricing

As biopharma companies have shifted their drug development away from primary care drugs used in broad populations to specialty medicines administered to much smaller numbers, development strategies have shifted. Companies still want to produce blockbusters, but the goal is to grow a blockbuster by gaining approval in multiple, different indications. The issue is a given drug will not provide the same benefits, and, therefore the same value, to payer and physician stakeholders across the various diseases for which its utilization is approved. In oncology, for example, the same drug may be used across a range of different cancers (e.g., breast cancer and gastric cancer) or subpopulations (e.g., the presence of absence of a specific biomarker such as EGFR expression). But the outcomes are often widely different.

For payers and providers, this can mean paying very high prices for poor or no results, while also exposing patients to unnecessary side effects. This realization has led some payers to test various flavors of indication-specific pricing [43,44].

Indication-specific pricing is not itself a new concept. It has been used in the past on a limited basis when drugs have utility in very different indications and can be formulated to create distinct medicines with their own brands and pricing strategies. For example, in 1998, Pfizer launched Viagra (sildenafil) for male erectile dysfunction; in 2005, the treatment was proven effective as a treatment for pulmonary arterial hypertension and Pfizer began marketing it under the new brand, Revatio. Similarly, Sanofi and its partner Regeneron developed and market the tyrosine kinase inhibitor aflibercept as two separate products under the brand names Eylea (for treatment of the wet form of age-related macular degeneration and other ophthalmic conditions) and Zaltrap (for treatment of colorectal cancer). The average net price per milligram of Eylea is about 60 times higher than that of Zaltrap [45–47].

The truth is, examples such as Viagra/Revatio and Eylea/Zaltrap are the exception rather than the rule. Most of the time it is not feasible to create two distinct product labels and brands with different dosing and pricing parameters, and that makes implementing indication-specific pricing much more complex. Payers and manufacturers must agree to preset reimbursement for different indications. They must also develop the data collection infrastructure to link drug use to specific known indications, which is challenging, especially in the United States, where most payers receive claims data that show what drug was prescribed but not why.

One way to reduce the administrative hurdles associated with indication-specific pricing is to create a single "weighted-average" price that takes into account estimates of indication use across the member population of a payer. Theoretical and actual use are then reconciled via rebates administered retrospectively at some predetermined time, say once annually. This type of approach has been used in England, Germany, and Italy, but the nonprofit research Institute for Clinical and Economic Review (ICER) called it "virgin territory" in the United States, given "robust data are still required for a retrospective review of claims" and the impact on government pricing models (e.g., Medicaid) is "unclear." Indeed, in a March 2016 report, ICER reported that successful indication-specific pricing models hinge on two key criteria: picking the right therapeutic situation and having a like-minded collaborator [48]. Given these uncertainties and the potential business risks associated with rapid embrace of this new pricing model, it seems likely that manufacturers will aim to first participate in individual pilots before broadly adopting the model.

One pilot that manufacturers and US payers are watching closely is the 2016 partnership between pharmacy benefits manager Express Scripts and Memorial Sloan Kettering Cancer Center to use indication-specific pricing for three oncology drugs on the PBM's 2016 preferred formulary. As part of the pilot, Express Scripts will pay different prices for a single drug, depending on how it performs in different tumor types. Which drugs are subject to the novel pricing model have not been disclosed, nor have preliminary results [49].

Urgency is growing in the payer community, however, to use new models to blunt the high costs of cancer treatments. A May 2016 analysis published in *Health Affairs* found that product competition, a situation that has limited pricing flexibility for hepatitis C and diabetes treatments, has thus far had little impact on oncology drug prices. Indeed, the researchers found that the costs of cancer medicines increased more than 5 percent annually above inflation from 2007 to 2013; however, direct competition for new cancer drugs only lowered their average monthly costs by 2 percent [50].

Bundled Payment Models

In other industries, consumers pay a single price for a desired package of goods or services. For instance, when customers buy a car or smartphone, they generally do not pay separate fees to separate manufacturers for the individual components; instead, they pay a single, fixed fee to a single entity for an all-inclusive experience. That is not usually the case in healthcare, where fee-for-service reimbursement systems mean patients receiving care from different physician groups or parts of a health system are billed for each individual interaction (e.g., the lab facility for diagnostic tests, the hospital for in-patient care, and the rehabilitation center for outpatient follow-up).

Currently, there is recognition that so-called bundled payments, where all drugs, devices, tests, and services required to treat a given condition are bundled into a single fee, is another mechanism that rewards outcomes delivered rather than volume of services rendered. Because bundled payments provide fixed reimbursement sums, they encourage providers to adhere to standardized treatment protocols that provide the most cost-effective care and the most efficient delivery, often via integrated, multidisciplinary practice units. If appropriately structured, bundled payments can also promote patient centricity, a topic discussed in Chapter 6, since the bundles of services and the outcomes achieved can be defined based on patient priorities, for instance, delivering a healthy child or reducing pain [51].

Much like indication-specific pricing, the concept is not new: bundled payments have been used to pay for care in certain niche areas such as organ transplantation and in self-pay scenarios, such as plastic surgery and in vitro fertilization, where patients pay for all the care out of pocket. There are currently a handful of bundled payment success stories, and evidence shows that the approach does not simply bend the cost curve downward but actually results in meaningful cost reductions. Thus, interest in implementing the concept is high across different countries, types of organizations, and therapeutic areas. In 2011, the Centers for Medicare and Medicaid Services (CMS) embraced the approach as a means of reducing costs and improving the quality of care associated with end-stage renal disease and has, via the Affordable Care Act, created a voluntary Bundled Payments for Care Improvement initiative that includes more than 14,000 bundles in 48 medical and surgical conditions. In 2016, CMS launched a mandatory bundled payment program for joint replacements covering 800 hospitals in more than 60 US metropolitan areas (Figure 7-10) [52,53].

Country	Pilot (Year initiated)	Analysis
Netherlands	Type 2 diabetes pilot (2007)	Covers a full range of diabetes-care services for one year, excluding certain complications. Lower cost of care and improved outcomes resulted from reduction in unnecessary services and prioritization of high-risk patients.
Sweden	County of Stockholm knee and hip replacement pilot (2009)	Over two years, reduced treatment costs by 17% and complication rate by 33%. Program expanded to include all major spine diagnoses requiring surgery.
United States	Acute Care Episode program (2009)	Bundled hospital and physician care for cardiac and orthopedic services, generating average projected savings to Medicare of 3.1%.
United States	Bundled Payments for Care Improvement (BCPI) (2011)	Creates bundled payments for 48 medical and surgical conditions. In 2016, bundled payments for joint replacements became mandatory in approximately 800 hospitals.
United States	Oncology episode-based payment model (2009)	Pilot tests use of bundled payments in breast, lung, and colon cancer. Reduced cancer costs by 34% compared with the control group, even though chemotherapy costs increased 179%. Pilot expanded in 2015.

Source: EY Analysis

Figure 7-10   Selected bundled payment experiments

Still, there remains skepticism that bundled payment models can be used outside acute settings, because defining which products and services are included in the bundle—and which are not—is significantly more complicated when treating chronic conditions such as diabetes or chronic obstructive pulmonary disease. Time-based bundles are one solution; providers and payer groups define the scope of services and products provided (also known as the episode of care) based on a discreet time span, say three months or one year. UnitedHealth Group, one of the largest commercial payers in the United States, sought to test the limits of this approach in a three-year pilot of more than 800 breast, lung, and colon cancer patients treated at five community oncology practices. The results, which were published in 2014, showed that a bundled payment approaches could reduce overall cancer treatment costs by 34 percent without affecting quality. Interestingly, the results seemed to suggest that improving the efficiency of care delivery, not reining in drug spending, is the best opportunity for cost savings (see text box, "Lessons from UnitedHealthcare's Bundled Payment Program in Oncology") [54,55].

Theoretically, the implementation of bundled payment models should put downward pressure on drug costs. Under this system, if cheaper generics provide the same outcomes as costlier branded medicines, physicians have no compelling reason to use the more expensive products. Moreover, with a fixed price for all goods and services in a defined cycle of care, providers and payers also have incentives to try and negotiate lower drug prices. Drug manufacturers, meanwhile, may be willing to provide rebates if they fear their medicines will not be prescribed because of cost.

For now, it is hard to know the full impact of bundled payment models on drug pricing. In its pilot, UnitedHealth did not include the drug costs in the overall bundle but reimbursed them separately. Moreover, it is clear that bundled payments work best in situations where clinical behavior is tightly controlled, so that care pathways are aligned around standardized treatment protocols. The administrative burden for such efforts remains high and the payout may only come years down the road. Employers are one group that may play a more forceful role in driving these experiments, a topic addressed in Chapter 8.

LESSONS FROM UNITEDHEALTHCARE'S BUNDLED PAYMENT PROGRAM IN ONCOLOGY

In 2009, UnitedHealthcare launched a pilot to test whether a time-based bundled payment approach could reduce the overall medical costs associated with the treatment of breast, lung, and colon cancer. Interestingly, a number of services or products were not included in the bundle: physician office visits, chemotherapy administration fees, and diagnostics were all reimbursed on a fee-for-service basis. Drug prices were not included in the bundle either; instead, UnitedHealth paid the average sales price for drugs, eliminating the 6 percent markup physicians charged under the so-called buy-and-bill program for physician-administered injectable and infused medicines. In 2014, the payer reported that shifting to an episode-of-care payment model had no impact on patient care. Medical expenditures were another story, even though some services were still paid via fee-for-service. Indeed, for this pool of patients, the total cost of care decreased by 34 percent, approximately $40,000 per patient.

Interestingly, the cost savings did not come from reduced spending on cancer drugs but appeared to result from lower hospitalization rates and reduced use of radiation therapy. Indeed, chemotherapy costs actually increased 179 percent during the pilot. This statistic seems to showcase a tenet biopharma executives have long maintained: drugs, even when expensive, can be one of the most cost-effective therapeutic options if they prevent or eliminate other costly types of care, especially emergency department visits and hospitalizations.

In order to better understand why the approach yielded cost-savings, United announced plans to expand the pilot, tripling the number of participating practices [56,57].

FINANCING THE FUTURE: AFFORDABILITY

While new payment models like UnitedHealth's bundled care experiment or Harvard Pilgrim's outcomes-based deal for Repatha make product pricing less transactional and more collaborative, the agreements fail to solve one of the most urgent issues payers face currently: near-term affordability. Indeed, as noted earlier, the most pressing issue related to Sovaldi has not been tied to concerns about the efficacy or cost effectiveness of the product but its upfront cost. Concerns about near-term affordability are also coming to a head because scientific advances make possible the creation of curative, one-time therapies for grievous rare diseases such as thalassemias or severe combined immunodeficiency. As researchers at RAND noted, this has created a dilemma for payers and policymakers: "Make treatment available and accept high short-term costs with the expectation of long-term savings or insist on budget discipline, forgo clinical benefit and long-term savings, and anger affected populations" [58].

Because neither option is particularly attractive, the RAND team proposed a third way: using debt-financing instruments to cover the acquisition cost of a breakthrough biopharmaceutical product. The instrument could be structured in various ways—as a bond, as a mortgage, or even as a credit line with fixed monthly payments. To make sure that such instruments did not simply result in a scenario that resulted in payment regardless of the results, the RAND team proposed linking ongoing reimbursement to demonstrations of real-world efficacy.

In a separate analysis, a team of researchers from the Massachusetts Institute of Technology and the Dana-Farber Cancer Institute have proposed the creation of consumer-focused healthcare loans that would be financed by investors who purchased bonds or equities issued by the organization that issued the credit. In essence, consumers who need expensive but curative therapies could take out loans to cover their co-payments from a special entity created to fund expensive drug purchases. The loan repayment would be amortized over time, similar to a car or house payment or student loan debt. The loan underwriter, meantime, would be financed by a pool of investors that purchased bonds and equities it had issued [59].

Currently, no payer or manufacturer has brokered either type of financing alliance. All of the uncertainties associated with other innovative pricing models remain—risks linked to data capture, revenue recognition, and best-pricing regulations. Moreover, structuring the debt correctly will require new capabilities such as cost-of-illness modelling, statistical analysis, and a deep understanding of financial products. Nevertheless, for high-cost, curative therapies for rare diseases, the financing model may soon emerge as an important alternative to other pricing strategies.

NEW TOOLS FOR OUTCOMES-DATA CAPTURE

As outcome-based pricing experiments become more common, both payers and biopharma manufacturers will need to adapt their business model and acquire new capabilities. In particular, manufacturers will need to leverage new digital and analytics tools, topics discussed in Chapters 9 and 10, to capture real-world data linked to outcomes. These data must be easy and inexpensive to measure and accumulate over a time frame that is consistent with payers' budget cycles. Process-based endpoints, for example, hospitalizations, are one of the easiest endpoints around which both parties can find common ground, inasmuch as such information is routinely collected via existing health claims and does not require mining individual patient records for unstructured clinical data. In the future, however, drug companies and payers will also be able to utilize new wearable and remote-sensor devices linked to smartphone or tablet applications to demonstrate product value.

For new outcomes-based partnerships to be successful, the partners must also agree up-front on the following: standard definitions of what is—or is not—an outcome and the party responsible for collecting and monitoring the data related to this outcome. Because trust between healthcare stakeholders is not high, it may be important for a neutral party to confirm the authenticity of the data and compliance with the outcome-based partnership. Drug manufacturers, meanwhile, may need to add actuarial capabilities so they have a better understanding a priori of what risks they can sensibly own, or not. Because revenue flows may change significantly under an outcomes-based partnership, biopharma companies will also need to alter their revenue forecasting methods. Finally, companies will need to educate and convince their shareholders that showing flexibility on the timing of revenues is a worthwhile compromise that builds healthier stakeholder relationships and avoids far more damaging scenarios such as mandated price controls.

CONCLUSION

The current debate about drug pricing requires that drug companies embrace different models now, when the risks are lower and there is an opportunity to be an active partner. Payers, even in the United States, are not waiting for companies to demonstrate value but are defining it themselves, using newly available tools to provide alternative definitions of worth that may or may not reflect the value assessments of patients. Absent credible data about product value, payers will use the information gleaned from such tools to demand deeper and deeper discounts in the marketplace. Such payer behaviors ultimately limit biopharma value creation, turning drugs into commodities and manufacturers into vendors. If biopharma companies want to shift their market access negotiations from price to value, and be engaged members of the ecosystem, they will have to alter their pricing strategies, putting greater emphasis on strategic payer engagement, a topic addressed in the Chapter 8.

SUMMARY POINTS

- Drugs remain one of the most efficient ways to deliver improved healthcare outcomes. However, drug pricing and its impact on the long-term sustainability of healthcare stakeholders remains a hotly debated topic and a target of government reforms. It is a top strategic issue for biopharma management teams.

- Market-specific reforms have resulted in markedly different pricing regulations around the world. It is therefore essential that biopharma companies adopt a global-local mentality, setting global pricing strategies that, because they are deployed locally, address the price sensitivities of the market in question.

- Consolidation among payers and providers will further pressure drug prices as these groups have more leverage in the marketplace because of the greater number of lives they manage.

- While all stakeholders value efficacy and safety, new determinants of value have emerged. These include the degree of targeting, real-word outcomes, up-front affordability, and, most especially, the total cost to the health system.
- When setting a price, companies must adopt a systematic approach that optimizes pricing flexibility in specific markets and takes into account newly emerged definitions of stakeholder value.
- Commercial teams need to fully investigate and understand which product attributes are most likely to have the greatest impact on patients and on patient outcomes, and thus on the ability of a biopharma to achieve maximum pricing flexibility at launch.
- Biopharma companies need to accept and embrace novel pricing structures that distribute reimbursement risk in closer alignment with the outcomes delivered. This will also improve their reputations with other stakeholders.
- Such novel value-based pricing arrangements are difficult to construct because of the need to invest in infrastructure to capture, analyze, and share data.
- Emerging digital tools that conveniently capture relevant real-world data of interest to biopharma companies, patients, and payers will be a critical enabler of these new value-based pricing models in the future.

CHAPTER 8

STRATEGIC PAYER ENGAGEMENT

In any sector, knowing the customer is key to commercial success. While payers are not the end users of drugmakers' products, they are among their most important partners. That is because their coverage and reimbursement decisions determine which patients will have access to their medicines. Biopharma has traditionally viewed physicians as their customers, not payers or indeed patients. However, this is changing as the costs of medicines rise, and as patients' roles in drug discovery, development, and access grow as a result of new patient-centered digital tools (see Chapter 6). Smart, sensor-enabled devices, combined with behavioral reminders, make it possible for consumers to proactively manage their own health and they are increasingly trying to understand which tools provide the greatest return on investment. In this context, payers, as broadly defined, are the gatekeepers.

PAYERS ARE NOT ALL ALIKE

The challenge for biopharma is that there is a wide range of payer types, each with different structures, preferences, and priorities. Some of this variation is determined by the country or region in which they operate: a European state payer, for example, works differently than a national US commercial payer, which in turn functions differently from a regionally based employer that self-insures its workforce. But even within a single nation or region, no two payers will look the same. They may cover different demographics and vary in their economic incentives, budgetary flexibility, profit motives, and, for commercial payers, in the medical benefits they offer their customers. A US payer that offers prescription drug coverage to citizens that qualify for Medicare, for instance, is looking solely to minimize drug costs and not to curb other medical expenses, while a private insurer offering full medical coverage to a 40-year-old individual may be

Managing Biotechnology: From Science to Market in the Digital Age, First Edition. Françoise Simon and Glen Giovannetti.
© 2017 John Wiley & Sons, Inc. Published 2017 by John Wiley & Sons, Inc.

more open to paying slightly more for a drug that is shown to reduce downstream complications, such as surgery.

In Europe, governments are the principal payers: most countries have taxpayer-funded national or regional health systems covering all or most of the population. In the United States, in contrast, federal and state government health spending accounts for less than half of overall health expenditure [1]. A patchwork of private (mostly for-profit) payers, intermediaries, and households make up the rest.

Nongovernment US payers can be broadly grouped into commercial insurers, such as UnitedHealthcare and Aetna, which sell health insurance plans to employers or individuals; pharmacy benefit managers (PBMs) such as Express Scripts, which manage coverage of pharmaceuticals, including negotiating pricing and access on behalf of health plans; and integrated delivery networks such as Kaiser Permanente, which comprise hospitals, physician groups, an insurer, and (often) a prescription drug purchaser all-in-one. Large employers are also increasingly behaving as payers. As workers' health costs become a more significant budget item, more companies are running their own health insurance for employees, including contracting directly with certain providers, thereby gaining greater control and leverage over component costs (Figure 8-1).

These players do not operate in isolation: they may interact in a variety of ways within a regional market that influences access to medicines. Moreover, any one payer may embrace multiple models simultaneously. For example, an insurer may administer only the medical claims for companies that prefer to manage their own drug spending (or negotiate with a PBM themselves), while managing both medical and drug benefit for other customers. Similarly, commercial insurers may manage Medicare/Medicaid-covered lives on behalf of the US government, as well as privately insured individuals or employees. The European payer landscape is somewhat less complex but also far from homogenous.

- **US Government:** Coverage via **Medicare** (seniors), **Medicaid** (low-income individuals), and **Veteran's Health Administration** (veterans). Medicare Part A covers hospital-based care, Part B covers doctors' visits and outpatient care, while Part D covers prescription drugs. Medicaid pays "best price" for drugs, defined as the lowest price paid by any purchaser.

- **Commercial Insurers:** Provide health plans to employers or individuals. Most are for-profit entities.

- **Pharmacy Benefit Managers:** Negotiate for prescription drugs on behalf of health plans.

- **Integrated Delivery Networks:** Combine health delivery and insurance in a coordinated care network. Have historically focused on wellness, disease prevention, and evidence-based care for patient members.

- **Employers:** Now designing their own health insurance programs to better control costs and incentives. May partner with commercial insurers for plan administration.

- **Providers:** Hospitals and physician practices (individuals or groups) in health systems that bear financial and cost-management responsibilities.

- **Individuals:** Individual households pay for a growing portion of their healthcare costs via insurance premiums, co-pays, and deductibles.

Source: EY Analysis

Figure 8-1 Key US payer types

NEW MARKET FORCES INCREASE PAYER POWER

This patchwork of payers, in addition to being complex, is constantly changing as the legislative, economic and competitive landscapes evolve. Escalating healthcare costs and the growth of high-priced, specialty drugs have driven aggressive drug price negotiations and coverage decisions among most payers in the United States, Europe, and beyond [2]. In the United States, the 2010 Affordable Care Act (ACA) catalyzed a shift toward paying for value, rather than volume, as well as expanding access to insurance across a wider portion of the population. This has forced payers to be more selective, focused on cost-effective care, and on therapies proven to deliver better outcomes. With increasing therapeutic competition in some areas—where several drugs with similar or identical mechanisms of action are approved within just weeks or months of one another—these dynamics have created a much more challenging commercial landscape for biopharmaceutical firms.

They have also driven widespread convergence and consolidation among payers, and between payers and providers, creating new kinds of customers for biopharmaceutical firms, not simply customers with more purchasing clout, but customers with different incentives, interests, and behaviors. These customers will each be driven to make different coverage decisions, based on their individual preferences and constraints as well as the geographies and competitive dynamics within which they operate.

Biopharmaceutical firms must therefore define and understand the key payer archetypes. They must segment them according to their structure and profit motive, the demographics and disease incidence within their covered population, their behavior and attitude to risk, and environmental factors such as consolidation and legislation. Then they must tailor their offerings to best meet the needs of each. This may involve prioritizing certain payers over others, at least in some therapy areas or for some types of product (Figure 8-2). "Smart payer segmentation strategies will soon be as important as smart physician and patient segmentation," writes Roger Longman, chief executive officer (CEO) of Real Endpoints, which has developed a drug valuation tool called RxScorecard. "Payers are the new powerbrokers. But they don't all make decisions in the same way" [3].

Segmenting this complex and rapidly changing payer environment is not easy. But it is increasingly necessary and also represents an important opportunity. For example, some integrated payer-provider networks may be open to engage in longer-term outcomes-based deals that link the price of a drug to the clinical results delivered, potentially supporting higher drug prices. And at the highest level, payers are, increasingly, driven by a common goal: demonstrable value and cost effectiveness. In that sense, European and US payers are becoming more alike: whether they are a government, an employer-employee sick fund, a commercial insurer, or an integrated delivery network, all want the best care at the lowest cost. That requires biopharma firms to show robust proof of value.

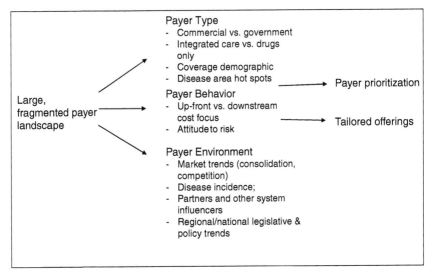

Figure 8-2   Payer segmentation

THE INCREASING IMPORTANCE OF THE CONSUMER IN THE UNITED STATES

As part of the expanded coverage under the Affordable Care Act (ACA), the legislation ushered in more competition among insurers. This happened primarily via the introduction of health exchanges—online marketplaces where individuals (without employee coverage) could shop for the most affordable (non-Medicare or Medicaid) health insurance (see text box, "Health Exchanges: Online Shopping for Health Plans"). By giving individuals more choice and more transparency about the kinds of health plans available to them, consumers are empowered to make better decisions about their care coverage, at a time when those already paying for coverage face increasing premiums as health plans struggle with higher costs. All of this, plus more widespread information on treatment cost and quality (outside of the exchanges), has made patients more discriminating, too. It has forced insurers to balance the more traditional business-to-business (B to B) model, toward selling directly to consumers (B to C).

HEALTH EXCHANGES: ONLINE SHOPPING FOR HEALTH PLANS

These online marketplaces for health insurance, mandated as part of the Affordable Care Act, have expanded insurance protection to more people in the US. They were intended to encourage competition among insurers and to promote accountability and transparency. The exchanges launched in late 2013; as of January 2017, 12.2 million people had signed up or renewed through these market places, according to the US Department of Health and Human Services [4].

A minority of US states, including California, Washington, and New York, set up their own exchanges, but most instead use healthcare.gov, established by the federal government. The ACA sets out various rules for any health plan offered via a health exchange, such as non-discrimination against individuals with pre-existing conditions, a requirement to justify any premium increases of more than 10 percent, and no caps on annual spending for essential health benefits. They also attract subsidies, though these are controversial.

Commercial insurers choosing to participate in the exchanges have had mixed experiences. On the one hand, these marketplaces offered up a huge new pool of potential customers. But selling to consumers is risky. Greater numbers of sicker (and, thus, more expensive) individuals are likely to be attracted to certain plans, and consumers can switch often, leaving insurers with higher costs and lower visibility on future costs. Several insurers, including UnitedHealth, the country's largest, and Humana have said they will pull out of health exchanges in many US states as a result, citing high costs and inadequate returns. Other insurers that specialize in care for low-income individuals, such as Centene, have fared better. Although these health exchanges are far from perfect, a 2017 analysis suggests participating insurers' decisions to enter or exit are consistent with normal competitive forces observed in dynamic markets [5,6]. But the idea is that several insurers participate on each of the exchanges, offering choice and competitive rates to consumers.

These dynamics—the quest for value and the impact of health reform laws— are driving payer consolidation. In order to offer the most competitive health plans and secure the most business, insurers are seeking greater economies of scale in their contracting with hospitals and other providers. Although a number of large insurance mergers were announced, anti-trust concerns have limited the number that have been finalized [7].

Large insurers are also strengthening their in-house PBM businesses to help drive down prices in negotiations with biopharma firms: UnitedHealth's $12.8 billion purchase of PBM Catamaran Corp. is one example [8]. PBMs themselves have consolidated, as their business model is threatened by payers and providers seeking to cut out the middleman, whose incentives are not always aligned with those of all its customers [9–11]. For instance, PBMs purport to lower drug acquisition costs for their clients. But they also generate a significant part of their drug-related profits from a complex system of rebates, negotiated with manufacturers. These rebates are calculated as a percentage of drug prices, meaning that PBM profitability is sometimes better served by higher, not lower, manufacturer drug prices [12]. Meanwhile, the fact that PBMs deal only in drugs, not other aspects of healthcare, runs counter to the trend toward more integrated (and, thus, cost-effective) care.

There are further examples of perverse incentives resulting from this complex web of payer types and intermediaries.

Providers Are Now Payers

The value-focused dynamics have also changed how providers (hospitals and physician groups) operate. Some are becoming payers in their own right. As such, the boundaries between payer and provider are blurring, creating new classes of payers—and more of them.

Many providers are now financially at-risk as a result of ACA-linked changes to how they are reimbursed for their services. Increasing numbers now receive a fixed fee (from a commercial insurer or from Medicare) for certain kinds of care, or for certain outcomes, rather than being paid per service or intervention. Many are organized into Accountable Care Organizations (ACOs), reimbursed (via one of a range of payment models, including capitation) according to care quality metrics and reductions in the total cost of care. Some ACOs get to share in any resulting savings.

This financial accountability means that providers need to control the entire continuum of care, rather than just one component of it. As a result they do not want to, for example, only deliver hip replacement operations. They want to ensure appropriate, coordinated follow-up care to avoid expensive hospital readmissions. This bid to deliver more cost-effective care across inpatient and outpatient settings requires reliable access to data generated at various steps along patients' care journey. Yet these data sets will often remain within independent providers with, until recently, little incentive to cooperate (not to mention the lack of inter-operability among data systems).

The drive for better operational efficiency and more comprehensive data is leading to provider consolidation—and raising further questions about the role of entities such as PBMs that deal with only one component of care. Hospitals have also been acquiring medical groups, including physician practices [13]. When provider groups become part of larger health systems, this organizational change reduces physician freedom to prescribe and creates new customers for biopharma firms elsewhere within provider management.

Vertical integration is also manifest in the growth and evolution of integrated delivery networks (IDNs). Organizations such as Kaiser Permanente and Intermountain Healthcare have until recently accounted for only a small, albeit high-profile, share of US health providers. Now, as providers reorganize, more IDNs—and new variations of these systems—are emerging. Some are embracing a broader range of collaborative partnerships and more patient involvement [14].

The next logical step for these growing providers is to sponsor or set up their own insurance plans, using internal metrics based on their participant populations rather than performance criteria tied to a far wider range of providers. Many are doing just that, effectively evolving into payers [15].

THE PBM PROBLEM: DRUG COSTS CANNOT BE CONSIDERED IN ISOLATION

The focus on outcomes and value is forcing providers to offer more integrated care, while minimizing overall costs (rather than the cost of any single intervention or drug). This, some argue, will challenge the positioning of entities like PBMs that deal with just one aspect of healthcare, prescription drugs. PBMs traditionally seek to drive down drug costs on behalf of their customers, the health plans, and the providers working within the confines of those plans. But doing so may not always be in the best longer-term interests of those customers—or society as a whole. Restricting access to an expensive treatment (or promoting another that comes with a sizeable rebate) may raise costs down the line. As providers are exposed to more financial risk, they will be more likely to want to make their own decisions about drug choice and access, or at least to want evidence that PBMs understand the full picture.

Employers Are Payers, Too

Employers are also becoming more important players in healthcare, as they, too, seek to curb growing costs. Already, some are teaming up with health plans and providers in more creative ways, often leveraging digital tools to help motivate their workers to stay healthy. Policies that allow individuals (and employers) to reduce their premiums by engaging in more daily physical activity, for example, as measured by a wearable tracking device, are gaining popularity. These policies shift responsibility and risk to consumers (employees). But employers, especially larger ones, may be able to drive a harder bargain with PBMs and payers, too, encouraging them to take on more risk around the cost and usage of certain drug classes [16]. After all, the choice of health benefits that employers offer is an important factor in workplace decisions [17]. Employers will not want to remain entirely at the mercy of traditional payers in the scope and nature of plans they can afford to offer their workers. If employers do step up with tougher demands from PBMs and payers, this will also affect how payers negotiate with drug companies.

These rapidly changing organizational dynamics, and the delivery of healthcare more generally, also vary considerably by geography. This variance is partly a function of local demographics, disease prevalence, local provider system setups, and state laws. Massachusetts, for instance, passed its own healthcare reform law in 2006, mandating that all citizens have minimum coverage. The ACA has strengthened the federal government's role in healthcare (Massachusetts' laws have been amended to be consistent with ACA), but it also left individual states with considerable autonomy in how they implement health reform. As such, the states are choosing to expand health insurance coverage in different ways (and some not at all).

The upshot of all this complexity is that, even within one country or region, biopharmaceutical firms need to assess their drugs' value and consider their pricing and product strategies, "not from the point of view of a mythical, unitary insurer," warns Real Endpoints' Roger Longman [18]. Instead, they must understand and respond in a more targeted fashion to a range of different payer types, with different priorities, constraints, and behaviors. Vertical integration theoretically means more openness to long-term cost savings, but, in reality, annual (or short-term) budget cycles can still dominate decision making.

EUROPEAN PAYERS: HIGH-LEVEL UNITY, LOW-LEVEL FRAGMENTATION

Europe's payers appear far more homogenous than their US counterparts, comprised of governments, or "sickness funds" working on behalf of governments, using general or specifically identified tax revenues to fund healthcare for the entire population. In part because of these budgetary constraints, Europe's payers have long been more cost-conscious than their US counterparts. Many are strongly influenced by national health technology assessment (HTA) agencies, which use a variety of tools to determine relative clinical and/or cost-effectiveness of drugs and medical devices.

These HTA agencies do not all assess new drugs in exactly the same way. Some, like the UK's National Institute for Health and Care Excellence (NICE), use the manufacturer's given price to calculate whether a drug exceeds a defined cost-effectiveness threshold. In Germany and France, the focus is on added clinical benefit relative to existing treatments, and the result feeds into subsequent pricing decisions. A common thread across all the systems, however, is the need for evidence of superior outcomes relative to existing treatments.

Beneath this degree of surface uniformity lies an increasingly complex network of regional and local payers and prescribers, all seeking to meet patients' needs within tightening budgetary constraints. The UK's National Health Service, for example, is free to all legal citizens. NICE, a public body, determines which medicines are cost effective and should be funded by the NHS. But actual drug purchasing decisions are made at the local level, by Clinical Commissioning Groups. Since reforms introduced in 2013, more than 200 of these statutory NHS bodies, made up of physicians and other clinicians, are responsible for planning and commissioning health services for their local area [19]. Thus, even though it may seem that NICE is the primary agency biopharmaceutical firms must convince of a drug's value, these companies also have to engage with local payer-prescribers as they determine care priorities. Market access in Spain and Italy is also highly decentralized; both markets have national gatekeepers as well as about 20 regional, semiautonomous payer committees, responsible for local formularies (Figure 8-3).

HTAs also feature in other developed markets, including Australia and Canada, both of which have government-funded systems covering the entire population. The Australian Pharmaceutical Benefits Advisory Committee (PBAC), rather like NICE, assesses proposed prices based on cost-effectiveness

	System Type	Health Technology Assessment Group	Centralized/Decentralized
UK	Universal coverage	The National Institute for Health & Care Excellence determines whether the NHS should fund novel therapies based on cost effectiveness	Mostly centralized: NICE guidance is binding in England and Wales; drug utilization may vary locally due to budgetary constraints
Germany	Universal coverage via sickness funds, nonprofit insurance collectives, funded by payroll taxes and government subsidies	Institute for Quality and Efficiency in Healthcare scores new drugs based on their additional benefit relative to existing treatments. Cost-effectiveness not specifically addressed.	Mostly centralized: Prices for new drugs are negotiated (using the added-benefit score) on behalf of the sickness funds. Biopharmas can contract with individual funds. Hospital drug prices are negotiated directly with hospitals or hospital groups
France	Universal coverage funded mainly by employer and employee contributions	Haute Autorite de Sante determines a drug's medical benefit. In 2012, the Commission d'Evaluation Economique et Santé Publique (CEESP) was created to examine cost-effectiveness of high-impact drugs but does not directly influence price	Centralized: Drug prices in France are negotiated based on added medical benefit score, cost effectiveness, and expected sales volume
Italy	Universal coverage funded by central and regional taxes	Central government defines drug's therapeutic value and economic impact; payment-by-results schemes exist for oncology drugs	Decentralized: Manufacturers must negotiate with some or all of the 21 regional payers
Spain	Universal coverage funded via regions	Prices and reimbursement are set nationally based on therapeutic utility, disease severity, and innovation. HTA operates both nationally and regionally, with no common standards around data or processes	Decentralized: Spain's regions are responsible for healthcare delivery and financing; several have their own HTA operations

Source: EY Analysis

Figure 8-3   Europe's top five payers: key characteristics

analyses and may deny reimbursement or restrict the target population [20]. HTA bodies are also being established across emerging economies in Asia and South America, despite challenges around a shortage of expertise and poor-quality local data in some markets [21].

UNITED STATES ADOPTS EUROPEAN-STYLE COST-EFFECTIVENESS HURDLES

As the US market evolves from the fee-for-service model to a fee-for-value framework, value-assessment bodies similar to Europe's HTAs are emerging. One example is the not-for-profit Institute for Clinical and Economic Review (ICER), which has published analyses of high-profile new medicines such as Novartis' heart drug Entresto (sacubitril/valsartan), the PCSK-9 inhibitors, and multiple myeloma drugs. As discussed in Chapter 7, other drug valuation tools designed to help clinicians, payers, and patients compare the clinical and cost effectiveness of drugs include the American Society of Clinical Oncologists' (ASCO) Value Framework, Memorial Sloan Kettering's Drug Abacus, Avalere/ Faster Cures' Patient Perspective Value Framework, and the National Comprehensive Cancer Network's Evidence Blocks [22].

Unlike in some European markets, US payers are not bound by the findings of these organizations (though many providers follow evidence-based guidelines developed by professional societies such as ASCO). Many of the larger payers also perform their own cost-effectiveness analyses. But the influence of cost-effectiveness analyses is growing as payers seek to validate coverage restrictions. Budgetary constraints and the flurry of novel, high-priced therapies in the market mean that payers simply cannot afford to cover all drugs, even if shown to be effective—and, in some cases, even if shown to be cost effective (see text box, "Value-Focused Price Not Enough for Entresto"). Indeed, the up-front costs of even a reasonably priced therapy may be too high, depending on the prevalence of the disease in the covered population (and, thus, the total costs to the payer) and the relative cost of existing treatment.

VALUE-FOCUSED PRICE NOT ENOUGH FOR ENTRESTO

Novartis' innovative heart-failure treatment Entresto is a rare thing: one that was fairly priced from the outset, at least according to a review by the US Institute for Clinical and Economic Review [23]. And its developer, Novartis, has shown a willingness to share financial risk if the drug does not deliver as expected by agreeing to reduce the price if the drug does not lower the rate of cardiovascular events among its users. Yet certain kinds of payers still do not want to buy Entresto, explains Roger Longman, CEO of Real Endpoints [24]. Medicare prescription drug plans, for example, which provide treatment coverage for elderly patients that qualify for Medicare, do not care about saving downstream costs; they seek only to reduce upfront drug bills. And because a relatively large proportion of their elderly demographic is likely to be at-risk for heart failure (and plenty of other high-cost comorbidities), making the drug easily available would simply encourage more patients at-risk for heart failure to use it—pushing up drug costs further for the plan. Hence, the importance of knowing the customer.

PAYER ENGAGEMENT STRATEGIES MUST BE TAILORED, SCALABLE, AND FLEXIBLE

To effectively engage with payers and achieve the best possible access for their products, biopharmaceutical firms require a more tailored approach, built on an understanding of each customer's preferences, restrictions, and ways of working. Even beyond the relatively clear-cut differences between, say, a US prescription drug plan seeking to purchase drugs at the lowest possible cost for its customers, an integrated delivery network working to reduce overall healthcare bills, and a European tax-funded state payer, there will be further variation in attitudes.

Value is in the eye of the beholder, even within Europe's HTA landscape: most payers like head-to-head trial evidence, but may seek comparisons with different standards of care. Many say they will consider patient-reported data supporting drug efficacy claims, but not all have established processes allowing them to weigh such evidence in their decision. Attitudes may vary by therapy area, in line with the characteristics of the covered population. Payers covering a high proportion of patients with chronic diseases may be more open to (and prepared to pay for) solutions offering proven support with medication adherence, for example. And while some payers have the resources and mindset to experiment with new payment models, others remain more conservative and focused on cost.

Faced with this complex, fragmented payer marketplace—multiple payer types and behaviors plus a fast-changing environment—biopharmaceutical firms need a payer engagement strategy that is systematic, manageable, and scalable, yet that can be adapted to optimally address the priorities of each payer. A logical approach to developing such a strategy is to rapidly identify the most relevant payers for any product or service. This could involve using basic data around disease incidence in a given region or regions, for example, and overlaying it with information on the payers and/or provider systems in those areas with the most covered lives for this disease. As the prevalence and sophistication of data sources grows, this exercise is becoming easier to do.

Geospatial mapping tools can also help: these overlay several types of data, including sociodemographic, payer, and provider data, for instance, on a geographical map to identify where the most critical payers are located. Structural information on whether and how specialists and other healthcare stakeholders such as pharmacies are interconnected can also be included to generate a more detailed picture of relevant targets [25].

Once this screening has identified a more manageable subset of high-opportunity payers, including their exposure to a particular demographic and/or therapy area, this smaller group can be segmented according to more specific measures associated with behavior and resources. These may include sensitivity to up-front drug costs versus downstream cost savings and outcomes, attitude to risk and to new approaches, strength of information technology (IT) infrastructure, and data access and expertise (Figure 8-4). Further, more detailed parameters around particular resource strengths or constraints, characteristics of care provision and patient pathways, and other budgetary pressure points may also be mapped at this stage (Figure 8-5). This mapping will generate a good understanding of which payers are most likely to be interested in a particular offering, as well as how best to position that offering.

A basic example is a stand-alone pharmacy benefit manager, which manages utilization of prescription medicines for health plans; this manager is likely to focus entirely on cost, specifically on procuring medicines as cheaply as possible on behalf of its health plan customers. That is because it is not responsible for downstream care outcomes (though it may soon be forced to consider them, as discussed in the text box, "The PBM Problem: Drug Costs Cannot Be Considered in Isolation"). Priorities may be somewhat different at a well-funded research hospital group, with established value-based payment systems and incentives, which is in charge of its own drug purchasing (as part of a group purchasing organization, for instance). Such an organization may be more interested in the

Segmentation by:

Payer Type/Characteristics	**Payer Behavior**	**Payer Environment**
- Commercial vs. government; IDN vs. PBM; regional vs. national payer	- Cost containment focus (up-front vs. downstream)	- Market trends (consolidation, competition)
- Coverage demographic; policy priorities	- Attitude to risk	- Disease incidence; referrals
- Disease area hot spots	- Engaged in new payment models?	- Partners and other system influencers
- Strength of IT infrastructure	- Degree of prescribing control	- Regional/national legislative and policy trends
- Resource constraints	- Data use/expertise	
- Clinical quality and care provision	- Level of clinical accountability	
	- Degree of patient involvement	

Prioritization and Engagement:

High Opportunity Payers	**New Opportunity Payers**	**Future Opportunity Payers**
Engage, explore, and expand new payment models, e.g., outcomes-based deals	Approach with tailored offerings; collaboration proposals	Track and observe payer policies/statements and evolution of landscape (e.g., health reform timelines)

Source: EY Analysis

Figure 8-4   Strategic payer segmentation and engagement

data supporting a drug's value proposition—including any evidence of down-stream savings—and its positioning within the treatment pathway.

In Europe, certain individual national or regional payers may, as a function of their experience, risk attitude, and data capabilities, be more willing to consider deals that tie drug pricing to outcomes. Italy, for example, has had outcomes-linked arrangements around certain cancer drugs; the Spanish region of Catalonia has recently engaged in similar deals for high-cost, specialist treatments. Reimbursement priorities of regional payers will also be strongly dictated by local budgets and money flow, despite national HTA guidelines. Some may not want or understand

Cost Containment
► How sophisticated are the cost-containment measures?
► Is there an HTA or tech assessment group?
► If so, what is the focus? (e.g., cost effectiveness)

Prescribing Control
► How tightly managed is physician prescribing? (e.g., step-edits)
► How much do HTA decisions influence product use?
► Do manufacturers have access to physicians?

Data Availability and Use
► What patient data are available?
► How sophisticated is the payer in integrating different data?
► Is the payer able to use the data predictively?
► How often is the payer sharing data with providers and patients?

Accountability & Autonomy
► What is the level of clinical autonomy?
► How does the payer's organizational structure affect coverage decisions?
► How transparent is the payer regarding its coverage process?

Clinical Quality
► How important are clinical guidelines in coverage decisions?
► Is the emphasis on short-term treatment or long-term prevention?
► Does the payer enable disease management, adherence or palliative care programs?

Figure 8-5   Mapping payers based on behaviors and preferences

the complex cost-effectiveness models sought nationally. Biopharmaceutical firms must understand those budgetary dynamics and resource and expertise constraints. They may find that certain regional payers in different countries share similarities that allow a common approach and shared learnings.

CHANGING BIOPHARMA-PAYER RELATIONSHIPS: FROM TRANSACTIONAL TO COLLABORATIVE

Whatever a payer's particular priorities at any given time, biopharmaceutical firms need to engage with them in a more collaborative, ongoing fashion than has previously been the case. Rather than a series of transactions typically focused on pricing in isolation, both sides could benefit from greater engagement with the others' needs and concerns (and those of other stakeholders elsewhere in the value chain). Many large pharmaceutical firms are expanding their R & D efforts to include services and other "beyond the pill" offerings; these should feature in discussions around how to improve outcomes and thus reduce overall costs.

Such offerings may support appropriate adherence to a particular product. As noted in Chapter 5, however, consumers are most interested in information and services that are product-agnostic and payers would like to apply them across a range of patients with a given disease. Biopharma needs to show that it understands that supporting cost-effective outcomes is ultimately in its own interest, even if these are not directly tied to increased prescriptions of proprietary drugs. The hard truth is that payers on the brink of bankruptcy will not be able to buy any new drugs, even if those medicines are effective.

A more collaborative relationship with payers would serve biopharma in several ways. Most importantly, it would help build trust. Without that foundation, a biopharma is unlikely to be able to convince payers that it is willing to engage beyond maximizing sales, and is thus unlikely to find receptivity for the often-expensive outcomes and/or patient-relevant data that prove value. Absent a relationship built on trust, payers are unlikely to believe any evidence supporting the oft-cited argument that paying for drugs upfront can generate significant savings downstream (see text box, "Trust: The Heart of the Matter).

TRUST: THE HEART OF THE MATTER

The biopharmaceutical industry has a trust problem. Despite the extraordinary advances it has brought to human health, the sector scores poorly in public perception surveys. Indeed, according to the 2017 Harris Poll, only 9 percent of more than 1,000 US adults surveyed believe biopharma companies prioritize patients over profits [26]. Other healthcare stakeholders (e.g., payers) also remain wary of the industry's motives. This is largely because the biopharmaceutical industry's behavior has fallen short in several high-profile cases of illegal kick-backs, dubious marketing practices, deals to stifle competition, and withholding negative clinical trial data (Figure 8-6) [27]. Against this backdrop, it is little wonder that rising drug prices have catalyzed such an intense public debate. How dare the industry charge the public what many perceive as unjustifiably high prices for its medicines?

While it should, and in many cases is, paying for those mistakes, the bio-pharmaceutical sector must not be blamed for its profit motive. That is the engine of a free-market economy and of innovation. How to ensure that the system, and society, continue to encourage beneficial healthcare innovations, yet can also afford to pay for them, is a critical challenge. Achieving ways to fairly and appropriately value (and price) new drugs is a big part of that.

Solving this challenge requires healthcare stakeholders to enter into new kinds of relationships and explore new routes toward achieving equitable access to drugs at reasonable prices. Forming new collaborations and partnerships requires mutual under-standing, and at least a certain degree of trust.

Trust, as with many things, is far easier and quicker to break than to build. But efforts to rebuild it have begun. Many senior executives at pharmaceutical firms acknowledge the trust deficit; most are trying to address it. Several have engaged with the AllTrials initiative to publish full trial data on their products. GlaxoSmithKline, in 2011, stopped linking sales representatives pay to prescriptions, instead rewarding them based on product knowledge and understanding the needs of patients and physicians. It has not been an easy transition, but the group is persevering [28].

"Pricing of medicines must balance the needs of multiple stakeholders, striking a fair balance between rewarding innovation, managing cost pressures in healthcare systems, and ensuring patient access to the medicines they need. Achieving that balance requires new thinking, improved collaboration and creativity," according to Andrew Witty, formerly the CEO of GlaxoSmithKline. Witty was speaking as a member of PharmaDiplomacy, a US/EU leadership initiative seeking to overcome the trust deficit between health systems and the biopharmaceutical industry. The program, which assembles over a dozen senior leaders from industry, payers and health

---

A series of past and current behaviors have contributed to public and stakeholder mistrust of biopharma:

- Unaffordable drug prices; opaque pricing mechanisms
- Potentially misleading drug advertising including, in the United States, direct-to-consumer ads
- Drug coupons (discounts given to patients for named drugs, encouraging them, via reduced out-of-pocket costs, to request these over potentially cheaper ones)
- Financial relationships with doctors/providers (disclosures are required under the 2010 Sunshine Act)
- Commercial team bonus structures incenting higher sales
- Failure to publish all clinical trials, especially negative or inconclusive ones

Source: EY Analysis

Figure 8-6   Biopharma's trust-breakers

systems, patient organizations, and investors, is one of several multi-stakeholder efforts to find solutions to the drug pricing question. In May 2016, it launched a framework designed to help stakeholders navigate multiple, often competing interests toward mutually acceptable drug pricing [29]. Key to the framework is the principle of continuous, iterative dialog between biopharma and payers enabling each side to understand and respond to concerns and priorities.

Trust will not alter the reality that payer objectives (to pay the lowest price for the best medicines) are different from those of biopharma (to get the highest price for the best medicines in order to achieve a return on its R & D investment commensurate with the risk taken). Nor will it alter the fact that payers work on short, annual budget cycles that are sensitive to the prices paid for medicines today but cannot easily factor in lower costs resulting from those medicines in later years. But a trusted relationship can improve the chances that real, reasonable efforts are made by both sides to try to accommodate those differences.

Biopharma companies and their investors have the most to lose from the trust deficit. Failure to reach some kind of solution to drug pricing could result in more draconian measures imposed by governments, including the US government. However credible the threat of government-imposed price controls, today or in the future, biopharma needs to rebuild trust among its customers and collaborators. Biopharma also needs the cooperation and goodwill of patients in order to develop its next generation of products and solutions. Developing patient-relevant products that address patient-reported needs (rather than only achieving certain clinical endpoints) is increasingly recognized as critical to successful outcomes, and thus to the industry's sustainable future. "To ensure the pharmaceutical industry continues to innovate and sustain the delivery of value to society, we must improve our stakeholder collaboration, which can only be done with a strong foundation of trust," said Jane Griffiths, company group chairman, Europe, Middle East, and Africa, Janssen, and part of the PharmaDiplomacy group [30].

NEW BIOPHARMA ORGANIZATIONAL MODELS NEEDED

As drug-buying decisions shift from individual doctors to teams within larger care networks, hospital committees, or payers, many biopharma firms have already refocused their commercial sales efforts. They have moved away from the traditional sales representative, typically focused on maximizing short-term sales of a single product, toward key account managers. These are individuals with strong interpersonal skills whose responsibility is to establish longer-term relationships with physicians and other payer budget-holders and decision makers, taking a portfolio rather than single-product approach.

This is a step in the right direction, but challenges remain. Key account managers require specific and broad skill sets and are often in short supply [31]. Their success depends on a degree of cross-functionality across different departments (e.g., medical affairs, account management, sales, and even R & D) that is still lacking in many current organizational models. Key account managers must also operate within a broader strategic and structural framework that recognizes not

---

Understanding the Payer Landscape

Highly fragmented and complex universe characterized by:
- Increased power to control drug utilization
- More widespread use of cost-effectiveness tools
- New kinds of payers, including provider-payers, employer-payers, integrated delivery networks

---

Biopharma-Payer Engagement
- Payer segmentation strategies that are flexible yet scalable
- Evolve from a one-off, transactional approaches toward more collaborative, ongoing relationships
- Greater focus on outcomes-based deals, especially for high-cost chronic diseases
- Rebuild trust via data co-creation, ethical behavior

New Biopharma Organizational Models
- More cross-functional flexibility
- Creation of commercial teams that operate within broader strategic payer-segmentation framework
- Creation of longer-term incentive structures

Source: EY Analysis

Figure 8-7   Understanding and engaging with payers

just individual customer concerns but also those of broader customer segments, including within specific regions. Furthermore, biopharma organizations must be sufficiently informed and flexible to not only understand and meet the current needs of payers but also to forecast how these might evolve, given health reform trends and competitive pressures. This forward-thinking perspective is also necessary to allow certain approaches to be efficiently scaled-up to a wider range of payers with similar interests.

In sum, biopharma must adopt more flexible, cross-disciplinary organizational models with longer-term incentive structures in order to make strategic and commercial sense of a rapidly shifting landscape (Figure 8-7).

BIOPHARMA-PAYER ENGAGEMENT MUST MOVE BEYOND EXPERIMENTATION

For now, some biopharma firms and an evolving cohort of US and European payers are experimenting around new, more collaborative pricing and access strategies that better support improved outcomes. Shifting payment models from volume to value, as is happening in the United States, will take time to evolve. Such a change requires a host of organizational, infrastructure, and cultural changes. Accountable Care Organizations are growing in number and reach, but data on how well they are improving care and saving costs remains mixed [32]. Health exchanges only opened for business in late 2013, and their effects on the insurance sector have not been fully realized [33].

The European payer market also continues to evolve. Established HTAs such as NICE, facing criticism from patients and the public and greater demands from the government health department, have called for a broad overhaul of how medicines are accessed and paid for, as well as how they are developed [34]. In France, efforts are being made to tie clinical effectiveness decisions more closely to pricing, another indirect bid to find value-focused prices. The German government is considering shutting off the single remaining free-pricing window in Europe by capping the prices that manufacturers can charge during the year before their products are subject to a stringent added-benefit assessment [35]. There have been whispers—though little more—about setting up a pan-European buying group for certain drugs.

Adjustments notwithstanding, the future direction for the healthcare market is clear. The resistance of payers to high drug pricing is here to stay in all markets; so is a focus on cost-effective outcomes, whatever the precise methods used to encourage them. The US government's aim is for 50 percent of all Medicare provider payments to be based on quality/value by 2018. In 2016, the Centers for Medicare and Medicaid Services proposed a range of new value-based payment pilots around drugs administered by physicians or in hospitals and even opened the door to outcomes-based risk-sharing deals with manufacturers [36]. Meanwhile, the data and digital revolutions are unstoppable and are providing new health data sources and novel data capture and analytics techniques. These technologies and the underlying data are challenging R & D strategies as well as commercial models. They also present unprecedented opportunities, for example, in enabling and driving greater patient-centricity, and in generating and supporting biopharma's value arguments, for instance, by allowing easier and more widespread outcomes-data capture.

Therefore, almost a decade after ACA, it is time for biopharma firms to start moving beyond experimentation. Those biopharmas that are in a position to expand payer engagement strategies may gain a competitive advantage over others that are slower to do so. Identifying and building relationships with long-term partners will create commercial advantages in some therapy areas, markets, and across some kinds of solutions.

Scaling-Up New Partnership Models

Expanding new partnership models will happen most easily—and fruitfully—with those payers that are open to change. As with any major market shifts, there will be early movers whose experiences can inform and reassure others. Thus, biopharma's payer segmentation exercise should include an assessment of willingness to engage in new pricing models or, in other words, their appetite for risk.

The US private payer market provides the most fertile ground. Some European payers, such as in Italy, have engaged in a handful of drug-specific outcomes-based deals but recent analysis suggests limited returns for the payers. For the most part, European and US state payers, covering large populations with taxpayer funds, are unlikely to take meaningful risks without seeing some evidence of workability. US commercial payers vary in size, number, and focus, providing a pool of potential partners for a range of models. Several have already begun to engage in outcomes-based deals (also known as risk-sharing arrangements) around particular drugs. These tie the price or discount given on a specific product to an agreed measure of the outcomes generated.

Thus, in November 2015, Massachusetts-based Harvard Pilgrim Health Care, a small, not-for-profit payer, entered into a pay-for-performance deal with Amgen around cholesterol-lowering Repatha (evolocumab). The deal promised greater discounts if the drug did not deliver the same cholesterol-lowering effect seen in clinical trials, and if usage exceeded a certain volume [37]. For Amgen, the deal helped Repatha gain a formulary head start over competitor Praluent, from Sanofi/Regeneron. Both are PCSK9 inhibitors, a novel class priced significantly higher than existing cholesterol treatments. For Harvard Pilgrim, the arrangement demonstrated a proactive approach to granting its customers access to novel therapies, differentiating the payer in a competitive marketplace where plans are competing for market share with individuals as well as employers.

In 2016, biopharmas collaborated with several larger payers, including Cigna, Aetna, and Express Scripts, on similar novel outcomes-based contracts. Harvard Pilgrim itself signed two other pay-for-performance contracts around Eli Lilly's diabetes drug Trulicity and Novartis' heart failure treatment Entresto. In the case of Trulicity, the drug, a GLP-1 agonist, is a late entrant into a crowded marketplace. In exchange for a formulary upgrade, Lilly has offered rebates if fewer Trulicity patients reach their blood sugar targets than those on other drugs [38]. For Entresto, Harvard Pilgrim gets a discount if the drug does not reduce hospitalization rates by a set amount [39].

The early examples of collaborations are focused on treatments entering highly competitive, price-sensitive indications, where traditional access models would likely fail. These arrangements require agreement on what outcomes to measure, a sufficiently robust IT infrastructure, and a willingness to invest in data analytics. For now, they are mostly limited to metrics, like cholesterol or blood sugar levels, that are reliable surrogate markers of outcomes and relatively easy to track via claims data.

Most payers rely on claims data; few but the most integrated payer-providers can access the clinical information held in electronic health records at hospitals and doctors' offices. Hospitalization rates and related cost offsets are less straightforward to track, but again feasible for integrated payer-providers. Says Michael Sherman, CMO at Harvard Pilgrim, "if the up-front drug cost is sufficiently high, I'm willing to dedicate internal resources to manually collect the data to determine if the success criteria have been met".

Because of these operational hurdles, it has been difficult to scale new value-based payment models beyond the pilot phase. Such performance-linked contacts will only become mainstream if biopharma and payers are able to come together in a safe forum to develop solutions to common hurdles related to defining and measuring outcomes and safe data sharing. In 2017, multiple consortia of bio-pharma, advocacy groups, policy makers, and payers emerged. These included the formation of a Learning Lab by UnitedHealth Group's Optum and Merck & Co. Inc. to learn how to design and conduct feasible, high quality outcome-based agreements that will be acceptable to all stakeholders [40].

Integrated Payers and Chronic, High-Cost Diseases Ripe for Outcomes-Based Deals

The challenges associated with managing outcomes-based contracts help identify payers most likely to engage in them. Payers that are optimally suited have tight links to, or are fully integrated with, hospital and physician networks, with robust IT systems for data gathering. This group is likely to include larger commercial insurers working with providers that have established electronic health records, integrated payer-provider networks, and perhaps some leading hospital systems with particular interest in new pricing models. (The US Department of Veterans Affairs, with its large, highly integrated system and data support, is another possible contender.) The behavior of groups such as these is, in turn, likely to influence others.

Payers must be willing to engage and invest. This is more likely if the products in question fall into the costliest therapy areas where there are many competing therapeutic options, including highly prevalent chronic diseases such as cardiovascular conditions and diabetes. These are, in any case, the areas where some biopharma companies are starting to invest in beyond-the-pill services or add-on technologies, including medication adherence tools, providing further avenues to track and improve long-term outcomes. Cancer is another high-cost area with, in some subcategories, several relatively undifferentiated medicines; prolonged survival rates mean some cancers are effectively chronic conditions. Payers have yet to tightly manage access to oncology medicines. However, budgetary pressures mean they may pilot indication-specific pricing or other models in the not-too-distant future. By segmenting payers according to their degree of integration, IT advancement, attitudes to risk, and the disease areas most pertinent to them, biopharma firms will be strongly placed to hone in on those most likely to engage on an ongoing basis.

Biopharma's attitudes must evolve, too, however. As Michael Sherman of Harvard Pilgrim notes, "most drug makers still view risk-sharing as a defensive strategy." The shift toward fee-for-value across healthcare means more providers and physicians are having to take on financial risk for delivering certain outcomes. With the vast majority of new drugs today entering competitive and/or highly price-sensitive therapy areas, biopharma firms will be required to do the same. Rather than viewing risk-sharing arrangements as a last resort, Sherman argues that biopharma should instead view them as an opportunity to enable greater patient access—and, for first movers, an opportunity to gain advantage over rivals, "as paying for outcomes becomes institutionalized across the country" [41].

Data Co-creation with Payers Leads to Greater Trust and Better Data

The success of some or all of these early deals will help build trust and, hopefully, transform a traditionally adversarial relationship into one that is more collaborative and mutually beneficial. Both sides have much to give to and learn from each other in order to enable more cost-effective, high-quality healthcare. By co-investing with biopharma in data collection and infrastructure to support outcomes tracking across multiple treatments, payers would gain a tool to help them understand relative treatment efficacy, learning from a partner with deep knowledge of data systems and data handling. Importantly, payers would also be able to offer their members potentially life-changing medicines. Biopharma, meanwhile, would gain real-world comparative data in a relevant therapy area, potentially supporting product access and pricing in other markets. Biopharma firms could also, depending on their portfolios, engage with a payer across more than one therapy or even indication, underlining their willingness to support care, not just drive prescriptions.

The right payer relationship could also encompass new digital tools and data sources already being investigated within biopharma R & D and provider settings, such as wearable technologies. Insights gained would allow both biopharma and payer to optimize their technology investments. For biopharma, that is critical in highly competitive fields where results-focused differentiation is key.

Reliable, meaningful, and accessible data are core to the achievement of value-based healthcare. Payers are, in any case, investing in systems and databases that may enable more proactive population health management, including more effective prevention [42]. Providers, with the burden of greater financial risk, are trying to evolve more integrated systems to better track the effectiveness and costs of patient journeys. Working with biopharmaceutical firms to optimize treatment targeting and usage is entirely consistent with these goals.

STRATEGIC PAYER ENGAGEMENT COMES IN MANY FORMS

Not every biopharmaceutical firm can engage collaboratively with every payer. Even those payers that are willing to embrace new payment models and have the capabilities to do so will lack the resources to engage on multiple fronts. Hence, biopharma should spread its net widely and creatively across select partners, ideally gaining familiarity across a range of payment models.

Once collaborations are underway and trust begins to build, solutions are more likely to be found as hurdles are, inevitably, met. Both sides by then have a vested interest in success. And those early successes will encourage others. Michael Sherman of Harvard Pilgrim says, "Risk sharing with pharma will only gain traction if there are some wins. That means taking small steps with the right partners" [43].

By definition, there are risks involved with these new access and payment models. Some will scale up well, others less so. Some will work in one market or therapy area, but not so well in another. But the risks of not engaging are greater. At its core, the new healthcare world order is simple: biopharma must develop patient-relevant, effective solutions whose prices reflect the value they deliver. Engaging effectively and consistently with those paying for and administering these solutions is paramount.

SUMMARY POINTS

- Payers are among the most important partners for biopharma; their coverage decisions are a key determinant of a product's commercial success at a time when new digital technologies create other business pressures for biopharma companies.

- Not all payers are alike: government payers differ from commercial payers; payers who buy only drugs differ from those who fund a broader range of health services.

- This fragmented landscape is changing fast: as healthcare reimbursement shifts from volume to value, payers are consolidating and new kinds of payers are emerging.

- All payers are more selective about what therapies they buy, and at what price. In this regard, US payers are beginning to look more similar to Europe's cost-conscious government payers.

- All payers are looking for value, but value may mean lower up-front prices for one, and long-term cost offsets for another.

- Biopharma firms need smart segmentation strategies to determine which approach best suits which kind of payer, and to stay abreast of the evolving needs of different payers.

- That means building more collaborative relationships, built on a stronger foundation of trust. Agreements such as outcomes-based deals, which tie the price (or rebate level) of a drug to the outcomes delivered, are challenging to create, but an option different stakeholders want to explore.

- Such deals require an investment in data infrastructure and other digital tools; they are most likely to succeed within more integrated payer systems, around high-cost chronic diseases with outcomes that can be measured in the near term.

- Outcomes-linked deals also demand and enable the kinds of data collection that will ultimately serve all healthcare stakeholders.

PART 3

NEW MODELS FOR DIGITAL HEALTH

CHAPTER 9

DIGITAL HEALTH STRATEGIES

INTRODUCTION

For the past several years, digital technology has transformed the healthcare landscape, from analytics-enabled research to Web-driven consumer empowerment. Biopharma R & D is being optimized by analytics tools such as IBM Watson Health, applying cognitive computing to genomic, clinical trial, and claims databases. Trials themselves are evolving, as randomized, double-blind models integrate patient-reported outcomes. Consumers are driving the rapid adoption of smartphones and biosensors such as Fitbit and the Apple Watch, and they are increasingly participating in product development through online patient communities. This new landscape reflects the convergence of infotech and healthcare, from Apple's ResearchKit, codeveloped with the Mayo Clinic and other health systems, to Samsung's bio-sensors and new entrants such as Proteus Digital Health.

This chapter will first cover the impact of digital health on the biopharma value chain, from R & D to commercial activities. It will then focus on consumer-driven trends including wearable sensors and social media. It will finally cover provider-centered telemedicine initiatives, from e-consults to remote drug monitoring and the rise of new, on-demand medical services. Chapter 10 examines how companies can leverage data and analytics to improve their agility across the same value chain.

BIOPHARMA DIGITAL STRATEGIES

New R & D Patient-Centric Models

The traditional drug development model follows a linear path, from discovery to the preclinical stage, leading to phase I, II, and III human trials to support approval by the Food and Drug Administration (FDA), the European Medicines Agency (EMA), and other regulators. A new model is emerging, involving patients as co-creators at each stage. Analytics allow a more predictive approach, often including biomarkers and companion diagnostics. Innovation itself is now more open, thanks to crowdsourcing technologies. Trials are optimized with e-

Managing Biotechnology: From Science to Market in the Digital Age, First Edition. Françoise Simon and Glen Giovannetti.
© 2017 John Wiley & Sons, Inc. Published 2017 by John Wiley & Sons, Inc.

recruitment and e-reporting. The supply chain is also enabled by real-time insight for forecasting, patient input for product formulation, and innovative cloud-based worldwide distribution.

As post-market data collection continues to blur the lines between research and commercial outreach, R & D supports marketing activities through an evidence-based communications strategy. The impact of digital technology on the value chain is summarized in Figure 9-1. In research, scientists can discover new care pathways by mining genetic and clinical data. In clinical care, big data may fuel a new paradigm for epidemiology by combining environmental data with user queries on search engines such as Google.

Online patient communities can also help find and recruit patients with rare diseases, but challenges remain for wider adoption of digital technologies in R & D. Electronic health records (EHRs) offer significant opportunities to optimize treatments on a broad scale, but they are still fragmented and may have large biases; for instance, they may exclude the populations served by understaffed hospitals without the necessary infrastructure [1]. In epidemiology, a new approach was pioneered in 2009 by Google as it published its Flu Trends initiative [2]. However, a subsequent paper reported that, for 2013, Google showed almost twice as many flu cases as were estimated by the Centers for Disease Control and Prevention (CDC) [3].

Optimizing Clinical Trials

Digital technology can transform several stages, including recruitment, remote monitoring, and post-marketing surveillance. According to the Institute of Medicine, 75 percent of US trials fail to enroll their target numbers, and 90 percent do

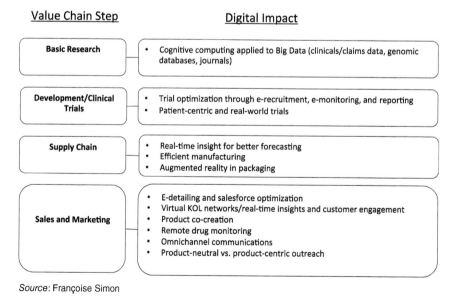

Source: Françoise Simon

Figure 9-1   Digital transformation

not reach that target within the specified time [4]. In addition to databases such as ClinicalTrials.gov, patients can now find trials through Google and Facebook ads, as well as online communities. For instance, Biogen has partnered with Patients-LikeMe and Fitbit to better understand the utility of wearables for tracking activity in multiple sclerosis patients and also to explore patient adherence to monitoring after the study. Apple's ResearchKit is used by many health systems, including Mount Sinai for their Asthma Health app; more than 8,000 participants enrolled in a clinical study within six months, and only 13 percent of them were located near the New York study site [5].

During trials, mobile devices allow real-time patient feedback, reducing in-person visits and giving an objective measurement of therapy response. Early signals of efficacy and safety can also help identify patient subsets with better responses and allow trial restructuring. Postlaunch, real-world evidence helps monitor efficacy and adverse events that may not have appeared within the limited scope of trials. For instance, Pfizer and IBM have launched a research project on Parkinson's disease, using sensors to provide real-time symptom information and medication timing and dosing, thus defining the digital signatures of individual patients. The study targets up to 200 participants including controls, and aims to discover which sensors can best provide correct insights and speed up trials. By 2019, Pfizer may apply this method to a phase III trial of a new compound and later extend it to other degenerative diseases such as Huntington's and Alzheimer's [6].

Role of Social Media in Trials

Patients are taking a direct role in trials. As noted in Chapter 6, PatientsLikeMe was launched in 2004 with a focus on amyotrophic lateral sclerosis (ALS) and has since expanded to more than 2,700 conditions, with over 500,000 members. In 2013, it launched its Open Research Exchange, funded by a grant from the Robert Wood Johnson Foundation to link scientists and members, who can log patient-reported outcomes (PROs) on it. This was expanded in 2015 with a $900,000 Robert Wood Johnson Foundation grant to fund a collaboration with the National Quality Forum, aiming to develop and test the broader use of PROs [7]. In 2016, PatientsLikeMe and informatics firm M2Gen started combining PROs with molecular and clinical data from patients in the Total Cancer Care Program at Ohio State University, with a focus on lung cancer. The alliance is funded by PatientsLikeMe partners AstraZeneca and Genentech [8].

Other patient communities have successfully funded trials in rare diseases and enabled rapid enrollment in such trials through their patient network. By the mid-2000s, the Leukemia and Lymphoma Foundation was deploying about $50 million annually to fund 350 research projects worldwide. In 2013–2014, pharmas contributed at least $600 million to further development for blood cancers [9]. Biopharmas are increasingly engaging in long-term collaborations to optimize research, not only with patient communities but also with infotech leaders.

NOVARTIS AND QUALCOMM: AN INNOVATION PARTNERSHIP

Qualcomm Ventures and Novartis announced in January 2015 their dRx Capital joint venture to target early-stage companies that offer mobile health applications, wearable devices, and clinical decision programs. They aim to invest up to $100 million, and have since funded companies including Omada Health, with a digital behavior management solution in diabetes, and Science 37, aiming to develop distributed clinical trials reaching dispersed populations in the United States.

Novartis and Qualcomm are also collaborating on a trial using Qualcomm's 2net platform to optimize home-based data collection in lung disease patients. The platform is FDA regulated and HIPAA compliant and will send sensor data collected via 2net Mobile to Qualcomm's cloud-based 2net platform. Novartis has market applications in this area, but the trial is not tied to a specific product [10].

While social media are helping optimize trials, some mixed reports are emerging. Apps developed for Apple's ResearchKit by health systems such as Mount Sinai (asthma) and Massachusetts General Hospital (diabetes) have enabled broader and faster enrollments (more than 70,000 participants in the first two months) [11]. However, active conversations within patient communities during trials may undermine data integrity in areas such as eligibility (patient coaching about how to meet criteria), blinding (advice on how to get into a therapy and not a control arm), and safety (sharing adverse events may trigger a false spike in safety reports) [12]. To mitigate these risks, sponsors may take into account the activity intensiveness of various communities, the study size (one e-participant may influence a small study to a larger degree), and possibly complement the e-consent process with patient education about these risks.

DIGITAL IMPACT ON SUPPLY CHAIN MANAGEMENT

In comparison with large retailers such as Walmart, the biopharma sector has been relatively slow in digitizing and integrating its supply chain. The evolution from siloed functions to a dynamic, patient-centric, and integrated global network will be increasingly supported by the Internet of Things (IoT). The healthcare IoT can be defined as platforms that collect and analyze actionable patient data to aid in the treatment and prevention of diseases beyond traditional care settings [13]. This can significantly reduce costs and connect market insights and patient outcomes back to the supply network, including contract manufacturers and suppliers. The IoT offers several advantages through the supply chain:

- *Pervasive visibility:* Monitoring a shipment in real time through a combination of radio frequency identification (RFID), connected devices, and channels (3G/4G, GPS).

- *Predictive maintenance:* Using sensors and connected devices to monitor and react to technical problems, coming close to machine-to-machine communications.

- *Forecasting and replenishment:* This is especially important in biopharma to avoid a stock-out that would endanger patient lives and cause enduring damage to a company reputation.

- *Asset tracking:* Smart labels include flat transponders fitted under conventional labels to transmit identifying data that are essential for security and compliance. In the current context of increasing risks such as opioid abuse in the United States, biopharmas are tightening control of their supply chains. For instance, Pfizer announced in May 2016 updated controls in its distribution channels to stop the use of its products in lethal-injection executions. The policy increases controls on wholesalers and distributors and sets up a monitoring system to ensure compliance. This is related to the 2015 Pfizer takeover of Hospira, which added several drugs used in lethal injections. While some states are still acquiring drugs from compounding pharmacies outside Pfizer's system, limits placed by several companies on their availability have partly contributed to a decline over several years in the use of the death penalty [14].

In manufacturing, an emerging technology is 3D printing, also called additive manufacturing, with uses in prosthetics and custom research tools. This creates a three-dimensional object by adding successive layers of material, guided by a computer. This market grew by 17 percent to $1.5 billion in 2015, and it is attracting specialized firms such as Stratasys and EOS GmbH, but also established players such as Hewlett-Packard. It announced a five-year initiative to develop a high-volume, more mainstream method allowing faster and cheaper production; it also took an equity investment in Shapeways. The first FDA approval for a 3D-manufactured drug was granted in March 2016 to Aprecia Pharmaceuticals for Spritam (levetiracetam) in epilepsy. Advantages of 3D printing include easier delivery for patients who have trouble swallowing pills and fast onset of action with rapid dissolution [15].

For distribution through a global network, cloud computing (the use of remote servers to store, access, and process data) can minimize capital investment and is best used in areas that have the greatest networking effect and share the least sensitive data; these include procurement, transportation management systems, store shelf optimization, and some sales and operations planning [16]. The impact of digital technology on the supply chain is illustrated in Figure 9-2.

DIGITAL TRANSFORMATION OF COMMERCIAL ACTIVITIES

Digitization is enabling a fundamental shift from a transactional mindset (selling a pill) to a patient-centric approach (meeting patient needs before, during, and after

▶ Collaborative and customer-centric with end-to-end visibility			
· Seamless connectivity and data sharing · Integrated local systems and functions		· Secured track and trace abilities · Proactive responses to potential issues	

Demand-driven	Manufacturing excellence	Advanced product design and packaging	Innovative distribution models
· Real-time insight for better demand forecasting · Innovation and responsiveness · Rapid ramp up/ down response	· Efficient manufacturing processes · 3D printing	· Smarter packaging for better customer experience · Identification via RFID · Compliance	· Innovative platforms to reach customers · Cloud-based services

Source: Françoise Simon

Figure 9-2   Intelligent supply chain

treatment and delivering positive outcomes that can support value for patients and payers). This entails an evolution from functional silos to an integrated system of care. While Web-connected patients have a primary need for long-term, product-neutral disease information, many digital activities fit within the marketing organization, with short-term budget cycles and sales objectives. In order for a new product to meet patient needs, a cross-functional approach must link development, economic, and marketing teams.

Care integration is being practiced by drug retailers and health systems. Among pharmacy chains, Walgreens is coordinating prescription refills, adherence tracking, and e-consults within a single smartphone app. It partnered with MDLive for telemedicine services and with WebMD for disease information, and it is incentivizing patients by integrating this into its Balance Rewards loyalty program. Among health systems, Duke University School of Medicine is piloting partnerships with Apple, Fitbit, and Withings to integrate patient-generated data such as blood pressure and weight with clinical data in its Epic electronic system, through the Apple HealthKit. For biopharmas, barriers to this integration include the lack of dedicated budgets and profit and loss ownership, and the significant overhead cost of pilot programs that may not be viable on a larger scale.

A 2016 survey of biopharmas showed that only 15 percent of senior managers could identify their company's main digital key performance indicators, fewer than 15 percent of companies had well-defined roles for digital leaders, and fewer than 30 percent could track their digital budget across business units. Many biopharmas tended to treat digital engagement as an aspect of execution, rather than as a central element of their strategy [17].

A key area for digital initiatives is diabetes, given its worldwide scope affecting over 350 million people. The major players have multipronged strategies, combining product-centric and product-neutral approaches.

- Novo Nordisk is by far the most diabetes-focused company, as the world's largest producer of insulin such as Levemir (insulin detemir) and NovoLog (insulin aspart), as well as Victoza (liraglutide) and a pipeline including an ultra-long-acting basal insulin and an oral long-acting GLP-1 analog [18]. Novo understood patient needs several years ago, as it developed an auto-injector branded as NovoPen, reflecting the commoditization of insulin in the patients' view, versus their clear preference for a user-friendly delivery system. Currently, its beyond-the-drug goals include helping discover demographic solutions. It teamed up with University College London and city leaders in several countries to analyze the sociological spread of diabetes in urban contexts through online and offline networking.

- Merck has the most comprehensive product-neutral resource across all therapeutic areas with its *Merck Manual*, now online, which has gained it a unique consumer recognition. It also runs an entire subsidiary, Vree Health, focused on healthcare service and delivery. Besides product promotion for Januvia (sitagliptin) and Janumet (sita-metformin), and a pipeline including omarigliptin (weekly DPP-IV inhibitor) and ertugliflozin (insulin glargine), Merck has wide-ranging initiatives in diabetes care innovation. It launched in 2014 a global outcomes registry to identify gaps in type 2 disease management. The three-year project, involving 20,000 patients and tracking glucose control, adherence, quality of life, and health resource utilization, is part of a broader commitment to generate real-world evidence [19].

- As AstraZeneca expands its portfolio from Bydureon (XR exenatide) to Forxiga (dapagliflozin) and Onglyza (saxagliptin), it aims to offer physicians a choice of treatments based on patient profiles and to provide customization to patients. In October 2014, It launched Fit2Me, a free diet and lifestyle support program including digital coaching, incentives, a progress log, and access to nurses across medication classes but still limited to AstraZeneca's products [20].

- Sanofi faces the patent loss of its flagship basal insulin Lantus (insulin glargine), a slower-than-expected uptake for its successor molecule Toujeo (high-concentration glargine), and biosimilars from Lilly and Boehringer Ingelheim. It is thus expanding the footprint of its Sanofi Patient Solutions (see the text box, "Sanofi Digital Portfolio in Diabetes").

SANOFI DIGITAL PORTFOLIO IN DIABETES

Sanofi is relying on diabetes as a change agent for a new integrated approach to care, including diagnostics as a value driver in patient outcomes. The company consulted patients and representative groups on issues such as caregiver experiences, trade-offs between injection phobias and side effects from oral therapies, and the consumer attractiveness of glucose-monitoring biosensors.

Sanofi proceeded on a step-by-step basis, addressing patient "pain points" through cross-functional teams. As one pain point was the failure of drugs and devices to interact in a way that minimized time and management burdens, Sanofi is building an integrated suite. Its iBGStar glucose meter, which connects to an iPhone, was developed with AgaMatrix and is used broadly by diabetes patients across Europe. Related offerings are MyStar Connect, custom software allowing physicians to evaluate patient hospital records through a secure portal, and the MyStar Extra device, launched in Europe in 2014, providing patients with on-demand coaching.

In France, the Diabeo management tool combines mobile apps and call centers for type 1 patients. The StarBem program in Brazil offers patient education across income levels. In China, with the world's largest population of diabetics, Sanofi is underwriting a five-year disease management program, the China Initiative for Diabetes Excellence, cosponsored by the Ministry of Health, with a clinically approved curriculum and hands-on instruction for 10,000 community physicians and healthcare workers. This is reinforced by Sanofi's alliance with Medtronic, building on the MiniMed implantable device, approved for type 1 patients by the EMA in 2013.

To support Sanofi's shift from pills to patients, five Centers of Excellence were set up, including Integrated Care and Patient Centricity, and a Chief Patient Officer was appointed [21]. The digital portfolio now ranges from the iBGStar to a diabetes blog and online glossary, Facebook and Twitter news posts, and the GoMeals diet app, in addition to the websites for Lantus and other products (Figure 9-3).

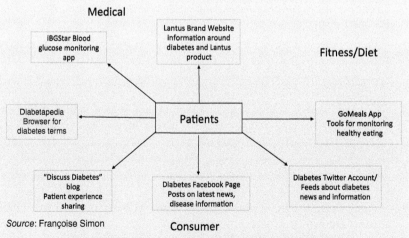

Source: Françoise Simon

Figure 9-3   Sanofi digital portfolio in diabetes

Other digital initiatives include Genentech's five-year partnership with PatientsLikeMe, with an initial focus on oncology. The network's clinical trial awareness tool may help with recruitment, and its Open Research Exchange program provides access to patient-reported outcomes, especially valuable in oncology for their potential to demonstrate value to payers and regulators [22].

Pfizer has also developed several product-neutral online initiatives. In September 2015, it launched "Breast Cancer: A Story Half Told" (www. storyhalftold.com) to encourage patients to share photos and messages of hope, in partnership with five advocacy groups, including the Cancer Support Community, Living Beyond Breast Cancer, and the Young Survival Coalition. This addresses the 150,000 to 250,000 US women suffering from metastatic breast cancer and aims to improve patient education [23]. Pfizer also announced in June 2015, together with the American Lung Association, the Quitter's Circle, a mobile app and online community designed to help smokers quit through educational, social, and financial support. Research had shown that only half of smokers spoke to their physicians about quitting, and they faced financial concerns such as doctor visits, counseling, and treatment costs. The initiative allows smokers to start a quit team with friends and family, crowdsource funds, and join the Quitter's Circle communities on Facebook and Twitter [24]. In 2012, Pfizer launched its first mobile logging tool, HemMobile, a free app helping hemophilia patients and caregivers log infusions and bleeds, regardless of what factor replacement product was used. The app allows users to set private reminders for infusions, physician appointments, and factor reordering, and also to enroll in the Hemophilia Village community. If patients opted out, Pfizer would not record any personal information [25].

While most companies now have such initiatives, there is still a significant gap between patients' needs for product-neutral disease information and bio-pharma offerings. A 2015 Accenture survey of 10,000 patients in Brazil, France, Germany, the United Kingdom, and the United States across seven areas (brain, bones, heart, immune system, lungs, metabolism, and cancer) showed that only 19 percent of patients were aware of biopharma services. Sixty-five percent of respondents stressed the pretreatment period as the most frustrating one in their patient journey and wanted guidance at that stage. While 85 percent preferred their physicians as the primary contact point, only 1 percent said it could be a pharma company [26].

Biopharmas continue to face structural barriers to being one-stop-shops for patient services because of functional silos and often of the lack of coordination between social and non-social communications. If social media are housed within marketing, the rotation of product managers and their short budget cycles may be issues. Ideally, patient communications should become part of a coordinated ecosystem that includes alliances with advocacy groups and offers real-time support around diseases, including prevention, moving beyond engagement only after a prescription has been issued.

CONSUMER-CENTERED TRENDS

Wearables: Growth and Challenges

In parallel with biopharma initiatives, market demand has driven two related trends: wearables (sensors worn on the body or in clothing to track activity and vital signs) and their link to social media. While wearables have shown exponential growth, company success has been uneven, in part because consumers are generally more satisfied with hardware (devices such as the Fitbit wristband) than software (fitness and health apps). According to BCC Research, mHealth, defined as "medical and public health practice supported by devices such as mobile phones, patient monitoring services and other wireless devices" [27], is expected to reach a global revenue of $21.5 billion by 2018, with Europe as the largest mHealth market [28].

Smartphones themselves, however, are showing signs of saturation. IDC (International Data Corporation) reported a flattening of global shipments, as Apple showed a first-ever decline in 2016 and Samsung (the largest maker of Android phones) also saw a fall in sales. As nearly 80 percent of Americans own smartphones, the market may be driven only by upgrades and conversion of the remaining nonusers [29].

A parallel trend is the proliferation of apps but a low level of satisfaction. Of the 165,000 health-related apps on Apple's iOS and Google's Android, most are rarely used and many are quickly abandoned. According to a 2015 IMS study, more than 50 percent of health apps have narrow functionality (often just information, without interpretation). Only 2 percent of apps have connectivity with provider systems.

Multiple barriers persist, including lack of integration between EHR systems, regulatory uncertainties, and privacy concerns. For physicians, the lack of infrastructure to handle massive patient inflows is compounded by liability and reimbursement issues.

Because of its fragmented healthcare system, the United States lags Europe. Denmark leads in mHealth utilization, level of digitization, and regulatory framework. In 2015, the National Health Service (NHS) in England launched a website and related app to treat depression and anxiety, and improve access to mental health services [30]. Some progress is being made in the United States, as the Mayo Clinic, Geisinger Health, Kaiser Permanente, Intermountain Healthcare, and Group Health formed, in 2015, the Care Connectivity Consortium to share patient data in a secure exchange.

A growing body of evidence is also being collected through collaborations. The Dana-Farber Cancer Institute and Fitbit announced, in April 2016, a partnered study of the impact of weight loss on cancer recurrence, sponsored by the National Cancer Institute and the Alliance for Clinical Trials in Oncology. The study aims to enroll more than 3,200 overweight women with early-stage breast cancer, to be randomized for a two-year weight loss and education program, versus health education alone. Fitbit is donating a fitness and heart rate tracker, smart scale, and software for video exercises on mobile devices [31]. It remains to be seen within what time frame the current vertical solutions can evolve from consumer-grade devices and apps to FDA-approved research-grade devices with curation of apps, provider buy-in, and interoperability across the care continuum, from patients to physicians and health systems.

BIOGEN, FITBIT, AND PATIENTSLIKEME: TRACKING MULTIPLE SCLEROSIS

In an earlier initiative, Fitbit partnered with Biogen and PatientsLikeMe to track progress in multiple sclerosis (MS). In July 2014, a group of patients with MS received a Fitbit activity tracker to use over three weeks and authorized PatientsLikeMe to access and transmit their activity data. The study aimed to help define baseline activity levels and attitudes toward biosensors. In MS, walking is an indicator of disease status, and tracking may allow changes to be detected earlier in relapsing MS. PatientsLikeMe recruited all participants in less than 24 hours, and a significant engagement level was shown, with 68 percent of participants reporting that the device helped them manage their MS and 54 percent wanting to continue sensor use. A University of California study, also conducted with Fitbit, supported a remote step-count monitoring as an exploratory outcome in MS trials. Future developments include a more detailed measurement of patients' gait and dexterity and an iPad app gauging cognitive function and vision [32].

Consumer concerns are also exacerbated by massive data breaches such as those of Anthem and Premera Blue Cross. Anthem alone suffered a breach of 78.8 million records in early 2015. Security experts agree that healthcare data has a much longer value than credit card information, as theft and misuse take a long time to show up in fraudulent billing and medical records [33]. Consumers are therefore reluctant to share data digitally. A 2013 Health Information National Trends survey of more than 3,000 patients showed that only 6 percent had actually shared health data through their devices, and that less than a quarter would be willing to do so for digital images or diagnostic information [34].

Some privacy risks may not even be publicly known. The *Journal of the American Medical Association* reported in 2016 a study of 211 Android diabetes apps that showed that 81 percent did not have privacy policies. Permissions (which users must accept to download an app) authorized collection and sharing with third parties of sensitive information such as insulin and blood glucose levels. There are no federal protections, including within HIPAA (the Health Insurance Portability and Accountability Act) against the sale or disclosure of data from apps to third parties [35].

The FDA has released several guidelines, including a 2015 guidance on electronic consent in trials, requiring clear information and ease of navigation [36]. It has stated its intent to calibrate regulation, overseeing only mobile apps and devices that could pose a safety risk if they malfunction, such as electrocardiography devices like AliveCor [37]. In its capacity to regulate false and deceptive advertising, the Federal Trade Commission (FTC) has already brought enforcement proceedings against two app developers, including one claiming to treat acne through light from a mobile phone. In addition, the Department of Health and Human Services (HHS) monitors HIPAA violations, and in July 2013 it fined WellPoint $1.7 million for failing to provide adequate safeguards for its online app database [38]. This conflicting pattern of rapid, mostly uncontrolled growth and related risks also applies to the evolution of social media in healthcare.

Social Media: From Insight Mining to Co-Creating

According to the Pew Research Center, 65 percent of American adults use social media, up from 7 percent in 2005, but the overall number of users has leveled off since 2013. While 90 percent of young adults use these sites, as many as 35 percent of those over 65 also do [39].

In its 2015 Cybercitizen Health US study, Decision Resources surveyed 6,601 US adults and found an overall demand for disease-oriented information, rather than drug data. Up to 38 percent of respondents had searched symptoms and conditions in the past 12 months, and up to 39 percent had done so through search engines versus 18 percent on social networks, only 12 percent on prescription drug websites, and even fewer (8 percent) on pharma corporate sites. The top site used was Facebook, closely followed by WebMD, with Twitter far behind. The top types of information sought were factual: prescription drugs' efficacy and side effects, followed by news feeds and provider ratings [40].

The use of private online physician ratings has greatly increased, with 8.9 million unique visitors for Healthgrades in September 2015 alone, partly because public websites such as Physician Compare include overly complex data or measures of clinical quality not meaningful to consumers, who are more interested in service components than mortality statistics [41].

In addition to provider ratings, the dominant need for disease information explains the growth of patient communities. Among others, PatientsLikeMe allows members to track their disease status and compare it with de-identified data from a large database, and to access customized clinical trial information. This trend is worldwide: in Europe, RareConnect is a site from EURORDIS (European Organization for Rare Diseases), with financing from public funds, events such as telethons, and corporate sources. PatientsLikeMe has partnered with the FDA to improve the reporting of adverse effects and has developed measurement tools through its Open Research Exchange. Given that 30 to 55 percent of patients with hypertension do not adhere to their medication regimen, PatientsLikeMe code-veloped with the Villanova College of Nursing a management instrument that would be free to physicians and would be completed during office visits to add PROs to clinical data [42].

The most advanced strategies belong to rare diseases, where some groups have actually funded trials and codeveloped breakthrough treatments. After its first investment in Aurora (later Vertex), leading to the 2012 FDA approval of Kalydeco (ivacaftor) for patients with a rare gene mutation, the Cystic Fibrosis Foundation is now funding research programs with Pfizer, Sanofi/Genzyme, and Shire. It has invested $425 million as part of its venture philanthropy model, and, in 2014, it sold its royalty rights for cystic fibrosis treatments developed with Vertex for $3.3 billion, to further develop new therapies and to provide online support of patients [43].

Given this rapid patient empowerment through social media, but also regulatory constraints, it would be prudent for biopharmas to adopt a stepwise approach. An indispensable first step is a sophisticated listening function, tracking what consumers are seeking online, but also what they are saying between themselves on social media. Beyond insights mining, companies can then reflect and shape the consumer demand for disease information with an unbranded portfolio ranging from blogs to compendia such as the *Merck Manual*. Some companies are issuing corporate posts on topics such as patient access information. Although practiced by a few biopharmas, branded messages remain a risk on uncontrolled social media. Facebook continues to allow pharma brands to disable comments, so many of the existing branded pages offer only the ability to share content but not respond [44]. These steps reflecting different degrees of risk are summarized in Figure 9-4.

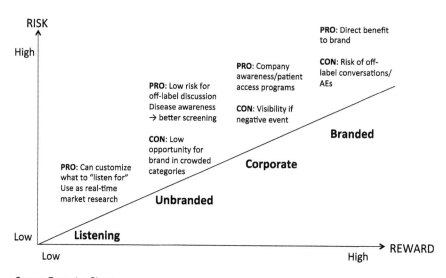

Source: Françoise Simon

Figure 9-4   Social content risk assessment

Best practices for biopharmas could also include the following steps:

- *Listen:* What conversations are happening around your disease and product?
- *Audit:* What are consumers' preferred platforms? Do they correspond to those you already use?
- *Create content:* Develop content that addresses patient pain points and their entire journey, including the pretreatment and posttreatment stages.
- *Integrate:* Pilot new initiatives and integrate them into overall social publishing
- *Coordinate:* Coordinate a consistent message across functions, from R & D to health economics and market access, customer relations, sales, and marketing.

In addition to extensive involvement with consumer trends and behaviors, eHealth success for biopharmas also depends on an understanding of provider-centered initiatives including telemedicine.

PROVIDER-CENTERED STRATEGIES: TELEHEALTH

The explosive growth of telehealth is supported by multiple trends, from an aging population with comorbidities weighing on an already cost-burdened system, to relaxing licensure regulation and mobile technology. The total addressable market for outpatient spending is now estimated at $57 billion by Cowen Equity Research [45]. While the terms *telehealth* and *telemedicine* are often used interchangeably, the latter is defined as "the use of electronic information and communication technologies to provide and support healthcare when distance separates participants." While telemedicine specifically refers to diagnosis and treatment, telehealth helps patients more broadly through self-care, education, and support systems [46]. The scope of telehealth is very broad, from standard e-consults to new on-demand services such as American Well and Teladoc.

Physician Digital Trends

While biopharmas aim to increase their patient and physician engagement, studies show a clear physician preference for other information sources. A 2015 Decision Resources study of 3,029 US practicing physicians showed that their clinical decisions are mostly influenced by conferences, colleagues, and journals, while pharma representatives were cited by less than a third of respondents. The professional apps most used were Epocrates, UpToDate, and Medscape, with their main attractiveness being quick access to information and ease of navigation. For online videos watched for clinical purposes, the same trend applied, with Medscape Professional Network and YouTube cited first versus only 8 percent using pharma websites. These videos were primarily for continuing medical education, seminars, medical procedures, and disease information [47].

Scope of Digital Services

Beyond these clear physician trends, the healthcare landscape is being fundamentally changed by a broad range of new and existing players, from on-demand services to device manufacturers (Figure 9-5). Several competitive threats are emerging for providers as well as biopharmas, as patients are partly migrating to on-demand services, content portals, and even pharmacy chains. These entities act to disintermediate communications between biopharmas and patients. For example, online portals like WebMD and Everyday Health are transitioning from content to service providers. WebMD offers a private wellness portal to self-insured employers and health plans. Its partnership with Walgreens integrates its content into the retailer's experience to track and reward healthy behavior. Everyday Health partners with Cigna for early risk identification in prenatal care, and it has also an alliance with the Mayo Clinic [48].

On-demand services represent a "convenience revolution," as they provide real-time consultations at about half the cost of standard visits. Players include MDLive, Doctor on Demand and American Well, and some firms such as AmeriDoc also offer lab testing services. Although some sites claim that they are reviewed by internal medical boards, most do not offer external validation or continuity of care.

A study published in May 2016 by *JAMA Dermatology* surveyed 16 online telemedicine companies, including seven general sites and nine focused on dermatology. Researchers created six fictitious scenarios and used stock images. Some sites misdiagnosed syphilis, herpes, and skin cancer, and two linked users to overseas doctors not licensed to practice where patients were located. Of the 14 clinicians who viewed photos of nodular melanoma, 11 correctly told the patient to see a doctor, but 3 diagnosed it as benign. According to the American Telemedicine Association (ATA), these services have grown rapidly, with more than one million e-visits expected in 2016. Many insurers cover them, generally for costs between $35 to $95. Given quality concerns, the ATA began an accreditation program in 2015. Although nearly 500 telemedicine companies applied, only 7 had been approved as of May 2016 [49].

Content Companies/Portals	On-Demand Services	Pharmacies	Insurers	Health Systems	Device Manufacturer
• WedMD/ employer portal • Everyday Health/Cigna Mayo partnerships	• American Well • Teladoc • MDLive • Doctor on Demand	• Walgreens/ MDLive • CVS Minute Clinics • Rite Aid	• Oscar Health • Anthem/Live Health Online • UnitedHealth/ Telehealth partners • Castlight comparison services	• Veterans Administration • John Hopkins • Partners Health Care • Kaiser Permanente	• Medtronic • Dexcom • AliveCor • Fitbit • Jawbone

Source: Françoise Simon

Figure 9-5   Scope of telehealth services

Faced with competition from new insurers such as Oscar Health, health plans have also developed online services. UnitedHealthcare has 16 telehealth partners and remotely monitors 20,000 members in their homes. Anthem also launched, in partnership with American Well, its LiveHealth program to be rolled out to its 33 million members, as a 24/7 service costing $49 per visit. These payer initiatives aim, in part, to minimize misuse of emergency rooms by patients with non-urgent issues.

Top therapeutic areas for telemedicine include mental health, dermatology, and cardiology through synchronous services (real-time consultations) and asynchronous services such as the transmission of radiology images.

Reimbursement from Medicare is slowly improving. Although there is no federal mandate, states have the option to reimburse for Medicaid teleservices, and many, including California, New York, and Pennsylvania, already cover video-conferencing. In addition, 21 states and the District of Columbia require private payer reimbursement, at varying cost levels [50].

Effectiveness of Telemedicine

Key issues for telemedicine remain its accuracy and cost effectiveness, which have been best analyzed by health systems. The Veterans Health Administration (VA) has a large program collecting data from over 17,000 participants, for illnesses ranging from diabetes to depression. It demonstrated high patient satisfaction, a 25 percent reduction in bed days, and a 19 percent reduction in hospital admission when compared with usual care.

Partners Healthcare conducted a randomized trial using a wireless pill bottle, together with feedback services and reminders for hypertension patients. Initial findings showed a 68 percent higher rate of medication adherence, compared with controls [51]. Similarly, in its Hospital at Home model, Johns Hopkins achieved comparable outcomes versus inpatients and yielded overall cost savings of 19 percent, generated, in part, from lower average length of stay and fewer diagnostic tests [52].

European initiatives have also generated positive results. In the United Kingdom, the Department of Health Whole System Demonstrator program, launched as early as 2008, was a 12-month study of 3,230 patients with diabetes, chronic obstructive pulmonary disease, or heart failure. Intervention participants, receiving telehealth equipment and monitoring services, showed fewer hospital admissions and lower mortality, also with lower costs per head.

In the United States, remaining barriers include licensure, privacy concerns, and broadband access, as some rural locations lack adequate network infrastructure. Only about 10 state medical boards issue licenses allowing interstate telehealth, but portability is expected to increase. A longer-lasting barrier may be liability fears. Teladoc and American Well both cover the cost of malpractice insurance, but risks persist if patients use telemedicine alone instead of as a complement to in-person visits [53]. Finally, interoperability remains a challenge, even though some EHRs have started exchange programs.

CONCLUSION

From consumer-driven trends, such as wearables and social media, to physician-centered strategies, such as on-demand services, and business-to-business initiatives from payers and EHR systems, digital technology is profoundly changing the healthcare landscape. Biopharma companies have launched initiatives, including those of Sanofi, Novo Nordisk, AstraZeneca, and Lilly in diabetes. They have also recognized the effectiveness of partnerships such as that of Biogen, Fitbit, and PatientsLikeMe in multiple sclerosis. However, these initiatives are still largely uncoordinated across functions and many are at the pilot stage.

Some significant gaps remain in biopharmas' understanding of the patient journey and of physician preferences. While multiple studies report an overwhelming information need from both groups for product-neutral information, biopharma digital portfolios are still often skewed toward product-centric communications. In addition, there is still not a clear business case for large-scale, long-term digital investments by biopharmas. Digital activities are still, in many cases, siloed by functions and business units, and the lack of metrics does not support investment.

SUMMARY POINTS

- Digital technology radically impacts the entire biopharma value chain, from new R & D models involving patients as co-creators to post-marketing surveillance optimized through continuous drug monitoring.

- EHealth also supports a growing consumer empowerment, especially as online communities take on an expanded role in collecting patient-reported outcomes and in actually funding clinical trials in rare diseases.

- Biopharmas and infotechs are increasingly partnering to fund technology start-ups and optimize data collection, as is shown by the dRx Capital joint venture between Novartis and Qualcomm.

- Biopharma supply chains are now increasingly supported by the Internet of Things, allowing better asset tracking, additive manufacturing, and cloud-based distribution.

- At the commercial end, biopharmas are developing digital portfolios including disease information and patient support, blogs, and wellness monitoring. However, there is a gap between consumer demand for product-neutral information and biopharma outreach that is still in great part product-centric.

- Consumer-driven trends include the growth of wearables such as Fitbit, but most apps are still limited by narrow functionality and lack of interoperability from patients to health systems.

- For providers, key digital information sources remain professional networks rather than biopharma companies. On-demand services represent new competition but suffer from uneven quality. While e-consultations are being increasingly reimbursed, the United States still lags Europe, due to limited interstate licensure, liability concerns, and privacy issues, especially in light of cyberattacks and uncertainties regarding cloud services.

CHAPTER 10

CREATING AGILITY THROUGH DATA AND ANALYTICS

INTRODUCTION

It is difficult not to get caught up in the statistics associated with big data. An estimated 2.5 billion bytes of data are collected daily by a growing cadre of sensor-based technologies, from mobile phones to the Internet of Things—from connected "smart" thermostats in homes to desktop computers [1]. Consumers worldwide used more than six billion connected "things" in 2016 [2]. As a result, analysts predict the digital universe, defined as the data created or copied yearly, will grow to 44 zettabytes, or 44 trillion gigabytes, by 2020 [3].

That staggering amount of data has the potential to disrupt a number of different businesses, including traditional biopharmas. This phenomenon has already altered the retail, banking, and transportation industries in fundamental ways, as organizations such as Amazon and Apple mine customer-generated information for insights about buying habits and behaviors in order to offer customized buying experiences [4]. Change in healthcare has not been quite as rapid. Appropriate concerns about patient privacy and a highly regulated product development environment have made it more difficult for biopharma companies to extract measurable value via the large-scale integration and analysis of data.

Yet data, and the analytics platforms that are critical to make sense of the wide variety of relevant data sets, have the potential to address the biggest challenges in healthcare. As noted in prior chapters, unsustainable cost inflation and budgetary pressures have fueled a shift in drug reimbursement from fee-for-service to paying-for-outcomes. At the same time, we have witnessed an explosion in the volume, variety, and velocity of health data. These data include electronic health record data, payers' claims data, gene sequencing data, real-time data generated by mobile technologies, and patient-reported data on social media sites such as Facebook and Twitter and from patient communities and advocacy organizations (e.g., PatientsLikeMe).

Managing Biotechnology: From Science to Market in the Digital Age, First Edition. Françoise Simon and Glen Giovannetti.

What if biopharmas could harness these data to identify the small percentage of individuals most likely to consume a disproportionate amount of healthcare resources and design appropriate therapies and behavioral interventions to keep them healthy? What if biopharmas could integrate these data into their R & D programs to identify better drug targets and further enhance the efficiency of clinical trials? What if new data types could inform commercial activities to better demonstrate the value patient, payer, and provider stakeholders say they want? Put more simply, what if biopharma companies could combine these different streams of data to see the "big picture"?

Such questions set up a compelling vision, in which the aggregation and utilization of real-world, real-time data harvested from diverse sources has the potential to transform every aspect of the biopharma value chain. Some of this is already happening. However, biopharmas are only at the beginning of understanding how best to use data and which kinds carry the most currency with stakeholders such as payers.

It is also true that drugmakers will only be able to extract value from data—estimated by some analysts to be greater than $1 billion across a medicine's life cycle—if they can transition to an analytics-driven culture [5]. Making that leap requires that drugmakers overcome significant cultural, technological, and, in some cases, regulatory barriers to create new business practices that can replace—or coexist with—complicated processes that developed in a pre-digital age. As Charles Hansen famously put it, "All the problems with digital are analog problems" [6].

This chapter reviews the opportunities and challenges represented by the current explosion in data and analytics technologies. It also addresses the multiple forces that require biopharma companies to have access to data analytics expertise. If, in the future, intellectual property is tied less to an actual product than the real-world evidence that product generates—and the algorithms used to uncover it—it will behoove biopharma companies to develop robust systems that allow them to shorten the cycle time between data generation and the creation of business insights.

MULTIPLE FORCES CONVERGE TO CREATE DATA AND ANALYTICS OPPORTUNITIES

If biopharmas and their collaborators want to take advantage of today's data rich environment, they cannot just be excellent data aggregators. They must also be excellent data analyzers. Advances in a host of enabling tools, from cloud-based storage to natural language processing and machine learning, have resulted in an unprecedented opportunity to analyze and link disparate types of structured and unstructured health data, both big and small. Indeed, four different forces have recently converged to make data analysis a core capability within biopharmas (Figure 10-1). These four forces are:

- Changing customer expectations
- Changing speed of data generation
- Changing reimbursement models
- Changing biopharma business models

As discussed in Chapters 5 and 8, the traditional customers of biopharma products, physicians, have less voice in the current climate than a decade ago, while payers and patients have increasing power—and increasing expectations— due to economic shifts that require better population management as well as patient cost-sharing for medicines. In this environment, these groups of super-consumers want more data, not simply about product safety and efficacy but also about outcomes. The democratization of information and the growing importance of patient centricity mean that patients are not only informed about treatment options but are important influencers in the prescribing decision, especially when side-effects might adversely affect quality of life.

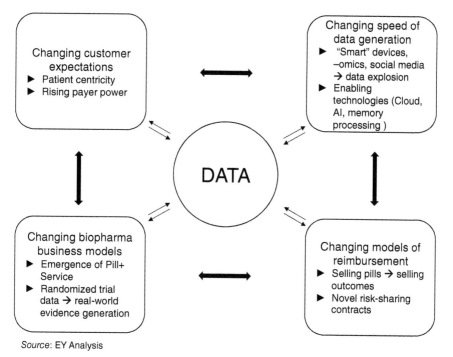

Source: EY Analysis

Figure 10-1   Multiple forces require biopharmas to become analytics experts

The changing speed of data generation is another important factor. As the wearable device revolution outlined in Chapter 9 accelerates, clinical-grade health data obtained by passive sensors linked to digital apps is improving. Indeed, Eric Schadt, the founding director of the Icahn Institute for Genomics and Multiscale Biology at New York's Mount Sinai Health System, predicts that as these devices grow more powerful "accurate information about your health will exist more outside the health system than inside the health system" [7]. That is both an opportunity and a challenge for biopharma companies. In order to take full advantage of this ever-larger pool of data, drugmakers must be able to mine it rapidly to make different business decisions.

Similarly, changes in healthcare reimbursement also require biopharmas to become more familiar with data analytics. As reimbursement is increasingly based on cost effectiveness and unique real-world value, data demonstrating that effectiveness are an intrinsic part of not only a product's value proposition but the basis for novel payment models that share risk between drugmakers and payers.

These changing customer expectations come at a time when biopharma business models are already under stress. R & D productivity has suffered as companies attack scientifically more challenging therapeutic areas such as Alzheimer's disease or attempt to develop breakthrough innovations in disease areas well served by generics (e.g., cardiovascular disease). Meanwhile, as drug spending becomes a greater concern in nearly every major market, companies have more limited ability to make regular price increases on existing products.

The end result is that as growth via traditional innovation has slowed, biopharmas are in the process of embracing new business models that go beyond selling products to creating solutions based on real-world data. At their core, these new business models are rooted in the ability to use data and analytics to adapt quickly to the evolving market. This ability to adapt becomes even more important as new entrants such as infotech companies enter the health space with their own data-driven solutions.

HEALTHCARE'S FOUR DATA VECTORS: VOLUME, VELOCITY, VARIETY, AND VERACITY

Since their beginnings, biopharma companies have been data-driven organizations. They are already adept at using data from randomized clinical trials to develop novel products that are safe and efficacious. In the evolving commercial landscape, biopharmas are now trying to simultaneously collect data to do the following: better segment patient populations, more accurately target high-prescribing physicians, collect real-world proof of outcomes to satisfy public and private payers, and incorporate these real-world findings into their discovery and research and development activities.

As data have grown in importance, the number of terms to describe it have likewise ballooned (see the box, "Important Definitions"). Most of the time, health data still do not clear the bar of being truly "big data" in terms of the amount of bytes being aggregated. The advent of large genetic data sets and information collected by Internet of Things (IoT) devices means the landscape is shifting rapidly, however.

IMPORTANT DEFINITIONS

The following definitions are important to keep in mind:

- *Big data:* A term coined in the 1990s for a collection of data sets so large and complex that they are difficult to analyze using traditional database management tools or data processing applications [8].

- *Small data:* Data comprising less than several gigabytes that connect people with timely information that is organized and packaged to be actionable for everyday tasks. Also called "the last mile of big data," in biopharma it refers to any data related to the development and commercialization of a specific product [9]. Small data are sometimes used to refer to data from consumer-facing wearables.

- *Real-world data:* Data that are not captured via clinical trials and are also not intended for research purposes. Real-world data comprise both small and big data, depending on the quantity of data and the number of sources that must be combined.

- *Structured data:* Data that can be stored, interrogated, queried, and analyzed by machine. Laboratory results, reimbursement codes, and patient health data (e.g., blood pressure, heart rate, body temperature) from electronic health records are examples of structured data.

- *Unstructured data:* Text- or image-rich data that are not organized in a predefined manner. Physician notes, medical images, and social media commentary are all examples of unstructured data.

- *Analytics:* A three-step process to discover and communicate meaningful patterns in data, whether big or small. The three steps are data collection, data sharing, and data analysis.

Health data can be classified along four different axes: volume, velocity, variety, and veracity (Figure 10-2) [10]. In addition to anonymized patient record data, imaging records, biometric sensor readings from wearables, genetic sequence information, and social media interactions have driven tremendous growth in the volume, velocity, and variety of health data now being generated. While each of these three parameters present challenges for biopharma companies, it is the third "V", variety, which has been the most difficult to manage.

Consider volume, first. While the explosion of healthcare data is a challenge, the obstacles biopharmas face are really no different from those other industries (e.g., retail or consumer) have confronted. This means analytics tools that have been well validated elsewhere can be adapted, or applied, to the biopharma space, while management teams build the organizational structures

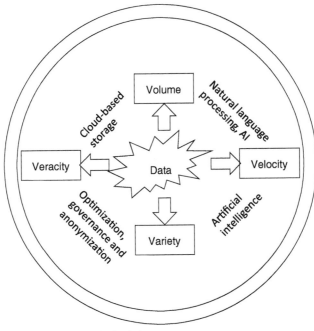

Source: EY Analysis

Figure 10-2 Enabling tools to leverage data's four vectors

required for analytics-driven cultures to flourish. Given healthcare's time frames, biopharma companies also do not need to use analytics to make decisions based on data generated in microsecond time frames. As such, managing the velocity of data generation in healthcare is not as big a concern as it is in industries such as finance or banking.

Instead, it is the variety of data biopharma companies must now assimilate that is the primary hurdle to clear. It is also one of the biggest opportunities. While each data type, for instance electronic health record data or genetic data or lifestyle data, has tremendous value on its own, it is only by linking these disparate pieces of information together that biopharma companies can achieve a step change in business as usual. As David Shaywitz, chief medical officer of DNAnexus, a leading provider of enterprise platforms for translational informatics, notes, "it is from the collisions of data where true insights arise" [11].

But each of these different data types exist in different formats and, because of patient privacy, have been stripped of identifying information. That makes combining the data into a credible whole challenging. Biopharmas must account for unstructured information—from social media commentary, physicians' notes in electronic health records, environmental readouts, and patient journey descriptions in clinical trials—while linking it to more structured data from the electronic health record in ways that can lead to new kinds of insights. In addition, the challenge of assimilating disparate data is made greater because most are owned by different players in the health ecosystem. Thus, if biopharma companies want to fully transform their businesses via integrating real-world data with patient health records, they must either purchase the information or partner with other healthcare stakeholders to access what they do not already own. As discussed later in the chapter, the dynamic market for healthcare data—and how best to partner with payers and providers, two groups that do not necessarily trust biopharmas—is of growing importance as the changing commercial landscape evolves to require integrated data covering the totality of the patient experience.

In addition to the three attributes described above, there is a fourth data characteristic that is critical to consider when evaluating health data: veracity. As biopharmas increasingly use unstructured data in their analytics efforts, they must take particular care to make sure the data are as error-free as possible and credible. As discussed later in the chapter, data quality is a particular challenge because unstructured data can be highly variable and inaccurate, for instance, due to mistranslation of a doctor's handwriting [12].

EXTRACTING VALUE FROM DATA REQUIRES NEW TOOLS

As healthcare transitions from paper records, prescriptions, and imaging films to digital technologies, the information needs to be collected and stored on a common platform. In this environment, cloud computing has become a key enabler of data management. It not only allows easy access to information regardless of where the data are generated but supports the storage of disparate types of data in a common location. That makes the bits and bytes easier to manipulate. In addition, the existence of secure clouds from third-party specialists such as DNAnexus or Medidata Solutions means biopharma companies do not have to spend the time and money investing in the creation and upkeep of large departments devoted to data management and storage. That lowers the barrier to entry for big data analytics, particularly for younger biopharma companies, allowing them to scale their activities more quickly.

Jeffrey Reid, Ph.D., Executive Director and Head of Genome Informations at the Regeneron Genetics Center, a division of Regeneron that is applying high throughput genomics to speed drug discovery and development, notes the company's data efforts would have had a much rockier growth curve in the absence of cloud computing. Just setting up the data storage center would have required a massive effort, from the purchasing of hardware to the creation of a dedicated facility with computer servers. "From a pure infrastructure standpoint, we were able to go from not having a center to establishing a top of the line capability in a time frame that would not have been possible without cloud computing," he says [13].

In addition to cloud computing, other tools capable of analyzing structured and unstructured data are essential as biopharma's pool of data grows. There is now a pervasive belief that having more data is always better. In reality, having more data can be a mixed blessing. "All you have really done," notes David

Davidovic, founder of the consultancy pathForward and a former senior executive at Merck & Co., Genentech, and Roche, "is build a bigger and bigger haystack of data that organizations do not know what to do with" [14]. Indeed, according to the market research firm IDC, "only about 5% of the data that are currently captured worldwide are ever analyzed" [15].

Getting a return from data will require deeper analysis of the other 95 percent of the information. Here tools that are making a difference include the divide-and-process approach of parallel computing, software platforms such as Apache Hadoop, the use of probabilistic statistical models, and advances in artificial intelligence (AI), including cognitive computing and machine learning. Such tools move beyond human-based applications to more predictive solutions that can both manage the proliferation of data and quickly generate meaningful insights to biopharma decision makers at a relevant point in time [16]. (See the boxes, "Using Machine Learning to Move from Experience-Based to Evidence-Based Medicine: The Evolution of GNS Healthcare" and "Artificial Intelligence: The Potential to Make Drugs Smarter, Faster, and for Less.")

USING MACHINE LEARNING TO MOVE FROM EXPERIENCE-BASED TO EVIDENCE-BASED MEDICINE: THE EVOLUTION OF GNS HEALTHCARE

GNS Healthcare, based in Cambridge, Massachusetts, was formed in 2000, when excitement about the sequencing of the human genome was at a fever pitch. For nearly a decade, the company, which uses Bayesian algorithms to reveal the complex, cause-and-effect relationships between variables in large data sets, focused on sifting through genetic and clinical data to help pharmaceutical companies discover novel drug targets, combination therapies, or new indications for existing products. As machine learning tools evolved, however, GNS expanded its approach, combining billions of patient data points into computer models to answer real-world questions about the effectiveness of therapies, medical procedures, and care management programs in individuals. "Our goal is to leverage data from multiple sources quickly to solve the ultimate matching problem: identifying de novo the right intervention for a patient to improve health outcomes and lower the total cost of care," says Colin Hill, GNS's co-founder, chairman, and chief executive officer [17].

Indeed, a number of studies indicate that billions of dollars are wasted annually in the United States alone because of wasted or inappropriate care [18]. Patients diagnosed with rheumatoid arthritis (RA), for instance, are prescribed one therapy, and then step through alternatives depending on their response and side effects. Despite having a range of therapeutic options to treat RA, optimizing the therapy is done not by science but via trial and error and the experience of the physician. This trial-and-error process is common across many diseases, including cancer, cardiovascular disease, and central nervous system disorders.

As machine learning and artificial intelligence have evolved, Colin Hill wants to change that paradigm. He believes that using causal machine learning (causal ML) and simulation to reveal complex causal relationships within large datasets will be a key enabler for value-based contracting between pharma and payers.

In 2012 the company partnered with Aetna to create causal models identifying patients with the greatest one-year risk of developing metabolic syndrome. The company used its causal ML and simulation platform known as REFS (Reverse Engineering and Forward Simulation), to transform de-identified medical, pharmacy, lab, and demographic data for 37,000 individuals at one of Aetna's employer customers into computer models of metabolic syndrome risk and response on an individual level. GNS' REFS platform found that certain combinations of factors were more meaningful than others. Indeed, the combination of waist circumference, blood glucose levels, and number of doctor's visits predicted with 88 percent accuracy which individuals would develop metabolic syndrome. Moreover, GNS was able to do this high-level analysis in just three months, creating the opportunity for meaningful patient intervention [19].

This causal analysis was possible because GNS can rapidly combine a variety of data and turn it into new kinds of evidence based on statistically significant responses observed in patients with one set of risk factors and not another. But GNS's researchers also played a vital role, notes Hill, by "being able to step back and ask important fundamental questions" about metabolic syndrome.

Moving forward, Hill believes payers and providers will increasingly use causal ML to make value determinations about which therapies and interventions should be applied to patient subpopulations and even down to the individual patient level. Biopharma companies could also use these data proactively to more confidently enter risk-sharing agreements with other stakeholders. "Biopharmas can interrogate the data to understand what other parameters are necessary for a positive health outcome. They are able to know more fully the risks they are owning in an outcomes-based contract," he says. As such, GNS is positioning itself to play the role of "honest broker" between biopharmas and payers.

What Hill is most excited about is the ability of causal ML to create new comparative knowledge that would not be practical (or affordable) given our current randomized clinical trial approach. "There is not the time, money or a large enough patient pool to answer many fundamental questions about the real world utility of medicines," says Hill. But computational approaches now offer the ability to quickly test hundreds of potentially relevant correlations to identify situations where A causes B. In that sense, causal ML is also a critical decision support tool in quantifying how and where scant healthcare dollars should be spent to maximize patient outcomes while minimizing the total cost of care [20].

THE ANALYTICS CONTINUUM: FROM DESCRIPTIVE TO PRESCRIPTIVE

If biopharmas are to fully utilize the power of data and analytics to transform their businesses, their capabilities need to evolve from being descriptive to prescriptive. In other words, companies need to shift from identifying what has happened (e.g., drug sales in a given market grew 20 percent in six months) to understanding what steps to take to make the event happen (e.g., by taking a more strategic approach to market the product selectively to certain top regional health systems, which currently have low awareness of the product, it will be possible to increase product

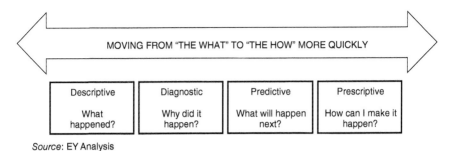

Source: EY Analysis

Figure 10-3   The analytics continuum

sales by the desired target). Moving from the "what" to the "how" occurs along a four-step continuum, which is described in Figure 10-3.

The first step in the process is the simplest: with *descriptive analytics*, biopharma companies need to consolidate data sources, creating systems that consistently collect, aggregate, and distribute structured and unstructured data from both internal and external sources. Mining the data typically requires real-time dashboards or other visual tools. At this stage, it may also be useful to perform *diagnostic analytics* to understand, based on past performance, why something happened. A biopharma preparing to launch a new cardiovascular product, for instance, might look at its three most recent launches to assess sales force deployment, advertising spend, use of co-pay cards, and other factors to gain a data-driven understanding of what worked—and what did not—in past launches. That understanding would allow the company to refine and further optimize its current launch strategy.

As biopharmas' expertise with data grows, they will advance to using analytics to identify past patterns that are predictive of future events. Such *predictive analytics* are particularly valuable when making complex forecasts, for instance, tied to a product or business unit's sales and marketing, as they help drive actual business decisions and help manage risk. Research shows even a modest improvement in the accuracy of predictions can result in significant savings or increased revenues. As Eric Siegel recounts in *Predictive Analytics: The Power to Predict Who Will Click, Buy, Lie, or Die*, one insurance company used predictive analytics to reduce its loss ratio, defined as the total amount it paid in claims divided by the total amount of premiums collected, by a half percentage point. The net effect of this small improvement was financially significant, worth around $50 million annually [21].

According to the technology research firm Gartner, only about 13 percent of businesses across all industries currently use predictive analytics. Fewer still, just 3 percent, utilize the most valuable form of analytics—*prescriptive analytics* [22]. Prescriptive analytics are designed to help answer specific questions, for instance, what combination of interventions, including drugs and behavioral change, could keep a patient with a history of heart disease, diabetes, and poorly controlled cholesterol healthy and out of the hospital? Having access to such data would obviously empower biopharma companies to make more informed investment decisions about services that might be wrapped around a product, or additional data to collect in the development phase to showcase value to stakeholders such as payers and health systems.

A cross-industry analysis by Forbes Insights suggests that when it comes to data capabilities, companies developing technology and consumer products have the most mature data and analytics capabilities, while biopharmaceuticals companies score close to the bottom, roughly on par with healthcare organizations and governments [23]. There are a number of reasons for this lower level of maturity. First, appropriately managing and manipulating health data requires access to a portfolio of analytics tools and skill sets that are different from the business intelligence tools biopharmas have traditionally employed. In addition, the highly fragmented healthcare market means considerable work is required to aggregate high-value data from different payers and providers, as well as patients and caregivers, to establish a complete picture of health needs and potential trends. Finally, healthcare is highly regulated and patient privacy remains a critical part of the social contract between patients and other stakeholders. How best to use algorithms to target high risk-patients while maintaining appropriate standards for sensitive, personally identifiable information is an issue yet to be adequately resolved [24].

ARTIFICIAL INTELLIGENCE: THE POTENTIAL TO MAKE DRUGS SMARTER, FASTER, AND FOR LESS

By Pamela Spence, Global Life Sciences Leader, EY

AI, defined as artificial or perhaps better labelled augmented intelligence, has the potential to greatly enhance scientific breakthroughs and medical research via the application of neural networks that promote deep learning. Powered by machine learning algorithms, computers can leverage big data to beat humans at video and board games and spot illnesses before symptoms appear. In 2016, DeepMind's "AlphaGo" bested humans in the ancient and complicated cognitive board game, a historic first. At Oxford University, Chris Holmes, a Bayesian biostatistician, has been using machine learning studies to understand the development of genetic diseases. Deep learning can make the connections that humans cannot put together. This type of AI learns from the shape of data, not just the discrete parts, which will increase the chances of breakthrough discoveries that can solve critical problems and have a positive long-term impact on humankind—if we let it.

Without doubt, one of the biopharma industry's biggest challenges is R & D productivity, with new molecules requiring more than $1 billion and 10–15 years to develop. There is universal appreciation that current levels of attrition during clinical development are not sustainable. The industry and regulators also have an overreliance on animal testing, which is assumed to be transferable to humans. Gene and disease function often do not transfer between species and gene-disease relationships are not understood.

AI can be applied to many different biopharma domains. It is a research assistant that can solve problems by systemic and relentless search at incredible speeds, never stopping. There are now vast amounts of biomedical data, from a growing body of literature to whole genome sequencing data, that can be rapidly analyzed for previously unidentified associations. Specific time-lapse comparisons between individual gene responses can now be analyzed at scale. Deep learning can be applied to predict symptomologies from gene and protein features and then applied in reverse to relate symptomologies back to gene function.

Using this fuller data set, biopharma companies can increase the probability of success and decrease the costs of failure. Indeed, it is now more possible to identify the right target, right compound, right safety profile, right patient, and right trial design. AI gives us a more streamlined and efficient process to drug discovery, better patient stratification, better predictability of disease progression, and better patient personalization.

Innovative drug discovery companies such as the London-based BenevolentAI, formed in 2013, are now bringing software engineers, data analytics experts, and scientists together to collaborate in "agile" ways on drug discovery and development. Such collaborative innovation enables companies to ask questions that never before were possible to ask. The opportunity today is to integrate seamlessly new combinations of skills.

DATA ANALYTICS ACROSS THE BIOPHARMA VALUE CHAIN

For data to actually transform the biopharma value chain, companies will need to build capabilities or partner to access a portfolio of different tools and technologies. Indeed, one of the challenges in creating an analytics-driven organization is that no one single technology or process provides all the analytics capabilities required to answer all the questions that arise across the biopharma value chain, from how to discover the most effective biological targets, to how to develop them efficiently, to how to optimize product sales (Figure 10-4). As discussed later in the chapter, the possibility of siloed information or expertise makes it imperative that companies establish governance structures that promote appropriate sharing and integration of data.

Improving Research and Discovery

Data analytics has perhaps the biggest potential to enable a new drug discovery and development paradigm, though currently the return on investment at this step of the value chain is hardest to measure. The advent of new genomic technologies has resulted in significant reductions in the cost of genome sequencing. According to the National Human Genome Research Institute, which collects data from the genome sequencing groups it funds, in mid-2015, it cost around $4,000 to create a high-quality draft whole human genome sequence. By late 2015, the price tag was dramatically lower—just $1,500; and if only the protein coding regions were desired—what scientists call the exome—the price tag was lower still, under

Stage of Value Chain	Role of Analytics	Example
Discovery	▶ Novel target and biomarker discovery ▶ Drug repurposing ▶ Identification of new services to treat unmet medical needs	Berg Health uses machine learning to find novel cancer target; Regeneron links genotypic and phenotypic data via cloud
Development	▶ Real-time analysis of data ▶ Incorporation of real-world data into clinical trials ▶ Targeted patient recruitment ▶ New trial designs: adaptive and virtual	Quintiles and Validic provide remote trials; Corcept Therapeutics partners with Liquid Grid to use social media to identify patients with rare diseases
Supply Chain	▶ Real-time insight into demand forecasting ▶ Efficient manufacturing processes ▶ Adverse event monitoring ▶ End-to-end coordination from manufacturer → pharmacy → patient	GSK and University of Cambridge's Institute for Manufacturing partner to build end-to-end supply project
Sales and Marketing	▶ Real-world data-driven solutions ▶ Payer segmentation ▶ Sales optimization by channel and geography ▶ Incorporation of social media data into commercial messaging	Big pharma optimizes patient out-of-pocket spending in 12 key US geographies to increase gross sales
Life Cycle Management	▶ Real-time messaging to maintain medication adherence; behavioral change ▶ Precision care pathways ▶ Predictive interventions	J&J, IBM, and Apple using AI to provide a virtual coach to patients; AstraZeneca uses real-world data to get better formulary placement of heart drug; Amgen, Novartis, and Pfizer create real-world evidence platforms for data capture

Source: EY Analysis

Figure 10-4   Analytics across the biopharma value chain (selected examples)

$1,000 per genome [25]. As sequencing technology at Illumina and other biotechs develops, costs are anticipated to drop further, potentially under $100. As sequencing costs fall, biopharmas are able to rethink how they identify and validate drug targets, leveraging big sets of genetic data to find interesting but rare biological signals that could be the basis for novel medicines.

This approach grows even more powerful if biopharma companies are able to link unstructured phenotypic data, for instance, from patient electronic health records, to genetic data. Combining the genetic data with unstructured historical data via powerful analytics, biopharma companies can uncover not just previously hidden biomarkers, but relate their molecular research to outcomes that previously were not recognized.

Tapping that opportunity is one of the reasons Regeneron formed its Regeneron Genetics Center (RGC) and partnered with Geisinger Health System to sequence the genomes of hundreds of thousands of Geisinger patients [26]. In March 2016, the partners published their first peer-reviewed paper, using sequence data linked to de-identified longitudinal health records to identify a specific genetic mutation that results in a significantly reduced risk of coronary artery disease [27]. The findings corroborate ongoing R & D efforts at Regeneron from animal studies, as well as biochemical and early human genetic experiments, about the novel target's importance in improving clinical outcomes. "This new evidence gives us a lot of confidence about our development strategy and the ability to identify game-changing opportunities," says Aris Baras, M.D., Head of the RGC [28].

In addition to Regeneron, start-ups such as Berg Health, TwoXAR and Sema4 are on their own, and in partnership with academic groups, bigger biopharmas, and infotechs, using cognitive computing and other big data tools to develop novel drugs for complex disease states [29–31].

Cancer has been one of the areas where these efforts to transform biopharma discovery have been most obvious; that is partly because the same trends driving convergence and precision medicine, topics outlined in Chapters 1 and 4, respectively, reinforce the demand for sophisticated analytics. As outlined in Chapter 1, IBM, via its Watson Health division, is making a clear bid to use cognitive computing to identify and personalize oncology therapies [32].

Going forward, this intersection of genetics and what has historically been health IT will merge and further drive the acceleration of efficient drug R & D. Critically, the failure rate for drugs in late-stage trials is still too high in a world of constrained resources. According to a team of researchers at Sagient Research Systems and the Biotechnology Innovation Organization (BIO), around 40 percent of all drugs fail in phase III [33]. Since the cost of R & D increases sharply from one phase to the next, such late-stage failures represent a very inefficient use of R & D capital. Because of historical pricing flexibility, biopharmas have not had the pressure to focus on R & D efficiency, but that situation is changing rapidly. In the future, biopharma companies will need to better use enabling tools such as artificial intelligence and causal machine learning to improve this portion of the value chain [34].

Improving Clinical Trials

There is no question the current clinical trials paradigm, defined as sequential phase I, II, and III studies punctuated by months of analyses and planning, is outdated. In sharp contrast to the technology and consumer sectors, where big data collected in real time routinely informs product formation, the basic framework for drug development has not changed since the 1960s [35]. Because of the high cost of late-stage drug failures, however, biopharmas are beginning to embrace analytics-driven clinical trial designs to increase the efficiency and success rates of their development programs. These so-called adaptive designs rely on Bayesian algorithms to enable preplanned adjustments to clinical trials to refine hypotheses and reallocate R & D dollars in real time based on clinical data [36].

In addition, as described in Chapter 9, the marriage of clinical data and social media (e.g., Twitter, Facebook, and YouTube, and especially online patient communities) creates a new opportunity to develop clinical descriptions of disease that can inform and accelerate clinical trial enrollment, while –omic data (e.g., genomic, proteomic, microbiomic, etc.) enable the identification of patients likely to respond. Similarly, the incorporation of digital technologies into trial designs allows the detection of early safety and efficacy signals. Indeed, data streams from wearables and sensors allow real-time feedback, creating an opportunity for continuous learning in clinical trials via analytics.

Biopharma companies are only now beginning to identify how to leverage analytical tools such as machine learning in this regard. Many of the first efforts are clustered in neurological disease areas where measuring product efficacy and disease progression have historically depended on subjective survey data. Teva Pharmaceutical Industries, for instance, teamed up with Intel in September 2016 to incorporate data from wearable devices in a phase II trial monitoring disease progression in Huntington's disease to generate objective scores measuring the severity of motor symptoms [37].

Creating the Agile Supply Chain

As cost pressures mount and competition from both start-ups and new entrants increases, larger biopharmas are increasingly focused on optimizing their operational performance, especially the activities tied to manufacturing and supply chain. Advanced analytics has a key role to play here. Beyond improving manufacturing efficiencies, analytics can help companies do a better job of creating real-time forecasts, reducing the need to carry costly excess inventory, as well as creating new drug distribution platforms.

A 2014 study shows that while most biopharmas amass significant amounts of historical manufacturing and supply-chain related data, the collected statistics are siloed across different parts of the organization and the available tools are too limiting to handle biopharma's complex manufacturing processes [38]. As streamlining business processes becomes more important in today's tougher climate, however, biopharma companies will look outside the industry to lessons learned in the retail and consumer technology sectors. Analytics-enabled flexible supply chains like the kind Apple employs to create its iPhones will become the norm. Steps that can optimize the hand-offs between the wholesaler, the retail pharmacy, and the patient encourage care coordination and adherence, which can ultimately promote a drug's value

To that end, GlaxoSmithKline in 2014 teamed up with Cambridge University's Institute for Manufacturing to build a more efficient end-to-end supply chain that brings together equipment manufacturers, regulators, knowledge transfer networks, and healthcare providers [39]. Three years earlier, the biopharmaceutical company also partnered with what, at the time, was a non-obvious player: the Formula One race car manufacturer McLaren. On the racetrack, every second counts, so pit crews use sophisticated data analytics to reduce the time required for tire changes and other repairs. GlaxoSmithKline wanted to adapt such methodology to its own processes, particularly in its consumer health business, where small-batch manufacturing leads to not just lost productivity but lower margins. After working with McLaren for about a year, GlaxoSmithKline reduced downtime in one particular manufacturing plant by 60 percent. Since 2011, the two organizations have worked to scale-up changes and have expanded their efforts to make R & D more efficient via the use of sophisticated sensors in clinical trials [40].

Using Analytics to Rethink Commercial Activities

The shift from fee for service to fee for value and the growth of digital technologies have made what was once one of the most straightforward parts of the biopharma value chain—sales and marketing and life cycle management—one of the most complicated. Indeed, estimates suggest that approximately two-thirds of new drugs fail to meet prelaunch sales expectations in their first year on the market and continue to underperform for the next two years [41].

As noted in Chapters 7 and 8, one reason so many recent drug launches have been suboptimal is the need to have, at launch, data showing real-world utility. Absent such information, increasingly skeptical payers and providers make medicines harder to obtain, either by putting them on expensive formulary tiers or by excluding them altogether [42]. (See the box, "Real-World Data—and Analytics—Play an Increasingly Important Role in Establishing Product Value.")

REAL-WORLD DATA—AND ANALYTICS—PLAY AN INCREASINGLY IMPORTANT ROLE IN ESTABLISHING PRODUCT VALUE

As shown in Figure 10-5, real-world data play an increasingly important role in determining product value and accelerating the uptake of medicines in the market. Such data may be linked to solutions that support treatment adherence, improved care coordination, precision medicine–linked care pathways, or predictive interventions. IMS estimates the potential value of these efforts is between $600 and $800 million, much of it due to direct revenue uplift [43].

Incorporating real-world data in earlier parts of the biopharma drug life cycle, for example, to improve the probability of success of phase III trials, is critical as well. Here, the payoffs are more difficult to quantify. It is difficult to put a dollar value on the

Stakeholder	Value to stakeholder
Biopharma	Accelerates market adoption and protects existing market share by... ▶ Demonstrating improved patient outcomes/efficacy ▶ Enhancing understanding of patients' unmet medical needs ▶ Exploring new indications ▶ Providing justification of reimbursement
Regulators	Supports safety and efficacy in the real world by... ▶ Detecting safety signals ▶ Validating long-term effectiveness
Providers	Optimizes patient treatments for highest quality care by... ▶ Providing evidence in local patient populations ▶ Enabling continued provider reimbursement ▶ Bolstering reputation in the community
Payers	Promotes more cost-effective allocation of resources to patient population by... ▶ Informing value and coverage determination ▶ Linking utilization of health resources to evidence of outcomes ▶ Developing better models for calculating cost versus benefit
Patients	Enables more personalized health experience by... ▶ Allowing more informed evaluation of individual risks and benefits ▶ Promoting selection of safer, more convenient medicines

Source: EY Analysis

Figure 10-5   Real-world evidence is central to all health stakeholders, but for different reasons

long-term benefit associated with reducing clinical trial design flaws or an improved product profile design. It is easier to see the impact on clinical trial recruitment, where incorporation of real-world data can accelerate patient recruitment in a two-step process that includes the identification of better responding patient subgroups and subsequent clinical trial restructuring. Indeed, IMS estimates a 30 percent improvement can result in cost savings of $100 to $200 million annually for a top 10 biopharma [44]. Moreover, as regulatory bodies embrace new conditional approval pathways that allow accelerated product launches, as well as their accelerated withdrawal, real-world data will become a *de minimis* requirement [45].

Of course, the translation of real-world data into usable and compelling evidence requires an analytics backbone that is able to reduce the time to actual business decisions. Having predefined tools that integrate data in compliance with patient privacy and do not require special programming capabilities is necessary, as they allow biopharmas to deploy their staff on value-added strategic tasks (e.g., clinical trial design or launch planning) rather than more routine processes such as data cleaning or aggregation. The payoffs are likely to be greatest in helping manage complicated chronic diseases such as diabetes or heart failure.

Beyond real-world evidence analysis, other commercial activities that will alter as a result of data analytics include strategic payer engagement, a topic discussed in Chapter 8, and the channel and geographic optimization of a biopharma's sales force via multichannel digital tools. Such analytics capabilities better enable drugmakers to interact with the right physicians, key opinion leaders, and health systems based on a therapy's clinical profile. As it becomes increasingly difficult to engage with already busy physicians, the ability to customize the message to the right prescribers is essential. On average, high-prescribing physicians are contacted by drugmakers nearly 3,000 times a year. But many of those interactions are overly general and come as physicians are struggling to deliver higher quality care in shorter appointment times [46].

While there is a major opportunity to make the experience for the provider more tailored and personal, the potential to optimize the patient experience could be even greater. Luca Foschini, Chief Data Scientist at Evidation Health, which develops predictive analytics tools for a variety of healthcare stakeholders, believes the same arc that has enabled customer-centricity in the online advertising and retail spaces will also fundamentally change the patient experience. "Personalization was completely absent 10 years ago and poorly understood five years ago," he says. "Now it is making a huge difference" [47]. Indeed, as organizations such as Netflix and Amazon have grown more data-savvy, they have embraced predictive analytics to mine a user's viewing or reading habits to make recommendations on future movies or books, further customizing the experience and changing consumer expectations [48].

As biopharmas develop their analytics capabilities, one can envision them taking similar strides to customize the patient experience either directly, where regulations permit, or through collaboration with providers. They might use wearable data to provide tailored interactions to patients based on their health status, for instance, to promote medication adherence or healthy behaviors such as better sleep hygiene. Data analytics could also be a valuable tool for connecting more directly with patients on aspects of disease education. Mining metadata from social media (e.g., Twitter, Facebook, and YouTube), biopharmas could begin to develop clinical descriptions of disease that are consistent with how patients themselves discuss their symptoms. This terminology can then be used to develop more meaningful education-based and patient-based portals.

Biopharmas interested in these new approaches must tread carefully, however. Guidance on how biopharmas can interact with patients safely and legally are still evolving, and there is clear evidence that patients want brand-agnostic information, not materials linked to a specific therapy. Indeed, success will depend partly on establishing a new social contract that makes patients more willing to share their personal data with non-provider stakeholders in the health space [49].

Future Uses

As drug companies fully integrate external and internal data to answer stake-holders' needs and gather product evidence about value, they have an opportunity to create new types of data-rich partnerships that are less transactional (selling pills) and more relational (engaging around health outcomes). (See the box, "The Dynamic Data Market.") These include new risk-sharing models, described in Chapters 7 and 8, as well as beyond-the-pill service models where the intellectual property is not a therapeutic but an algorithm.

Consider that biopharmas can partner with payers to combine the latter's claims and authorization data with its proprietary clinical trial data and develop algorithms to forecast the monetary impact associated with using a novel but relatively untested product versus the potential benefits. The biopharma could devise a pricing contract that preserves pricing flexibility but limits the potential monetary risk to the payer if utilization exceeds the forecast. This kind of analytics-based outcomes payment can improve the biopharma's productivity, accelerating the collection of valuable outcomes data while simultaneously generating revenue. An added but important bonus: by sharing data in this manner, the biopharma strengthens its relationship with a critical customer.

Companies are already edging into this arena. For example, Vifor Frese-nius Medical Care Renal Pharma, a joint venture between Vifor Pharma and Fresenius Medical Care, is developing an outcomes-based service to predict, and ultimately prevent, debilitating anemia in patients with chronic kidney disease. The service hinges on structured data collected from laboratory reports. As enabling technologies such as cloud computing and machine learning evolve, however, future algorithms will also take advantage of environmental and personal data as well [50].

THE DYNAMIC DATA MARKET

Because biopharma companies are inherently data driven, there has always been a focus on accumulating data to show product value. As definitions of value have evolved to include real-world effectiveness and cost effectiveness, however, the kinds of data biopharmas must access have altered. This shift, in addition to technological shifts in the volume, velocity, and variety of data generation, have further accelerated changes in an already dynamic data market. The end result is a land-grab mentality, as different players in the data space align to try to lock up access to key data sources as well as capabilities. A case in point: the $9 billion merger between Quintiles and IMS in 2016 to create a leading data aggregator of real-world evidence and patient data [51].

QuintilesIMS has taken advantage of the desire of payers, pharmacy benefits managers, and providers to monetize what has now become a core value driver, de-identified data. But it is hardly the only company with this strategy, as a host of different companies develop the tools and infrastructure platforms necessary to make data faster to collect, analyze, and use in day-to-day business decisions. Siemens Healthineers, for instance, signed a five-year partnership with IBM Watson in 2016 to develop a data-driven population health service. That is just one of a number of data-driven deals IBM Watson has brokered since creating its life sciences focused business unit in 2015, with acquisitions that include Truven Health Analytics, Explorys, and Merge Healthcare [52].

In addition to IBM, other infotech giants like Oracle and Cisco view owning a slice of the growing life sciences data market as a revenue-generating opportunity. On the more innovative end of the spectrum, start-ups such as Evidation Health, Zephyr Health, Veeva, and Treato want to become dominant players in their own right.

As the universe of data aggregators, analyzers, and tools providers expands, biopharmas have a range of partners to choose from, as well as to vet as possible collaborators. This expansion has been further accelerated by the creation of multi-stakeholder consortia, which increasingly include public and private organizations. For instance, the US-based not-for-profit Health Care Cost Institute is combining payer claims data and utilization data to provide a more informed picture of US healthcare spending trends, while multiple governments are helping drive genomic data collection programs to accelerate precision medicine (see Chapter 4) [53].

DATA AND ANALYTICS CHALLENGES

As biopharmas gain expertise with data analytics, there are a number of challenges they must overcome (Figure 10-6). These challenges can be grouped into the following categories:

- *Data integration:* How can companies abolish data silos and integrate external and internal data across the organization?
- *Data quality:* With the huge increase in data volume, how can companies prevent inconsistencies that skew the analysis?

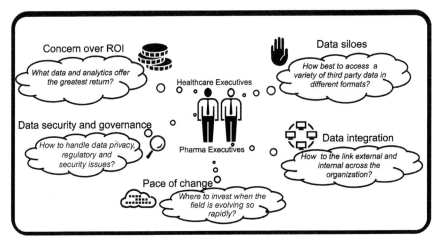

Source: EY Analysis

Figure 10-6   Challenges blocking wider usage of data and analytics

- *Data privacy:* How can companies remain compliant with privacy, regulatory, and security issues?
- *Pace of change:* With the field advancing so quickly, where are the biggest returns and how should biopharmas invest?
- *Organizational and cultural barriers:* How can incentives be created that promote a data-first business orientation when return on investment is still unclear?

Data Integration

The first two challenges, data integration and data quality, are largely technological hurdles that companies have started, albeit slowly, to address. Because of the fragmented nature of health data generation—via wearables, medical records, lab tests, and payer claims—one of the first steps is gaining access to the relevant data. As biopharmas invest more heavily in real-world evidence collection post-launch, they will generate some of these data themselves. Other types of data, for instance, anonymized electronic health record information or claims data, will come via partnerships with providers or payers. As noted, biopharmas are already active in this arena. Still other data, for example, air quality forecasts or consumer search patterns, can be purchased from third-party sources, including infotech players.

In addition to obtaining access to the needed data, biopharmas must create a common platform, whether via a third-party cloud or an internally built warehouse, to promote those all-important collisions of data (Figure 10-7). That common location encourages users to make connections between different types of data that were historically stored in discrete so-called "data lakes" inside or outside the

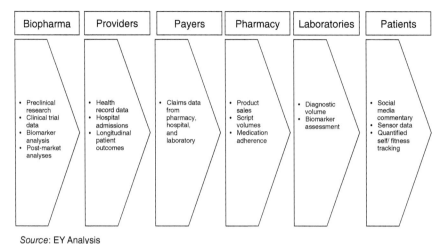

Biopharma	Providers	Payers	Pharmacy	Laboratories	Patients
• Preclinical research • Clinical trial data • Biomarker analysis • Post-market analyses	• Health record data • Hospital admissions • Longitudinal patient outcomes	• Claims data from pharmacy, hospital, and laboratory	• Product sales • Script volumes • Medication adherence	• Diagnostic volume • Biomarker assessment	• Social media commentary • Sensor data • Quantified self/ fitness tracking

Source: EY Analysis

Figure 10-7   Data remain siloed within healthcare's diverse ecosystem

organization. By integrating those different flows of data, the objective is to turn individual lakes into a larger data ocean. At even the most sophisticated bio-pharmas, however, the current level of in-house analytics capabilities makes this prospect more an aspirational goal than a reality.

To encourage data sharing, especially across large biopharma organizations, management teams will need to develop systems that consistently structure data in ways that preserve contextual relationships, even when the information has been de-identified due to privacy regulations. This is particularly important for unstructured data, as well as non-health data that has an impact on patient wellness (e.g., environmental data related to air quality for patients with asthma or chronic obstructive pulmonary disease). As such, strict data governance protocols, includ-ing using master data management techniques that resolve inconsistencies in how data are defined, are important to establish early on. Indeed, researchers at the MIT Sloan Center for Information Systems Research recommend that bigger companies consider designating a "data dictator" to establish common definitions and data management protocols for the safe and appropriate handling of data [54].

Data Quality

For data to be useable and generate new insights, it has to be of high quality. This is not exactly a new problem for biopharma data teams, but it has been made worse by the volume of data being generated and the tendency for it to be stored in silos. The problem is, if the "small data" are not trustworthy, having a bigger pool does not necessarily help. It just increases the risk that biopharmas draw erroneous conclu-sions based on their analyses. Moreover, if biopharmas are to avoid the garbage in, garbage out phenomenon, they must actively avoid what researchers at Northeastern

University and Harvard University term "big data hubris," in which "big data are a substitute for, rather than a supplement to, traditional collection and analysis" [55]. (See the box, "Google Flu Trends' Unanticipated Big Data Lesson.")

GOOGLE FLU TRENDS' UNANTICIPATED BIG DATA LESSON

As noted in Chapter 1, Google Flu Trends (GFT) was an effort to use big data—the frequency of consumer web searches for a defined number of flu-related terms—as a mechanism to forecast the real-time prevalence of flu. In 2013, it became apparent that GFT had significantly and consistently overestimated the size of its flu forecasts. One explanation for the lapse: an uptick in media coverage about the flu led to a larger-than-expected increase in flu-related web searches by non-symptomatic individuals. Because the algorithm underpinning GFT did not account for this behavioral shift, it over-estimated the prevalence of the illness.

There was another, bigger issue at work, however, related to the validity and reliability of the data GFT used to make its assessment. GFT did not incorporate historical, but highly accurate, data from the Centers for Disease Control about current flu prevalence into its model. Had GFT incorporated this information, which was based on actual on-the-ground data collection, the team from Northeastern and Harvard noted GFT "could have largely healed itself" [56].

While just a single anecdote, the GFT parable illustrates how important it is to take a step back and make sure the big data in any data set are also the right data. Unfortunately, this process is more of an art than a science. Indeed, biopharma companies big and small struggle to know which data are likely to be the most reliable and informative for a given aspect of product development.

Validating health data and developing consistent standards to judge their reliability are two essential activities going forward. Absent these capabilities, there is a very real danger that analytics applied to vast volumes of data result not in an interesting or accurate finding, but a spurious correlation that results in a flawed conclusion. In our highly regulated health space, such inaccurate judgments can have detrimental consequences—for patients and for biopharma companies' reputations. This is why many biopharma companies have been cautious about investing in massive big data programs. Indeed, most efforts are, for now, focused on using analytics to improve target discovery and trial design in highly defined populations where the risks associated with data integration are more easily managed.

Data Privacy

In many markets, privacy regulations require healthcare organizations to remove patient identifying information before the information is shared. That can make it more difficult to conduct the predictive and prescriptive analytics most likely to offer the biggest return on investment. For instance, a biopharma company may want to demonstrate the value of a new cardiovascular medicine that might compete with older, cheaper generics. It could use predictive and prescriptive analytics to identify the 20 percent of the patient population that is at greatest risk of a costly adverse event and begin to conduct clinical and observational trials to showcase the value. But to build a complete picture, the biopharma will likely want to integrate a range of different data, for instance, information transmitted from digitally enabled scales or activity trackers. Without established processes for data governance and integration, it could be difficult to combine the data in meaningful ways that give a complete and actionable picture.

There are also emerging compliance risks for biopharma companies. As data are combined from different organizations, there is still the risk of re-identification, particularly if health data are combined with governmental information such as US voter registration details. To limit the risks, data management techniques that include the aggregation of smaller sample sizes are helpful [57].

But biopharmas will also have to review their own cybersecurity plans to make sure adequate safeguards exist for the highly sensitive patient data stored within their organizations or in the cloud. Data generated from IoT-enabled devices such as smart asthma or glucose monitors could be particularly vulnerable to hacks by cybercriminals who might use details to commit fraud [58]. Indeed, even if no hack actually occurs, the threat of a potential cybercrime can damage a company's reputation and its product revenues. That is what happened to Hospira in 2015, when the US Food and Drug Administration issued a warning about software vulnerabilities associated with the manufacturer's Symbiq drug pumps. Although Hospira initially worked on software updates to prevent remote hacking, it ultimately decided to remove the product from the market [59].

Though many biopharmas clearly understand the potential business risks cyber threats pose, a 2015 survey by EY found significant gaps in capabilities. Interestingly, 65 percent of life sciences organizations surveyed revealed a significant cyber incident that was not otherwise identified by their security team; a similar percentage, 61 percent, also noted they do not have a dedicated cybersecurity role to focus on threats tied to emerging technologies. Closing this capability gap will be important as biopharmas rely more heavily on big data [60].

Pace of Change

In addition to the challenges described above, biopharmas developing data analytics capabilities face a fourth major challenge: the pace of change. It may be surprising, but just five years ago, electronic health records were not widely implemented across health systems, and wearable usage was limited to early adopters. Since then, there have been dramatic improvements in enabling technologies that ease data access and integration, and specific analytics tools required to make sense of the information are now available. The question for biopharma companies in this dynamic environment is, how do you invest in data analytics in ways that are flexible and scalable?

This is not a trivial question. Typically, these kinds of information technology investments take months, if not years, to implement, along with large amounts of capital. Given the velocity with which technology standards and platforms change, and the fact that biopharma business models themselves are evolving because of macroeconomic forces, there is a real risk that, by the time a biopharma creates an internal analytics engine, it will no longer be fit for purpose. That is a potential problem when revenue growth at many of the biggest biopharmas in the industry is already slowing.

Organizational and Cultural Barriers

It is relatively easy to create a narrative that draws a direct line between improved data analytics and better market performance. Unfortunately, the data proving the value of data largely do not yet exist; one exception, perhaps, is the use of data analytics to optimize marketing to key providers. Given the potential significant upfront costs associated with creating analytics expertise, this lack of clarity about return on investment creates a further disincentive to accelerate investment.

In addition, there are other cultural and organizational barriers that might limit willingness to invest in analytics. Big data analytics is not a core capability for most biopharma organizations. Traditionally, data experts sat in a backroom buying and manipulating databases. Data was not seen as a strategic imperative that will accelerate work across all aspects of the biopharma value chain. This siloed thinking makes it more difficult to integrate different kinds of data across the biopharma organization and, thus, reap full value for the investment.

Biopharma firms also need new kinds of expertise, particularly data scientists able to extract meaning from various types of structured and unstructured data. Not only do such individuals understand the limitations of different types of data, but they are capable of quickly building predictive models to reflect real-time changes, for example, in product sales or clinical trial recruitment.

Individuals with these capabilities are a rare commodity: the strategic consulting firm McKinsey predicts a global excess demand of 1.5 million data scientists [61]. And since many data scientists come from mathematics or engineering backgrounds, these executives will also need healthcare-specific training [62].

BUILDING AN ANALYTICS-FIRST ORGANIZATION: CULTURAL NOT TECHNICAL HURDLES

A 2015 survey of nearly 3,000 managers in different industries in MIT Sloan Management Review found that the chief obstacle to extracting value from analytics was *not* technological in nature, for example, data management or complex modeling skills. Instead, it was translating analytics into actual behavior change, or moving from big data to bigger insights [63]. So what should biopharma companies do to derive full value from their analytics efforts and create agility? There are three critical steps:

1. Make analytics a strategic imperative
2. Encourage the right behaviors
3. Partner where possible for flexibility

Analytics as a Strategic Imperative

Inexpensive computing power, the cloud, and increasingly robust algorithms powered by artificial intelligence are the primary technological drivers behind the current data analytics opportunity. However, these technology advances should be viewed as necessary, but not sufficient, for success. The overarching goal is to institutionalize a set of behaviors that promote using analytics as a core competency to generate better business insights. Such sweeping behavior change will only come about when biopharma's senior leadership views analytics as a strategic imperative.

That means having a top-level executive committed to analytics initiatives, who is capable of advocating for resources and elevating the subject to the board as appropriate. This person could be a chief information officer (CIO) or a chief data officer (CDO). The title is less important than the ability to have someone responsible at a business-wide level for articulating how analytics will support the overall business strategy. "We see many organizations that have spun up initiatives and are spending a lot of money, (but) do not necessarily have a clear point of view on how value will be delivered," notes Chris Mazzei, chief analytics officer for EY [64]. Indeed, a CIO or CDO can help connect the dots between interesting ongoing pilots so the companies can reduce duplication and translate successful initiatives to other groups in the organization.

Changing Behaviors

One of the key jobs for management is to create the incentives that promote the appropriate sharing of data and analytics tools across the organization. This is both a people management issue as well as a technological issue. For larger companies, one way to accelerate the process is to prioritize the creation of a center of excellence focused on developing certain crucial analytics processes. This senior management team would be responsible for doing the following: developing protocols for data governance and aggregation; centralizing methods, tools, and models so they can be shared easily across the organization; creating shared metrics for success; and promoting new innovations. By focusing on these kinds of activities, senior management can drive behavior change, promoting an environment where the results of prior analyses are factored into new analytics projects. Importantly, biopharma companies that use this approach spend less time searching for the right data and tools and more time performing analyses to drive important business decisions.

For this approach to succeed, however, the activities of the center of excellence must be closely integrated with the actual business. Having a team of data scientists produce multiple product launch scenarios that are then handed off to a biopharma brand unit to assess and implement is less likely to succeed than if the sales and marketing people interact with the analysts as a single team to develop a precision launch plan. Only by working together can the analysts and the business organization build credibility with each other and establish clear alignment between the end analyses and the business unit's priority—in this example, a successful launch. Indeed, absent a strong working relationship between business leaders and data scientists, there is a real risk that biopharma decision makers revert to business as usual, making decisions that are not driven by analytics and evidence but rooted in their preconceived notions and historical biases.

Partner for Flexibility

Bigger biopharmas face the option of building their own in-house capabilities either organically or via acquisitions, while smaller, earlier-stage biotechs, because of capital constraints, will almost certainly need to partner to access the data, the platform-enabling analytics tools, and the human expertise. However, just because bigger companies have the wherewithal to "go it alone" does not mean they should. Building a robust analytics engine requires significant up-front investments in time and money to create the appropriate infrastructure and capabilities. Because the technology is changing so fast, there is a real risk of spending hundreds of millions of dollars to create a platform that is unusable or out of date given the changing healthcare market.

To maintain flexibility, companies should consider whether an "as a service" model can be applied to various aspects of data analytics (Figure 10-8). Many biopharmas already outsource certain elements of their business, partnering with third parties around manufacturing or aspects of research like assay development. Why not analytics as well?

Companies can partner with various third parties to get access to the capabilities that are most valuable based on their maturity and life cycle. A pre-commercial biotech in late-stage clinical trials could begin working with a commercial analytics specialist to develop analytics to optimize a pending product launch; a commercial biotech with just a handful of products might partner with an analytics provider to develop more customized pricing agreements with key health systems. Even larger biopharmas might be interested in working with bigger analytics players to integrate patient-centric data into their clinical trial design given changing regulations about when and how such data should be used. Simply put, by taking an analytics-as-a-service approach, biopharmas can scale-up—or scale-down—their use of analytics assets based on their changing needs. They can also limit their risks by contracting with a third party that can help generate the analytical insights.

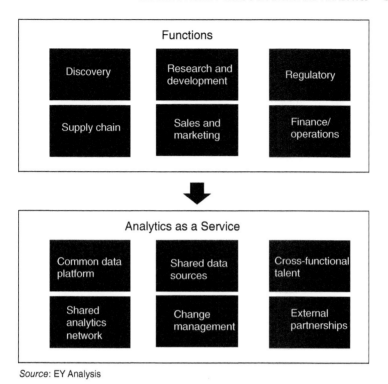

Source: EY Analysis

**Figure 10-8   Building the agile, analytics-enabled biopharma
organization**

Many of the biggest biopharmas will examine the analytics as a service option and decide that data-driven insights are such a core part of their business that they need to "own" these capabilities. Indeed, companies that are serious about moving beyond the pill may find that an essential component of their intellectual property is an algorithm designed to maximize product sales following launch. In this instance, companies will want to retain full control of the algorithm, and that means keeping the capabilities in house.

Even in this situation, given the variety of data that play a role in health, biopharma companies will need to establish partnerships with third parties. At a minimum, this means reaching outside the organization to access different types of relevant data to combine it with internally available data. But it also may mean sharing data with partners or suppliers to create new ways of doing business, for example, working with a payer to create an outcomes-based pricing model for a new but expensive drug. As the need to pursue such partnerships grows, companies will want to structure these agreements so that they retain control of the processes resulting in their data-driven insights.

CONCLUSION

Data and analytics will be a core competency for biopharmas going forward. For companies that are only now building these capabilities, the good news is that it is not too late. Those companies that grasp how data and analytics can improve fundamental aspects of the biopharma business, and, as a result, change their practices, will have a competitive advantage, outperforming the competition. However, to be successful, management teams must focus on how data and analytics enhance the value proposition of their companies' medicines. In doing so, they can actively avoid being edged out by infotechs that play an increasingly outsized role in health data generation via consumer-focused devices and software. As is true for so many other areas of biopharma drug development, from marketing to pricing to alliance building, context is everything.

SUMMARY POINTS

- Data, and the analytics that underpin them, have the potential to identify new solutions to some of healthcare's biggest challenges.
- As business models put increasing primacy on customers' definitions of drug value, combining new types of data to generate outcomes-based insights is an essential skill for biopharmas.
- Big data and analytics will alter every aspect of the biopharma value chain, especially commercial practices.
- The return on investment for analytics capabilities is intuitive but, as yet, difficult to quantify, especially for earlier stages of drug development.
- To build an analytics-first culture that takes full advantage of big data, biopharmas must access, or build, key capabilities, including tools to aggregate and analyze data.
- As part of the process, senior biopharma leaders must remain focused on the questions that they want to answer, while avoiding data overload. The question of greatest importance is, "what is the business issue we really want to solve?"
- To be successful, biopharma companies will need to take a portfolio approach, marrying specific types of big data and analytical tools depending on the disease area and competitive market dynamics.

CONCLUSION

The trends sweeping health systems and the biopharmaceutical industry present daunting challenges for management teams, but they also offer significant opportunities for those who are able to adjust their strategies and business models. These trends include the emergence of new digital technologies, new entrants into healthcare, rising expectations of consumers, and changing payment models. Our analysis yields key findings for biopharmaceutical companies seeking to make the shift from a linear view of value creation to one that surrounds the patient. This requires three distinct shifts, which have been addressed throughout this book.

MOVING FROM PRODUCT-CENTRICITY TO PATIENT-CENTRICITY

- Future success will depend on moving from a model focused on the attributes of the product to one focused on patient needs and informed by a deep understanding of the patient journey—from pre-diagnosis through post-treatment stages. Such understanding will occur, in part, by listening to increasingly connected and vocal patients and through enhanced interactions with patient advocacy groups.

- This deeper understanding will help identify unmet needs, drive product development and clinical trial design strategies, and ultimately form the basis for building the case for a product's value to patients, providers, and, most critically, payers.

- Creating a patient-centric organization requires leadership commitment and consistency across all functions. At the commercialization end, this will include communications and pricing policies that focus on building trust with stakeholders.

- Precision medicine is inherently a patient-centric strategy but is no longer limited to diagnostic-drug pairs. Rather, precision medicine can be thought of as encompassing a variety of approaches, including those that leverage

Managing Biotechnology: From Science to Market in the Digital Age, First Edition. Françoise Simon and Glen Giovannetti.
© 2017 John Wiley & Sons, Inc. Published 2017 by John Wiley & Sons, Inc.

digital technologies and connectivity to allow treatments to be more precisely targeted to patient needs and thereby achieve better outcomes.

MOVING FROM UNITS TO OUTCOMES

- Companies at all stages of development must embrace the new reality that success will no longer be measured by the number of units consumed but rather by a holistic view of the outcomes achieved.

- For patients, outcomes will include evidence of effectiveness in addressing true unmet needs in real-world settings. For payers, outcomes will include both achieved cost offsets and the medicine's upfront affordability in light of constrained budgets.

- Outcomes- (or risk-) based pricing arrangements will become more common, with payment based on measurably improved outcomes at the patient level, the system level, or both. This reality will require new and varied sources of data.

- Generating this data will require new capabilities and a shared view of success. It is important that biopharma company data be trusted and that commercial strategies do not diminish trust in the enterprise or its data.

MOVING FROM TRANSACTIONAL TO RELATIONSHIP ORIENTATION

- The complexity of these challenges will require biopharma companies to enter into more, and more varied, strategic relationships, both with traditional industry players and nontraditional partners such as infotech companies and payers. Such relationships will require a move from a transactional mind-set focused on maximizing short-term benefits, to a longer-term relationship orientation based on shared risk and mutually beneficial outcomes.

- Infotech companies have entered the healthcare arena and have the potential to disrupt relationships and the traditional biopharma business model. However, some of these companies may be reticent to develop medical affiliations for fear of regulatory constraints, presenting collaboration opportunities.

- Payers are among biopharma companies' most important partners; their coverage decisions are a key determinant of a product's commercial success. Yet they vary in their areas of focus and definitions of value, which requires relationship strategies that are customized and the creation of more collaborative relationships, built on a stronger foundation of trust.

- Finally, being truly patient-centric also will require rebuilding trust with consumers. This will mean taking a longer-term view of the patient relationship (especially for chronic conditions) and making decisions accordingly, including the willingness to invest in co-creating solutions that address real patient needs and to share product-neutral health information through digital platforms or other means.

REFERENCES

CHAPTER 1

1. Evens R, Kaitin K. "The Evolution of Biotechnology and Its Impact on Health Care." *Health Affairs*. 2015;34(2):210–219.
2. Jinek M, Chylinski K, Fonfara I, Hauer M, Doudna JA, Charpentier E. "A Programmable Dual-RNA-Guided DNA Endonuclease in Adaptive Bacterial Immunity." *Science*. 2012;337 (6096):816–821. See also Platt RJ, Chen S, Zhou Y, et al. "CRISPR-Cas9 Knockin Mice for Genome Editing and Cancer Modeling." *Cell*. 2014;159(2):440–455. See also Ruby T, Singh N. "Realizing the Potential of CRISPR: Three Healthcare Executives Share Industry Perspectives on the Future of Genome Editing." McKinsey, January 2017.
3. Paine J, Shipton CA, Chaggar S, et al. "Improving the Nutritional Value of Golden Rice through Increased Pro-vitamin A Content." *Nature Biotechnology*. 2005;23(4):482–487. See also Simon F, Kotler P. *Building Global Biobrands: Taking Biotechnology to Market*. New York: Free Press; 2003; p. 4.
4. Greenwood J. "Unleashing the Promise of Biotechnology to Help Heal, Fuel and Feed the World." In: Shimasaki C, ed. *Biotechnology Entrepreneurship: Starting, Managing and Leading Biotech Companies*. Waltham, MA: Elsevier; 2004: 3–13. See also Friedman Y. *Building Biotechnology*. Washington, DC: Logos Press; 2014.
5. Clark D, Strumpf D. "Tech Stalwarts Soar to New Highs." *Wall Street Journal*. October 24, 2015; Eisen B, Dieterich C, "Apple Market Cap Tops $800 Billion". *Wall Street Journal*. May 10, 2017; market cap for Johnson & Johnson, *Capital IQ*, May 2017.
6. World Health Organization. *MHealth: New Horizons for Health through Mobile Technologies*. Global Observatory for eHealth Series, volume 3, 2011; cited in IMS Health Research Institute, Patient Adoption of mHealth, September 2015.
7. PWC Health Research Institute. *Health Wearables: The Early Days*. 2014.
8. Dormehl L. "Why the Anthem Security Breach Was Such a Wake-Up Call for the Health Industry." *Fast Company*. February 6, 2015.
9. Steinberg D, Horwitz G, Zohar D. "Building a Business Model in Digital Medicine." *Nature Biotechnology*. 2015;33(9):910–920.
10. Forrester Research. The State of Consumers and Technology: Benchmark 2015, US.
11. IMS Institute for Healthcare Informatics. Patient Adoption of mHealth, September 2015.
12. Steinberg D, Horwitz G, Zohar D. "Building a Business Model in Digital Medicine." *Nature Biotechnology*. 2015;33(9):910–920.
13. Miller R. "Proteus Seeks Pharma Partnerships for Ingestible Sensors." *The Gray Sheet*. July 15, 2015.
14. Neil R. "The Digital Healthcare Revolution Picks Up Speed." *MedTech Insight*. July 14, 2015.

Managing Biotechnology: From Science to Market in the Digital Age, First Edition. Françoise Simon and Glen Giovannetti.
© 2017 John Wiley & Sons, Inc. Published 2017 by John Wiley & Sons, Inc.

15. Etherington D. "Apple Boasts over 3500 Apple Watch Apps Already Available." TechCrunch Website. https://techcrunch.com/2015/04/27/apple-boasts-over-3500-apple-watch-apps-already-available/. Published April 27, 2015. Accessed April 18, 2017. Cited in Husson T. "Beyond the Apple Watch Hype–Early Lesson for B2C Marketers." June 22, 2015.

16. Michael O'Reilly, VP Medical Technology, Apple, interview by Françoise Simon and Ellen Licking, October 20, 2015.

17. O'Reilly interview, ibid. See also Apple. "Apple Announces New ResearchKit Studies for Autism, Epilepsy and Melanoma." https://www.apple.com/pr/library/2015/10/15Apple-Announces-New-ResearchKit-Studies-for-Autism-Epilepsy-Melanoma.html. Published October 15, 2015. Accessed April 18, 2017; for CareKit, see Genes N, "The First CareKit Apps Are Out. What's Next?", *Telemedicine Magazine*, March 7, 2017.

18. Jack Young, former leader of dRx Capital at Qualcomm, interview by Françoise Simon, September 16, 2015. Don Jones, Chief Digital Officer, Scripps Translational Research Institute, interview by Françoise Simon, October 2, 2015; see also dRX Capital website, http://www.dRxcapital.com.

19. Simon F, Kotler P. *Building Global Biobrands: Taking Biotechnology to Market*, Free Press, New York, 2003; p. 35.

20. Paul Grundy, IBM Global Director of Healthcare Transformation, interview by Françoise Simon, October 22, 2015.

21. IBM Annual Report/SEC Form 10 K, February 24, 2015; see also IBM Annual Report 2016.

22. Apple. "Japan Post Group, IBM and Apple Deliver iPads and Custom Apps to Connect Elderly in Japan to Services, Family and Community." https://www.apple.com/pr/library/2015/04/30Japan-Post-Group-IBM-and-Apple-Deliver-iPads-and-Custom-Apps-to-Connect-Elderly-in-Japan-to-Services-Family-and-Community.html. Published April 30, 2015. Accessed April 18, 2017.

23. Medtronic. "IBM and Medtronic Partner to Improve Diabetes Care." http://newsroom.medtronic .com/phoenix.zhtml?c=251324&p=irol-newsArticle&ID=2034597. Published April 13, 2015. Accessed April 18, 2017.

24. Rubenfire A. "IBM's Watson Targets Cancer and Enlists Prominent Providers in the Fight." *Modern Healthcare*. May 5, 2015.

25. Lohr S. "Google to End Health Records Service after It Fails to Attract Users." *New York Times*. June 24, 2011. Available at http://www.nytimes.com/2011/06/25/technology/25health.html?_r=1. Accessed April 18, 2017.

26. Verel D. "Google to Reshape How It Provides Health Information, Mayo Clinic Joins as Partner," *MedCity News*. http://medcitynews.com/2015/02/google-seeks-bring-accuracy-online-health-information/. Published February 10, 2015. Accessed April 18, 2017.

27. Ginsberg J, Mohebbi M, Patel R, Braumer L, Smolinski M, Brilliant L. "Detecting Influenza Epidemics Using Search Engine Query Data." *Nature* 2009;457(7232):1012–1014. Available at http://www.nature.com/nature/journal/v457/n7232/full/nature07634.html. Accessed April 18, 2017. See also Lazer D, Kennedy R, King G, Vespignani A. "The Parable of Google Flu Traps in Big Data Analysis." *Science*. March 14, 2014;343: 1203–1205. Available at https://gking .harvard.edu/files/gking/files/0314policyforumff.pdf. Accessed April 18, 2017. Cited in Hopkins B. "Google Flu Trends–A Big Data Fail? Not Exactly." *Forrester Research*. https://www.forrester .com/Google+Flu+Trends+A+Big+Data+Fail+Not+Exactly/fulltext/-/E-RES116507. Published June 20, 2014. Accessed April 18, 2017.

28. Sanofi. "Sanofi to Collaborate with Google Life Sciences to Improve Diabetes Health Outcomes." http://www.news.sanofi.us/2015-08-31-Sanofi-to-Collaborate-with-Google-Life-Sciences-to-Improve-Diabetes-Health-Outcomes. Published August 31, 2015. Accessed April 18, 2017; see also Roland D, Landauro I, "Companies Join to Fight Diabetes", *Wall Street Journal*, September 13, 2016.

29. Comstock J. "DexCom Taps Google for Smaller, Cheaper Diabetes Devices." *MobiHealthNews*. http://mobihealthnews.com/46008/dexcom-taps-google-for-smaller-cheaper-diabetes-devices/. Published August 11, 2015. Accessed April 18, 2017.

30. Winslow R. "Google Joins Heart Research Effort." *Wall Street Journal.* November 9, 2015: B5. See also "Google to Collect Data to Define Healthy Human." *Wall Street Journal.* July 24, 2014. Available at http://online.wsj.com/articles/google-to-collect-data-to-define-healthy-human-1406246214. Accessed April 18, 2017. See also "Johnson & Johnson Announces Formation of Verb Surgical Inc, in Collaboration with Verily", press release December 10, 2015. Available at https://www.jnj.com/media-center/press-releases/johnson-johnson-announces-formation-of-verb-surgical-inc-in-collaboration-with-verily. Accessed July 8, 2017.
31. GSK. "GSK and Verily to Establish Galvani Bioelectronics–A New Company Dedicated to the Development of Bioelectronic Medicines." http://us.gsk.com/en-us/media/press-releases/2016/gsk-and-verily-to-establish-galvani-bioelectronics-a-new-company-dedicated-to-the-development-of-bioelectronic-medicines. Published August 1, 2016. Accessed April 18, 2017.
32. Calico. "AbbVie and Calico Announce a Novel Collaboration to Accelerate the Discovery, Development and Commercialization of New Therapies." http://www.calicolabs.com/news/2014/09/03/. Published September 3, 2014. Accessed April 18, 2017.
33. GV Portfolio (https://www.gv.com/portfolio/) and Google Capital company data (https://www.capitalg.com).
34. Macmillan D. "Google Backs Health Insurance Start-Up." *Wall Street Journal.* September 7, 2015: B1, B8.
35. Caradigm. "Caradigm Partners with Eliza Corporation to Improve Patient Outcomes Care Efficiency." https://www.caradigm.com/en-us/news-and-events/caradigm-partners-with-eliza-corporation-to-improve-patient-outcomes-care-efficiency/. Published April 13, 2015. Accessed April 18, 2017.
36. Robinson M. "Johns Hopkins Joins Forces with Microsoft to Improve Critical Care." http://www.microsoft.com/en-us/health/blogs/johns-hopkins-joins-forces-with-microsoft-to-improve-critical-care/default.aspx#fbid=QY6nldkv8EJ. Published October 19, 2015. Accessed April 18, 2017. See also Chase D. "Microsoft Ends Another Vertical Market Dalliance—This Time in Healthcare." *TechCrunch.* http://techcrunch.com/2011/12/10/microsoft-ends-dalliance-healthcare/. Published December 10, 2011. Accessed April 18, 2017.
37. Tan T, "Big Pharma Helps Pour $900 Million Into Grail," MedTech Insight, March 1, 2017. Available at https://medtech.pharmamedtechbi.com/MT104520/Big-Pharma-Helps-Pour-$900m-Into-Grail. Accessed July 8, 2017.
38. Friend S. "App-Enabled Trial Participation: Tectonic Shift or Tepid Rumble?" *Science Translational Medicine.* 2015;7(297):297ed10.

CHAPTER 2

1. Hay M, Thomas D, Craighead J, Economides C, Rosenthal J. "Clinical Development Success Rates for Investigational Drugs." *Nature Biotechnology.* 2014;32(1):40–51.
2. Mathers E. "If You Build It, Will It Matter?" *Beyond Borders: Matters of Evidence.* EY Biotechnology Annual Report. 2013: 5. Available at http://www.ey.com/Publication/vwLUAssets/Beyond_borders/$FILE/Beyond_borders.pdf. Accessed April 19, 2017.
3. Pharmaceutical Research and Manufacturers of America (PhRMA). *Medicines in Development: Biologics 2013 Report.* Washington, DC: PhRMA 2013; 6. Available at http://phrma.org/sites/default/files/pdf/biologicsoverview2013.pdf. Accessed April 19, 2017.
4. Tufts Center for the Study of Drug Development. *How the Tufts Center for the Study of Drug Development Pegged the Cost of a New Drug at $2.6 Billion.* Boston: Tufts University; 2014. Available at http://csdd.tufts.edu/files/uploads/cost_study_backgrounder.pdf. Accessed April 19, 2017.
5. Data derived from the respective companies' financial statements, available at US Securities and Exchange Commission Website, EDGAR Company Search. http://www.sec.gov/edgar/searchedgar/companysearch.html. Accessed April 19, 2017.

6. Bosley K."Life of a Start-up CEO: Priorities and Preparation." In: EY, *Beyond Borders: Reaching New Heights. Biotechnology Industry Report 2015*. Available at http://www.ey.com/Publication/vwLUAssets/EY-beyond-borders-2015/$FILE/EY-beyond-borders-2015.pdf. Accessed April 19, 2017.

7. EY analysis based on data from Capital IQ and VentureSource databases.

8. Bosley K. "Life of a Start-up CEO: Priorities and Preparation." In: EY, *Beyond Borders: Reaching New Heights. Biotechnology Industry Report 2015*. Available at http://www.ey.com/Publication/vwLUAssets/EY-beyond-borders-2015/$FILE/EY-beyond-borders-2015.pdf. Accessed April 19, 2017.

9. Mass Medical Angels MA2 Website. http://www.massmedangels.com/. Accessed April 19, 2017. See also Life Sciences Angels Website. http://lifescienceangels.com/about/. Accessed April 19, 2017.

10. Sohl J. "The Angel Investor Market in Q1Q2 2015: Modest Changes in Deals and Dollars." Center for Venture Research. https://paulcollege.unh.edu/sites/paulcollege.unh.edu/files/webform/Q1Q2%202015%20Analysis%20Report%20FINAL.pdf. Published January 15, 2016. Accessed April 19, 2017.

11. Timmerman L. "Crowdfunding Is Coming to Biotech, so Get Ready for a Wild Ride." *Xconomy*. http://www.xconomy.com/national/2013/01/28/crowdfunding-is-coming-to-biotech-so-get-ready-for-a-wild-ride/. Published January 28, 2013. Accessed April 19, 2017.

12. Bancroft D."Biotech Crowdfunding in Europe: Trendy but Only 0.2% of Total VC Money Raised since 2010." Labiotech. European Biotech News Website. http://labiotech.eu/biotech-crowdfunding-in-europe-trendy-but-only-0-2-of-total-vc-money-raised-since-2010/. Published July 9, 2015. Accessed April 19, 2017. See also Kelly E."Life Science Start-Ups Turning to Crowdfunding," Science Business News Website. http://www.sciencebusiness.net/news/77188/Life-science-start-ups-turning-to-crowdfunding. Published September 10, 2015. Accessed April 19, 2017.

13. EY analysis based on various primary data sources, including review of the financial statements included in the relevant IPO documents and Capital IQ and VentureSource databases.

14. Booth B."Debunking Corporate Venture Capital in Biotech." Life Sci VC Website. https://lifescivc.com/2011/09/debunking-corporate-venture-capital-in-biotech/. Published September 15, 2011. Accessed April 19, 2017.

15. Google Ventures (GV) Life Sciences Portfolio Investments Website. https://www.gv.com/portfolio/#life. Accessed June 2016.

16. WebMD. "Cystic Fibrosis—Topic Overview." http://www.webmd.com/children/tc/cystic-fibrosis-topic-overview. Accessed April 19, 2017.

17. Cystic Fibrosis Foundation Website. "CF Foundation Venture Philanthropy." https://www.cff.org/Our-Research/Our-Research-Approach/Venture-Philanthropy/. Accessed April 19, 2017.

18. Aurora Biosciences Corporation Form 10-K for Year ended December 31, 1999. http://www.sec.gov/Archives/edgar/data/1010919/0000912057000011002/0000912057-00-011002.txt. Accessed April 19, 2017.

19. Pollack A. "Deal by Cystic Fibrosis Foundation Raises Cash and Some Concern." *New York Times*. November 19, 2014. Available at https://www.nytimes.com/2014/11/19/business/for-cystic-fibrosis-foundation-venture-yields-windfall-in-hope-and-cash.html?_r=0. Accessed April 19, 2017.

20. Walker J, Rockoff J. "Cystic Fibrosis Foundation Sells Drug's Rights for $3.3 Billion: The Biggest Royalty Purchase Ever Reflects Group's Share of Kalydeco Sales." *Wall Street Journal*. November 19, 2014. Available at http://www.wsj.com/articles/cystic-fibrosis-foundation-sells-drugs-rights-for-3-3-billion-1416414300?alg=y. Accessed April 19, 2017.

CHAPTER 3

1. Czerpak EA, Ryser S. "Drug Approvals and Failures: Implications for Alliances." *Nature Reviews Drug Discovery.* 2008;7: 197–198.

2. Booth B. "Transformational Late Stage Drugs Delivered through Deal-Making," *Life Sci* VC Website. http://lifescivc.com/2014/03/transformational-late-stage-drugs-delivered-through-deal-making/. Published March 21, 2014. Accessed April 20, 2017.

3. Berkrot B. "Success Rates for Experimental Drugs Falls: Study." Reuters Health News Website. http://www.reuters.com/article/us-pharmaceuticals-success-idUSTRE71D2U920110214. Published February 14, 2011. Accessed April 20, 2017.

4. Lo A, Pisano G. "Lessons from Hollywood: A New Approach to Funding R&D." *MIT Sloan Management Review.* 2015;57 (2). Bernal L. "Why Pharma Must Go Hollywood." *The Scientist.* 2017;21 (2):42–45.

5. Morgan Stanley Research. "Pharmaceuticals: Exit Research and Create Value." January 20, 2010.

6. Bluestein A. "Will Johnson & Johnson's New Innovation Centers Point the Way Toward Its Future?" *Fast Company.* http://www.fastcompany.com/3025556/keeping-up-with-the-johnsons. Published January 20, 2010. Accessed April 20, 2017. Senior M. "J&J Courts Biotech in Clusters." *Nature Biotechnology.* 2013;31; 769–770.

7. Index Ventures. "Index Ventures Launches New €150 Million Life Sciences Fund." https://indexventures.com/news-room/news/index-ventures-launches-new-%E2%82%AC150m-life-sciences-fund. Published March 21, 2012. Accessed April 20, 2017.

8. Jarvis J. "Pfizer's Academic Experiment." *Chemical & Engineering News.* 2012;90 (40):28–32. http://cen.acs.org/articles/90/i40/Pfizers-Academic-Experiment.html. Accessed April 20, 2017.

9. UCB Pharma. "UCB Leads Epilepsy Hackathon to Support Patient Needs through Digital Tools and Services." http://www.cureepilepsy.org/downloads/articles/UCB-hackathon.pdf. Published February 18, 2015. Accessed April 20, 2017.

10. EY. "Firepower Index and Growth Gap Report 2016." http://www.ey.com/GL/en/Industries/Life-Sciences/EY-vital-signs-firepower-index-and-growth-gap-report-2016. Accessed April 20, 2017.

11. For example, the page on Merck's website that describes licensing, available at http://www.merck.com/licensing/home_licensing.html. Accessed April 20, 2017.

12. Carroll J."Novartis Options Proteon Therapeutics for $550 M." FierceBiotech Website. http://www.fiercebiotech.com/story/novartis-options-proteon-therapeutics-550m/2009-03-05. Published March 5, 2009. Accessed April 20, 2017.

13. Carroll J."Constellation Inks $95 M Discovery Deal, Buyout Option with Genentech." FierceBiotech Website. http://www.fiercebiotech.com/story/constellation-inks-95m-discovery-deal-buyout-option-genentech/2012-01-16. Published January 16, 2012. Accessed April 20, 2017. Fidler B."Constellation Pharma Plots IPO Run as Genentech Passes on Buyout Deal." Xconomy Website. http://www.xconomy.com/boston/2015/08/24/constellation-pharma-plots-ipo-run-as-genentech-passes-on-buyout-deal/. Published August 24, 2015. Accessed April 20, 2017.

14. McBride R."Updated: Fueled by Sanofi, Warp Drive Bio Takes off with $125 M Deal." FierceBiotech Website. http://www.fiercebiotech.com/story/fueled-sanofi-warp-drive-bio-takes-125m-deal/2012-01-10. Published January 10, 2012. Accessed April 20, 2017.

15. Genentech. "Genentech and Roche Holding Ltd. Form Pioneering Relationship; Roche to Own 60 Percent of an Independent Genentech." http://www.gene.com/media/press-releases/4305/1990-02-02/genentech-and-roche-holding-ltd-form-pio. Published February 2, 1990. Accessed April 20, 2017.

16. Genentech. "Genentech Stockholders Approve Roche's Extended Buyout Option." http://www.gene.com/media/press-releases/4728/1995-10-25/genentech-stockholders-approve-roches-ex. Published October 25, 1995. Accessed April 20, 2017.

17. Infinity Pharmaceuticals. "Infinity Announces Global Strategic Alliance with Purdue Pharma and Mundipharma Encompassing Infinity's Early Clinical and Discover Programs." Nasdaq Global-Newswire Website. https://globenewswire.com/news-release/2008/11/20/388767/155108/en/Infinity-Announces-Global-Strategic-Alliance-With-Purdue-Pharma-and-Mundipharma-Encompassing-Infinity-s-Early-Clinical-and-Discovery-Programs.html. Published November 20, 2008. Accessed April 20, 2017.

18. Pierson R. "Sanofi to Buy 12 Percent of Alnylam, Expands Rare-Disease Drug Deal." *Reuters* Website. http://www.reuters.com/article/us-sanofi-alnylam-idUSBREA0C07K20140113. Published January 13, 2014. Accessed April 20, 2017.

19. Roche. "Roche Enters a Broad Strategic Collaboration with Foundation Medicine in the Field of Molecular Information in Oncology." http://www.roche.com/media/store/releases/med-cor-2015-01-12.htm. Published January 12, 2015. Accessed April 20, 2017.

20. Menzel G, Xanthopoulos K. "Securing a Partner Is Only the Beginning—You then Have to Put Substantial Effort and Resources into Keeping the Collaboration Functioning and Productive." Bioentrepreneur (Nature Biotechnology) Website. http://www.nature.com/bioent/2012/120201/full/bioe.2012.2.html. Published February 23, 2012. Accessed April 20, 2017.

CHAPTER 4

1. Personalized Medicine Coalition *The Case for Personalized Medicine*. 4th ed. Washington, DC: Personalized Medicine Coalition; 2014. Available at http://www.personalizedmedicinecoalition.org/Userfiles/PMC-Corporate/file/pmc_the_case_for_personalized_medicine.pdf. Accessed April 21, 2017.

2. Biotechnology Industry Organization, Biomedtracker, Amplion. *Clinical Development Success Rates: 2006–2015*. Report, June 2016. Available at https://www.bio.org/sites/default/files/Clinical%20Development%20Success%20Rates%202006-2015%20-%20BIO,%20Biomedtracker,%20Amplion%202016.pdf. Accessed April 21, 2017.

3. About the Precision Medicine Initiative Cohort Program, National Institutes of Health webpage (https://www.nih.gov/precision-medicine-initiative-cohort-program).

4. Naylor S. "What's in a Name? The Emergence of P-Medicine." The Journal of Precision Medicine. October/November 2015; 15–29. Available at http://www.thejournalofprecisionmedicine.com/wp-content/uploads/2015/10/NAYLOR.pdf. Accessed April 21, 2017.

5. Mara Aspinall, Executive Chairman of GenePeeks and CA Therapeutics and cofounder of the School of Biomedical Diagnostics, personal correspondence, February 2016.

6. Tozzi J. "Drugs Could Soon Come with a Money-Back Guarantee." *Bloomberg Businessweek*, October 8, 2015. Available at http://www.bloomberg.com/news/articles/2015-10-08/drugs-could-soon-come-with-a-money-back-guarantee. Accessed April 21, 2017.

7. Senior M. "How Patients Are Transforming Pharma R&D." In Vivo Website. Published May 9, 2016. https://invivo.pharmamedtechbi.com/IV004513/How-Patients-Are-Transforming-Pharma-RampD. Accessed April 21, 2017.

8. National Institute for Health and Care Excellence Technology Appraisal Guidance, 2014. https://www.nice.org.uk/process/pmg19/chapter/1-acknowledgements.

9. Kolata G, "F.D.A. Approves Repatha, a Second Drug for Cholesterol in a Potent New Class." *New York Times*. August 27, 2015. Available at http://www.nytimes.com/2015/08/28/health/fda-approves-another-in-a-new-class-of-cholesterol-drugs.html?_r=0. Accessed April 21, 2017.

10. Hirschler B, "New Heart Drugs Struggle to Win Sales as Doctors Hold Back." Reuters Health News Website. http://www.reuters.com/article/us-health-heart-drug-idUSKCN0XI0T6. Published April 21, 2016. Accessed April 21, 2017.

11. Lincoln Nadauld, Director, Cancer Genomics at InterMountain Healthcare, personal correspondence, February 2016.

12. Nadauld L, Van Norman SB, Fulde G, et al. "Precision Medicine to Improve Survival Without Increasing Costs in Advanced Cancer Patients." *Journal of Clinical Oncology*. 2015; 33. (suppl; abstr e17641). Available at http://meetinglibrary.asco.org/content/152750-156. Accessed April 21, 2017.

13. Kaiser Permanente."Connectivity: Comprehensive Health Information at Your Fingertips." https://share.kaiserpermanente.org/total-health/connectivity/. Accessed April 21, 2017.

14. Minor L. "We Don't Just Need Precision Medicine, We Need Precision Health." *Forbes*. http://www.forbes.com/sites/valleyvoices/2016/01/06/we-dont-just-need-precision-medicine-we-need-precision-health/#60f6ddb6415e. Published January 6, 2016. Accessed April 21, 2017.

15. US Food and Drug Administration "FDA Approves New Pill to Treat Certain Patients with Non-Small Cell Lung Cancer." http://www.fda.gov/NewsEvents/Newsroom/PressAnnouncements/ucm472525.htm. Published November 13, 2015. Accessed April 21, 2017.

16. Boggs J. "AstraZeneca Concedes NSCLC Drug Iressa in U.S. Withdrawal." BioWorld Website. http://www.bioworld.com/content/astrazeneca-concedes-nsclc-drug-iressa-us-withdrawal. Published May 29, 2012. Accessed April 21, 2017.

17. Dennis B, Bernstein L. "Cancer Trials Are Changing. That Could Mean Faster Access to Better Drugs." *The Washington Post*. June 1, 2015. Available at https://www.washingtonpost.com/national/health-science/paradigm-change-in-the-development-of-cancer-drugs/2015/06/01/09fcb4c4-086e-11e5-95fd-d580f1c5d44e_story.html. Accessed April 21, 2017.

18. "The Top 15 Best-Selling Drugs of 2016," *Genetic Engineering News*, March 6, 2017. Available at http://www.genengnews.com/the-lists/the-top-15-best-selling-drugs-of-2016/77900868.

19. US Food and Drug Administration "FDA Approves First Companion Diagnostic to Detect Gene Mutation Associated with a Type of Lung Cancer." May 13, 2014.

20. Staton T. "BMS' Opdivo Gets a Jump on Keytruda with Another Early FDA Approval." FiercePharma Website. http://www.fiercepharma.com/regulatory/bms-opdivo-gets-a-jump-on-keytruda-another-early-fda-approval. Published October 12, 2015. Accessed April 21, 2017.

21. Loftus P, Rockoff J, Steele A. "Bristol Myers: Opdivo Failed to Meet Endpoint in Key Lung-Cancer Study." *Wall Street Journal*. August 5, 2016. Available at http://www.wsj.com/articles/bristol-myers-opdivo-failed-to-meet-endpoint-in-key-lung-cancer-study-1470400926. Accessed April 21, 2017. See also U.S. Food & Drug Administration. "FDA Approves First Cancer Treatment for Any Solid Tumor with a Specific Genetic Feature." U.S. Department of Health and Human Services website. Published May 23, 2017. Available at: https://www.fda.gov/newsevents/newsroom/pressannouncements/ucm560167.htm. Accessed July 17, 2017.

22. Rockoff J, Loftus P. "Bristol-Myers Bucks Trend Toward Precision Medicine." *Wall Street Journal*. March 13, 2016. Available at http://www.wsj.com/articles/bristol-bucks-trend-toward-precision-medicine-1457912801. Accessed April 21, 2017.

23. Armour A, Watkins C. "The Challenge of Targeting EGFR: Experience with Gefitinib in Non-Small Cell Lung Cancer." *European Respiratory Review*. 2010;19: 186–196. Available at http://err.ersjournals.com/content/19/117/186. Accessed April 21, 2017.

24. De Bock A."Iressa (gefitinib): The Journey." A presentation by AstraZeneca Portfolio Leader Oncology/Infection Anne De Bock, May 2011. Available at https://ec.europa.eu/research/health/pdf/event06/12052011/anne-debock_en.pdf. Accessed April 21, 2017.

25. Schattner E. "Companion Diagnostics? For Cancer Care, We Need Better Ones." *Forbes*. http://www.forbes.com/sites/elaineschattner/2015/11/19/companion-diagnostics-why-we-need-more-and-better-ones-to-optimize-cancer-care/#5b2ce2996003. Published November 19, 2015. Accessed April 21, 2017.

26. Relling M, Evans W. "Pharmacogenomics in the Clinic." *Nature*. 2015;526:343–350. Available at http://www.nature.com/nature/journal/v526/n7573/full/nature15817.html. Accessed April 21, 2017.

27. Audette J. "Biomarker Trends: 73% Growth in the Use of Companion Diagnostic Biomarkers." Amplion Website. http://www.amplion.com/biomarker-trends/73-growth-in-use-of-companion-diagnostic-biomarkers/. Published October 19, 2015. Accessed April 21, 2017.

28. Getz K, Stergiopoulos, Kim JY. "The Adoption and Impact of Adaptive Trial Designs." R&D Senior Leadership Brief. Boston, MA: Tufts Center for the Study of Drug Development, February 13, 2013. Available at https://www.iconplc.com/icon-files/docs/thought-leadership/premium/TuftsCSDD_Adaptive-Design-Trials-Sr-Mgmt-Brief_May2013.pdf. Accessed April 21, 2017. See also Woodcock J, Lavange L. "Master Protocols To Study Multiple Therapies, Multiple Diseases, Or Both." *New England Journal Of Medicine* 2017; 377:62-70. Accessed July 17, 2017.

29. Schork N. "Personalized Medicine: Time for One-Person Trials." *Nature.* 2015;520: 609–611. Available at http://www.nature.com/news/personalized-medicine-time-for-one-person-trials-1.17411. Accessed April 21, 2017. See also Demeyin W, Frost J, Ukoumunne O, Briscoe S, Britten N. "N of 1 Trials and the Optimal Individualisation of Drug Treatments: A Systematic Review." *Systematic Reviews* 2017 6:90. Accessed July 17, 2017.

30. Hayes D, et al. "Breaking a Vicious Cycle." *Science Translational Medicine.* 2013;5, 196cm6.

31. Schork N. "Personalized Medicine: Time for One-Person Trials." *Nature.* 2015;520: 609–611. Available at http://www.nature.com/news/personalized-medicine-time-for-one-person-trials-1.17411. Accessed April 21, 2017.

32. Food & Drug Administration *In Vitro Companion Diagnostic Devices: Guidance for Industry and Food and Drug Administration Staff.* Rockville, MD: US Department of Health and Human Services, August 6, 2014. Available at http://www.fda.gov/downloads/MedicalDevices/DeviceRegulationandGuidance/GuidanceDocuments/UCM262327.pdf. Accessed April 21, 2017.

33. Pothier K, Gustavsen G. "Combating Complexity: Partnerships in Personalized Medicine." *Personalized Medicine.* 2013;10(4):387–396.

34. Hayes D, et al. "Breaking a Vicious Cycle." *Science Translational Medicine.* 2013;5, 196cm6.

35. National Institute of Health and Care Excellence "EGFR-TK Mutation Testing in Adults with Locally Advanced or Metastatic Non-Small-Cell Lung Cancer." NICE Diagnostics Guidance. https://www.nice.org.uk/guidance/dg9/chapter/3-Clinical-need-and-practice. Published August 2013. Accessed April 21, 2017.

36. Domchek SM, Bradbury A, Garber JE, Offit K, Robson ME. "Multiplex Genetic Testing for Cancer Susceptibility: Out on the High Wire Without a Net?" *Journal of Clinical Oncology.* 2013;31(10):1267–1270.

37. Thermo Fisher Scientific "Thermo Fisher Scientific Signs Development Agreement for Next-Generation Sequencing-Based Companion Diagnostic." http://news.thermofisher.com/press-release/life-technologies/thermo-fisher-scientific-signs-development-agreement-next-generation. Published November 18, 2015. Accessed April 21, 2017.

38. Global Genomics Group "Global Genomics Group (G3) Partners with Sanofi to Identify New Signaling Pathways in Atherosclerotic Cardiovascular Diseases." PR Newswire Website. http://www.prnewswire.com/news-releases/global-genomics-group-g3-partners-with-sanofi-to-identify-new-signaling-pathways-in-atherosclerotic-cardiovascular-diseases-300195426.html. Published January 5, 2016. Accessed April 21, 2017.

39. Human Longevity, Inc "Human Longevity, Inc. Announces 10 Year Deal with AstraZeneca to Sequence and Analyze Patient Samples from AstraZeneca Clinical Trials." http://www.humanlongevity.com/human-longevity-inc-announces-10-year-deal-with-astrazeneca-to-sequence-and-analyze-patient-samples-from-astrazeneca-clinical-trials/. Published April 21, 2016. Accessed April 21, 2017. See also Mack H. "Verily, Stanford, and Duke Kick Off Project Baseline Study to Develop Broad Reference to Human Health." *Mobihealth News,* April 20, 2017. Available at: http://www.mobihealthnews.com/content/verily-stanford-and-duke-kick-project-baseline-study-develop-broad-reference-human-health. Accessed July 17, 2017.

40. Lung-MAP Clinical Trial http://www.lung-map.org. Accessed April 21, 2017.

41. US Food & Drug Administration Biomarker Qualification Program https://www.fda.gov/Drugs/DevelopmentApprovalProcess/DrugDevelopmentToolsQualificationProgram/BiomarkerQualificationProgram/default.htm. Accessed April 21, 2017.

42. About PrecisionFDA https://precision.fda.gov/about. Accessed April 21, 2017.

43. Mike Capone, COO, Medidata, personal correspondence, March 7, 2016.
44. Molteni M. "Medicine Is Going Digital. The FDA Is Racing to Catch Up." *Wired*. Published May 22, 2017. https://www.wired.com/2017/05/medicine-going-digital-fda-racing-catch. Accessed July 17, 2017. See also European Medicines Agency. *"Work Programme 2016*. London: European Medicines Agency. July 5, 2016. Available at http://www.ema.europa.eu/docs/en_GB/document_library/Work_programme/2016/03/WC500202857.pdf. Accessed April 21, 2017.
45. Foundation Medicine "IMS Health and Foundation Medicine Announce Collaboration to Optimize Targeting of Precision Therapies in Oncology." http://investors.foundationmedicine.com/releasedetail.cfm?releaseid=918859Published June 22, 2105. Accessed April 24, 2017.
46. Oracle "Oracle Powers Precision Medicine Delivery with New Solution Connecting Research, Pathology and Clinical Care." https://www.oracle.com/corporate/press/oracle-precision-medicine-012516.html. Published January 25, 2016. Accessed April 24, 2017.
47. National Academies of Sciences, Engineering, Medicine "Roundtable on Genomics and Precision Health." http://www.nationalacademies.org/hmd/Activities/Research/GenomicBasedResearch.aspx. Accessed April 24, 2017.
48. Independence Blue Cross "Independence Blue Cross Becomes First Major Insurer to Cover Next-Generation Whole Genome Sequencing for a Variety of Cancers." http://news.ibx.com/independence-blue-cross-becomes-first-major-insurer-to-cover-next-generation-whole-genome-sequencing-for-a-variety-of-cancers/.) Published January 11, 2016. Accessed April 24, 2017.
49. Buzyn A. "How INCa Is Supporting the Development of Personalized Medicine." Presented at WIN2013, July 10–12, 2013. Available at http://www.winsymposium.org/wp-content/uploads/2013/07/WIN2013_Agnes-Buzyn-REVISED.190713.pdf. Accessed April 24, 2017.
50. Personalized Medicine Coalition *"The Case for Personalized Medicine."* 4th ed. Washington, DC: Personalized Medicine Coalition; 2014. Available at http://www.personalizedmedicinecoalition.org/Userfiles/PMC-Corporate/file/pmc_the_case_for_personalized_medicine.pdf. Accessed April 24, 2017.
51. Qiagen "QIAGEN and Lilly Collaborate to Co-Develop Companion Diagnostics for Simultaneous Analysis of DNA and RNA Biomarkers in Common Cancers." PR Newswire Website. http://www.prnewswire.com/news-releases/qiagen-and-lilly-collaborate-to-co-develop-companion-diagnostics-for-simultaneous-analysis-of-dna-and-rna-biomarkers-in-common-cancers-261199831.html. Published May 30, 2014. Accessed April 24, 2017.
52. Adaptive Biotechnologies Corporation. "Adaptive Announces a Biomarker Discovery Agreement with Johnson & Johnson Innovation." PR Newswire Website http://www.prnewswire.com/news-releases/adaptive-announces-a-biomarker-discovery-agreement-with-johnson–johnson-innovation-239926921.html. January 13, 2014. Accessed April 24, 2017.
53. Senior M. "How Patients Are Transforming Pharma R&D." In Vivo Website. Published May 9, 2016. https://invivo.pharmamedtechbi.com/IV004513/How-Patients-Are-Transforming-Pharma-RampD. Accessed April 21, 2017.
54. Tom Miller, cofounder and managing partner, GreyBird Ventures, personal correspondence, February 8, 2016.
55. Mara Aspinall, executive chairman of GenePeeks and CA Therapeutics and cofounder of the School of Biomedical Diagnostics, personal correspondence, February 2016.
56. Chen C. "Google's Huber to Lead Illumina Cancer-Detecting Startup Grail." Bloomberg Technology. http://www.bloomberg.com/news/articles/2016-02-10/google-s-huber-to-lead-illumina-cancer-detecting-startup-grail. Published February 10, 2016. Accessed April 24, 2017.

CHAPTER 5

1. Loftus P. "US Drug Spending Climbs." *Wall Street Journal*. April 14, 2016; B3; see also Aitken M, "Medicines Use and Spending in the US," Quintiles IMS Institute, May 2017.

2. Aitken M, Outlook for Global Medicines Through 2021, Quintiles IMS Institute, December 2016.
3. Birth A."Whether Prescribed or Over-The-Counter, Americans Prefer Generics." Harris Poll. December 2, 2015.
4. IMS Institute for Healthcare Informatics. "Medicines Use and Spending in the US: A Review of 2015 and Outlook to 2020." IMS Health Website. http://www.imshealth.com/en/thought-leadership/quintilesims-institute/reports/medicines-use-and-spending-in-the-us-a-review-of-2015-and-outlook-to-2020. Accessed April 26, 2017; see also Aitken M, "Medicines Use and Spending in the US," op. cit.
5. Experts in Chronic Myeloid Leukemia, Abboud C, Berman E, et al. "The Price of Drugs for Chronic Myeloid Leukemia (CML) Is a Reflection of the Unsustainable Prices of Cancer Drugs: From the Perspective of a Large Group of CML Experts." *Blood.* 2013;121(22):4439–4442.
6. Bennette C, Richards C, Sullivan S, et al. "Steady Increases in Prices for Oral Anticancer Drugs after Market Launch Suggest a Lack of Competitive Pressures." *Health Affairs.* 2016;35 (5):805–812.
7. Knutsen RM."Rare Disease Drugs Facing Questions Over Prices, Incentives." Medical Marketing and Media website. http://www.mmm-online.com/rare-disease-drugs-facing-questions-over-prices-incentives/printarticle/478088/. February 22, 2016. Accessed April 26, 2017. For drug sales, see "The Top 15 Best-Selling Drugs of 2016," *Genetic Engineering News,* March 6, 2017. Available at http://www.genengnews.com/the-lists/the-top-15-best-selling-drugs-of-2016/77900868.
8. Kaplan H."Preparing for the Zero Moment of Truth: Managing Early Awareness in Rare Disease Drug Commercialization." *In Vivo.* April 13, 2016.
9. "Patient Engagement and Patient Use of Evidence." *Health Affairs.* 2016; 35(4):744.
10. Wenzel M, Hall C."Opposites Attract: Pairing R&D and Commercial Teams." *Pharmaceutical Executive.* May 5, 2015. Available at http://www.pharmexec.com/opposites-attract-pairing-rd-and-commercial-teams. Accessed April 26, 2017. See also Bailey CJ. "Why Is Exubera Being Withdrawn?" *British Medical Journal.* 2007; 335(7630):1156.
11. Wenzel M, Hall C, ibid.
12. Magids S, Zorfas A, Leemon D."The New Science of Customer Emotions." *Harvard Business Review.* 2015. (November): 68–76. Available at https://hbr.org/2015/11/the-new-science-of-customer-emotions. Accessed April 26, 2017.
13. Edelman D."Branding in the Digital Age: You're Spending Your Money in All the Wrong Places." *Harvard Business Review.* 2010; (December): 2–8. Available at https://hbr.org/2010/12/branding-in-the-digital-age-youre-spending-your-money-in-all-the-wrong-places. Accessed April 26, 2017.
14. Fox B, Hofmann C, Paley A."How Pharma Companies Can Better Understand Patients." McKinsey & Company Website. http://www.mckinsey.com/industries/pharmaceuticals-and-medical-products/our-insights/how-pharma-companies-can-better-understand-patients. Published May 2016. Accessed April 26, 2017. See also Bell D, Fox B, Olohan R. *Pharma3D: Rewriting the Script for Marketing in the Digital Age.* Google, McKinsey & Company, 2016.
15. Simon F, Kotler P. *Building Global Biobrands: Taking Biotechnology to Market.* New York: Free Press; 2003: 109–110.
16. Simon F, Kotler P, op. cit., 118–120.
17. "The Top 15 Best-Selling Drugs of 2016," *Genetic Engineering News,* March 6, 2017. Available at http://www.genengnews.com/the-lists/the-top-15-best-selling-drugs-of-2016/77900868.
18. Simon F, Kotler P, op. cit, 142–143. See also Merrill J."Among New Drug Launches, Oncology Scores Big While CV Lags." *Pink Sheet.* March 28, 2016. Sutter S."Pitting Crestor Against Lipitor Misses the Mark." *Pink Sheet.* September 5, 2011. For Crestor sales, see Pharmacompass, "Top Drugs by Sales Revenue in 2015, Who Sold the Biggest Blockbuster Drugs," March 10, 2016. Available at https://www.pharmacompass.com/radio-compass-blog/top-drugs-by-sales-revenue-in-2015-who-sold-the-biggest-blockbuster-drugs. Accessed April 26, 2017.
19. The Top 15 Best-Selling Drugs of 2016, op. cit.
20. Longman R."The Shrinking Value of Best-in-Class and First-in-Class Drugs," *In Vivo.* July 20, 2015. Available at https://www.pharmamedtechbi.com/publications/in-vivo/33/7/the-shrinking-value-of-bestinclass-and-firstinclass-drugs. Accessed April 26, 2017.

21. Dysart J. "Diagnostic Companions." *Medical Marketing and Media*. June 2014; 26–30; for Xalkori sales, see Datamonitor/Decision Resources Group database, 2016.

22. Crow D, "Lung Cancer Drug Failure in Trials Deals $23bn Blow to Bristol-Myers Squibb", *Financial Times*, August 6/7, 2016; see also "FDA Approves First Cancer Treatment For Any Solid Tumor with a Specific Genetic Feature", FDA news release, May 23, 2017 (https://www.fda .gov/newsevents/newsroom/pressannouncements/ucm560167.htm); Helfand C, "In Unexpected Blow, Merck Halts Keytruda Myeloma Trial Enrollment to Probe Patient Deaths", Fierce Pharma, June 13, 2017 (http://www.fiercepharma.com/pharma/merck-halts-keytruda-myeloma-study-enrollment-to-gather-info-trial-deaths); Helfand C, "With Asco Data Tallied, Bristol-Myers Loses Ground to Merck in I-O Field, Fierce Pharma, June 7, 2017 (http://www.fiercepharma.com/ pharma/asco-data-tallied-bristol-myers-falls-farther-behind-merck-i-o-field); "Phase III Study Evaluating The Safety and Efficacy of Adjuvant Opdivo in Resected High-Risk Melanoma Patients Meets Primary Endpoint", Bristol-Myers press release, July 5, 2017.

23. Schnipper L, Abel G. "Direct-to-Consumer Drug Advertising in Oncology Is Not Beneficial to Patients or Public Health." *JAMA Oncology*. 2016; 2(11):1397–1398.

24. Simon F, Kotler P, op. cit, 114–116.

25. Simon F, Kotler P, op. cit, 149–151.

26. Dobrow L. "Community Clash." *Medical Marketing and Media*. April 2017; 31–39.

27. Vranica S. "Catch Me If You Can." *Wall Street Journal*. June 22, 2016; R1; Sharma A. "Big Media Needs to Embrace Digital Shift – Not Fight It." *Wall Street Journal*. June 22, 2016; R1, R2.

28. American Medical Association. "AMA Calls for Ban on Direct to Consumer Advertising of Prescription Drugs and Medical Devices." https://www.ama-assn.org/content/ama-calls-ban-direct-consumer-advertising-prescription-drugs-and-medical-devices. Published November 17, 2015. Accessed April 26, 2017.

29. Dobrow L, "Gut Check," *Medical Marketing and Media*, April 2016, 27–33.

30. Mahoney S. "How to Seize Your Omnichannel Moment." *Medical Marketing and Media*. March 15, 2016. Available at http://www.mmm-online.com/features/how-to-seize-your-omnichannel-moment/article/481839/. Accessed April 26, 2017.

31. Darling P. "Commercial Models for a New Healthcare Ecosystem." PharmExec.com website. http://www.pharmexec.com/commercial-models-new-healthcare-ecosystem. Published January 28, 2016. Accessed April 26, 2017.

32. Vranica S, op. cit., R1, R2.

33. Mayo Clinic Staff. "Type 2 Diabetes." Mayo Clinic website. http://www.mayoclinic.org/diseases-conditions/type-2-diabetes/diagnosis-treatment/treatment/txc-20169988. Accessed June 24, 2016.

34. Merck Manuals Online. https://www.merckmanuals.com/. Accessed June 24, 2016. Porter RS. *The Merck Manual*. 19th Ed. West Point, PA: Merck & Co., 2011.

35. Greenwood T. "Sales and Marketing: Reaching the Unreachables." Modern Marketing Concepts website. http://www.mmcweb.com/sales-marketing-reaching-the-unreachables/. Published January 16, 2016. Accessed April 26, 2017.

36. Groebel R. "Cloud Marketing: Faces in the Cloud." Medical Marketing and Media website. http:// www.mmm-online.com/cloud-marketing-faces-in-the-cloud/printarticle/440390. Published September 25, 2015. Accessed April 26, 2017.

37. Edmunds R, Danner S, Padilla N. "Tomorrow's Selling Strategies: Invest and Test." *Pharmaceutical Executive*. 2015;35(3). Available at http://www.pharmexec.com/tomorrow-s-selling-strategies-invest-test. Accessed April 26, 2017.

38. Cohen J. "Biosimilars: Improving Patient Access to Biologics While Bending the Cost Curve." In Vivo Pharma Intelligence website. https://invivo.pharmamedtechbi.com/IV004385/Biosimilars-Improving-Patient-Access-To-Biologics-While-Bending-The-Cost-Curve. Published June 8, 2015. Accessed April 26, 2017.

39. Celia F. "Brand Development Strategies: Golden Oldies." Medical Marketing and Media website. http://www.mmm-online.com/features/brand-development-strategies-golden-oldies/article/ 433923/. Published August 26, 2015. Accessed April 26, 2017.

40. Subramanian R, Baqri R."Branding: When One Is Not Enough." Pharmaceutical Executive website. http://www.pharmexec.com/branding-when-one-not-enough. Published February 3, 2016. Accessed April 26, 2017.
41. Laffler MJ."Roche: Slow and Steady Wins the Race." *Pink Sheet.* April 19, 2016.
42. Simon F, Kotler P. Building Global Biobrands, op. cit., 164.
43. Scala S, Miner K, Issi L, et al. "Pharmaceutical Industry Pulse." *Cowen Equity Research Report,* March 2016; 212–221.
44. Buck Luce, C, Jaggi G. *Progressions: Building Pharma 3.0.* Report, EY; 2011: 46–47.
45. Simon F, Kotler P, op. cit., 186–187, 195, 199–200.
46. Cohen J., op. cit.
47. Zhan P, Bolger T, Renjen V."The Birth of an Orphan Biosimilar Market." In Vivo Pharma Intelligence website. https://invivo.pharmamedtechbi.com/IV004469/The-Birth-Of-An-Orphan-Biosimilar-Market. Published February 17, 2016. Accessed April 26, 2017.

CHAPTER 6

1. Coulter A. "Patient Engagement—What Works?" *Journal of Ambulatory Care Management.* 2012;35(2):80–89; see also Coulter A, Ellins J. "Effectiveness of Strategies for Informing, Educating and Involving Patients. " *British Medical Journal.* 2007;335(7609):24–27.
2. Senior M."Outcomes-Focused Payers, New Technologies and Empowered Consumers Are Pushing Pharma Towards Patient-Centric Drug Development and Commercialization." Datamonitor Healthcare Trends Report, 2016.
3. Perlin J, Baker D, Brailer D, Fridsma D, Frisse M, Halamka J, et al. "Information Technology Interoperability and Use for Better Care and Evidence." National Academy of Medicine discussion paper, September 19, 2016. Available at https://nam.edu/information-technology-interoperability-and-use-for-better-care-and-evidence-a-vital-direction-for-health-and-health-care/. Accessed May 1, 2017.
4. Parsons S, Starling B, Mullan-Jensen C, Tham SG, Warner K, Wever K. "What the Public Knows and Wants to Know About Medicines Research and Development: A Survey of the General Public in Six European Countries." *British Medical Journal Open.* 2015;5: e006420. (doi: 10.1136/bmjopen-2014-006420); see also European Patients Academy website https://www.eupati.eu/.
5. Janssen. "Janssen Launches Three New Research Platforms Focused on Redefining Healthcare." https://www.jnj.com/media-center/press-releases/janssen-launches-three-new-research-platforms-focused-on-redefining-healthcare. Published February 12, 2015. Accessed May 1, 2017.
6. Insel R, Dunne J, Atkinson M, Chiang J, Dabelea D, Gottlieb P, et al. "Staging Presymptomatic Type 1 Diabetes: A Scientific Statement of JDRF, the Endocrine Society and the American Diabetes Association." *Diabetes Care.* 2015;38: 1964–1974.
7. Janssen E."UCB Wins Award for 'Hack Epilepsy' Initiative." UCB website. http://www.ucb.com/patients/magazine/article/UCB-wins-award-for-%E2%80%98Hack-Epilepsy%E2%80%99-initiative. Published March 22, 2016. Accessed May 1, 2017; see also UCB. "UCB Leads Epilepsy Hackathon to Support Patient Needs through Digital Tools and Services." UCB website. http://www.ucb.com/stories-media/press-releases/article/UCB-leads-epilepsy-hackathon-to-support-patient-needs-through-digital-tools-and-services. Published February 18, 2015. Accessed May 1, 2017.
8. Dreyer N, Reites J, Smurzynski M."Engaging and Retaining Patients in Long-Term Observational Studies." In Vivo Pharma Intelligence website. https://invivo.pharmamedtechbi.com/IV004302/Engaging-And-Retaining-Patients-In-LongTerm-Observational-Studies. Published November 19, 2015. Accessed May 1, 2017.

9. Senior M."How Patients Are Transforming Pharma R&D." In Vivo Pharma Intelligence website. https://invivo.pharmamedtechbi.com/IV004513/How-Patients-Are-Transforming-Pharma-RampD. Published May 9, 2016. Accessed May 1, 2017.

10. "NIH Awards $55 Million to Build Million-Person Precision Medicine Study." National Institutes of Health. https://www.nih.gov/news-events/news-releases/nih-awards-55-million-build-million-person-precision-medicine-study. Published July 6, 2016. Accessed May 1, 2017.

11. Crew D."Niche Treatments Become Big Business." *Financial Times*. September 28, 2015:2.

12. Wicks P, Lowe M, Gabriel S, Sikirica S, Sasane R, Arcona S. "Increasing Patient Participation in Drug Development." *Nature Biotechnology*. 2015;33(2):135–136.

13. "Using Social Media to Improve Patient Recruitment." *Access Point*. January 2016; 34(11):7. Available at http://www.imshealth.com/files/web/Global/RWE/RWE-Collateral/IMS%20RWE%20AccessPoint.pdf. Accessed May 1, 2017.

14. Looney W."Patient-Centered Strategies for Clinical Trials and Treatments." Pharmaceutical Executive website. http://www.pharmexec.com/patient-centered-strategies-clinical-trials-treatment. Published September 9, 2016. Accessed May 1, 2017.; for ruxolitinib, see Basch E. "Toward Patient-Centered Drug Development in Oncology." *New England Journal of Medicine*. 2013;369(5): 397–400.

15. Looney W., ibid.

16. Lipset C. "Engage with Research Participants About Social Media." *Nature Medicine*. 2014;20(3): 231. Available at www.nature.com/nm/journal/v20/n3/pdf/nm0314-231.pdf. Accessed May 1, 2017.

17. "A Third of People Track Their Health or Fitness. Who Are They and Why Are They Doing It?" GfK website. http://www.gfk.com/insights/press-release/a-third-of-people-track-their-health-or-fitness-who-are-they-and-why-are-they-doing-it/. Published September 29, 2016. See full study at http://www.gfk.com/global-studies/global-study-overview/. Accessed May 1, 2017.

18. Carman K, Murer M, Mangrum R, Yang M, Ginsburg M, Sofaer S, et al. "Understanding an Informed Public's Views on the Role of Evidence in Making Healthcare Decisions." *Health Affairs*. 2016;35(4):566–574.

19. "Patients' and Consumers' Use of Evidence, *Datagraphic.* " *Health Affairs*. 2016;35(4):564–565; Ranard B, Werner R, Antanavicius T, Schwartz A, Smith R, Meisel Z, et al. "Yelp Reviews of Hospital Care Can Supplement and Inform Traditional Surveys of the Patient Experience of Care." *Health Affairs*. 2016;35(4):697–705.

20. Centers for Medicare and Medicaid Services. "First Release of the Overall Hospital Quality Star Rating on Hospital Compare." https://www.cms.gov/newsroom/mediareleasedatabase/fact-sheets/2016-fact-sheets-items/2016-07-27.html. Published July 27, 2016. Accessed May 1, 2017; see also Budryk Z."CMS Releases Hospital Star Ratings Amid Industry Criticism." Fierce Healthcare website. http://www.fiercehealthcare.com/healthcare/cms-releases-hospital-star-ratings-amid-industry-criticism. Published July 27, 2016. Accessed May 1, 2017.

21. Findlay S. "Consumers' Interest in Provider Ratings Grows, and Improved Report Cards and Other Steps Could Accelerate Their Use." *Health Affairs*. 2016;35(4):688–695.

22. Kaul A."We Are Engaged! A Commitment To Patients." Health Affairs Blog. http://healthaffairs.org/blog/2015/05/11/we-are-engaged-a-commitment-to-patients/. Published May 11, 2015. Accessed May 1, 2017.

23. Ibid.

24. Volpp K, Mohta N."Patient Engagement Survey: Far to Go for Meaningful Participation." NEJM Catalyst website. http://catalyst.nejm.org/patient-engagement-initiatives-survey-meaningful-participation/. Published September 8, 2016. Accessed May 1, 2017.

25. CancerCare. "2016 CancerCare Patient Access and Engagement Report." Available at http://www.cancercare.org/accessengagementreport. Accessed May 1, 2017.

26. Merlino J, Raman A. "Health Care's Service Fanatics." *Harvard Business Review*. May 2013: 2–10.

27. Sullivan HW, Aikin KJ, Squiers LB. "Quantitative Information on Oncology Prescription Drug Websites." *Journal of Cancer Education.* September 2, 2016: 1–4. Available at http://link.springer.com/article/10.1007/s13187-016-1107-1. Accessed May 1, 2017.

28. Romito T."Patient Services: Pharma's Best Kept Secret." Accenture report, 2015; cited in Dobrow L, "Revolution." Medical Marketing and Media, September 2015: 33–36.

29. Khedkar P, Sturgis M."Want Better Access to Physicians? Understand What's Top of Mind: How to Broaden Your Reach—And Target Your Messaging—To Engage Healthcare Providers." ZS Associates, 2016. Available at https://www.zs.com/-/media/pdfs/ph_mar_wp_afm_acm_2016_es_v4.pdf?la=en. Accessed May 1, 2017.

30. Gupta M, Seiter S, Von Allmen H, Jaffe H."A New Foundation for Designing Winning Brand Strategies: The Patient Journey Re-Envisioned." IMS Consulting Group White Paper, 2014. Available at http://www.imshealth.com/files/web/Global/Services/Services%20Resource%20Center/IMSCG_Patient_Journey_WP_090714F.pdf. Accessed May 1, 2017.

31. Fox B, Hofmann C, Paley A."How Pharma Companies Can Better Understand Patients." McKinsey & Company website. http://www.mckinsey.com/industries/pharmaceuticals-and-medical-products/our-insights/how-pharma-companies-can-better-understand-patients. Published May 2016. Accessed May 1, 2017.; see also Bell D, Fox B, Olohan R. *Pharma3D: Rewriting the Script for Marketing in the Digital Age.* McKinsey e-book, April 2016. Available at www.pharma3D.com. Accessed May 1, 2017.

32. Elton J, O'Riordan A. *Healthcare Disrupted: Next Generation Business Models and Strategies.* Hoboken, NJ: John Wiley & Sons, 2016:97–99.

33. Viswanathan M, Golin CE, Jones CD, Ashok M, Blalock S, Wines R, et al. "Interventions to Improve Adherence to Self-Administered Medications for Chronic Disease in the United States." *Annals of Internal Medicine.* 2012;157:785–795.

34. Ibid.

35. Robinson R. "Pharma's Role in Personalized Smart Health." *PharmaVoice.* May 2016:12–16.

36. Wang R, Blackburn G, Desai M. "Accuracy of Wrist-Worn Heart Monitors." *JAMA Cardiology.* October 12, 2016. (doi: 10.1001/jamacardio.2016.3340).

37. Beetsch J, Vice President Patient Advocacy, Celgene, personal communication with Françoise Simon, October 12, 2016.

38. "Celgene Corporation and Sage Bionetworks Announce Technology Collaboration to develop Observational Study Using the Apple ResearchKit Framework." Celgene website. http://ir.celgene.com/releasedetail.cfm?releaseid=994085. Published October 18, 2016. Accessed May 1, 2017.

39. Bell D, Fox B, Olohan R. *Pharma3D: Rewriting the Script for Marketing in the Digital Age.* McKinsey e-book, April 2016. Available at www.pharma3D.com. Accessed May 1, 2017.

40. Matthias A."The Secret to True Patient Centricity from Big Pharma's First Chief Patient Officer." PM360 Panorama website. https://www.pm360online.com/the-secret-to-true-patient-centricity-from-big-pharmas-first-chief-patient-officer/. Published March 18, 2015. Accessed May 1, 2017; see also LaMotta L."What Is the Prescription for Patient Centricity?" *Pink Sheet.* November 24, 2014. Available at https://pink.pharmamedtechbi.com/PS076672/What-Is-The-Prescription-For-Patient-Centricity. Accessed May 1, 2017.

CHAPTER 7

1. Frazier K."The Pharma All-Stars." Panel discussion at the Forbes Healthcare Summit 2015, New York, NY, December 3, 2015.

2. Tefferi A, et al. "In Support of a Patient-Driven Initiative to Lower the High Price of Cancer Drugs." *Mayo Clinic Proceedings.* 2015; 90: 996–1000.

3. Weismann R."Doctors Challenge Vertex over the High Price of Cystic Fibrosis Drug." *The Boston Globe.* July 20, 2015. Available at http://www.bostonglobe.com/business/2015/07/20/researcher-

and-group-doctors-challenge-vertex-price-new-cystic-fibrosis-drug/d5PZMlj6T6uzq0usm2xLEL/
story.html. Accessed May 3, 2017.

4. Carroll A."The EpiPen, Case Study in Health System Dysfunction." *The New York Times*. August 23, 2016. Available at http://www.nytimes.com/2016/08/24/upshot/the-epipen-a-case-study-in-health-care-system-dysfunction.html. Accessed May 3, 2017.

5. Saunders B."Our Social Contract with Patients." Allergan website. https://www.allergan.com/news/ceo-blog/september-2016/our-social-contract-with-patients. Published September 6, 2016. Accessed May 3, 2017.

6. Thomas K."New Online Tools Offer Path To Lower Drug Prices." *The New York Times*. February 9, 2016. Available at https://www.nytimes.com/2016/02/10/business/taming-drug-prices-by-pulling-back-the-curtain-online.html.

7. "Drugs in America: Seizure-Inducing." *The Economist*. September 3, 2016. Available at http://www.economist.com/news/business/21706347-row-over-mylans-epipen-allergy-medicine-raises-fresh-questions-about-how-drugs-are. Accessed May 3, 2017.

8. Tufts Center for the Study of Drug Development. "Cost to Develop and Win Marketing Approval for a New Drug Is $2.6 Billion." Press release, November 18, 2014. Available at http://csdd.tufts.edu/news/complete_story/pr_tufts_csdd_2014_cost_study. Accessed May 3, 2017.

9. Berkrot B."New Incentives Needed to Develop Antibiotics to Fight Superbugs." Reuters website. http://www.reuters.com/article/us-health-superbug-antibiotics-idUSKCN0YI2MZ. Published March 27, 2016. Accessed May 3, 2017.

10. Brooks M."Big Pharma Pledges to Develop New Antibiotics, with Help." Medscape website. http://www.medscape.com/viewarticle/857627. Published January 21, 2016. Accessed May 3, 2017.

11. Silverman E."Vermont Poised to Become First State to Require Pharma to Justify Pricing." STAT website. https://www.statnews.com/pharmalot/2016/05/19/vermont-drug-costs-pharmaceutical/. Published May 19, 2016. Accessed May 3, 2017.

12. Organisation for Economic and Co-operative Development. "Pharmaceutical Spending (Indicator)." https://data.oecd.org/healthres/pharmaceutical-spending.htm. Accessed December 22, 2016.

13. Aitken M, Kleinrock M. "Understanding The Dynamics of Drug Expenditures." QuintilesIMS Institute. Published July 11, 2017. Accessed July 12, 2017.

14. Long D."The Balance Between Innovation and Smarter Spending." Presentation at the Health and Human Services Pharmaceutical Forum, Washington, DC, November 20, 2015.

15. World Health Organization. "2015 Global Survey of Health Technology Assessments by National Authorities." Available at http://ec.europa.eu/health/technology_assessment/docs/2014_strategy_eucooperation_hta_en.pdf. Accessed May 3, 2017.

16. European Medicines Agency and EUnetHTA, "Report on the Implementation of the EMA-EUnetHTA Three Year Work Plan 2012–2015." March 23, 2016. Available at http://www.ema.europa.eu/docs/en_GB/document_library/Report/2016/04/WC500204828.pdf. Accessed May 3, 2017.

17. Vogler S, Habl C, Bogut M, Voncina L. "Comparing Pharmaceutical Pricing and Reimbursement Policies in Croatia to the European Union Member States," *Croatian Medical Journal*. 2011; 52: 183–197.

18. WHO Collaboration Centre for Pharmaceutical Pricing and Reimbursement Policies. "Glossary." http://whocc.goeg.at/Glossary/About. Accessed May 3, 2017.

19. Gemeinsamer Bundesausschuss. "Reference Prices and How They Are Set." http://www.english.g-ba.de/special-topics/pharmaceuticals/reference/. Accessed May 3, 2017.

20. Ruggeri K, Nolte E."Pharmaceutical Pricing: The Use of External Reference Pricing." RAND Corporation, 2013. Available at http://www.rand.org/content/dam/rand/pubs/research_reports/RR200/RR240/RAND_RR240.pdf. Accessed May 3, 2017.

21. Nagano Y."Japan's 2014 Drug Price Reforms Extend Price Premium Program." *PharmAsia News*. January 23, 2014.

22. EY. "Life Sciences Quarterly Update, Asia-Pac and Japan." April 2016. http://www.ey.com/GL/en/Industries/Life-Sciences/EY-vital-signs-life-sciences-sector-update-for-asia-pacific-and-japan.

23. "The 2016 Drug Trend Report." Express Scripts, March 2017.

24. "Anthem Announces Definitive Agreement to Acquire Cigna Corporation." BusinessWire website. http://www.businesswire.com/news/home/20150724005167/en/Anthem-Announces-Definitive-Agreement-Acquire-Cigna-Corporation. Published July 24, 2015. Accessed May 3, 2017.

25. "Aetna to Acquire Humana." Aetna website. https://news.aetna.com/2015/08/aetna-to-acquire-humana/. Published July 3, 2015. Accessed May 3, 2017.

26. "Centene to Combine with Health Net in Transaction Valued at $6.8 Billion." HealthNet website. http://newsroom.healthnet.com/press-release/centene-combine-health-net-transaction-valued-approximately-68-billion. Published July 2, 2015. Accessed May 3, 2017.

27. Humer C."Express Scripts Drops Gilead Hep C Drugs for Cheaper AbbVie Rival," Reuters Health News website. http://www.reuters.com/article/us-express-scripts-abbvie-hepatitisc-idUSKBN0K00-7620141222. Published December 22, 2014. Accessed May 3, 2017.

28. Miller S."The $4 Billion Return on a Promise Kept." The Lab: Express Scripts Insights. http://lab.express-scripts.com/lab/insights/specialty-medications/the-4-billion-return-on-a-promise-kept. Published January 27, 2015. Accessed May 3, 2017.

29. Shrank W, Barlow J, Brennan T. "New Therapies in the Treatment of High Cholesterol: An Argument to Return to Goal-Based Lipid Guidelines." *Journal of the American Medical Association.* 2015; 314 (14): 1443–1444. Available at http://jamanetwork.com/journals/jama/article-abstract/2427467. Accessed May 3, 2017. See also "Landmark Outcomes Study Shows That Repatha Decreases LDL-C To Unprecedented Low Levels and Reduces Risk of Cardiovascular Events with No New Safety Issues," PR Newswire website. https://www.amgen.com/media/news-releases/2017/03/landmark-outcomes-study-shows-that-repatha-evolocumab-decreases-ldlc-to-unprecedented-low-levels-and-reduces-risk-of-cardiovascular-events-with-no-new-safety-issues. Published March 17, 2017. Accessed July 12, 2017.

30. Senior M."Scoring Value: New Tools Challenge Pharma's U.S. Pricing Bonanza." In Vivo Pharma Intelligence website. https://invivo.pharmamedtechbi.com/IV004434/Scoring-Value-New-Tools-Challenge-Pharmas-US-Pricing-Bonanza. Published October 21, 2015. Accessed May 3, 2017.

31. Neumann P, Cohen J. "Measuring the Value of Prescription Drugs." *New England Journal of Medicine.* 2015; 373: 2595–2597.

32. Simon F, Kotler P. *Building Global Biobrands: Taking Biotechnology to Market.* New York: Free Press, 2003.

33. Schleifer L."The Pharma All-Stars." Panel discussion at the 2015 Forbes Healthcare Summit, New York, New York, December 3, 2015.

34. Garrison L, Carlson J, Bajaj P, Towse, A, Neumann P, Sullivan S, et al. "Private Sector Risk-Sharing Agreements in the United States: Trends, Barriers, and Prospects." *American Journal of Managed Care.* 2015; 21 (9): 632–640.

35. John M, Hirschler B."France Pegs Gilead Hepatitis C Drug at Lowest Price in Europe." Reuters website. http://www.reuters.com/article/health-hepatitis-gilead-solvadi-idUSL6N0TA2TA20141120#QRzmDbgzqdBH7rIM.97. Published November 20, 2014. Accessed May 3, 2017.

36. Vioix, H, Franzen S, Selby D, Collomb D, Hauch O, Emmas C. "Three Years of the Gefitinib UK Single Patient Access Scheme (SPA); Duration of Treatment for Patients with EGFR Mutation Positive NSCLC in NHS Clinical Practice." *Value in Health.* 2013; 16 (7): A425.

37. Vioix H, Franzen S, Selby D, et al. "Duration of Gefitinib Treatment in EGFR Mutation Positive NSCLC Patients in a UK Single Payment Access Scheme." Presented at ISPOR, June 3–7, 2012.

38. Pollack A."Pricing Pills by the Results." *New York Times.* July 14, 2007. Available at http://www.nytimes.com/2007/07/14/business/14drugprice.html?_r=0. Accessed May 3, 2017.

39. Thomas K, Ornstein C. "Considering The Side Effects of Drugmakers' Moneyback Gaurantees," *New York Times.* July 10, 2017. Available at https://www.nytimes.com/2017/07/10/health/prescription-drugs-cost.html. Accessed July 11, 2017.

40. McAllister E."Results May Vary." *BioCentury.* February 2, 2016.

41. Sherman M, interview by E. Licking, January 4, 2016.

42. Garfield S, Sherman M, Longman R, Shiff S, and Licking E. "The Value Lab: Moving Value-Based Health Care from Theory to Practice." In press. In Vivo Pharma Intelligence Website.

43. Merrill J. "Multi-Indication Pricing: Big Hurdles and Actionable Options." *The Pink Sheet*. May 30, 2016.

44. Bach P. "Indication-Specific Pricing for Cancer Drugs." *Journal of the American Medical Association*. 2014; 312 (16): 1629–1630.

45. Revatio [package insert]. New York: Pfizer, Inc.; June 2005.

46. Viagra [package insert]. New York: Pfizer, Inc.; November 1988.

47. Center for Drug Evaluation and Research Application Number 125418Orig1s000 [memorandum]. Food and Drug Administration. July 27, 2012.

48. Pearson S, Dreitlein B, Henshall C. "Indication-Specific Pricing of Pharmaceuticals in the United States Health Care System." *Institute for Clinical and Economic Review*. March 2016.

49. Miller S. Panel presentation at the Health and Human Services Pharmaceutical Forum, Washington DC, November 20, 2015.

50. Bennette C, Richards C, Sullivan S, Ramsey S. "Steady Increase in Prices for Oral Anticancer Drugs after Market Launch Suggests a Lack of Competitive Pressure." *Health Affairs*. 2016; 35: 805–812.

51. Porter M, Kaplan R. "How to Pay for Health Care." *Harvard Business Review*. July-August 2016. Available at https://hbr.org/2016/07/how-to-pay-for-health-care. Accessed May 3, 2017.

52. Mechanic R. "Medicare's Bundled Payment Initiatives: Considerations For Providers." American Hospital Association [issue brief], January 19, 2016.

53. Centers for Medicare and Medicaid Services. "Bundled Payments for Care Improvement Initiative." https://innovation.cms.gov/initiatives/bundled-payments/. Accessed May 3, 2017.

54. Newcomer L. "Innovative Payment Models and Measurement for Cancer Therapy." *Journal of Oncology Practice*. 2014; 10: 187–189.

55. Conway L. "What Can We Learn from United's Medical Oncology Episode-Based Payment Pilot?" Advisory Board Blog. *Oncology Rounds*. July 17, 2014.

56. Newcomer L. "Innovative Payment Models and Measurement for Cancer Therapy." *Journal of Oncology Practice*. 2014; 10: 187–189.

57. Appelby J. "United Healthcare Expands Effort to Rein in Rising Costs of Cancer Treatment." *Kaiser Health News*. October 29. 2015.

58. Mattke S, Hoch E. "Borrowing for the Cure." RAND Corporation, 2015.

59. Montazerhodjat V, Weinstock D, Lo A. "Buying Cures versus Renting Health: Financing Health Care with Consumer Loans." *Science Translational Medicine*. 2016; 8: 1–8.

CHAPTER 8

1. Centers for Medicare and Medicaid Services "National Health Expenditure Fact Sheet, Historical (2014) and Projected (2015-25)." https://www.cms.gov/research-statistics-data-and-systems/statistics-trends-and-reports/nationalhealthexpenddata/nhe-fact-sheet.html. Accessed May 5, 2017.

2. Senior M. "Sovaldi Makes Blockbuster History, Ignites Drug Pricing Unrest." *Nature Biotechnology*. 2014;32, 501–502. Available at http://www.nature.com/nbt/journal/v32/n6/full/nbt0614-501.html?WT.feed_name=subjects_pharmacoeconomics. Accessed May 5, 2017.

3. Longman R. "The Myth of the Payer." Published in EY Annual Biotechnology Report *Beyond Borders 2016: Returning to Earth*. June 2016. Available at http://www.ey.com/GL/en/Industries/Life-Sciences/EY-vital-signs-the-myth-of-the-payer. Accessed May 5, 2017.

4. Centers for Medicare and Medicaid Services. "Health Insurance Marketplaces 2017 Open Enrollment Period Final Enrollment Report: November 1, 2016 - January 31, 2017." March 15, 2017. Available at: http://www.cms.gov/Newsroom/MediaReleaseDatabase/Fact-sheets/2017-Fact-Sheet-items/2017-03-15.html. Accessed July 10, 2017.

5. Johnson C."UnitedHealth Group to Exit Obamacare Exchanges in All but a 'Handful' of States." *Washington Post.* April 19, 2016. Available at https://www.washingtonpost.com/news/wonk/wp/2016/04/19/unitedhealth-group-to-exit-obamacare-exchanges-in-all-but-a-handful-of-states/?utm_term=.9c0a38ae396c. Accessed May 5, 2017.

6. Von Ebers P."Mega-Health Insurance Mergers: Is Bigger Really Better?" Health Affairs Blog. http://healthaffairs.org/blog/2016/01/22/mega-health-insurance-mergers-is-bigger-really-better/. Published January 22, 2016. Accessed May 5, 2017. See also Garthwaite C and Graves J. "Success And Failure In The Insurance Exchange." *New England Journal of Medicine* 2017; 376: 907–910.

7. Humer C, Bartz D. "Aetna, Humana Drop Merger; Cigna Wants To End Anthem Deal." Reuters website. http://www.reuters.com/article/us-humana-m-a-aetna-idUSKBN15T1HN. Published February 14, 2017. Accessed July 10, 2017.

8. Mathews A, Walker J. "UnitedHealth to Buy Catamaran for $12.8 Billion in Cash." *Wall Street Journal.* March 30, 2015. Available at https://www.wsj.com/articles/unitedhealth-to-buy-catamaran-for-12-8-billion-in-cash-1427709601. Accessed May 5, 2017.

9. Staton T."Heavyweight PBMs Mean Trouble for Big Pharma's Pricey New Meds." FiercePharma website. http://www.fiercepharma.com/pharma/heavyweight-pbms-mean-trouble-for-big-pharmas-pricey-new-meds. Published March 31, 2015. Accessed May 5, 2017.

10. Gottlieb S."What a Drug Price Debate Reveals about Obamacare." Forbes website. https://www.forbes.com/sites/scottgottlieb/2015/01/08/what-a-drug-price-debate-reveals-about-obamacare/#7f2735971a21. Published January 8, 2015. Accessed May 5, 2017.

11. Japsen B."If Anthem Splits with Express Scripts, a New PBM May Emerge." Forbes website. http://www.forbes.com/sites/brucejapsen/2016/03/22/if-anthem-splits-with-express-scripts-a-new-pbm-may-emerge/#7b8eba0014bf. Published March 22, 2016. Accessed May 5, 2017.

12. Galvin R, Longman R."Who Has the Power to Cut Drug Prices? Employers." *Harvard Business Review.* December 1, 2015.

13. Book R."Why Are Hospitals Buying Physician Practices and Forming Insurance Companies?" American Action Forum website. https://www.americanactionforum.org/research/why-are-hospitals-buying-physician-practices-and-forming-insurance-companies/. Published February 11, 2016. Accessed May 5, 2017.

14. Lenzke L."How Are You Responding to Changes in the Healthcare System?" EY presentation, 2015.

15. Herman B."More Health Systems Launch Insurance Plans, Despite Caveats." Modern Healthcare website. http://www.modernhealthcare.com/article/20150404/MAGAZINE/304049981. Published April 4, 2015. Accessed May 5, 2017.

16. Galvin R, Longman R. "Who Has the Power to Cut Drug Prices? Employers." *Harvard Business Review.* December 1, 2015.

17. Gruessner V."Why a Competitive Health Insurance Plan Matters to Employees." HealthPayer Intelligence website. http://healthpayerintelligence.com/news/why-a-competitive-health-insurance-plan-matters-to-employees. Published January 14, 2016. Accessed May 5, 2017.

18. Longman R,"The Myth of the Payer," June 2016. Published in *Beyond Borders Biotechnology Industry Report: Returning to Earth,* EY. Available at http://www.ey.com/GL/en/Industries/Life-Sciences/EY-vital-signs-the-myth-of-the-payer. Accessed May 5, 2017.

19. NHS Clinical Commissioners "About Clinical Commissioning Groups." http://www.nhscc.org/ccgs/. Accessed May 5, 2017.

20. Paris V, Belloni A."Value in Pharmaceutical Pricing. Country Profile: Australia." OECD Report, November 2014. Available at https://www.oecd.org/health/Value-in-Pharmaceutical-Pricing-Australia.pdf. Accessed May 5, 2017.

21. Asia Pacific Observatory on Health Systems and Policies. "Policy Brief: Conducive Factors to HTA Development in Asia." Available at http://www.wpro.who.int/asia_pacific_observatory/resources/policy_briefs/hta/en/. Accessed May 5, 2017.

22. Senior M."Scoring Value: New Tools Challenge US Pricing Bonanza." In Vivo Pharma Intelligence website. https://invivo.pharmamedtechbi.com/IV004434/Scoring-Value-New-Tools-Challenge-Pharmas-US-Pricing-Bonanza. Published October 21, 2015. Accessed May 5, 2017. See also Institute for Clinical and Economic Review. "Final Value Assessment Framework For 2017–2019." ICER website. Available at https://icer-review.org/final-vaf-2017-2019/. Accessed July 10, 2017.

23. Institute for Clinical and Economic Review. "CardioMEMS HF System (St. Jude Medical) and Sacubitril/Valsartan (Entresto, Novartis) for Management of Congestive Heart Failure: Effectiveness, Value, and Value-Based Price Benchmarks." Revised Draft Review, October 9, 2015. Available at https://icer-review.org/wp-content/uploads/2016/01/CHF_Revised_Draft_Report_100915.pdf. Accessed May 5, 2017.

24. Longman R, "The Myth of the Payer," June 2016. Published in *Beyond Borders Biotechnology Industry Report: Returning to Earth*, EY. Available at http://www.ey.com/GL/en/Industries/Life-Sciences/EY-vital-signs-the-myth-of-the-payer. Accessed May 5, 2017.

25. EY "Progressions: Navigating the Payer Landscape." Global Pharmaceutical Report, 2014. Available at http://www.ey.com/Publication/vwLUAssets/EY-progressions-2014-navigating-the-payer-landscape/$FILE/EY-progressions-2014.pdf. Accessed May 5, 2017.

26. The Harris Poll. "The 2016 Harris Poll Study of Reputation Equity and Risk Across the Health Care Sector." Available at http://www.theharrispoll.com/health-and-life/Pharma-Biotech-Patients-Over-Profits.html. Accessed July 11, 2017.

27. Kessel M. "Restoring the Pharmaceutical Industry's Reputation." *Nature Biotechnology*. 2014;32, 983–990. Available at http://www.nature.com/nbt/journal/v32/n10/full/nbt.3036.html. Accessed May 5, 2017.

28. Silverman E."Glaxo to Change Its Compensation Program for U.S. Sales Reps." The Wall Street Journal Pharmalot Blog. https://blogs.wsj.com/pharmalot/2015/04/13/glaxo-to-change-its-compensation-program-for-u-s-sales-reps/. Published April 13, 2015. Accessed May 5, 2017.

29. Meteos Ltd. "Principles for Collaborative, Mutually-Acceptable Drug Pricing." Report of Conclusions from the Pharmadiplomacy Dialogue, May 2016. Available at http://www.meteos.co.uk/resources/principles-for-collaborative-mutually-acceptable-drug-pricing/. Accessed May 5, 2017.

30. Meteos Ltd., ibid.

31. Coyle B, Chapman B."Overcoming the Key Account Management Talent Shortage in Pharma." PM360 Online. https://www.pm360online.com/overcoming-the-key-account-management-talent-shortage-in-pharma/. Published December 18, 2013. Accessed May 5, 2017.

32. Muhlestein D."Growth and Dispersion of Accountable Care Organizations In 2015." Health Affairs Blog. http://healthaffairs.org/blog/2015/03/31/growth-and-dispersion-of-accountable-care-organizations-in-2015-2/. Published March 31, 2015. Accessed May 5, 2017.

33. Nussbaum A."Health Insurance Exchanges." Bloomberg Quick Take. http://www.bloomberg.com/quicktake/health-insurance-exchanges. Updated August 3, 2016.

34. National Institute of Health and Care Excellence "NICE Calls for a New Approach to Managing the Entry of Drugs into the NHS." https://www.nice.org.uk/news/press-and-media/nice-calls-for-a-new-approach-to-managing-the-entry-of-drugs-into-the-nhs. Published September 18, 2014. Accessed May 5, 2017.

35. Thomas A. "Germany Mulls Limiting Prices Drug Firms Can Charge to Health System." *Wall Street Journal*. April 22, 2016. Available at http://www.wsj.com/articles/germany-mulls-limiting-prices-drug-firms-can-charge-to-health-system-1461307437. Accessed May 5, 2017.

36. Centers for Medicare and Medicaid Services "CMS Proposes to Test New Medicare Part B Prescription Drug Models to Improve Quality of Care and Deliver Better Value for Medicare Beneficiaries." https://www.cms.gov/Newsroom/MediaReleaseDatabase/Fact-sheets/2016-Fact-sheets-items/2016-03-08.html. Published March 8, 2016. Accessed May 5, 2017.

37. "Harvard Pilgrim Negotiates First-in-the Nation Innovative Contract for Blockbuster Cholesterol Drug Repatha." Businesswire website. http://www.businesswire.com/news/home/20151109006090/en/Harvard-Pilgrim-Negotiates-First-In-The-Nation-Innovative-Contract. Published November 9, 2015. Accessed May 5, 2017.

38. Staton T. "Lilly's Trulicity Joins Pay-for-Performance Trend with Harvard Pilgrim Deal." Fierce-Pharma website. http://www.fiercepharma.com/pharma/lilly-s-trulicity-joins-pay-for-performance-trend-harvard-pilgrim-deal. Published June 28, 2016. Accessed May 5, 2017.

39. Humer C. "Novartis Sets Heart-Drug Price With Two Insurers Based On Health Outcome." Reuters website. http://www.reuters.com/article/us-cigna-novartis-drugpricing-idUSKCN0VH25K. Published February 9, 2016. Accessed May 5, 2017.

40. Sherman M. "It's Time for Biopharma to Embrace Risk-Sharing." June 2016. Published in *Beyond Borders Biotechnology Industry Report: Returning to Earth*, EY. Available at http://www.ey.com/GL/en/Industries/Life-Sciences/EY-its-time-for-biopharma-to-embrace-risk-sharing. Accessed May 5, 2017.

41. Sherman M., ibid.

42. Morse S. "Dartmouth-Hitchcock, Harvard Pilgrim Join Forces on Population Health." HealthcareIT News website. http://www.healthcareitnews.com/news/dartmouth-hitchcock-harvard-pilgrim-analytics-population-health-benevera-health. Published October 5, 2015. Accessed May 5, 2017.

43. Sherman M. "It's Time for Biopharma to Embrace Risk-Sharing." June 2016. Published in *Beyond Borders Biotechnology Industry Report: Returning to Earth*, EY. Available at http://www.ey.com/GL/en/Industries/Life-Sciences/EY-its-time-for-biopharma-to-embrace-risk-sharing. Accessed May 5, 2017.

CHAPTER 9

1. Fallik D. "For Big Data, Big Questions Remain." *Health Affairs*. 2014;33(7):1111–1113.

2. Ginsberg J, Mohebbi MH, Patel RS, Braumer L, Smolinski MS, Brilliant L. "Detecting Influenza Epidemics Using Search Engine Query Data." *Nature*. 2009;457(7232):1012–1014.

3. Butler D. "When Google Got Flu Wrong." *Nature*. 2013;494(7436):155–156.

4. Institute of Medicine, "Transforming Clinical Research in the United States: Challenges and Opportunities," Workshop Summary. National Academies Press, 2010; cited in Validic and Fierce Markets, "Advancing Drug Development with Digital Health: Four Key Ways to Integrate Patient-Generated Data into Trials." March 2016.

5. Lee SM. "How an IPhone Medical Research App Is Helping People with Asthma." BuzzFeed News, September 29, 2015; cited in Validic, op. cit.

6. Lorenzetti L. "Pfizer and IBM Launch Research Project to Transform Parkinson's Disease." *Fortune*. April 7, 2016. Available at http://fortune.com/2016/04/07/pfizer-ibm-parkinsons. Accessed May 8, 2017.

7. "Robert Wood Johnson Foundation Awards Grant to PatientsLikeMe to Develop New Measures for Healthcare Performance." PatientsLikeMe website. http://news.patientslikeme.com/press-release/rwjf-awards-grant-patientslikeme-develop-new-measures-healthcare-performance. Published December 8, 2015. Accessed May 8, 2017.

8. PatientsLikeMe press release, "PatientsLikeMe and M2Gen Announce Partnership and Plans for Landmark Cancer Experience Study." PatientsLikeMe website. http://news.patientslikeme.com/press-release/patientslikeme-and-m2gen-announce-partnership-and-plans-landmark-cancer-experience-stu. Published March 8, 2016. Accessed May 8, 2017.

9. Lott R. "New Players Join in the Drug Development Game." *Health Affairs*. 2014;33(10): 1711–1713.

10. Al-Faruque F. "Novartis and Qualcomm Partner in mHealth." In Vivo Pharma Intelligence website. https://www.pharmamedtechbi.com/publications/in-vivo/33/1/novartis-and-qualcomm-partner-in-mhealth?p=1. Published January 27, 2015. Accessed May 8, 2017; Zimmerman Carolyne, Executive Director, Global Business Development and Licensing and Novartis Lead for dRx Capital, personal communication with Françoise Simon, October 20, 2015.

11. Friend SH. "App-Enabled Trial Participation: Tectonic Shift or Tepid Rumble?" *Science Translational Medicine*. July 22, 2015; Vol. 7: 297ed10: 1–3.

12. Lipset C. "Engage with Research Participants about Social Media." *Nature Medicine*. 2014; 20(3):231; Lipset Craig, Head of Clinical Innovation for Worldwide Research & Development, Pfizer; personal communication with Françoise Simon, October 15, 2015.

13. Roman DH, Conlee KD. *The Digital Revolution Comes to US Healthcare*. Goldman Sachs report, June 29, 2015.

14. Matthews C, Jones A. "Pfizer Blocks the Use of Drugs in Executions." *Wall Street Journal*. May 14/15, 2016: A3.

15. Clark D. "HP Bets on 3-D Printers to Make Innovative Mark." *Wall Street Journal*. May 18, 2016: B4. See also "First FDA-Approved Medicine Manufactured Using 3D Printing Technology Now Available." Aprecia website. https://www.aprecia.com/pdf/ApreciaSPRITAMLaunchPress Release__FINAL.PDF. Published March 22, 2016. Accessed May 8, 2017; Hicks J. "FDA Approved #D Printed Drug Available in the US." Forbes website. http://www.forbes.com/sites/jenniferhicks/2016/03/22/fda-approved-3d-printed-drug-available-in-the-us/print/. Published March 22, 2016. Accessed May 8, 2017.

16. EY. *EY Digital Overview Report*. 2015.

17. Rosenberg R, VanLare J, Reinholt B, Rao S, Dertouzos J. "Capturing Value from Connected Health." In Vivo Pharma Intelligence website. https://www.pharmamedtechbi.com/Publications/In-Vivo/33/6/Capturing-Value-From-Connected-Health?resut-3&total-32&searchquery-0%253fg%253dcapturin. Published June 18, 2015. Accessed May 8, 2017; see also Fox B, Paley A, Prevost M, and Subramanian N. "Closing the Digital Gap in Pharma," McKinsey, November 2016.

18. Senior M. "The End of Drug Innovation in Diabetes?" In Vivo Pharma Intelligence website. https://www.pharmamedtechbi.com/publications/in-vivo/33/2/the-end-of-drug-innovation-in-diabetes. Published February 3, 2015. Accessed May 8, 2017.

19. Senior M., ibid.

20. AstraZeneca. "Fit2Me: Managing Type 2 Diabetes." http://www.fit2me.com/managing-type-2-diabetes.html.

21. Looney W. "Sanofi's Big Bet on Integrated Patient Care." Pharmaceutical Executive website. http://www.pharmexec.com/sanofi-s-big-bet-integrated-patient-care. Published January 9, 2015. Accessed May 8, 2017.

22. Kelly C. "Genentech Social Media Collaboration Will Focus on Patient Experiences in Cancer." The Pink Sheet. https://www.pharmamedtechbi.com/publications/the-pink-sheet-daily/2014/4/8/genentech-social-media-collaboration-will-focus-on-patient-experiences-in-cancer. Published April 8, 2014. Accessed May 8, 2017.

23. "Pfizer Partners with Breast Cancer Leaders to Chronicle the Lives of Women with Metastatic Breast Cancer." Pfizer website. http://press.pfizer.com/press-release/pfizer-partners-breast-cancer-leaders-chronicle-lives-women-metastatic-breast-cancer-t. Published September 30, 2015. Accessed May 8, 2017.

24. "New Online Community Quitters Circle Helps Smokers Trade Cigarettes for Real Time Support." Pfizer website. https://investors.pfizer.com/investor-news/press-release-details/2015/New-Online-Community-Quitters-Circle-Helps-Smokers-Trade-Cigarettes-for-Real-Time-Support/default.aspx. Published June 23, 2015. Accessed May 8, 2017.

25. "Pfizer Hemophilia: The Way You Log Is About to Change." Hemophilia Federation of America website. http://www.hemophiliafed.org/news-stories/2012/12/pfizer-hemophilia-the-way-you-log-is-about-to-change/. Published December 4, 2012. Accessed May 8, 2017.

26. Accenture 2015 survey; cited in Dobrow L. "Revolution." *Medical Marketing & Media*. September 2015: 33–36.

27. World Health Organization."mHealth: New Horizons for Health through Mobile Technologies." Global Observatory for eHealth Series, Vol. 3, 2011; cited in IMS Institute for Healthcare Informatics, Patient Adoption of mHealth, September 2015.

28. "Things Are Looking App." *The Economist*. March 12, 2016: 59–60.

29. Gallagher D. "Google Clicks in a Peak Smartphone Age." *Wall Street Journal*. May 16, 2016: C6.

30. IMS Institute for Healthcare Informatics, Patient Adoption of mHealth, September 2015.

31. "Dana Farber and Fitbit Partner to Test If Weight Loss Can Prevent Breast Cancer Recurrence." Dana-Farber Cancer Institute website. http://www.dana-farber.org/Newsroom/News-Releases/dana-farber-cancer-institute-and-fitbit-partner-to-test-if-weight-loss-prevent-breast-cancer-recurrence.aspx. Published April 27, 2016. Accessed May 8, 2017.

32. McCaffrey K."Biogen, PatientsLikeMe Use Fitbit to Better Understand Multiple Sclerosis." Medical Marketing & Media website. http://www.mmm-online.com/digital/biogen-patients likeme-use-fitbit-to-better-understand-ms/article/409279/. Published April 15, 2015. Accessed May 8, 2017; see also Block VJ, Lizee A, Crabtree-Hartman E, Bevan CJ, Graves JS, Bove R, Green AJ, Nourbakhsh B, Traublay M, Gourraud PA, et al., "Continuous daily assessment of multiple sclerosis disability using remote step count monitoring," *J. Neurology* (2017) 264:316–326 (doi 10. 1007/s00415-016-8334-6), published online November 28, 2016.

33. Epper Hoffman K. "First Sign of Defense." *Medical Marketing & Media*. April 2016: 40–41.

34. Serrano K, Yu M, Riley W, Patel V, Hughes P, Marchesini K, et al. "Willingness to Exchange Health Information Via Mobile Devices: Findings from a Population-Based Survey." *Annals of Family Medicine*. 2016;14(1):36–40.

35. Blenner S, Kollmer M, Rouse A, Daneshvar N, Williams C, Andrews L. "Privacy Policies of Android Diabetes Apps and Sharing of Health Information." *Journal of the American Medical Association*. 2016;315(10):1051–1052.

36. FDA Draft Guidance, Use of Electronic Informed Consent in Clinical Investigations, March 2015, Center for Drug Evaluation and Research. Silver Spring, MD.

37. Cortez M, Cohen G, Kesselheim A. "FDA Regulation of Mobile Health Technologies." *New England Journal of Medicine*. 2014;371(4):372–379.

38. Yang T. Silverman R. "Mobile Health Applications: The Pattern of Legal and Liability Issues Suggests Strategies to Improve Oversight." *Health Affairs*. 2014;33(2); 222–227.

39. Pew Research Center."Social Media Usage: 2005–2015." http://www.pewinternet.org/2015/10/08/social-networking-usage-2005-2015/. Published October 8, 2015. Accessed May 8, 2017.

40. Decision Resources Group. *Cybercitizen Health®* U.S. 2015.

41. Findlay S. "Consumers' Interest in Provider Ratings Grows, and Improved Report Cards and Other Steps Could Accelerate Their Use." *Health Affairs*. 2016;35(4):688–705.

42. Kear T, Harrington M, Bhattacharya A. "Partnering with Patients Using Social Media to Develop a Hypertension Management Instrument." *Journal of the American Society of Hypertension*. 2015;9 (9):725–734.

43. Cystic Fibrosis Foundation."The Cystic Fibrosis Foundation's Drug Development Model." https://www.cff.org/Our-Research/Our-Research-Approach/Venture-Philanthropy, 2015. Accessed May 8, 2017.

44. Chase J."Lack of Expertise Limits Pharma's Facebook Use." Medical Marketing & Media website. http://mmm-online.com/lack-of-expertise-limits-pharmas-facebook-use/printarticle/461035/. Published December 23, 2015. Accessed May 8, 2017.

45. Rhyee C, Auh J, Wachter Z. *Telehealth: Bringing Health Care to Your Fingertips*. Ahead of the Curve Series. Cowen Equity Research. February 20, 2015.

46. Schwamm L. "Telehealth: Seven Strategies to Successfully Implement Disruptive Technology and Transform Healthcare." *Health Affairs*. 2014;33(2):200–206; See also Kvedar J, Coye MJ, Everett W. "Connected Health: A Review of Technologies and Strategies to Improve Patient Care with Telemedicine and Telehealth." *Health Affairs*. 2014;33(2):194–199.

47. Decision Resources Group.*Taking the Pulse U.S. 2015 Physician Research Module. Physician Mobile Strategy in 2016: Optimizing Fundamentals and Driving Innovation;* see also Rhyee C, Wachter Z, Auh J. *Online Content Providers: From Portal to Platform.* Ahead of Curve Series. Cowen Equity Research, September 16, 2015.
48. Rhyee C, et al., Online Health Content Providers, op. cit.
49. Beck M. "Websites Misdiagnose Ailments." *Wall Street Journal.* May 16, 2016: A6.
50. Rhyee, C et al, *Telehealth: Bringing Healthcare to Your Fingertips.* op. cit.
51. Kvedar J, Coye MJ, Everett W."Connected Health." op. cit.
52. Cryer L, Shannon S, Van Amsterdam M, Leff B. "Costs for 'Hospital at Home' Patients Were 19 Percent Lower, with Equal or Better Outcomes Compared to Similar Inpatients." *Health Affairs.* 2012;31(6):1237–1243.
53. Rhyee C. *Telehealth: Bringing Healthcare to Your Fingertips,* op. cit.

CHAPTER 10

1. Siegel E. *Predictive Analytics: The Power to Predict Who Will Click, Buy, Lie, or Die.* Hoboken, NJ: John Wiley & Sons, 2016.
2. Gartner Group. "Gartner Says 6.4 Billion Connected 'Things' Will Be in Use in 2016, Up 30% From 2015." http://www.gartner.com/newsroom/id/3165317. Published November 10, 2015. Accessed May 9, 2017.
3. IDC Technologies "The Digital Universe of Opportunities: Rich Data and the Increasing Value of the Internet of Things." http://www.emc.com/leadership/digital-universe/2014iview/executive-summary.htm. Published 2014. Accessed May 9, 2017.
4. Kiron D, Prentice PK, Ferguson RB."Raising the Bar with Analytics." *MIT Sloan Management Review.* Winter 2014.
5. Hughes B, Kessler M, McDonell A. *The $1 Billion RWE Opportunity.* IMS Health White Paper. https://www.imshealth.com/files/web/Global/Services/Services%20TL/rwes_breaking_new_ground_d10.pdf. Published August 2014. Accessed May 9, 2017.
6. Lavorgna M. "There's No Such Thing as Digital: A Conversation with Charles Hansen, Gordon Rankin, and Steve Silberman." Audiostream website. http://www.audiostream.com/content/draft#XArQrlELGYJSdpw6.99. Published June 24, 2013. Accessed May 9, 2017.
7. McKinsey & Co. "The Role of Big Data in Medicine." http://www.mckinsey.com/industries/pharmaceuticals-and-medical-products/our-insights/the-role-of-big-data-in-medicine. Published November 2015. Accessed May 9, 2017.
8. Miller L."The Origins of Big Data: An Etymological Detective Story." *New York Times.* February 1, 2013. Available at http://bits.blogs.nytimes.com/2013/02/01/the-origins-of-big-data-an-etymological-detective-story. Accessed May 9, 2017.
9. Bonde A. "Small Data: A Brief History and New Design Philosophy." Presentation at SPARK Boston, July 11, 2016. Available at https://smalldatagroup.com/2016/07/11/a-new-design-philosophy-my-talk-at-spark-boston/. Accessed May 9, 2017.
10. IBM Big Data and Analytics Hub "The Four V's of Big Data." http://www.ibmbigdatahub.com/infographic/four-vs-big-data. Accessed May 9, 2017.
11. Dr. David Shaywitz, Chief Medical Officer, DNANexus, interview by E. Licking, July 15, 2016.
12. EY. *Progressions: Navigating the Payer Landscape.* Global Pharmaceutical Report, 2014. Available at http://www.ey.com/Publication/vwLUAssets/EY-progressions-2014-navigating-the-payer-landscape/$FILE/EY-progressions-2014.pdf. Accessed May 9, 2017.
13. Reid J. Personal interview by E. Licking. September 6, 2016.
14. Davidovic D. Personal interview by E. Licking. July 25, 2016.

15. IDC Technologies *The Digital Universe of Opportunities: Rich Data and the Increasing Value of the Internet of Things.* 2014. Available at https://www.emc.com/collateral/analyst-reports/idc-digital-universe-2014.pdf. Accessed May 9, 2017.

16. Perjasamy M,. Raj P. "Big Data Analytics: Enabling Technologies and Tools." In Mahmood Z, *Data Science and Big Data Computing.* New York: Springer International Publishing, 2016: 221–243.

17. Hill C. Personal interview by E. Licking. August 9, 2016.

18. Gawande A. "Overkill." *New Yorker.* May 11, 2015. Available at http://www.newyorker.com/magazine/2015/05/11/overkill-atul-gawande. Accessed May 9, 2017.

19. Steinberg G. "Using Big Data to Predict—and Improve—Your Health." Aetna website. https://news.aetna.com/2014/06/big-data-can-predict-and-improve-health/. Published June 2014. Accessed May 9, 2017.

20. Hill C. Personal interview by E. Licking. August 9, 2016.

21. Siegel E. *Predictive Analytics: The Power to Predict Who Will Click, Buy, Lie, or Die.* Hoboken, NJ: John Wiley & Sons, 2016.

22. Robb D. "Gartner Taps Predictive Analytics as Next Big Business Intelligence Trend." EnterpriseApps Today website. http://www.enterpriseappstoday.com/business-intelligence/gartner-taps-predictive-analytics-as-next-big-business-intelligence-trend.html. Published April 17, 2012. Accessed May 9, 2017.

23. EY and Forbes Insights. *Analytics: Do Not Forget the Human Element.* November 2015. Jersey City, NJ: Forbes Insights. 2015. Available at http://www.ey.com/Publication/vwLUAssets/EY-Forbes-Insights-Data-and-Analytics-Impact-Index-2015/$FILE/EY-Forbes-Insights-Data-and-Analytics-Impact-Index-2015.pdf. Accessed May 9, 2017.

24. Lazarus D. "'Big Data' Could Mean Big Problems for People's Health Care Privacy." *Los Angeles Times.* October 11, 2016. Available at http://www.latimes.com/business/lazarus/la-fi-lazarus-big-data-healthcare-20161011-snap-story.html. Accessed May 9, 2017.

25. National Human Genome Research Institute, "The Cost of Sequencing a Human Genome." https://www.genome.gov/27565109/the-cost-of-sequencing-a-human-genome/. Published July 6, 2016. Accessed May 9, 2017; see also Herper M. "Illumina Promises to Sequence Human Genome for $100–But Not Quite Yet." *Forbes*, January 9, 2017. Accessed July 6, 2017.

26. Pollack A. "Aiming to Push Genomics Forward in New Study." *New York Times.* January 13, 2014. Available at https://www.nytimes.com/2014/01/13/business/aiming-to-push-genomics-forward-in-new-study.html. Accessed May 9, 2017.

27. Dewey FE, et al. "Inactivating Variants in *ANGPTL4* and Risk of Coronary Artery Disease." *New England Journal of Medicine.* 2016;374:1123–1133.

28. Baras A. Personal interview by E. Licking. September 6, 2016.

29. Sanati C. "How One Company Is Using Artificial Intelligence to Develop a Cure for Cancer." Fortune website. http://fortune.com/2015/04/16/cancer-cure-artificial-intelligence/. Published April 16, 2015. Accessed May 9, 2017.

30. Radin A. "Mission Possible: Software Driven Drug Discovery." Life Science Leader website. http://www.lifescienceleader.com/doc/mission-possible-software-driven-drug-discovery-0001. Published April 1, 2016. Accessed May 9, 2017.

31. Warren M."The Cure for Cancer Is Data—Mountains of Data." Wired website. https://www.wired.com/2016/10/eric-schadt-biodata-genomics-medical-research/. Published October 19, 2016. Accessed May 9, 2017.

32. Lorenzetti L."Here's How IBM Watson Health Is Transforming the Health Care Industry." Fortune website. http://fortune.com/ibm-watson-health-business-strategy/. Published April 5, 2016. Accessed May 9, 2017.

33. Hay M, Thomas D, Craighead J, Economides C, Rosenthal J. "Clinical Development Success Rates for Investigational Drugs." *Nature Biotechnology.* 2014;32:40–51.

34. Akmaev S. Personal interview by E. Licking. July 28, 2016.

35. Bhatt A. "Evolution of Clinical Research: A History Before and Beyond James Lind." Perspectives in Clinical Research. 2010;1(1): 6–10.

36. EY. *Beyond Borders: Unlocking Value*. Biotechnology Industry Report 2014. Available at http://www.ey.com/Publication/vwLUAssets/EY-beyond-borders-unlocking-value/$FILE/EY-beyond-borders-unlocking-value.pdf. Accessed May 9, 2017.

37. "Teva, Intel to Develop Huntington Wearable Tech and Machine Learning Platform." Center-Watch News Online website. https://www.centerwatch.com/news-online/2016/09/20/teva-intel-develop-huntington-wearable-tech-machine-learning-platform/. Published September 20, 2016. Accessed May 9, 2017.

38. Auschitzky E, Santagostino A, Otto R. "Advanced Analytics Improve Biopharma Operations." Pharmaceutical Manufacturing website. http://www.pharmamanufacturing.com/articles/2014/advanced-analytics-improve-biopharma-operations/. Published November 13, 2014. Accessed May 9, 2017.

39. "REMEDIES Moves on to the Next Stage." REMEDIES website. https://remediesproject.com/2015/08/27/remedies-moves-on-to-next-stage/. Published August 27, 2015. Accessed May 9, 2017.

40. Ward A. "McLaren Speeds up GSK with Racetrack Expertise." *Financial Times*. December 10, 2014. Available at https://www.ft.com/content/3e2b7874-6f36-11e4-8d86-00144feabdc0. Accessed May 9, 2017.

41. Ahlawat H, Chierchia G, van Arkel P. "The Secret of Successful Drug Launches." McKinsey & Company website. http://www.mckinsey.com/industries/pharmaceuticals-and-medical-products/our-insights/the-secret-of-successful-drug-launches. Published March 2014. Accessed May 9, 2017.

42. Licking E, Garfield S. "A Road Map to Strategic Drug Pricing." *In Vivo*. 2016;34(3): 2–11. Available at http://www.ey.com/Publication/vwLUAssets/ey-in-vivo-a-road-map-to-strategic-drug-prices-subheader/$FILE/ey-in-vivo-a-road-map-to-strategic-drug-prices-subheader.pdf. Accessed May 9, 2017.

43. Hughes B, Kessler M, McDonell A. *Breaking New Ground with RWE: How Some Pharmacos Are Poised to Realize a $1 Billion Opportunity*. IMS Health White Paper. August 2014. Available at https://www.imshealth.com/files/web/Global/Services/Services%20TL/rwes_breaking_new_ ground_d10.pdf. Accessed May 9, 2017.

44. Hughes B, Kessler M, McDonell A., ibid.

45. Eichler HG. et al. "From Adaptive Licensing to Adaptive Pathways: Delivering a Flexible Life-Span Approach to Bring New Drugs to Patients." *Clinical Pharmacology and Therapeutics*. 2015; (97):234–246.

46. "Data Analytics Create Better Commercial Strategies." PharmaVOICE website. http://www.pharmavoice.com/article/2016-06-data-analytics/. Published June 2016. Accessed May 9, 2017.

47. Foschini L. Personal interview by E. Licking. June 25, 2016.

48. Arora S. "Recommendation Engines: How Amazon and Netflix Are Winning the Personalization Battle." MTA Martech Advisor website. https://www.martechadvisor.com/articles/customer-experience/recommendation-engines-how-amazon-and-netflix-are-winning-the-personalization-battle/. Published June 28, 2016. Accessed May 9, 2017.

49. Ahmed L. "Who's Afraid of a Tweet and a Pin? Strategies to Start Engaging Online," Scrip Pharma Intelligence website. https://scrip.pharmamedtechbi.com/SC065067/Whos-Afraid-Of-A-Tweet-And-A-Pin-Strategies-To-Start-Engaging-Online. Published May 6, 2016. Accessed May 9, 2017.

50. Frank H.P. "Building Connected Health Services." In *Pulse of the Industry: Medical Technology Report 2016*. EY, October 2016. Available at http://www.ey.com/Publication/vwLUAssets/ey-pulse-of-the-industry-2016/$FILE/ey-pulse-of-the-industry-2016.pdf. Accessed May 9, 2017.

51. Grover N. "Quintiles, IMS Health to Merge in $9 Billion Deal." Reuters, May 3, 2016.

52. IBM "IBM Watson Health Announces Plans to Acquire Truven Health Analytics for $2.6B, Extending Its Leadership in Value-Based Care Solutions." PR Newswire website. http://www .prnewswire.com/news-releases/ibm-watson-health-announces-plans-to-acquire-truven-health-analytics-for-26b-extending-its-leadership-in-value-based-care-solutions-300222147.html. Published February 18 2016. Accessed May 9, 2017.
53. Senior M. *Data in Healthcare: Underpinning the Shift to Value.* Datamonitor Healthcare. November 22, 2016.
54. "Lessons from Becoming a Data-Driven Organization." *MIT Sloan Management Review.* October 18, 2016.
55. Lazer D, Kennedy R, King G, Vespignani A. "The Parable of Google Flu: Traps in Big Data Analysis." *Science.* 2014;343:1203–1205.
56. Lazer D, Kennedy R, King G, Vespignani A., ibid.
57. Berger M, Axelsen K, Subedi P."The Era of Big Data and Its Implications for Big Pharma." Health Affairs Blog. http://healthaffairs.org/blog/2014/07/10/the-era-of-big-data-and-its-implications-for-big-pharma/. Published July 10, 2014. Accessed May 9, 2017.
58. Miller J. "Big Pharma's Bet on Big Data Creates Opportunities and Risks." Reuters website. http://www.reuters.com/article/us-pharmaceuticals-data-idUSKCN0V41LY. Published January 26 2016. Accessed May 9, 2017.
59. Kovacs E."FDA Issues Alert over Vulnerable Hospira Drug Pump." Security Week website. http://www.securityweek.com/fda-issues-alert-over-vulnerable-hospira-drug-pumps. Published August 3, 2015. Accessed May 9, 2017.
60. EY. "The 'New Normal' in Today's Digital Landscape." Vital Signs, EY Perspectives on Life Sciences. http://www.ey.com/gl/en/industries/life-sciences/ey-vital-signs-the-new-normal-in-todays-digital-landscape. Accessed May 9, 2017.
61. Lund S, Manyika J, Nyquist S, Mendonca L, Ramaswamy M. *Game Changers: Five Opportunities for US Growth and Renewal.* McKinsey Global Institute, July 2013.
62. Senior M. *Data in Healthcare: Underpinning the Shift to Value.* Datamonitor Healthcare. November 22, 2016.
63. Kiron D, Kirk Prentice P, Ferguson RB. "The Analytics Mandate." Findings from the 2014 Data and Analytics Global Executive Study and Research Report. *MIT Sloan Management Review.* 2014; Winter: 3–21.
64. EY and Forbes Insights. *Analytics: Do Not Forget the Human Element.* November 2015. Jersey City, NJ: Forbes Insights. 2015. Available at http://www.ey.com/Publication/vwLUAssets/EY-Forbes-Insights-Data-and-Analytics-Impact-Index-2015/$FILE/EY-Forbes-Insights-Data-and-Analytics-Impact-Index-2015.pdf. Accessed May 9, 2017.

INDEX

Abbott Molecular, 106
AbbVie, 20, 25, 109, 113, 153
Abilify (aripiprazole), 12
accountable care organizations
        (ACOs), 110, 178, 188
active ingredient-based groups, 151
Actonel (risedronate), 103
Actos (pioglitazone), 115
acute myeloid leukemia (AML), 99
Aetna, commercial insurers, 164, 174,
        190, 223
affordability, 130, 141, 142, 145, 156,
        169
  of prescription drugs, 145
  up-front of medicine, 154
Affordable Care Act (ACA), 21, 149, 167,
        175, 176, 179, 189
Afrezza inhaler, 97
AG-221 (enasidenib), 99
AgaMatrix, 204
Agency for Healthcare Research and
        Quality (AHRQ), 131
Aggarwal, R, 129
agile supply chain, creating, 229
algorithms, 216, 225, 232
  Bayesian, 222, 228
AliveCor, 8, 12, 204
alliance. see also strategic alliances
  acquisition continuum, 58
  biotech companies, 50
  Celgene, 49, 54, 55, 84, 95, 98, 99,
        107, 140
  contract, 62
  contractual, 59
    arrangement, 64

pharma companies, 50
transactions, 59
Alnylam
  cash raising, 27
  financing strategies, 26–28
  funding, 26
  RNA interference (RNAi) based
        therapies, 26
Alphabet, 6, 8, 12, 17, 18, 20–22, 37,
        84, 85
  healthcare portfolio, 18
ALS (amyotrophic lateral sclerosis), 102,
        127, 129, 199
Alzheimer's disease, 218
Amazon, 21, 215, 231
American Lung Association, 205
American Society of Clinical Oncologists'
        (ASCO) Value Framework, 181
American Telemedicine Association
        (ATA), 211
  accreditation, 211
American Well, 210–212
AmeriDoc, 211
Amgen, 4, 46, 49, 54, 73, 103, 113, 117,
        123, 164, 190, 227
amyotrophic lateral sclerosis (ALS), 102,
        127, 129
analytics, 219
  across biopharma value chain, 227
  continuum, 224
  descriptive, 224
  driven organization, 226
  enabled biopharma organization, 241
  first organization building, 238
    as strategic imperative, 239

Managing Biotechnology: From Science to Market in the Digital Age, First Edition. Françoise Simon
and Glen Giovannetti.
© 2017 John Wiley & Sons, Inc. Published 2017 by John Wiley & Sons, Inc.